REBELLIOUS FAMILIES

International Studies in Social History
General Editor: Marcel van der Linden,
International Institute of Social History, Amsterdam

Trade Unions, Immigration, and Immigrants in Europe, 1960–1993
Edited by Rinus Penninx and Judith Roosblad

Class and Other Identities
Edited by Lex Heerma van Voss and Marcel van der Linden

Rebellious Families
Edited by Jan Kok

REBELLIOUS FAMILIES

Household Strategies and Collective Action
in the Nineteenth and Twentieth Centuries

EDITED BY
JAN KOK

Berghahn Books
New York • Oxford

First published in 2002 by

Berghahn Books
www.BerghahnBooks.com

Library of Congress Cataloging-in-Publication Data
Rebellious families : household strategies and collective action in the nineteenth and twentieth centuries / edited by Jan Kok.
    p. cm. -- (International studies in social history ; v. 3)
    Includes bibliographical references and index.
    ISBN 1-57181-528-7 (cloth : alk. paper) -- ISBN 1-57181-529-5
(pbk. : alk. paper)
    1. Family--Economic aspects.   2. Family--political aspects.
3. Labor movement.   4. Collective behaviour   I. Kok, J. (Jan)   II.
Series

HQ518 .R4 2002
306.85--dc21   2002018266

British Library Cataloguing in Publication Data
A catalogue record for this book is available
from the British Library.

Printed in the United States on acid-free paper.

ISBN 1–57181–528–7 (hardback)
ISBN 1–57181–529–5 (paperback)

CONTENTS

LIST OF TABLES, FIGURES AND MAPS

Tables

Figures

Maps

PREFACE

Jan Kok

How do wage workers perceive their interests and how do they acknowledge that these interests can be served by collective action? Until recently, most labour historians looked for answers to these questions only in the sphere of wage work itself. They located the organisational drive in changing labour relations and in processes operative at the workfloor, such as deskilling. Labour organisations were studied mainly by analysing their internal mechanisms and their effectiveness in defending their members' interests. However, newly developed fields of history, in particular family, gender and ethnic studies, have generated important insights in showing how identities are constructed, how interests are perceived and how others are seen as allies or enemies. For men and women alike, the 'home sphere' of household, family and community appears to be of central importance for their interactions with the labour market and with labour organisations. To understand the strategies of workers to improve their living conditions, we have to know what is going on in the 'home sphere'. How do men and women perceive the adequacy of their current efforts to sustain their families? What shifts occur in the prevailing household strategies? And how were forms of collective action adopted in the family repertoire?

In 1997, the research department of the International Institute of Social History (Amsterdam, The Netherlands) decided to elaborate these questions by launching a programme called 'Living Strategies'. At least for the next five years, this topic was to be the link between ongoing research and the starting-point for new projects. In November 1997, the programme started with a workshop that explored the ways in which families 'mixed' various strategies in order to survive or to gain better positions. Specialists on specific working-class strategies, such as migration, reliance on charity, pawning and the use of kinship networks, were invited to share their thoughts on the strategic choices of families. In the workshop, much attention was paid to sources, methods and definitions appropriate to this new terrain as well. In May 1999, the meeting had a sequel in a workshop with a slightly different angle. This time, case studies were requested of specific incidences or forms of collective action. This could include the decline of organisations or even the rejection of collective strategies. The contributors were asked to look at the development of group action from the perspective of family interests.

In this volume, we compile these case studies, most of them written for the second 'Living Strategies' workshop. However, our thinking on the subject has been aided enormously by the theoretical and methodological discussions on strategies in the first workshop. Therefore, we thank the following experts who kindly participated in the workshops, either by presenting a paper themselves or by commenting: Gita Deneckere, Patricia van den Eeckhout, Raelene Frances, Karl Christian Führer, Francisca de Haan, Lex Heerma van Voss, Marco van Leeuwen, Jan Lucassen, Kees Mandemakers, Andrew Miles, Heidi Rosenbaum, Ratna Saptari and Willem van Schendel. Subsidies for the workshops were granted by the Royal Netherlands Academy of Arts and Sciences (KNAW) and the Netherlands Organization for Scientific Research (NWO). Finally we thank the staff of the International Institute for providing all the facilities that enable pleasant and fruitful discussions.

CHAPTER 1

INTRODUCTION

Marcel van der Linden

Why do people rebel?[1] This is one of the most important questions historians and social scientists have been grappling with over the years. It is a question to which no satisfactory answer has been found, despite more than a century of research. While research into social protest and social movements has boomed, especially since the 1960s, in most cases that research has focused on what people do *if* they rebel.[2] The logically prior question of *why* people decide to rebel was generally answered in socio-psychological terms, or simply deemed unimportant.[3] The essays in this volume attempt to offer an alternative perspective. They presuppose the need for a Copernican change in how we think about collective action. The principal weakness of even the most advanced analyses is that they tend to focus on those people who engaged in collective action in a specific situation. The institutional context in which protesters acted, the resources they mobilised, how they attempted to legitimise their action, etc., have been studied in great detail. However, the people who, in that same situation, did *not* engage in collective action and so kept their distance have rarely attracted the attention of scholars.[4]

A teleological approach like this can be misleading. Suppose we want to know why people from a certain social group engaged in a particular form of collective action at a particular time. Research may show that the group of people so engaged had all manner of grievances and also had access to certain organisational resources, and they therefore resolved to engage in collective action. Such a reconstruction gives the impression that the combination of grievances and resources leads almost automatically to collective action. The fallacy of this impression would become apparent if we were also to study the people from that same social group who did *not* join in that collective action. Assuming they had the same grievances and resources, we soon see that participation in collective action was not the only option available to those involved; these options usually remain outside the discussion. Such a result-oriented reconstruction also implies that those who preferred an alternative option were merely making a negative choice: they did not join, they showed no solidarity, etc. There are very strong empirical indications to suggest that this was not in fact the case. In almost all situations people have access to a broad range of options to alleviate or resolve material misfortune. This becomes clear only if we begin not with the results themselves but with the problems of which the results are an expression. In other words, we cannot answer the question 'Why do people rebel?' unless we also know why they do not.

Once this line of reasoning has been embarked on, it becomes clear that it is also necessary to break with the traditional approach in a second respect. Students of collective protest tend to treat rebellious people as coalitions of isolated individuals. That was true as far back as Karl Marx, who referred to 'the dot-like isolation [*Punktualität*]' of the 'free worker'.[5] The same assumption is also prevalent among modern theorists of 'rational choice', 'resource mobilisation', etc.[6] Of course all these scholars *know* that most people belong to families or other small-scale communities and that they are members of a wide range of social networks (religious communities, neighbourhoods, etc.), but these same scholars attach hardly any consequences for the analysis of collective behaviour to this fact. The essays in this collection are an attempt to change this view. They analyse rebellious and non-rebellious people as members of families and as members of other social networks.

Since these essays explore a new research perspective, they do not focus on all family types and social networks to the same extent. The authors have deliberately opted to concentrate on families, particularly families for which wages were the key source of income. Joseph Schumpeter once claimed, in another context, that: 'The family, not the physical person, is the true unit of class and class theory'.[7] This is too simplistic of course, since not only does it present the family household as 'a unit defined a priori' rather than as a concept derived analytically, it also neglects the fact that there are, as noted earlier, other social networks that might be of social, cultural, economic or political importance for individuals.[8] Nonetheless, Schumpeter's remark is not entirely without foundation since the family does seem to be crucial to an understanding of many social conflicts. The authors of the essays presented here believe that an understanding of the entire range of economic options available to rebellious and non-rebellious families is a pre-condition for studying many forms of collective protest – or their failure to materialise – particularly those with economic causes.

The authors focus on working-class families in a broad sense.[9] The disadvantage of this self-imposed restriction is that only a selection of historical experiences will receive attention. There is, however, also an advantage to this approach, namely that in limiting the range of types slightly it becomes easier to compare results and relatively easier to develop fragments of theory. An additional advantage is that the study of working-class families and their strategies is fairly well advanced, and there is therefore a fairly large quantity of material available that can be drawn on by new analyses.

One should note though, that there are serious limitations to this material. Just as the historians of workers' protests have tended to exclude families from their analyses, so, conversely, the students of family strategies have seldom studied workers' protests. This is all the more surprising since scholarly interest in family strategies was actually a response to working-class protest. Almost immediately after the first major manifestations of labour conflict in nineteenth-century Europe, observers began to take an interest in the economy of proletarian households. The wave of protest that swept across continental Europe over a century-and-a-half ago and that culminated in the revolutions of 1848 prompted the first large-scale budget surveys.[10] In the words of George Stigler: 'The agitation and violence of the working classes led to an increasing concern for their economic condition and thus to the collection of economic data, including budgetary data'.[11] Budget studies were carried out in Saxony and Prussia in 1848, and in 1855 a Belgian study, by Edouard Ducpétiaux, was published with full details on almost two hundred household budgets. The motive for these studies was generally a simple view of the relationship between household budget and collective action: if the first were inadequate, the second would surely follow. The key pioneers of budget surveys, such as Ernst Engel and Frédéric Leplay, claimed there was a direct relationship between people's real income and their well-being.[12] Such views have been extraordinarily persistent and continued to influence scholars until late into the twentieth century.[13]

So many researchers have explicitly claimed a direct relationship between high levels of unemployment and high food prices on the one hand and social protest on the other. Edward Thompson, who has referred sardonically in this context to the 'spasmodic school', once remarked that: 'This contains a self-evident truth (people protest when they are hungry): and in much the same way a 'sexual tension chart' would show that the onset of sexual maturity can be correlated with a greater frequency of sexual activity. The objection is that such a chart, if used unwisely, may conclude an investigation at the exact point at which it becomes of serious sociological or cultural interest: being hungry (or being sexy), what do people do?'[14]

While the relationship between household budget and collective action was often oversimplified in the past, conventional analyses of household budgets have also failed to give us much insight into the problem either. In the first place these analyses usually took the family's income as a given and simply examined how the family employed its resources. How that income was obtained was beyond the scope of these studies; it seemed to originate from a black box. If sources of income were considered at all, it was at best as a secondary consideration, by including an inventory of the various means by which households obtained money.[15] Since the question of how income was acquired and the considerations that played a role in acquiring it are of the greatest importance in understanding household strategies, any satisfactory understanding of collective action is inevitably difficult then, if not impossible.

Principles

Before we can develop an alternative analysis, it will be useful to describe the central concepts involved in more detail. By *families* I mean the small social units based on marriage or descent from common ancestors ('lineage'). These should be distinguished from *households*. This second concept is rather ambiguous and has been subject to extensive terminological debate[16]. To avoid a digression into this issue, I will use the description given in McGuire et al., namely that households are 'those sets of relationships, historically variable yet relatively constant, that have as one of their principal features the sharing of sustenance gained from the widest possible variety of sources'.[17] This description is loose enough to cover a wide variety of situations. It stresses the budget-pooling aspect of households, an approach that serves the purpose of my project.

The following reservations apply to using the designation of households:

- Households do not necessarily consist of two or three generations of one family. They may include several families, other types of biological kinship (such as siblings), or members not related by blood or marriage.
- Households do not necessarily entail co-residence, not even according to Donald Bender's definition, which calls for 'a proximity in sleeping arrangements and a sentiment similar to that expressed in our folk concept of home'.[18] For example, at least one member of a household of seasonal migrants is likely to live elsewhere for months at a time and will nevertheless contribute substantially to the household budget. (In the absence of co-residence, it is possible to form what I will call secondary households.[19])
- This focus on economic aspects should not diminish the role of households as culturally significant units shaped by symbolic processes.[20]
- Rather than being predetermined, the composition of households is a product of negotiations. Factors affecting the composition of a household may include income, marriage prospects for men and women, employment opportunities, arrangements for the care of elderly parents, and government factors such as legislation and taxation.[21]
- Households should not be considered anthropomorphic entities through being designated as products of collective will. Members do not necessarily work for the common good of the household; on the contrary, they may be driven by selfish motives. Conflicts of interest are also possible, as well as oppression and resistance against oppression.[22] Both dependency and authority may vary according to the member of the household. Laslett pointed out that infants and children have the greatest stake in the household's survival, 'since their life chances depend almost wholly on its existence and persistence, on their being accepted and retained as members. But children also have the least power to affect the household's decisions and none whatever to carry them out'.[23] This statement about influencing household decisions implies that while we should not arbitrarily ascribe a collective will to households, members nevertheless try to find a variety of ways to control their fate whenever possible. To this end, they negotiate to devise a strategy for generating and allocating the common budget.

In everyday language hardly any distinction is made between families and households. There is much to be said for this since households are generally based on marriage and/or real or fictive kinship. But it is useful nonetheless to make an analytical distinction between the two concepts. There are enough examples of non-kin-related household members, and kinship can extend beyond just the household, as is shown by the case of male labourers working in the agricultural industry in Madagascar who are members of more than one family at the same time.[24]

The third central concept is that of *household strategies*. This is a somewhat controversial notion. Some scholars argue that the term 'strategy' implies the existence of a 'master plan', which households and families use to ensure their survival. Of course this is not the case. In fact, the 'strategy' to be adopted is a matter for continual negotiation between household members, and occasionally the plans of some members are even opposed by other members in no uncertain terms. We have considered a number of alternatives ('coping methods' for example), but they were not really much of an improvement. Furthermore, the concept of 'household (or family) strategies' is now fairly well established in the academic literature, and so we have decided to retain it, despite some reluctance. By 'strategies' we mean here the one-off or repetitive and coordinated use of resources to achieve a particular purpose.[25] Within each strategy one can there-fore make a distinction between the following: (i) the resources mobilised, i.e., the various resources, such as time, money, land, means of communication and networks, used to achieve that purpose; (ii) the purpose of the strategy, i.e., what the actors wish to achieve; and (iii) how the resources are combined to achieve that purpose (who decides, who carries it out, what resources are to be used, and how). We must be wary though, of tautologies; not all actions carried out by household members are household strategies, only those intended to contribute directly to the welfare of that household.[26]

The fourth and final concept is *collective action*. Collective action can be defined as the more or less coordinated actions of a group of people intended to achieve a particular purpose that none of them acting on their own and with the resources at their disposal could achieve in the same space of time. This def-inition is exceptionally wide, since it also includes the participation of a team in a football competition. Not all forms of collective action are intended to pro-mote the interests of households by any means. The collective actions of house-holds examined in this book are primarily socio-economic in nature and vary from food riots and wildcat strikes, through mutual aid societies, producer or consumer co-operatives, to trade unions and political parties. In this context, the reference to 'more or less coordinated actions' of a group of workers is by no means meant to suggest the existence of a formal organisation. It could just as easily be an extremely short-lived ad-hoc coalition formed specifically for that one action and which collapsed once that action had ended. The difference between formal and informal organisations is sometimes vague. Moreover, a collective action does not necessarily need to have the character of a protest. There are many types of collective action that are not regarded as protests either by the workers involved or the authorities.[27] Whether an action entails a violation of existing rules is determined solely by the specific historical context. The authorities repeatedly redefine these rules (partly in response to the pres-sure of collective action), and so actions that at one moment constitute a seri-ous breach of the law might at some other time be completely legal.

Individual workers and their families always combine a number of activities to be able to cope with problems related to waged labour. Not only does a great deal of subsistence labour take place every day in every family (especially, but not exclusively, performed by women),[28] there are usually also several forms of activity remunerated with money. The social budget pooling function of households entails income and expenditure. This process need not be exclusively monetary: it may also consist of goods and services.

The pattern of *expenditure* in independent households is composed of at least five types of expenses:[29]

- Support of household members involved in productive labour.
- Support of these same individuals during periods of disability or unemployment.
- Support of older household members who used to be involved in productive labour.
- Support of younger household members not yet involved in productive labour.
- Payments to third parties (such as taxes, duties, and payment of debts).

This list includes the possibility of economies of scale arising from common use of certain goods. (Whether a household consists of two members or five, its members can make do with one vacuum cleaner.)

The income of independent households is derived from at least seven sources:[30]

- Labour remunerated in wages or in kind.
- Non-commercial labour (directly consumable goods), including home-made clothing, raising domestic animals such as pigs and poultry,[31] and gathering rubbish for direct reuse.[32]
- Petty commodity production or petty commerce, including manufacturing cottage-industry textiles, raising livestock for sale, peddling,[33] and professional scavenging.[34]
- Providing resources such as land, tools for labour, accommodation, and money; this may include income received from renting out beds or rooms.[35]
- Transfer payments, received without immediate reciprocal exchange of labour or commodities, including support from friends and acquaintances in times of need, charity, and social benefits.
- Theft, including both conventional methods of stealing and especially pilfering at the workplace.[36]
- Credit, including billing in instalments, deferred payments, or pawning personal property.[37]

Working-class households are households where the first of these sources of income (remunerated labour) prevails. This does *not* exclude the role of other sources of income. On the contrary, working-class households usually rely on a variety of sources of income, virtually all members generate a reliable income, and individual members (especially over the course of their entire lives) tend to provide income from numerous sources. While these observations do not imply the absence of a clear correlation between age and gender on the one hand, and revenue-producing activities on the other, it is likely that the degree of correlation varies according to the source of income.[38]

The various reproductive activities of the household have a gendered nature. Some are typically male, some typically female. These gendered definitions may be flexible, depending on the circumstances. There are many examples of gender transgressions, with men doing 'women's work' and vice versa.[39] The management of the household is a distinct type of work and is normally done by a woman. As far as I am aware, there is no satisfactory comparative historical analysis of this management.[40]

A Range of Strategies

What are the potential strategies for survival and improvement available to a working-class household? Let us begin with the means for self-improvement at the disposal of *individual* households. First, they might move to another neighbourhood, city, or country in the hope of finding more satisfactory conditions. Millions have already chosen this option.[41] Secondly, they can take advantage of better times to take precautionary measures for the hard times that lie ahead. These measures may include saving money[42] or purchasing a house.[43] Thirdly, households may reduce expenses through measures such as living (still more) frugally, not paying their debts, and expelling non-productive members.[44] Fourthly, they can change the way they obtain their income, for example by seeking other work or by diversifying their sources of income.

In addition to measures taken by households themselves to improve their living conditions, there are several strategies involving help from outside sources. As a first strategy, households may appeal to *relatives*. Many authors have indicated the value of kinship for households. Tamara Hareven wrote that to many American immigrants and urban workers, kin were 'the main, if not the only, source of assistance and survival. In the absence of public welfare agencies and social security, kin were the exclusive source of social insurance. Kin assistance was crucial in handling personal and family crises (such as child-bearing, illness, and death), and in coping with the insecurities imposed by the industrial system (such as unemployment, accidents, and strikes)'. Furthermore, '[s]trategies for kin assistance required both short-term and long-term investments over the life-course. Short-term investments entailed assistance in the workplace, in housing, in loaning money or tools, and trading skills, goods, or services. Among the long-term investments, the most pervasive exchange was that between parents and children – old-age support in return for childrearing'.[45]

Kinship relations *outside* one's immediate surroundings often proved especially important. An interesting method of distributing the risks involves mutual assistance between rural-agrarian and urban relatives. Heidi Rosenbaum described an example of this system when she mentioned the importance 'of family support from relatives in the countryside' for workers in Linden (Germany) in the early twentieth century.[46] Jean Peterson showed how the reverse currently holds true for Philippine peasantry: 'some families explicitly plan to establish some siblings ... as wage-earners in the city' to generate revenue in cases of crop failure or poor harvests.[47]

A second source of relief lies in *personal communities*. These communities consist of informal networks based on companionship, emotional aid, and small services in daily life. While the networks may be locally based (neighbourhoods), this restriction is not essential to their operation. Personal communities also include kinship networks and require the same investment as strategies for short-term kin assistance (relatively small and readily available skills and services).[48] Personal communities have always appeared gendered, although their focus varies depending on the time, the place, and the culture.[49] There is often a fluid boundary between blood relatives and personal communities, as proved by frequent transformations of friendships into fictitious kinship relations, as with the *compadrazgo* (fictitious parenthood usually involving the relationship between parents and godparents to a child) in Latin America[50] and the selection of *Taufpaten* (godparents) among the nineteenth-century German working class.[51]

Acceptance of *patronage* is a third strategy. Whereas the first two forms of social insurance are generally horizontal (the actors pertained to similar social classes), this approach is clearly vertical. As Y. Michal Bodemann has written, it involves 'a form of class rule and class struggle and at the same time its concealment'.[52] Weak subalterns seek protection from higher, more powerful individuals who help them in emergencies in return for material or other types of services. This relationship is not merely economic but sociocultural as well, as patrons receive their clients' loyalty and esteem in return for their protection and help. Forms of patronage may vary from political clientelism to patriarchal enterprise.[53]

Then there is the fourth and final strategy, which forms the core of our discussion: collective action to bring about overall improvement in the conditions of segments of the working class. There are at least eight ways in which households can improve their circumstances, whether on their own accord or with outside help. *How* households devise their strategy is of course crucial. Several factors need to be considered. The preceding description is *taxonomic* in that it covers opportunities that *may* arise over time. The various options are actually limited to specific historical contexts. Paternalism, for example, is less likely in highly developed industrial societies than in less-developed ones.[54] Each actual situation will therefore present fewer opportunities than those described here. On the other hand, each strategy consists of several options: those who wish to join social movement organisations can sometimes choose from a wide range of possibilities. It is also possible (and even common) to use several strategies at once. Furthermore, the strategies described here are interrelated and can alternatively undermine or reinforce one another. Frequent geographical mobility can work against the establishment of powerful unions in some cases, whereas it might actually form the basis of organisations in other cases.[55] Strategies may even intermingle.

Extremely close non-kin relationships can, for example, be transformed into fictitious kinship relations.[56] Alternatively, kinship and personal communities may provide a valuable basis for a social movement organisation.[57]

The Transition to Collective Action

The crucial question running through this book is how the transition to collective action is made. It would be helpful here to consider for a moment the concept of labour movements. Three types of organisation should be distinguished: household-centred, enterprise-centred, and state-centred labour organisations. *Household-centred organisations* entail measures taken by wage labourers to accomplish more with the material means at their disposal without necessarily eliciting confrontations with entrepreneurs or the authorities. Mutual aid societies, which use a communal fund from several households to provide some protection in cases of unemployment, illness, old age, or death, are one example of this type of activism. Consumer co-operatives that purchase goods for several households at once are another.[58] *Enterprise-centred organisations* involve efforts to alter the economic balance of power between workers and entrepreneurs. Changes may occur either through battles against capitalist industry for higher wages or improved working conditions (traditionally the unions' job), or through attempts to establish and maintain producer cooperatives. Finally, *state-centred organisations* aim to guide or obtain improvements from the state that would be impossible (or far more difficult) to achieve through household- or enterprise-centred activism. The most obvious organisational instruments for this purpose are, of course, political parties, although it is possible for other organisations to focus their efforts on the state.

Once again, these forms of activism overlap. Mutual aid societies often became unions, and consumer co-operatives have at times become actively involved in national politics. Based on this brief characterisation of organisational types and subtypes, which each possess their own contextual repertoire of collective action, we can examine how they relate to the interests of households. The first question is where the freerider problem surfaces, or which organisations make it attractive to benefit from them without joining. As mutual benefit societies, consumer and producer co-operatives offer direct advantages only to the households involved; they do not have a freerider problem. Trade unions and political parties are a different matter, however, as their activities can also benefit non-members.[59] It is common knowledge that organisations can try to solve the freerider problem through selective incentives (second-order collective goods), such as providing goods and services (e.g. free legal aid) to members only. This approach may make it considerably more attractive to join an organisation.[60]

Next comes the degree of risk associated with participation in an organisation and its actions. Membership of mutual benefit societies or consumer co-operatives generally entails a smaller financial risk than participation in producer co-operatives, as households involved in the first two kinds of organisations invest – and therefore risk losing – small sums, whereas their stake in producer co-operatives is far greater. Repression by the state or entrepreneurs is another major factor. Substantial repression through an acute danger of imprisonment or unemployment will obviously be a far greater deterrent to joining an organisation than more tolerant conditions. It seems plausible that the degree of repression faced by household-centred organisations (and producer co-operatives), which tend to avoid conflicts, is almost always less than that faced by trade unions and workers' parties. At the same time, when unions and parties are consolidated and integrated, the degree of repression they face can decrease considerably. As the threat of repression increases, the financial risk to households rises. Table 1.1 summarises a few of the considerations briefly described here.

Table 1.1 *Workers' organisations*

Type	Focus	Freerider problem	Financial risk	Repression
Mutual benefit society	Household	No	Low	Low
Consumer cooperative	Household	No	Low	Low
Producer cooperative	Enterprise	No	High	Low
Trade union	Enterprise	Yes	Low-high	Low-high
Worker's party	State	Yes	Low-high	Low-high

As mutual benefit societies and consumer co-operatives were the easiest kinds of association for households to join, it is understandable that they were by far the largest working-class organisations (even though their relative size was sometimes exceeded by unions offering selective welfare-state-type incentives); and because workers' parties rarely offer selective incentives, their membership is usually small (even if they receive a high percentage of the vote), unless trade unions are also party organisations (as in Great Britain and Sweden until recently). Producer co-operatives never seem to have appealed to more than a small minority of the working class, which suggests that the permanent substantial financial risk that this organisation entails is a major barrier.[61]

Even the most comprehensive organisations have never succeeded in organising *all* wage labourers in households, except in situations involving economic or legal force. There always seems to be some segment (whether large or small) of the working class that opts for household strategies different from those offered by labour movements. Examining these non-organised groups can enhance our understanding of the motives of the organised segments.

The Essays

The observations made above arose in the course of discussions at the International Institute of Social History in Amsterdam during the 1990s. At the time, I summarised them in a position paper, which served as the starting-point for two international workshops held on 28–29 November 1997 and 28–29 May 1999.[62] Eight of the nine essays included in the current collection were originally presented there in draft form. Henk Wals's contribution (Chapter 8) was included later. All of them comment on the arguments presented here and explore them further.

Eileen Janes Yeo (Chapter 2) offers a number of qualifications to the central thesis, based on the development of early British labour movements. She points out that the needs articulated by the family – of security, dignity and justice ('along with others which are sometimes ignored, like pleasure') – were always gendered, contested and shifting. Labour movements attempted to meet these complex needs through a wide range of activities, varying from cooperative stores to dignified funerals, from tea parties to theatre performances. Men and women from the same families participated in these activities according to a gendered division of labour. Their decision to participate was based in part on how they saw 'the interests of the family at different times' and 'how they assessed labour movement provision compared with other realistic alternatives in a particular context'.

Christina von Hodenberg (Chapter 3) discusses the rebellion among proto-industrial cotton weavers in Silesia in 1844. She describes the range of household strategies available to the weavers' families and points to the importance of local networks at village level. These formed the context in which specific notions of justice – and injustice – and respectability were developed and which at the same time ensured that a number of individual strategies (migration, switching to another occupation) were rendered impossible. They formed, too, the background to the gendered allocation of responsibilities during the rebellion: the younger men were responsible for 'public' protest, while the women had a sort of auxiliary function. The collective protest developed step by step; violence against employers was only the final stage in a process of escalation.

Bruce Scates (Chapter 4) focuses on the household strategies of poor single mothers in Melbourne during the depression of the early 1890s. These single mothers could take on 'unskilled' work, seek charitable assistance, take in boarders or washing and sewing, prostitute themselves, etc. Their children could also work, or scavenge or steal on the street, etc. During the depression, however, it was sometimes impossible to make ends meet, even when expenditure was kept to a bare minimum. In that case, more drastic measures were resorted to, and the size of the family was reduced. The collective protest of single mothers and their families was usually 'spontaneous' and took the form of demonstrations. Unlike protests by male breadwinners, it focused primarily on charity and the city government rather than employers and work sites, and it was combined with other strategies.

Justin Byrne (Chapter 5) examines one particular all-male group of workers, the bricklayers in Madrid, along with their families and household strategies. The bricklayers' trade union *El Trabajo* grew explosively after 1897 and Byrne argues that the growth of this organisation and its activities can be understood properly only if one analyses not just the developments in the building industry but also the domestic lives of the workers. The union was not a replacement for other household strategies; it built upon them, with kinship networks and personal communities, maintained primarily by women, playing a crucial role in the mobilisation process. The mutual insurance offered by the union also made membership attractive to many women. The demands made by the union, and expressed in gendered terms, reflected the priorities within households; the fact that both men and women were providers makes it clear why bricklayers could afford to struggle for a reduction in hours rather than higher wages.

Theresa Moriarty (Chapter 6) discusses the celebrated lockout in Dublin in 1913–14 and observes that collective action and household strategies became 'inseparable'. She shows how the Irish Transport and General Workers' Union and working-class families enjoyed a symbiotic relationship for a period of several months. In particular, she draws attention to one remarkable household strategy, namely the organised removal of children from the scene of the industrial conflict by placing them with 'host families'. This method, employed earlier by textile workers in Lawrence (Massachusetts), was consistent with an established household practice, but elevated it to a more politicised level.

Bonnie Stepenoff (Chapter 7) describes the combination of various forms of waged labour within working-class families in Northeast Pennsylvania around 1900. While many fathers earned a living in anthracite mining, their daughters often worked in silk mills. When the fathers went on strike, their daughters did the same – with their permission. Nonetheless, it was much more difficult to organise the daughters within trade unions than it was to organise their fathers. Stepenoff's explanation for this is that the daughters had to operate in a cultural context in which they were regarded as weak, as incapable of acting independently, and in which their contribution to the family economy was considered of minor importance.

In his study of Amsterdam building labourers in the early twentieth century, Henk Wals (Chapter 8) investigates the considerations that played a role in deciding whether or not to join a trade union. He points out that ideological considerations tended to be of little importance. Emotional grounds (for example, an abhorrence of hazardous and damaging strikes, or, on the contrary, sympathy with the fighting spirit of radical unions) played a role, but the main considerations were rational ones. Wals makes a good case for claiming that most working-class families carried out a cost-benefit analysis in which account was taken for example of the level of union dues, of allowances obtainable through the union in the event of sickness, unemployment and strikes, and of the higher wages that might ensue from membership. Wals also makes it clear that such a cost-benefit analysis was 'carried out' against a normative background (respectability, security) and might well be accompanied by conflicts between men and their wives. Justin Byrne's conclusion, that the majority of the Madrid bricklayers appear to have been interested largely in 'improving their lot in the here and now', also applies, Wals claims, to their colleagues in the Amsterdam building trade.

In her case study of Philippine plantation workers who were involved in 'high-cost' guerilla activism that ran partly counter to the interests of their household, Rosanne Rutten (Chapter 9) questions the assumption of a direct link between poor people's household interests and activism. She points out that social ties with people *outside* the household can create obligations that might prevail over household interests. Individual household members are involved in shifting social networks, 'of which the household is only one', and it is these 'multiple embeddings' that make forms of high-risk and high-cost activism intelligible.

Finally, unlike the other authors, Mark Pittaway (Chapter 10) is concerned not so much with the *origin* of collective protest as its *disappearance*. His essay focuses on Hungary in the early 1950s, where labour protests increasingly gave way to household strategies in the private sphere. Pittaway argues that the explanation for this development must be sought not simply in the considerable degree of state repression, but also in the unsuccessful 'socialistic' policy of industrialisation, which compelled working-class families to seek additional resources outside the formal state sector to supplement their wage income. In doing so, women attached more importance to social privatisation than men, because 'they coped with the consequences of socialist industrialisation not only as workers but as home-makers and consumers'.

These nine essays offer a wealth of new perspectives and reveal many aspects so far neglected by social historians. They also include a number of suggestions for achieving a deeper insight into the factors that encourage collective protest among families.

Translation: Chris Gordon and Lee Mitzman

Notes

1. I am grateful to Patricia van den Eeckhout, Francisca de Haan, Lex Heerma van Voss, Marian van der Klein, Jan Lucassen, Alice Mul, Rosanne Rutten and Ratna Saptari for their helpful comments on earlier versions of (parts of) this chapter. Jan Kok and Henk Wals read the penultimate draft and suggested helpful amendments.
2. See for example the excellent survey in Sidney Tarrow, *Power in Movement: Social Movements and Contentious Politics*, Cambridge, UK, 1998.
3. A well-known example of a socio-psychological explanation is Ted Robert Gurr's *Why Men Rebel*, Princeton, NJ, 1970, which is based on a frustration-aggression hypothesis. A number of influential theorists of the 'resource mobilisation' school have argued that what motivates rebellious people is not very relevant since subaltern groups always have sufficient reason to engage in collective action; all that matters is the resources available to these groups to articulate their discontent. A classic exposition of this view can be found in John D. McCarthy and Mayer N. Zald, 'Resource Mobilization and Social Movements: A Partial Theory', *American Journal of Sociology* 82 (1976–77): 1212–41. Often this 'logistical' interpretation is expressed only implicitly; for example, Charles Tilly distinguishes five components in the analysis of social movements: 'interest, organization, mobilization, opportunity, and collective action itself'. Charles Tilly, *From Mobilization to Revolution,* Reading, MA, 1978, 7. As Craig Calhoun has aptly remarked: 'this leaves out self-understanding and emphasizes instrumental pursuits'. Craig Calhoun, '"New Social Movements" of the Early Nineteenth Century', *Social Science History* 17 (1993): 385–427, here 387.
4. As long ago as 1975 Charles Tilly et al. rightly defended the proposition that 'an explanation of protest, rebellion, or collective violence that cannot account for its absence is no explanation at all'. Charles Tilly, Louise Tilly and Richard Tilly, *The Rebellious Century*, Cambridge, MA, 1975, 12. However, Fox Piven and Cloward have argued that Tilly's own work also takes insufficient account of this methodological admonition. Frances Fox Piven and Richard

A. Cloward, 'Collective Protest: A Critique of Resource-Mobilization Theory', in *Social Movements: Critiques, Concepts, Case-Studies,* ed. Stanford M. Lyman, Basingstoke and London, 1995, 137–167, here 147.

5. Karl Marx, *Grundrisse: Foundations of the Critique of Political Economy (Rough Draft),* trans. Martin Nicolaus, Harmondsworth, 1973, 485.

6. See for instance Mancur Olson, *The Logic of Collective Action: Public Goods and the Theory of Groups,* Cambridge, MA and London, 1965, who assumes explicitly and throughout that people are 'self-interested individuals'.

7. Joseph Schumpeter, 'Social Classes in an Ethnically Homogeneous Environment' (1927), in Joseph Schumpeter, *Imperialism and Social Classes*, Oxford, 1951, 148.

8. Diane Wong, 'The Limits of Using the Household as a Unit of Analysis', in *Households and the World-Economy,* eds Joan Smith, Immanuel Wallerstein and Hans-Dieter Evers, Beverly Hills, 1984, 56–63; the quotation is on 62.

9. The non-Eurocentric and gendered conceptualisation of this 'working class in a broad sense' is in itself a theoretical problem of some importance. I have discussed several aspects of it in more detail in my essay 'El fin del eurocentrismo y el futuro de la historia del trabajo: O por qué debemos y podemos reconceptualizar la clase obrera', in *Cultura social y política en el mundo del trabajo,* eds Javier Paniagua, José A. Piqueras and Vicent Sanz, Valencia, 1999, 301–22.

10. Small-scale budget surveys had been carried out before, of course, and the phenomenon is at least as old as F.M. Eden's *The State of the Poor,* 1797.

11. George J. Stigler, 'The Early History of Empirical Studies of Consumer Behavior', in George J. Stigler, *Essays in the History of Economics*, Chicago and London, 1965, 198–233, here 201.

12. Carle E. Zimmerman, 'The Family Budget as a Tool for Sociological Analysis', *American Journal of Sociology* 33 (1927–28): 901–11, here 903.

13. See too the interesting survey of attempts to identify budgetary 'laws' in Carle E. Zimmerman, 'Laws of Consumption and Living', *American Journal of Sociology* 41 (1935–36): 13–30.

14. Edward P. Thompson, 'The Moral Economy of the English Crowd in the Eighteenth Century', in Edward P. Thompson, *Customs in Common*, Harmondsworth, 1993, 185–258, here 187.

15. This tradition goes back at least to Ernst Engel's *Rechnungsbuch*. See, based on this, Stephan Bauer, 'Konsumtion II: Das Konsumtionsbudget der Haushaltung', *Handwörterbuch der Staatswissenschaften*, vol. 5, Jena, 1900: second revised edition, 316–33, here 323.

16. It is difficult to provide a generally valid definition of households. Attempts to find 'a precise, reduced definition' have been unsuccessful, as households are 'inherently complex, multifunctional institutions imbued with a diverse array of cultural principles and meanings'. Sylvia Junko Yaganisako, 'Family and Household: The Analysis of Domestic Groups', *Annual Review of Anthropology* 8 (1979): 161–205, 200.

17. Randall H. McGuire, Joan Smith and William G. Martin, 'Patterns of Household Structures and the World-Economy', *Review* 10, no. 1 (1986): 75–97, 76.

18. Donald R. Bender, 'A Refinement of the Concept of Household: Families, Co-Residence, and Domestic Functions', *American Anthropologist* 69 (1967): 493–504, 498.

19. Examples of secondary households include the Canadian bushworker camps in Ian Radforth's *Bushworkers and Bosses: Logging in Northern Ontario, 1900–1980,* Toronto, 1987, ch. 5, and the travelling groups of German brickmakers in Piet Lourens and Jan Lucassen, *Arbeitswanderung und berufliche Spezialisierung: Die lippischen Ziegler im 18. und 19. Jahrhundert,* Osnabrück, 1999, 73–86.

20. Sylvia Junko Yaganisako, 'Explicating Residence: A Cultural Analysis of Changing Households among Japanese-Americans', in *Households. Comparative and Historical Studies of the Domestic Group,* eds Robert M. Netting, Richard R. Wilk and Eric J. Arnould, Berkeley, 1984, 330–52.

21. Yaganisako, 'Family and Household', 167–75; David J. Maume and R. Gregory Dunaway, 'Determinants of the Prevalence of Mother-Only Families', *Research in Social Stratification and Mobility* 8 (1989): 313–27; Michael Mitterauer, 'Faktoren des Wandels historischer Familienformen', in: Michael Mitterauer, *Familie und Arbeitsteilung. Historischvergleichende Studien*, Vienna, 1992, 214–55.

22. Judith Bruce, 'Homes Divided', *World Development* 17 (1989): 979–991; Diane L. Wolf, 'Daughters, Decisions and Domination: An Empirical and Conceptual Critique of House-

hold Strategies', *Development and Change* 21 (1990): 43–74. In 'The Limits of Using the Household as a Unit of Analysis' (57) Diane Wong distinguishes two levels of inner-household struggle: (i) who is to control child labour, and (ii) who is allowed to reproduce, that is 'to establish a family and a household'.

23. Peter Laslett, 'The Family as a Knot of Individual Interests', in Netting, Wilk and Arnould, *Households*, 353–79, here 370–1.

24. Jean-Claude Rabeherifara, 'Réseaux sociaux et familiaux: détournement du salarial?', in *Classes ouvrières d'Afrique noire*, eds Michel Agier, Jean Copans and Alain Morice, Paris, 1987, 183–213. For Ghanaian examples of activities that cut across several households see Prudence Woodford-Berger, 'Women in Houses: The Organization of Residence and Work in Rural Ghana', *Antropologiska Studier*, no.30–31 (1981): 3–35; Roger Sanjek, 'The Organization of Households in Adabraka: Toward a Wider Comparative Perspective', *Comparative Studies in Society and History* 24 (1982): 57–103; Dorothy Dee Vellenga, 'Women, Households, and Food Commodity Chains in Southern Ghana', *Review* 8 (1984–85): 293–318.

25. An example of a one-off strategy is the desertion of unfree wage labourers, about which Robin Cohen and others have written. Robin Cohen, 'Resistance and Hidden Forms of Consciousness amongst African Workers', in Robin Cohen, *Contested Domains: Debates in International Labour Studies,* London and New Jersey, 1991, 91–109. Wage labour on the other hand is a repetitive strategy.

26. Diane Wolf has criticised the concept of household strategies because of its alleged tautological character: 'A strategy is everything a household does, and everything a household does is a strategy'. Diane L. Wolf, *Factory Daughters: Gender, Household Dynamics, and Rural Industrialization in Java*, Berkeley, 1992, 20.

27. Some historians tend to interpret every form of workers' collective action as a protest, even when the workers involved did not. This seems to me 'one of the subtler forms of condescension in historical writing' about which John Stevenson has written. See his *Popular Disturbances in England, 1700–1832*, second edition, Harlow, 1992, 4.

28. Men often contribute too, of course. The subsistence labour of children has less often been studied. See, however, Anna Davin, 'Working or Helping? London Working-Class Children in the Domestic Economy', in Smith, Wallerstein and Evers, *Households and the World-Economy*, 215–32; Maria Papathanassiou, *Zwischen Arbeit, Spiel und Schule. Die ökonomische Funktion der Kinder ärmerer Schichten in Österreich 1880–1939*, Vienna and Munich, 1999, chs 5, 7 and 8.

29. This distribution is based in part on Claude Meillassoux's three categories of reproduction costs: 'The value of labour power is derived from three factors: supporting workers during periods of employment (*retaining* the existing workforce), *maintaining* workers during periods of idleness (such as unemployment or illness), and replacing workers by providing for their progeny (known as *reproduction*)'. Claude Meillassoux, *Femmes, Greniers & Capitaux*, Paris, 1975, 152.

30. Kathie Friedman listed the first five of these sources of income in 'Households as Income-Pooling Units', in Smith, Wallerstein and Evers, *Households and the World-Economy*, 37–55, 46.

31. Bettina Bradbury, 'Pigs, Cows, and Boarders: Non-Wage Forms of Survival among Montreal Families, 1861–91', *Labour/Le Travail* no. 14 (Fall 1984): 9–46; Béatrice Cabedoce, 'Jardins ouvriers et banlieue: le bonheur au jardin?', in *Les Premiers Banlieusards. Aux Origines des Banlieues de Paris 1860–1940*, ed. Alain Faure, Paris, 1991, 249–79.

32. See James R. Barrett, *Work and Community in the Jungle. Chicago's Packinghouse Workers 1894–1922*, Urbana and Chicago, 1987, 104.

33. John Benson, *The Penny Capitalists. A Study of Nineteenth-Century Working Class Entrepreneurs*, Dublin, 1983; Serge Jaumain, 'Contribution à l'histoire comparée: les colporteurs belges et québécois au XIXe siècle', *Histoire sociale/Social History* no. 39 (1987): 49–77.

34. Alain Faure, 'Classe malpropre, classe dangereuse? Quelques remarques à propos des chiffoniers parisiens au XIXe siècle et de leurs cités', *Recherches* no. 29 (December 1977): 79–102; Chris Birkbeck, 'Self-Employed Proletarians in an Informal Factory: The Case of Cali's Garbage Dump', *World Development* 6 (1978): 1173–85; Daniel T. Sicular, 'Pockets of Peasants in Indonesian Cities: The Case of Scavengers', *World Development* 19 (1991): 137–61.

35. Bradbury, 'Pigs, Cows, and Boarders'; John Modell and Tamara Hareven, 'Urbanization and the Malleable Household: An Examination of Boarding and Lodging in American Families', *Journal of Marriage and the Family* 35 (1973): 467–479; Franz Brüggemeier and Lutz Niethammer, 'Schlafgänger, Schnapskasinos und schwerindustrielle Kolonie. Aspekte der Arbeiterwohnungsfrage im Ruhrgebiet vor dem ersten Weltkrieg', in *Fabrik, Familie, Feierabend. Beiträge zur Sozialgeschichte des Alltags im Industriezeitalter*, eds Jürgen Reulecke and Wolfhard Weber, Wuppertal, 1978, 153–74; Josef Ehmer, 'Wohnen ohne eigene Wohnung. Zur sozialen Stellung von Untermietern und Bettgehern', in *Wohnen im Wandel. Beiträge zur Geschichte des Alltags in der bürgerlichen Gesellschaft*, ed. Lutz Niethammer,Wuppertal, 1979, 132–50.

36. See Gerald Mars, 'Dock Pilferage: A Case Study in Occupational Theft', in *Deviance and Social Control*, eds Paul Rock and Mary McIntosh, London, 1974, 209–28, and Jason Ditton, *Part-Time Crime: An Ethnography of Fiddling and Pilferage*, London, 1977. Historical case studies include Michael Grüttner, 'Working-Class Crime and the Labour Movement: Pilfering in the Hamburg Docks, 1888–1923', in *The German Working Class 1888–1933. The Politics of Everyday Life*, ed. Richard J. Evans, London and Totowa, New Jersey, 1982, 54–79; Peter d'Sena, 'Perquisites and Casual Labour on the London Wharfside in the Eighteenth Century', *London Journal* 14 (1989): 130–47; Adrian J. Randall, 'Peculiar Perquisites and Pernicious Practices. Embezzlement in the West of England Woollen Industry, c. 1750–1840', *International Review of Social History* 35 (1990): 193–219; Anna Green, 'Spelling, Go-Slows, Gliding Away and Theft: Informal Control over Work on the New Zealand Waterfront, 1915–1951', *Labour History* no. 63 (1992): 100–14. William Freund reveals the possibility of a smooth transition to theft as a collective act in 'Theft and Social Protest Among the Tin Miners of Northern Nigeria', *Radical History Review* 9, no. 26 (1982): 68–86.

37. Michelle Perrot, *Les ouvriers en grève. France 1871–1890*, vol I, Paris and The Hague, 1974, 210–12; Melanie Tebbutt, *Making Ends Meet. Pawnbroking and Working-Class Credit*, New York, 1983; Paul Johnson, *Saving and Spending. The Working-Class Economy in Britain 1870–1939*, Oxford, 1985, ch. 6; Karl Christian Führer, 'Das Kreditinstitut der kleinen Leute: Zur Bedeutung der Pfandleihe im deutschen Kaiserreich', *Bankhistorisches Archiv* 18 (1992): 3–21.

38. Joan Smith and Immanuel Wallerstein, 'Households as an Institution of the World-Economy', in Joan Smith et al., *Creating and Transforming Households. The Constraints of the World-Economy,* Cambridge, 1992, 3–23, 11–12.

39. See for example Susan Porter Benson, 'Living on the Margin: Working-Class Marriages and Family Survival Strategies in the United States, 1919–1941', in *The Sex of Things: Gender and Consumption in Historical Perspective*, eds Victoria de Grazia and Ellen Furlough, Berkeley, 1996, 212–43, esp. 233–4.

40. After studying these financial aspects in more detail one might concur with Richard Wilk, who distinguishes three components of the household budget: (i) an 'obligated fund' for a specific purpose that is not open to negotiation; (ii) a 'personal fund' under the control of a single person and not designed for a particular purpose; and (iii) an unobligated 'general fund' that is available for any number of uses in the future. Many or all members of the household can have a claim on general funds. Richard Wilk, 'Inside the Economic Institution: Modeling Budget Structures', in *Anthropology and Institutional Economics,* ed. James M. Acheson, Lanham, 1994, 365–90, 375–78. See also James M. Acheson, 'Household Organization and Budget Structures in a Purepecha Pueblo', *American Ethnologist* 23, 1996, 331–51. One should be wary though of being too quick to generalise. For example, it is by no means the case that every household has an undivided obligated fund. We also know of cases of households in which the obligated fund comprises two elements: one managed by the woman and the other by the man. See, for example, Philomene E. Okeke, 'Female Wage Earners and Separate Resource Structures in Post Oil Boom Nigeria', *Dialectical Anthropology* 22 (1997): 373–87; Georg Elwert, 'Conflicts Inside and Outside the Household: A West African Case Study', in Smith, Wallerstein and Evers, *Households and the World-Economy*, 272–96.

41. For an interpretation of certain migration patterns from the perspective of the household see, for example, Arjan de Haan, 'Migration as Family Strategy: Rural-Urban Labor Migration in India during the Twentieth Century', *The History of the Family* 2 (1997): 481–505.

42. Günther Schulz, "'Der konnte freilich ganz anders sparen als ich'". Untersuchungen zum Sparverhalten industrieller Arbeiter im 19. Jahrhundert', in *Arbeiterexistenz im 19. Jahrhundert. Lebensstandard und Lebensgestaltung deutscher Arbeiter und Handwerker*, eds Werner Conze and Ulrich Engelhardt, Stuttgart, 1981, 487–515; Jos De Belder, 'Het arbeiderssparen 1850–1890', in *De Belgische Spaarbanken. Geschiedenis, Recht, Economische Funktie en Instellingen*, eds August Van Put et al., Tielt, 1986, 91–119; Johnson, *Saving and Spending*, ch. 4.

43. Barrett, *Work and Community in the Jungle*, 104–107.

44. Still very useful in this context is Helen Bosanquet, 'The Burden of Small Debts', *Economic Journal* 6, 1896, 212–25, an article marred unfortunately by an anti-Semitic passage. Isabelle Devos describes how in Belgium around 1900 parents invested less in their young daughters because they earned least. This, combined with their heavy workload, led to girls dying young more often than boys. Isabelle Devos, 'Te jong om te sterven. De levenskansen van meisjes in België omstreeks 1900', *Tijdschrift voor Sociale Geschiedenis* 26 (2000): 55–75.

45. Tamara K. Hareven, 'A Complex Relationship: Family Strategies and the Processes of Economic and Social Change', in *Beyond the Marketplace. Rethinking Economy and Society*, eds Roger Friedland and A.F. Robertson, New York, 1990, 215–44.

46. Heidi Rosenbaum, *Proletarische Familien. Arbeiterfamilien und Arbeiterväter im frühen 20. Jahrhundert zwischen traditioneller, sozialdemokratischer und kleinbürgerlicher Orientierung*, Frankfurt am Main, 1992, 153.

47. Jean Treloggen Peterson, 'Interhousehold Exchange and the Public Economy in Three Highland Philippine Communities', *Research in Economic Anthropology* 11 (1989): 123–42, 136.

48. Barry Wellman, Peter J. Carrington and Alan Hall, 'Networks as Personal Communities', in *Social Structures. A Network Approach*, eds Barry Wellman and S.D. Berkowitz, Cambridge, 1988, 130–84, 163.

49. Compare personal communities in London between 1870 and 1914 in Ellen Ross, 'Survival Networks: Women's Neighbourhood Sharing in London Before World War I', *History Workshop Journal* no.15 (Spring 1983): 4–27, with those in Lebanon in the 1970s in Suad Joseph, 'Working-Class Women's Networks in a Sectarian State: A Political Paradox', *American Ethnologist* 10 (1983): 1–22. See also Michael John, '"Kultur der Armut" in Wien 1890–1923. Zur Bedeutung von Solidarstrukturen, Nachbarschaft und Protest', *Zeitgeschichte* 20 (1993): 158–86; Leslie Page Moch and Rachel G. Fuchs, 'Getting Along: Poor Women's Networks in Nineteenth-Century Paris', *French Historical Studies* 18 (1993): 34–49.

50. Sidney W. Mintz and Eric R. Wolf, 'An Analysis of Ritual Co-Parenthood (Compadrazgo)', *Southwestern Journal of Anthropology* 6 (1950): 341–68.

51. Hartmut Zwahr, *Zur Konstituierung des Proletariats als Klasse. Strukturuntersuchungen über das Leipziger Proletariat während der industriellen Revolution*, Berlin, 1978, 163–89.

52. Y. Michal Bodemann, 'Relations of Production and Class Rule: The Hidden Basis of Patron-Clientage', in Wellman and Berkowitz, *Social Structures. A Network Approach*, 198–220, 215.

53. For a comprehensive analysis of industrial paternalism, see Alvarez Sierra, *El obrero soñado. Ensayo sobre el paternalismo industrial (Asturias 1860–1917)*, Madrid, 1990, 7–164. Important case studies are: Patrick Joyce, *Work, Society and Politics: The Culture of the Factory in Victorian England*, Brighton, 1980; and Mark W. Steinberg, *Moral Communities: The Culture of Class Relations in the Russian Printing Industry, 1867–1907*, Berkeley, 1992.

54. Robin Theobald and Michael A. Korovkin debate the historical conditions necessary for patronage in Robin Theobald, 'The Decline of Patron-Client Relations in Developed Societies', *Archives Européennes de Sociologie* [hereafter: *AES*] 24 (1983): 136–47; Michael A. Korovkin, 'Exploitation, Cooperation, Collusion: An Enquiry into Patronage', *AES* 29 (1988): 105–26; Robin Theobald, 'On the Survival of Patronage in Developed Societies', *AES* 33 (1992): 183–91.

55. Joan Wallach Scott, *The Glassworkers of Carmaux. French Craftsmen and Political Action in a Nineteenth-Century City*, Cambridge, MA, 1974, 68, 83–7; Humphrey Southall, 'Mobility, the Artisan Community and Popular Politics in Early Nineteenth-Century England', in *Urbanising Britain. Essays on Class and Community in the Nineteenth Century*, eds Gerry Kearns and Charles W.J. Withers, Cambridge, 1991, 103–53.

56. The discussion of personal communities provided some examples of this transformation. It may also occur with patronage – patrons and patronesses can become godfathers or god-

mothers respectively – or self-help organisations. Emily Honig's example of female textile workers in Shanghai during the first half of the twentieth century illustrates this point: 'After working together for several years, six to ten women would formalize their relationship with one another by pledging sisterhood. Once they had formed a sisterhood, the members would call each other by kinship terms based on age: the oldest was 'Big Sister', the next oldest 'Second Sister', and so forth.... Often the sisterhoods functioned as an economic mutual aid society'. Emily Honig, 'Burning Incense, Pledging Sisterhood. Communities of Women Workers in the Shanghai Cotton Mills, 1919–1949', *Signs* 10 (1984): 700–14, 700–1. Better known than this case of surrogate kinship among women are the countless fraternal organisations that have sprung up in workers' movements over time. For examples, see Mary Ann Clawson, *Constructing Brotherhood: Class, Gender, and Fraternalism*, Princeton, 1989.

57. See Zwahr, *Zur Konstituierung des Proletariats*. Furthermore, in 'The Dutch Social Democratic Workers' Party in the Province of Zeeland, 1898–1920', *Tijdschrift voor Sociale Geschiedenis* 18 (1992): 389–403, 401, Bert Altena convincingly argues that 'family acquaintance played an important part' in the formation of early working-class organisations.

58. For a long time historians have neglected mutual benefit societies and consumer cooperatives. I have attempted a synthesis of existing knowledge in my essays 'Mutual Workers' Insurance: A Historical Outline', *International Social Security Review* 46, no. 3 (1993): 5–18, and 'Working-Class Consumer Power', *International Labor and Working-Class History* 46 (1994): 109–21.

59. There is now an extensive literature on the freerider problem. Directly relevant studies include Colin Crouch, *Trade Unions: The Logic of Collective Action*, Isle of Man, 1982; and Michael Hechter, *Principles of Group Solidarity*, Berkeley, 1987, especially 104–24.

60. The Swedish union movement is a good example, as its unusually strong organisation is due mainly to an arrangement with the state entitling it to provide certain services, including unemployment benefits.

61. The negative correlation between the number of producer co-operatives established annually and the economic situation also reflects their low appeal. Economic deterioration and rising unemployment seem to decrease reluctance to join this type of organisation.

62. Marcel van der Linden, 'Households and Labour Movements', *Economic and Social History in the Netherlands* 6 (1994): 129–44; this is an expanded version of 'Connecting Household History and Labour History', in *The End of Labour History?*, ed. Marcel van der Linden, Cambridge, 1993, 163–73.

Bibliography

Acheson, J.M. 'Household Organization and Budget Structures in a Purepecha Pueblo'. *American Ethnologist* 23 (1996): 331–51.

Altena, B. 'The Dutch Social Democratic Workers' Party in the Province of Zeeland, 1898–1920', *Tijdschrift voor Sociale Geschiedenis* 18 (1992): 389–403.

Barrett, J.R. *Work and Community in the Jungle. Chicago's Packinghouse Workers 1894–1922*. Urbana and Chicago, 1987.

Bauer, S. 'Konsumtion II: Das Konsumtionsbudget der Haushaltung', *Handwörterbuch der Staatswissenschaften*, 5, second revised edition. Jena 1900, 316–33.

Bender, D.R. 'A Refinement of the Concept of Household: Families, Co-Residence, and Domestic Functions', *American Anthropologist* 69 (1967): 493–504.

Benson, J. *The Penny Capitalists. A Study of Nineteenth-Century Working Class Entrepreneurs*. Dublin, 1983.

Benson, S.P. 'Living on the Margin: Working-Class Marriages and Family Survival Strategies in the United States, 1919–1941', in *The Sex of Things: Gender and Consumption in Historical Perspective*, eds V. de Grazia and E. Furlough. Berkeley, 1996, 212–43.

Birkbeck, C. 'Self-Employed Proletarians in an Informal Factory: The Case of Cali's Garbage Dump', *World Development* 6 (1978): 1173–85.

Bodemann, Y.M. 'Relations of Production and Class Rule: The Hidden Basis of Patron-Clientage', in: Wellman and Berkowitz, *Social Structures. A Network Approach*, 198–220.

Bosanquet, H. 'The Burden of Small Debts', *Economic Journal* 6 (1896): 212–25.

Bradbury, B. 'Pigs, Cows, and Boarders: Non-Wage Forms of Survival among Montreal Families, 1861–91', *Labour/Le Travail* 14 (Fall 1984): 9–46.

Bruce, J. 'Homes Divided', *World Development* 17 (1989): 979–91.

Brüggemeier, F., and Niethammer, L. 'Schlafgänger, Schnapskasinos und schwerindustrielle Kolonie. Aspekte der Arbeiterwohnungsfrage im Ruhrgebiet vor dem ersten Weltkrieg', in *Fabrik, Familie, Feierabend. Beiträge zur Sozialgeschichte des Alltags im Industriezeitalter*, eds J. Reulecke and W. Weber. Wuppertal, 1978, 153–74.

Cabedoce, B. 'Jardins ouvriers et banlieue: le bonheur au jardin?', in *Les premiers banlieusards. Aux origines des banlieues de Paris 1860–1940*, ed. A. Faure. Paris, 1991, 249–279.

Calhoun, C. '"New Social Movements" of the Early Nineteenth Century', *Social Science History* 17 (1993): 385–427.

Clawson, M.A. *Constructing Brotherhood: Class, Gender, and Fraternalism*. Princeton, 1989.

Cohen, R. 'Resistance and Hidden Forms of Consciousness amongst African Workers', in R. Cohen, *Contested Domains: Debates in International Labour Studies*. London and New Jersey, 1991, 91–109.

Crouch, C. *Trade Unions: The Logic of Collective Action*. Isle of Man, 1982.

Davin, A. 'Working or Helping? London Working-Class Children in the Domestic Economy', in Smith, Wallerstein and Evers, *Households and the World-Economy*, 215–32.

de Belder, J. 'Het arbeiderssparen 1850–1890', in *De Belgische Spaarbanken. Geschiedenis, Recht, Economische Funktie en Instellingen*, eds A. van Put et al. Tielt, 1986, 91–119.

Dee Vellenga, D. 'Women, Households, and Food Commodity Chains in Southern Ghana', *Review* 8 (1984–85): 293–318.

Devos, I. 'Te jong om te sterven. De levenskansen van meisjes in België omstreeks 1900', *Tijdschrift voor Sociale Geschiedenis* 26 (2000): 55–75.

Ditton, J. *Part-Time Crime: An Ethnography of Fiddling and Pilferage*. London, 1977.

Eden, F.M. *The State of the Poor*. London, 1797.

Ehmer, J. 'Wohnen ohne eigene Wohnung. Zur sozialen Stellung von Untermietern und Bettgehern', in *Wohnen im Wandel. Beiträge zur Geschichte des Alltags in der bürgerlichen Gesellschaft*, ed. L. Niethammer.Wuppertal, 1979, 132–50.

Elwert, G. 'Conflicts Inside and Outside the Household: A West African Case Study', in Smith, Wallerstein and Evers, *Households and the World-Economy*, 272–96.

Faure, A. 'Classe malpropre, classe dangereuse? Quelques remarques à propos des chiffoniers parisiens au XIXe siècle et de leurs cités', *Recherches* no. 29 (December 1977): 79–102.

Fox Piven, F., and Cloward, R.A. 'Collective Protest: A Critique of Resource-Mobilization Theory', in *Social Movements: Critiques, Concepts, Case-Studies*, ed. S.M. Lyman, Basingstoke and London, 1995, 137–67.

Friedman, K. 'Households as Income-Pooling Units', in Smith, Wallerstein and Evers, *Households and the World-Economy*, 37–55.

Freund, W. 'Theft and Social Protest Among the Tin Miners of Northern Nigeria', *Radical History Review* 9, no. 26 (1982): 68–86.

Führer, K.C. 'Das Kreditinstitut der kleinen Leute: Zur Bedeutung der Pfandleihe im deutschen Kaiserreich', *Bankhistorisches Archiv* 18 (1992): 3–21.

Green, A. 'Spelling, Go-Slows, Gliding Away and Theft: Informal Control over Work on the New Zealand Waterfront, 1915–1951', *Labour History* no. 63 (1992): 100–14.

Grüttner, M. 'Working-Class Crime and the Labour Movement: Pilfering in the Hamburg Docks, 1888–1923' in *The German Working Class 1888–1933. The Politics of Everyday Life*, ed. R.J. Evans. London and Totowa, 1982, 54–79.

Gurr, T.R. *Why Men Rebel*. Princeton, NJ, 1970.

Haan, A. de, 'Migration as Family Strategy: Rural-Urban Labor Migration in India during the Twentieth Century', *The History of the Family* 2 (1997): 481–505.

Hareven, T.K. 'A Complex Relationship: Family Strategies and the Processes of Economic and Social Change', in *Beyond the Marketplace. Rethinking Economy and Society*, eds R. Friedland and A.F. Robertson. New York, 1990, 215–44.

Hechter, M. *Principles of Group Solidarity*. Berkeley, 1987.

Honig, E. 'Burning Incense, Pledging Sisterhood. Communities of Women Workers in the Shanghai Cotton Mills, 1919–1949', *Signs* 10 (1984): 700–14.

Jaumain, S. 'Contribution à l'histoire comparée: les colporteurs belges et québécois au XIXe siècle', *Histoire sociale/Social History* no. 39 (1987): 49–77.

John, M. '"Kultur der Armut" in Wien 1890–1923. Zur Bedeutung von Solidarstrukturen, Nachbarschaft und Protest', *Zeitgeschichte* 20 (1993): 158–86.

Johnson, P. *Saving and Spending. The Working-Class Economy in Britain 1870–1939*. Oxford, 1985.

Joseph, S. 'Working-Class Women's Networks in a Sectarian State: A Political Paradox', *American Ethnologist* 10 (1983): 1–22.

Joyce, P. *Work, Society and Politics: The Culture of the Factory in Victorian England*. Brighton, 1980.

Junko Yaganisako, S. 'Family and Household: The Analysis of Domestic Groups', *Annual Review of Anthropology* 8 (1979): 161–205.

———. 'Explicating Residence: A Cultural Analysis of Changing Households among Japanese-Americans', in Netting, Wilk and Arnould, eds, *Households*, 330–52.

Korovkin, M.A. 'Exploitation, Cooperation, Collusion: An Enquiry into Patronage', *Archives Européennes de Sociologie* 29 (1988): 105–26.

Laslett, P. 'The Family as a Knot of Individual Interests', in: Netting, Wilk and Arnould, eds, *Households*, 353–79.

Linden, M. van der, 'Mutual Workers' Insurance: A Historical Outline', *International Social Security Review* 46, no. 3 (1993): 5–18.

———. 'Connecting Household History and Labour History', in *The End of Labour History?*, ed. M. van der Linden. Cambridge UK, 1993, 163–73.

———. 'Working-Class Consumer Power', *International Labor and Working-Class History* 46 (1994): 109–21.

———. 'Households and Labour Movements', *Economic and Social History in the Netherlands* 6 (1994): 129–44.

———. 'El fin del eurocentrismo y el futuro de la historia del trabajo: O por qué debemos y podemos reconceptualizar la clase obrera', in *Cultura social y política en el mundo del trabajo*, eds J. Paniagua, J.A. Piqueras and V. Sanz. Valencia, 1999, 301–22.

Lourens, P., and Lucassen, J. *Arbeitswanderung und berufliche Spezialisierung: Die lippischen Ziegler im 18. und 19. Jahrhundert.* Osnabrück, 1999.

Mars, G. 'Dock Pilferage: A Case Study in Occupational Theft', in *Deviance and Social Control*, eds P. Rock and M. McIntosh. London, 1974, 209–28.

Marx, K. *Grundrisse: Foundations of the Critique of Political Economy (Rough Draft)*, trans. Martin Nicolaus. Harmondsworth, 1973.

Maume, D.J., and Dunaway, R.G. 'Determinants of the Prevalence of Mother-Only Families', *Research in Social Stratification and Mobility* 8 (1989): 313–27.

McCarthy, J.D., and Zald, M.N. 'Resource Mobilization and Social Movements: A Partial Theory', *American Journal of Sociology* 82 (1976–77): 1212–41.

McGuire, R.H., Smith, J., and Martin, W.G. 'Patterns of Household Structures and the World-Economy', *Review* 10, no.1 (1986): 75–97.

Meillassoux, C. *Femmes, Greniers & Capitaux*. Paris, 1975.

Mintz, S.W., and Wolf, E.R. 'An Analysis of Ritual Co-Parenthood (Compadrazgo)', *Southwestern Journal of Anthropology* 6 (1950): 341–68.

Mitterauer, M. 'Faktoren des Wandels historischer Familienformen', in: M. Mitterauer, *Familie und Arbeitsteilung. Historischvergleichende Studien*. Vienna, 1992, 214–55.

Modell, J. and Hareven, T. 'Urbanization and the Malleable Household: An Examination of Boarding and Lodging in American Families', *Journal of Marriage and the Family* 35 (1973): 467–79.

Moch, L.P., and Fuchs, R.G. 'Getting Along: Poor Women's Networks in Nineteenth-Century Paris', *French Historical Studies* 18 (1993): 34–49.

Netting, R.M., Wilk, R.R., and Arnould, E.J, eds. *Households. Comparative and Historical Studies of the Domestic Group*. Berkeley, 1984.

Okeke, P.E. 'Female Wage Earners and Separate Resource Structures in Post Oil Boom Nigeria', *Dialectical Anthropology* 22 (1997): 373–87.

Olson, M. *The Logic of Collective Action: Public Goods and the Theory of Groups*. Cambridge, MA and London, 1965.

Papathanassiou, M. *Zwischen Arbeit, Spiel und Schule. Die ökonomische Funktion der Kinder ärmerer Schichten in Österreich 1880–1939*. Vienna and Munich, 1999.

Perrot, M. *Les ouvriers en grève. France 1871–1890*, I. Paris and The Hague, 1974.

Peterson, J. T. 'Interhousehold Exchange and the Public Economy in Three Highland Philippine Communities', *Research in Economic Anthropology* 11 (1989): 123–42.

Rabeherifara, J.-C. 'Réseaux sociaux et familiaux: détournement du salarial?', in *Classes ouvrières d'Afrique noire*, eds M. Agier, J. Copans and A. Morice. Paris, 1987, 183–213.

Radforth, I. *Bushworkers and Bosses: Logging in Northern Ontario, 1900–1980.* Toronto, 1987.

Randall, A.J. 'Peculiar Perquisites and Pernicious Practices. Embezzlement in the West of England Woollen Industry, c. 1750–1840', *International Review of Social History* 35 (1990): 193–219.

Rosenbaum, H. *Proletarische Familien. Arbeiterfamilien und Arbeiterväter im frühen 20. Jahrhundert zwischen traditioneller, sozialdemokratischer und kleinbürgerlicher Orientierung*. Frankfurt am Main, 1992.

Ross, E. 'Survival Networks: Women's Neighbourhood Sharing in London Before World War I', *History Workshop Journal* 15 (Spring 1983): 4–27.

Sanjek, R. 'The Organization of Households in Adabraka: Toward a Wider Comparative Perspective', *Comparative Studies in Society and History* 24 (1982): 57–103.

Schulz, G. "'Der konnte freilich ganz anders sparen als ich". Untersuchungen zum
   Sparverhalten industrieller Arbeiter im 19. Jahrhundert', in *Arbeiterexistenz im 19.
   Jahrhundert. Lebensstandard und Lebensgestaltung deutscher Arbeiter und Hand-
   werker*, eds W. Conze and U. Engelhardt. Stuttgart, 1981, 487–515.
Schumpeter, J. 'Social Classes in an Ethnically Homogeneous Environment' (1927),
   in J. Schumpeter, *Imperialism and Social Classes*. Oxford, 1951.
Scott, J.W. *The Glassworkers of Carmaux. French Craftsmen and Political Action in a
   Nineteenth-Century City*. Cambridge, MA, 1974.
Sena, P. d', 'Perquisites and Casual Labour on the London Wharfside in the Eigh-
   teenth Century', *London Journal* 14 (1989): 130–47.
Sicular, D.T. 'Pockets of Peasants in Indonesian Cities: The Case of Scavengers',
   World Development 19 (1991): 137–61.
Sierra, A. *El obrero soñado. Ensayo sobre el paternalismo industrial (Asturias 1860–1917)*.
   Madrid, 1990.
Smith, J, and Wallerstein, I. 'Households as an Institution of the World-Economy',
   in Joan Smith et al., *Creating and Transforming Households. The Constraints of the
   World-Economy*. Cambridge, 1992, 3–23.
Smith, J., Wallerstein, I. and Evers, H.-D. *Households and the World-Economy*. Beverly
   Hills, 1984.
Southall, H. 'Mobility, the Artisan Community and Popular Politics in Early Nine-
   teenth-Century England', in *Urbanising Britain. Essays on Class and Community in
   the Nineteenth Century*, eds G. Kearns and C.W.J. Withers. Cambridge, UK,
   1991, 103–53.
Steinberg, M.W. *Moral Communities: The Culture of Class Relations in the Russian
   Printing Industry, 1867–1907*. Berkeley, 1992.
Stevenson, J. *Popular Disturbances in England, 1700–1832*, second edition. Harlow,
   1992.
Stigler, G.J. 'The Early History of Empirical Studies of Consumer Behavior', in G.J.
   Stigler, *Essays in the History of Economics*. Chicago and London, 1965, 198–233.
Tarrow, S. *Power in Movement: Social Movements and Contentious Politics*. Cambridge,
   UK, 1998.
Tebbutt, M. *Making Ends Meet. Pawnbroking and Working-Class Credit*. New York,
   1983.
Theobald, R. 'The Decline of Patron-Client Relations in Developed Societies',
   Archives Européennes de Sociologie 24 (1983): 136–47.
———. 'On the Survival of Patronage in Developed Societies', *Archives Européennes
   de Sociologie* 33 (1992): 183–91.
Thompson, E.P. 'The Moral Economy of the English Crowd in the Eighteenth Cen-
   tury', in E.P. Thompson, *Customs in Common*. Harmondsworth, 1993, 185–258.
Tilly, C. *From Mobilization to Revolution*. Reading, MA, 1978.
Tilly, C., Tilly, L. and Tilly, R. *The Rebellious Century*. Cambridge, MA, 1975.
Wellman, B., Carrington, P.J., and Hall, A. 'Networks as Personal Communities', in
   Wellman and Berkowitz, *Social Structures. A Network Approach,* 130–84.
Wilk, R. 'Inside the Economic Institution: Modeling Budget Structures', in *Anthro-
   pology and Institutional Economics,* ed. J.M. Acheson. Lanham, 1994, 365–90.
Wolf, D.L. 'Daughters, Decisions and Domination: An Empirical and Conceptual
   Critique of Household Strategies', *Development and Change* 21 (1990): 43–74.
———. *Factory Daughters: Gender, Household Dynamics, and Rural Industrialization in
   Java*. Berkeley, 1992.
Wong, D. 'The Limits of Using the Household as a Unit of Analysis', in Smith,
   Wallerstein and Evers, *Households and the World-Economy*, 56–63.

Woodford-Berger, P. 'Women in Houses: The Organization of Residence and Work in Rural Ghana', *Antropologiska Studier*, no. 30–31 (1981): 3–35.

Zimmerman, C.E. 'The Family Budget as a Tool for Sociological Analysis', *American Journal of Sociology* 33 (1927–28): 901–11.

———. 'Laws of Consumption and Living', *American Journal of Sociology* 41 (1935–36): 13–30.

Zwahr, H. *Zur Konstituierung des Proletariats als Klasse. Strukturuntersuchungen über das Leipziger Proletariat während der industriellen Revolution*. Berlin, 1978.

CHAPTER 2

EARLY BRITISH LABOUR MOVEMENTS IN RELATION TO FAMILY NEEDS

Eileen Janes Yeo

In the northern city of Bradford in the 1920s, Jack Reynolds' family was too poor to join the local Co-operative store; but a better-off neighbour would take him along with her children to collect her shopping Dividend and used it to treat them all to a lovely meal of fish and chips. Reynolds remembered 'Divi Day' as an occasion of exquisite pleasure. This vignette, although from a hundred years later, raises some key and continuing issues about labour movements and family need, including the motives for using labour movement facilities, gender in relation to labour movement strategies, and the conditions favouring or discouraging the involvement of families in collective action. These issues are particularly interesting to consider in relation to Britain not only because it developed into an industrial capitalist society earliest and in a particularly brutal way, but most importantly, British working people also created the widest range of labour movements to cater for the broadest spectrum of cultural need.

This chapter will consider the issues under four main headings. Firstly, it will explore articulated family need, and here examine the motivations of security, dignity and justice highlighted by Marcel van der Linden, together with others which are sometimes ignored, such as pleasure. Then it will assess the relevance of early labour movements to these needs, and examine the alternative options available during the years between 1820 and 1850. Thirdly, it will explore the difficulties which movements had in servicing the needs they identified. Finally, it will consider change over time, and stress the increasing amount of gender dissonance which could be expressed publicly and the increasingly real rivalry from other cultural providers.

Articulated Family Needs 1820–1850

Contemporaries often called the period between 1820 and 1850 in Britain one of 'Crisis' or 'revolution'. Indeed the co-operative and socialist movement, which also contained the Grand National Consolidated Trade Union, named its newspaper the *Crisis* between 1832 and 1834. Historians would point to this period as being the particularly painful phase of British industrial capitalist take-off. In both the newly mechanised factory sector and the older artisan crafts, capitalists made their profits by means of a low-wage strategy at home and export markets abroad. Until obstructed by evangelical Christians in their own class, capitalists tried to use women and children in the public workforce in new ways to undercut men's wages. At the same time, both capitalists and the state attacked the defences of labour, including trades unions and protective legislation which regulated entry, conditions of employment and wages in the various trades.

A massive proliferation of labour movements, unprecedented in size and geographical spread, was one response to this crisis. These movements ranged from the friendly societies which provided mutual insurance and spawned national affiliated orders after 1830, to trade unions which sometimes mushroomed into a spectacular national federation (like the Grand National Consolidated Trade Union), to the Co-operative movement which overlapped with the Owenite socialist movement and spread nation-wide, to campaigns for a ten-hour working day (which Marx claimed as the first victory of the political economy of labour over capital), to the national Chartist movement with its demand for universal (male!) suffrage and parliamentary reform.

These movements analysed the experience of crisis in several different ways. Within the co-operative movement, the economics developed by thinkers like John Gray and William Thompson in the 1820s,[1] stressed that the profit-making logic, which pitted capitalists against workers, was integral to the new 'competitive' system. Robert Owen, whose ideas were also publicised by socialist pamphlets and local periodicals, put great emphasis on the way machinery would be substituted for human labour, leading to recurrent crises of over-production coupled with under-consumption. These analyses were saturated with moral evaluations dignifying the manual workers as the useful and productive members of society and denigrating the useless, non-productive parasites, who included most of the middle classes and all of the upper classes. Membership in labour movements turned workers into 'honourable' labour while the capitalists who refused to recognise labour combinations were seen as 'dishonourable' employers.[2]

The very terms that van der Linden has pinpointed as motivating interest in collective action were much used in the period. The Co-operative and socialist movement made security, defined in several different ways, a clear objective. Security meant the certainty of a subsistence for families, but also 'individual security' meant each worker receiving the value he had created while 'social security' described a situation where the community as a whole could appropriate the collective fruits of its labour and be able to distribute these according to need.[3] Dignity was not only desirable but was being flagrantly transgressed in many areas of social life, including in educational and religious systems which taught about human nature and its potential. Thus the Sunderland Chartists held reading groups to consider rival 'works by which human nature may be elevated by the consciousness of its dignity' and which would hasten the time 'when every man (*sic*) is fit to be his own leader'.[4] Chartists were quite eager to develop a radical Christianity, which contained a labour-value theology, a castigation of oppressors and a determination 'to erect their own temples, and offer their own worship, to the God of Justice, whom they serve'.[5]

Working people continually articulated a sharp sense of class oppression in many areas of social life. Not only was there economic exploitation, sometimes expressed in the language of class, but also social, educational, recreational and religious oppression. The biblical and constitutional idioms were often used to conceptualise this wide-ranging oppression. Biblical bondage involving oppressors and slaves was reinforced by constitutional language repudiating tyrants who turned freeborn Britons into slaves. Another key concept, that was also contrasted to oppression, was 'independence' which connoted the collective capacity of a group to have significant control over their own lives. Embroiled in wide-ranging cultural politics, socialists and Chartists expressed the need for control over their own space where 'really useful knowledge' and really rational recreation (meaning under their own control) could take place. The Worcester Socialists, perhaps not famous in the annals of class struggle, argued in their prospectus for a local Hall of Science that:

> the working classes in this city cannot be accommodated with any commodious place of meeting without it is for such purposes as the classes above them approve of: we propose to raise an Institution that shall be open to all parties. The want of large public rooms wherein the working class might assemble with their wives and children, to acquire and communicate useful knowledge, and wherein they might have innocent recreation and rational amusement at so trifling an expense as to be within the means of the poorest when employed, has been long felt, and is generally admitted.[6]

Whatever historians may decide were the needs of working families, how families expressed their needs is important. Their own interpretations form a fundamental element of their discontent and of their willingness to join in collective action which they judge appropriate to their experience. So far I have presented analyses and symbolic systems from the labour movements themselves, which all left copious published remains, especially newspapers, and which provide one window onto the self-expression of family need; but this window may produce distorted views. Some of the most intractable problems involve inhibitions on women's public speech. In Britain, as in much of Europe in the eighteenth and nineteenth centuries, a public man meant an active citizen with political rights and powers. By contrast, a public woman meant a prostitute.

Chartist women tried to go public and maintain self-esteem while remaining respectable in the eyes of their male kinfolk and other men of their class, without concern for those watching from above. They chose their stance and words with care. In their highly stylised addresses to the *Northern Star* newspaper, the Chartist women presented themselves in their family roles as wives, daughters, mothers and sisters, and stressed the absolute necessity of entering politics to restore family well-being. The 'Address of the Female Political Union of Newcastle', which set the pattern for others, observed:

> We have been told that the province of woman is her home, and that the field of politics should be left to men; this we deny; the nature of things renders it impossible, and the conduct of those who give the advice is at variance with the principles they assert. Is it not true that the interests of our fathers, husbands, and brothers, ought to be ours? If they are oppressed and impoverished, do we not share those evils with them?[7]

The women went on to detail a scenario where 'the husband's earnings could not support his family', and, as a consequence, the wife left their home neglected 'and with her infant children, (to) work at a soul and body degrading toil'. Insecurity, indignity and injustice were rampant: 'the fear of want hangs over our heads; the scorn of the rich is pointed towards us; the brand of slavery is on our kindred, and we feel the degradation'.

In this period both capitalists and the state appeared to be waging a sustained offensive against customary family life. Women and children had always worked but they were now being pushed into the labour force in ways which disrupted ideas of proper family roles and authority patterns. To compound insult and injury, the New Poor Law of 1834 insisted on minimal relief only in the workhouse (popularly dubbed the 'bastille') where husbands would be separated from wives, and children from parents. It was a measure of the hatred of this law, and the stalwart resistance to it, that the indoor relief clause was never fully implemented. The Newcastle women lamented that they had seen:

> a law enacted to treat poverty as a crime, to deny misery consolation, to take from the unfortunate their freedom, to drive the poor from their homes and their fatherland, to separate those whom God has joined together, and tear the children from their parents' care.

With family life under attack, women found it difficult between 1830 and 1850, to target inequality within working-class families and, e.g., press for easier divorce. Class unity was prioritised over gender conflict. Although the socialists had an analysis of patriarchal power within the nuclear family, and Owenite lecturers attracted large audiences on the subject, they had to accept that many women listeners feared that socialism would mean a Casanova's charter. Self-enacted 'moral' marriages and divorces like that between Eliza Sharples and Richard Carlile were frowned upon in radical labour circles.[8] The public stance of most Chartist and socialist women alike was as devoted and militant family members.

Disrupted families and especially inter-class rape became a potent symbol of the effects of class exploitation for labour men, as well as women. Chartist and trade unionist Richard Pilling, conducting his defence at a trial for seditious conspiracy, told the court:

I have seen husbands carrying their children to the mill to be suckled by their mothers, and carrying their wives' breakfasts to them. I have seen this in Bradshaw's mills, where females are employed instead of men. I was one of a deputation to Mr. Orrell, and also to Mr. Bradshaw, requesting them to allow men to work at their mills, but they refused. One female requested most earnestly that her husband might be allowed to go and work alongside of her, but she was refused. These are a few instances that came within my own knowledge; but there are thousands of others. In consequence of females being employed under these circumstances, the overlooker, managers, and other tools, take most scandalous liberties with them.[9]

Here Pilling was using language that would be persuasive to the authorities, but which also conveyed most vividly to his own comrades the degradation that they experienced.

The Relevance of Labour Organisations

In the years between 1820 and 1850, virtually the whole range of labour movements engaged in some form of collective self-provision of goods and services beyond their explicit aims. Indeed it becomes difficult to slot them neatly into van der Linden's three categories of household, enterprise and political organisations because of this tendency to provide for any aspect of social life that might come within their influence. Thus Friendly Societies were supposed to offer the security of financial benefits at times of sickness, unemployment and death; but the sociability aspect of the monthly club night was as popular with the members as it was frowned upon by the authorities. Trade unions in this period often also ran social insurance schemes.

The Co-operative and socialist movement, like a giant vacuum cleaner sucked up virtually every other labour initiative in the period 1824–34, including consumer and producer co-operatives, labour exchanges,[10] trade unions and communities in the countryside. From 1835–45, the reorganised socialist movement continued to engage in cultural politics on an even grander scale mounting the most complete schedule of alternative cultural activities in their local meeting places and halls of science.

The political Chartist movement, aiming for universal (male) suffrage and parliamentary reform, operated 'ulterior measures' from 1839–49, every time its constitutional strategy of mass petitioning failed. The ulterior strategy first involved carrying out a boycott of banks, taxable articles, hostile shopkeepers and churches, as well as withdrawing from work in a general strike. Soon this strategy developed into self-provision in Chartist co-operative stores, chapels, schools, land schemes and in the Land and Labour bank.[11] This proliferation of activity partly reflected the extent to which movements tried to respond to family anxieties and hopes, and partly the degree to which alternative provision was meaningfully available. Between 1820 and 1850, movements were conspicuously responsive to family need (although not necessarily successful in meeting it on a large scale) while the nature of alternative provision from the state and philanthropists was often profoundly unacceptable to working people. The Friendly Societies were among the movements which attracted the largest membership with their promise of security in times of distress. It is worth noting that members were overwhelmingly male although a death benefit was universally paid to the widow and dependants.

The only alternative institutional provision, since private insurance was not targeted at a working-class market until the early twentieth century, was the cold hand and hard heart of the New Poor Law. Even moral-force Chartists who eschewed violence, like John Love of Norwich, were quite capable of provoking fully fledged fist fights with authorities who tried to separate husband from wife when they had to enter the bastille. Families would go to great lengths to keep out of the workhouse if possible, and those too poor to join Friendly Societies relied on informal generosity, ranging from raffles to support sick persons, to interest-free loans among London Irish neighbours, to kind friends who allowed even poorer families to squat in their dwellings to tide them over periods of unemployment.[12]

Death was a very sensitive issue. As a result of the Anatomy Act of 1832, if families could not afford to bury relatives who had died in the workhouse, then the authorities could turn the corpses over to schools of anatomy for dissection by medical students. This was experienced as horrifying degradation which violated strong taboos.[13] The Newcastle women Chartists ended their eloquent litany of woes with this climax:

> we are oppressed because we are poor – the joys of life, the gladness of plenty, and the sympathies of nature, are not for us; the solace of our homes, the endearments of our children, and the sympathies of our kindred are denied us – and even in the grave our ashes are laid with disrespect.

Not only the Friendly Societies, but the socialists, the Chartists and even the Trade Unions provided large and dignified funerals for their members. The Grand National Consolidated Trade Union felt this was a trump card in their recruiting drive; a London bricklayer's funeral procession 'had an imposing effect. It had already reconciled many of the Operatives to the Union'. The funeral of a Barnsley linenweaver provoked the remark 'if this be union. I will be made a member next Saturday night'.[14]

Labour movements offered a range of activities relevant to family need, from self-employment to education for the children, from recreation to the support for political victims and their dependants. Socialism and Chartism offered a setting where desired family life could be reconstituted if only for an evening, and where women's housewifery skills with the needle to sew banners, as cooks to do catering, and as teachers of children were valued and utilised. All the movements were aware of the problem of scarcity of time and money in working-class life. While better-off workers, usually with trade union clout, could command a weekly wage of 21 shillings or more, wages went into freefall for more vulnerable workers, often plummeting to 5 shillings a week in the dying hand trades or the non-unionised sections of the artisan trades.

Working hours were long, whether in the 'advanced' mechanised factory sector or in the dishonourable branch of the older trades (which contained, by

Mayhew's reckoning, 90 percent of London artisans). Leisure time was often unemployment time without money, while in many trades, such as building or dock work, casual work and thus intermittent pay was the rule. Frequent national depressions (1824–5, 1836–7, especially 1842 and 1847–8) compounded the problems of seasonal cycles of work. Labour movements tried to respond to these constraints by offering ways in which people could relate intermittently to activities, even if fully paid-up membership was beyond financial reach. As Birmingham socialist Hawkes Smith put it, modes were needed which would enable 'depressed labourers' to 'feel themselves participators in the great onward movements, without imposing on their minds or their pockets any requirements which they cannot with perfect convenience and facility comply'.[15]

Recreational activities were well attended by families and usually offered a packed experience for a small outlay of money.[16] The main form of festivity was the 'tea party soirée and ball' which provided food, in the form of sandwiches and cakes, dancing, music and even theatrical entertainment. The teetotal nature of the occasion may have made them more accessible to women, for Bronterre O'Brien observed that 'working men may more conveniently take their wives and sisters to soirées than to public dinners', which were both more expensive and more alcoholic. The soirée wove politics into the festivities by means of the tea, which was also a political gesture of depriving the state of revenue from alcohol, and by means of the decorations including the portraits of radical heroes, the banners and placards, the movement songs, addresses and inverted toasts. Where orthodox public dinners always opened the toasting with 'the Queen', Chartist toast-masters first saluted 'The People, the legitimate source of all power'. Soirées were good fund-raising occasions.

When money was needed for imprisoned comrades, entry charges were at their highest averaging one shilling for men, ninepence for ladies and sixpence for children;[17] but there were also cheaper functions: holiday concerts could cost as little as threepence (ninepence with tea), and regular weekly musical entertainments halfpenny. These admissions were not bad value even compared with the pub, where a whole evening could be spent nursing a fourpenny-halfpenny quartern of ale or a twopenny pint of porter, or compared with commercial entertainment. A theatrical in Rochdale at reduced prices charged half a crown for boxes, one and sixpence for the pit, and sixpence for the gallery; the Great Magician visiting Leeds charged two shillings for front seats, one shilling for back, and half-price for children. Even the London Penny Gaffs, frequented by poor street sellers, cost twopence for front places. All these entertainments supplied no food or drink for the price. Labour movements at this time offered an attractive alternative to commercial recreation and a distinctly more pleasurable experience than philanthropic provision where fun was repressed by evangelical earnestness (in the words of the poet Blake: 'priests with black gowns were walking their rounds/and binding with briars my joys and desires').

Co-operative stores were a feature of socialism and Chartism for reasons both of virtue and necessity. Early socialism operated a plebeian strategy of starting co-operative stores which aimed to keep any surplus intact in the hope of adding co-operative production and finally, when capital had accumulated sufficiently, to buy land and establish a virtually self-sufficient community. In fact the pressure was always towards dividing the surplus immediately. The obstacles to postponed gratification were enormous, and people often defaulted on their community contributions in order to pay for the local halls of science, which offered an immediate although partial experience of the New Moral World. In Chartism, part of the ulterior measures was exclusive dealing, which meant trading with shopkeepers friendly to the cause; this rapidly developed into Chartist co-operative stores.

As women were the family shoppers, these stores had to appeal to them. There is contradictory evidence about whether or not they did. In the early socialist movement a recurrent complaint was that wives refused to abandon their usual shopping habits, which included buying food on credit regardless of its quality and buying used clothing in rag markets. In Chartism, the women's associations, which were prevalent in 1839, all committed themselves to exclusive dealing and continued to support co-operative stores, especially as the Chartists, unlike the socialist enterprises, allowed for paying for shares through shopping (as in Sunderland) and sometimes permitted shopping on credit (the case in Great Horton).[18] In Calton, it was the women Chartists who first launched the idea of the Chartist Provision Store. With the establishment of the National Charter Association in 1840, women's groups no longer existed separately so it was less easy to glimpse them in action, although women joined the land plan as members in their own right.[19]

When both early socialism and Chartism were defeated, the consumer co-operative movement carried many of the impulses towards collective self-provision through the mid-nineteenth into the early twentieth century when the Co-operative Wholesale Society ranked as one of the ten largest business enterprises in the world. The most clear revelation of the continuing problems that labour consumption strategies had to face came at the turn of the twentieth century when the Women's Co-operative Guild took up the challenge of bringing co-operation to the poor. They defined the poor as 'those who get regular low wages and irregular high wages – say, with an average family, wage of from eighteen shillings to twenty-one shillings in large towns',[20] comprising the whole of the unskilled labouring class and seasonally employed artisans. It was impossible for these families to shop at Co-ops which had a predilection for high quality, high prices and high dividends. Instead, poor families bought in tiny quantities before each meal, at low prices regardless of the quality of the food, and preferred shopping at 'trust' shops where credit was available. They also relied heavily on a range of loan facilities, especially pawn shops where the rate of interest was usually 25 percent for loans under £2.

The Guild's General Secretary, Margaret Llewelyn Davies, continually urged upon the movement that they could win 'our poorer neighbours' by creating special people's stores with low prices and dividends, less excellent quality merchandise, cooked take-away food (and even co-op cafes and clubs as eat-in venues), abolition of entrance fees and full membership rights upon payment of a shilling instalment towards full shares. She urged that women should be store managers and put special emphasis on recruiting women as members: 'it is they we have to persuade to buy'. Although no credit was to be allowed, penny banks and a loan fund charging low interest was to be created to service members.[21] Some people's stores were founded, and ran successfully although they remained controversial with men in the movement. The Sunderland People's Store on Coronation Street had a devoted following of women, who enjoyed the Tuesday night parties which 'might almost be called a baby show', and of children, who monopolised the penny bank. Sales were buoyant: the cooked meat department had the lowest working expenses and highest profits per pound of sales in the town.[22] By contrast, in the early co-operative movement, store affairs had been discussed by men and these issues were never so directly or fully problematised.

The most trying times for a family were when the main breadwinners were sacked or worse imprisoned for their labour movement activity. Nearly five-hundred Chartists were arrested in 1839 resulting in over 250 imprisonments and six death sentences which were commuted to life transportation to Australia; after the 1842 general strike, transportations alone numbered some twohundred. Chartism shows how, paradoxically, this was at once the most precarious time for movements and yet called out their most supportive impulses towards families and thus generated activity which kept the movement going through the time of repression, until the next moment of revival, often occasioned by the freeing of the victims.

Women were always invited to take the leading role in collecting funds and disbursing them to the victimised families; published weekly lists of donations attested to this regular activity. Chartists were urged to patronise enterprises where wives often took over their husbands' jobs to keep the family income incoming; James Mitchell's wife ran their pub during his imprisonment – Peter Hoey's wife continued their weaving business.[23] Special collections were often raised for the wives of notable leaders, like Mrs William Lovett or Mrs John Frost; but even the families of humble ordinary members received help. A national collection enabled Mrs Roberts of Birmingham to buy a mangle so that she could take in washing; the wife of transported Leicester Chartist William Sherrat Ellis was first supported by subscription and then relocated to a London house and a shop bought for her. Yet, however much the movement tried to help families in distress, the lesson taken was that repression should be avoided if at all possible. Thus Chartism like other early labour movements went to great lengths to try to keep themselves legal as well as to occupy the moral high ground.

Labour Movement Problems of Meeting Family Needs

The difficulties of manoeuvring within state frameworks of legislation and policing were just one set of problems that labour movements had continually to face. Most labour movements in this period aimed to attract 'numbers unlimited' to their ranks, the socialists to squeeze the competitive system into the margins of national life, the Chartists to mount a massive constitutional strategy which would win their demands through intimidation. Yet this ambition had to confront the stubborn facts of poverty in working-class life, which ramified into the viability of the movements themselves. Working-class movements were navigating in treacherous waters full of contradictory currents: a movement's accessibility was often in tension with its quality and autonomy, and both were in conflict with its solvency.

Patronage was one possible way of short-circuiting the problems about money; but as the reading room movement in Carlile showed, patronage often brought unwelcome interference. One benefactor, Mr Mounsey, threatened to retract his gift if infidel literature went into the library, while local shopkeepers on the reading-room committee refused the Co-operative Society permission to meet there. It is a measure of their social creativity that movements deliberately tried to develop a variety of ways to raise money from working-class people and side-step the evils of curtailing the range of activities or of losing control.

For projects which needed capital, like co-operative stores or meeting halls, the one-pound (twenty shillings) share was a standard method of raising money, with payment possible in small weekly instalments; but it often took a long time to sell a share issue to local individuals. A month before opening in 1840, the Manchester Hall of Science had raised only one-half its £6,000 costs from among 800 shareholders. Attempts were also made to go beyond a single locality or indeed a single movement. The Friendly Societies, in command of large sums of money, gave mortgages and loans to other movements. The Bradford Long Pledge Temperance Hall (where the Chartists also met), was built with a mortgage from the Odd-Fellows in the nearby village of Shelf; a north London Lodge lent thirty pounds to the London socialists in 1844.

Nonetheless the struggle to survive was constant, calling for continual ingenuity. The Bradford Long Pledge Hall had to charge for lending their tea kettle and trestle tables. If they ordered too much food for a party, the surplus had to be sold or returned; the margin was wafer-thin. While Chartism was more sensitive than early socialism to the needs of poorer working-class families, their policy of keeping charges low to allow for accessibility made their financial position precarious – the salaries of the National Executive could rarely be paid. The Sheffield branch of socialists was also warned that their policy of 'low payments and low charges inevitable under democratic regulations ... will always keep them poor and in a decaying position'.[24] The prospects for longer-term survival were brightest when a movement managed to finance itself from supplying the basic necessities which working people would anyway have to buy elsewhere if the movement did not sell them. Co-operative stores pre-eminently fitted this description and were for that reason continually re-utilised (thus the Sheffield socialists used their store to finance their hall). It was a mark of the commitment to Chartism and socialism for example, and a sign of the inflexibility of capitalist and state encirclement, that many of the movements and halls managed to survive at all.

In any period, state policy will play a large part in determining what will be more or less dangerous choices for labouring families. Van der Linden distinguishes between high- and low-risk strategies, and identifies trade unions as the most risky choice and household-centred organisations as the safest because the least provocative to those holding economic or political power. Paradoxically in Britain, after the 1824 repeal of the Combination Acts, trade unions were in a more recognised legal position than a number of the other movements. Legal protection was not available to labour combinations which sat on large amounts of money, like the Friendly Societies or the Chartist Land Company and its Land and Labour Bank.

These movements wished to have a national organisation with some autonomy or self-government for local branches, a democratic formula not permitted under the Seditious Meetings Act.[25] Neither the affiliated national orders of Friendly Societies, nor the Chartist enterprises were permitted to register under the Friendly Societies or Companies Acts, with the result that when a local treasurer absconded with the funds or when the whole National Land Company, which had more than 44,000 shareholders, came crashing down, the life savings of many poor people were irretrievably lost. However, it is true that overt repression was more directed towards trade union and political associations in this period. Union militancy brought harsh penalties, including transportation to Australia in the famous cases of the Tolpuddle Martyrs (1834) and the Glasgow cotton spinners (1836); but even joining the 'household'-oriented movements involved considerable risk.

Changing Contexts for Nineteenth-Century Labour Movements

Over the rest of the nineteenth century, while some of the legal restraints on labour movements eased, rival providers of activities became more active and attractive. Both philanthropists and commercial leisure providers learned lessons from the early labour movements, and started to emulate and consciously to compete with them. By the mid 1840s philanthropists were beginning to offer counter-attractions, not only in the form of more pleasurable activities but in the form of newly accessible public territory for leisure use, such as public parks and libraries. Indeed the Manchester Hall of Science was transferred from one domain to the other. Always difficult to sustain financially, it was sold cheaply in 1850 to the public library movement which eventually turned it over to the Town Council to become the first free public library in Britain: in 1877 it was torn down to be replaced by a bigger, better building without any inconvenient historical associations.

Working-class effort had revealed a new market which commercial populists were not slow to exploit particularly after 1850. Charles Morton rebuilt the Canterbury in Lambeth, usually considered the first London music hall, in 1854 using a formula already tested in labour movements with a hall (capacity 1,500), a library and reading room and a picture gallery. Morton was one of the new wage of publican-entrepreneurs who called themselves 'caterers' in the double sense that they supplied food and satisfied the taste of the people. Given this entry of private capital into an area where working people had trouble floating their own enterprises, it is not surprising that commercial enclosure of working-class property sometimes also took place. Thus William

Lovett's Chartist National Hall, which tried unsuccessfully to procure a drinking licence, was evicted from its building in Holborn and the premises then reopened as Weston's Music Hall which was not only licensed but had magistrates as guests at its opening festivities.

Perhaps the most spectacular attempt to take over the possibilities disclosed by the labour movement, was the ongoing effort to displace, and just recently to buy, the national retail Co-operative movement. By the first decade of the twentieth century, the Co-op had the largest share of sales of basic commodities such as milk, tea, sugar, soap and coal, to working-class families. Its more modern production methods and efficient distribution networks had already pushed firms like the Huntley and Palmer biscuit company into a luxury niche market. Lord Lever, the founder of what became the international conglomerate Lever Brothers, became paranoid about the Co-op's refusal to stock his Sunlight Soap and took repeated legal action again the Co-op's supposed restraint of trade.[26] The twentieth-century story has been one of concerted attempts by private manufacturers, traders and state legislators to push co-operatives into more conventional capitalist retailing modes.[27] Even the current New Labour government is unwilling to give legislative protection to mutual forms like building societies and prevent their conversion into banks, although the take-over bid for the Co-operative Wholesale Society by a plucky young adventurer collapsed into a morass of industrial espionage and criminal charges implicating some venerable merchant banks of the City of London who instantly ran for cover.[28]

As much as the issue of alternative providers, the question of how different members of 'the family' articulated need is important in considering the attractiveness of collective strategies in labour movements. Although a more developed feminist analysis of patriarchy was present in early socialism, the changed context of government and voluntary policy towards family issues in the late nineteenth century, made it possible for some labour women to allow the cracks in the family romance to show. In the European eugenic panic before the First World War, when the quantity and quality of the national race became an obsession, labour women seized the moment to unveil terrible experiences of family violence and obstetric tragedy, and to demand full citizenship rights to cope with these. Such demands sometimes led to friction with the male movement; e.g. the Women's Co-operative Guild was refused a large annual subsidy from the Co-operative Union (on the insistence of Catholic men) because of its commitment to easier divorce.[29] Or else, sometimes, women voted with their feet. Hannah Mitchell a stalwart socialist, active in the Labour Church, the Independent Labour Party and the Clarion movement, got fed up with male insensitivity to gender issues in the family, and instead put her active energy into the suffragette movement for a time. She complained that socialist men 'expected Sunday dinners and huge teas with home-made cakes, potted meat and pies, exactly like their reactionary fellows' and assumed that a socialist girlfriend 'would change all her ways with her marriage ring and begin where their mothers left off'.[30]

A complex skein of factors need to be unravelled to straighten out why families chose collective activity in labour movements. These strands include how different members saw the interests of the family at different times, and how they assessed labour movement provision compared with other realistic alternatives in a particular context. As the twentieth century unfolded, and especially during the Thatcher years, labour movements for a variety of reasons, have lost ground in Britain; and yet they sometimes seem to have a capacity for resurgence in surprising ways. Unison, the trade union with the largest membership of women, has become increasingly family friendly, offering child care facilities to all officers and members on training courses. One of the fastest growing banks at the moment is the Co-operative Bank, which advertises itself as the ethical bank, investing only in enterprises which are fair to their employees, which do not exploit families in the global factory and do not damage the environment.[31] Instead of aping capitalist modes, the bank seems to be resuscitating the social morality which has lain, historically, at the heart of the Co-operative movement. Is this a sign of a movement back to the future?

Notes

1. See N. Thompson, *The People's Science: The Popular Political Economy of Exploitation and Crisis, 1816–34*, Cambridge, 1985; G. Claeys, *Machinery, Money and the Millennium: From Moral Economy to Socialism, 1815–60*, Cambridge, 1987.
2. See e.g., E.P. Thompson and E. Yeo, eds, *The Unknown Mayhew: Selections from the Morning Chronicle*, London, 1971, 182.
3. W. Pare, *An Address Delivered at the Opening of the Birmingham Co-operative Society, 17 Nov. 1828*, Birmingham Co-operative Society, Birmingham, n.d., 8 for security; W. Thompson, *An Inquiry into the Principles of the Distribution of Wealth Most Conducive to Human Happiness* (London, 1824, reprint, New York, 1963) 78, 384 ff. for individual and social security.
4. *Northern Star*, 22 August 1840.
5. Revd. Hill editor in ibid., 3 April 1841; also E. Yeo, 'Christianity and Chartist Struggle, 1838–42', *Past and Present*, no. 91 (1981), 109–39.
6. *New Moral World*, 20 July 1839; *Northern Star*, 22 August 1840 for the Sheffield Chartists.
7. All references to this 'Address' are in ibid, 9 February 1839.
8. H. Rogers, '"The Prayer, the passion and the reason" of Eliza Sharples: freethought, women's rights and republicanism, 1832–52', in *Radical Femininity: Women's Self-Representation in the Public Sphere*, ed. E.J. Yeo, Manchester, 1998, 69–71; Barbara Taylor, *Eve and the New Jerusalem. Socialism and Feminism in the Nineteenth Century*, London, 1983, 206–9; A. Clark, *The Struggle for the Breeches, Gender and the Making of the British Working Class*, London, 1995, 187.
9. Feargus O'Connor, ed., *The Trial of Feargus O'Connor and 58 other Chartists on a Charge of Seditious Conspiracy at Lancaster*, 1843.
10. Depots where products could be exchanged on the basis of the labour value they contained.
11. For a detailed examination of Chartist self-provision, see E. Yeo, 'Some Practices and Problems of Chartist Democracy', in *The Chartist Experience. Studies in Working-Class Radicalism and Culture, 1830–1860*, eds J. Epstein and D. Thompson, London, 1982, 346–49, 366–70.
12. Thompson and Yeo, eds, *The Unknown Mayhew*, 14 February 1850, 262, 264 for squatting; *London Labor and the London Poor*, London, 1861, reprint, London, 1968, vol. I, 115 for informal help in the Irish community.
13. R. Richardson, *Death, Dissection and the Destitute*, London, 1987, chs 1, 11.
14. *Crisis*, 29 March 1834, 5 April 1834.
15. *New Moral World*, 1 September 1838.
16. For a fuller discussion of how movements tried to address the constraint of scarcity, see my 'Culture and Constraint in Working-Class Movements, 1830–1855', in *Popular Culture and*

      Class Conflict. Essays in the Exploration of Labour and Leisure, eds E. and S. Yeo, Sussex, 1981, 163–8.
17. Twelve pence equalled one shilling, and twenty shillings made up one pound sterling.
18. H. Hodgson, *Fifty Years of Co-operation in Great Horton and District*, Manchester, 1909, 101; for problematising the inclusion of poorer families, *Northern Liberator*, 21 September 1839; *Northern Star*, 1 February, 17 October, 21 November 1840; 15 August 1840 for Calton.
19. All the land schemes of the period aimed at independence; members would be able to emancipate themselves from capitalist wage labour either in the Owenite community which would undertake both agricultural and industrial production or in the Chartist settlements where peasant proprietorship (of three acres) would be available to those lucky enough to win the lottery for a place.
20. M. Llewelyn Davies, *Co-operation in Poor Neighbourhoods*, Women's Co-operative Guild Sectional Conferences, 1899, Kirkby Lonsdale, 6–7.
21. Ibid., also her *A Co-operative Relief Column or How to Adapt Co-operation to the Needs of Poor Districts*, Women's Co-operative Guild, Woolwich Congress, June 1900; *A Co-operative Colony. Papers, reprinted from the 'Co-operative News', dealing with a Scheme of Co-operation for Poor Neighbourhoods*, Women's Co-operative Guild, Kirkby Lonsdale, n.d.
22. *Co-operative News*, 14 February, 23 March, 9 May 1903.
23. See J. Schwarzkopf, *Women in the Chartist Movement*, London, 1991, 147–50.
24. W. Newall to G.J. Holyoake, 15 July 1841, Holyoake Papers, Co-operative Union, Manchester, no. 20.
25. For a fuller discussion, see my 'Some Practices and Problems of Chartist Democracy'.
26. P. Redfern, *The New History of the C.W.S.*, London and Manchester, 1938, 55.
27. N. Killingback, 'Limits to Mutuality: Economic and Political Attacks on Co-operation during the 1920s and 1930s', in *New Views of Co-operation*, ed. S. Yeo, London, 1988, ch.12.
28. *Guardian*, 23 April 1997, 24; section G2, 2–3; *The Observer*, 13 July 1997, 3.
29. See G. Scott, *Feminism and the Politics of Working Women. The Women's Co-operative Guild, 1880s to the Second World War*, London, 1998, ch. 5.
30. H. Mitchell, *The Hard Way Up. The Autobiography of Hannah Mitchell Suffragette and Rebel*, ed. G. Mitchell, London, 1977, 96, 125–6.
31. *Guardian*, 8 April 1998, 22; Consume with Passion. Ethical Spending and Investing in the Nineties, *Observer* in association with the Co-operative Bank, n.d.

Bibliography

Claeys, G. *Machinery, Money and the Millennium: From Moral Economy to Socialism, 1815–60*. Cambridge, 1987.

Clark, A. *The Struggle for the Breeches, Gender and the Making of the British Working Class*. London, 1995.

Hodgson, H. *Fifty Years of Co-operation in Great Horton and District*. Manchester, 1909.

Mayhew, H. *London Labour and the London Poor* vol. I. London, 1861; reprint, London, 1968.

Killingback, N. 'Limits to Mutuality: Economic and Political Attacks on Co-operation during the 1920s and 1930s, in *New Views of Co-operation*, ed. S. Yeo. London, 1988.

Mitchell, H. *The Hard Way Up. The Autobiography of Hannah Mitchell Suffragette and Rebel*, ed. G. Mitchell. London, 1977.

O'Connor, F. ed. *The Trial of Feargus O'Connor and 58 other Chartists on a Charge of Seditious Conspiracy at Lancaster*. 1843.

Redfern, P. *The New History of the C.W.S.* London and Manchester, 1938.

Richardson, R. *Death, Dissection and the Destitute*. London, 1987.

Rogers, H. '"The Prayer, the passion and the reason" of Eliza Sharples: freethought, women's rights and republicanism, 1832–52', in *Radical Femininity: Women's Self-Representation in the Public Sphere*, ed. E.J. Yeo. Manchester, 1998.

Scott, G. *Feminism and the Politics of Working Women. The Women's Co-operative Guild, 1880s to the Second World War.* London, 1998.

Schwarzkopf, J. *Women in the Chartist Movement.* London, 1991.

Taylor, B. *Eve and the New Jerusalem. Socialism and Feminism in the Nineteenth Century.* London, 1983.

Thompson, E.P., and Yeo, E., eds. *The Unknown Mayhew: Selections from the Morning Chronicle.* London, 1971.

Thompson, N. *The People's Science: The Popular Political Economy of Exploitation and Crisis, 1816–34.* Cambridge, 1985.

Thompson, W. *An Inquiry into the Principles of the Distribution of Wealth Most Conducive to Human Happiness.* London, 1824; reprint, New York, 1963.

Yeo, E. 'Christianity and Chartist Struggle, 1838–42', *Past and Present*, no. 91 (1981): 109–139.

———. 'Culture and Constraint in Working-Class Movements, 1830–1855', in *Popular Culture and Class Conflict. Essays in the Exploration of Labour and Leisure*, eds E. and S. Yeo. Sussex, 1981.

———. 'Some Practices and Problems of Chartist Democracy', in *The Chartist Experience. Studies in Working-Class Radicalism and Culture, 1830–1860*, eds J. Epstein and D. Thompson. London, 1982.

CHAPTER 3

WEAVING SURVIVAL IN THE TAPESTRY OF VILLAGE LIFE

STRATEGIES AND STATUS IN THE SILESIAN WEAVER REVOLT OF 1844

Christina von Hodenberg

In early June 1844, hundreds of cottage workers, armed with clubs and fence posts, stormed the homes and businesses of their manufacturers in Peterswaldau and Langenbielau. Cotton weavers were protesting against continued wage cuts and the hiring of workers from other villages. They smashed the furnishings of the offices and homes belonging to the textile merchants, ripped up accounting books and later stole the goods in stock. Three semi-mechanical weaving looms were also destroyed at the hands of the protesters. The manufacturers fled from the angry crowd. Eventually troops were sent in to suppress the revolt, at the cost of twelve lives.[1]

The Silesian Weavers' Revolt of 1844 became famous both in Germany and abroad. Even today, the Silesian weaver is a symbol of a worker pauperised through no fault of his own, and the revolt in the mountainous region known as the *Eulengebirge* is often considered to be the archetypal antagonistic protest against technology and mechanisation. However, such popular perceptions of the revolt correspond little with the historical background of this uprising, which is very similar to many other, less spectacular factory revolts during the period of early industrialisation. The numerous myths that surround the weavers' revolt are based on the fact that this particular protest set off the first major public discussion of the 'social question' in Germany. The German press began an intensive examination of this topic, which not even the censors could prevent.[2] Karl Marx interpreted the 1844 revolt as the long-awaited precursor to the organised German workers' movement. Heinrich Heine wrote his famous *Weberlied*, a lyric in which the Silesian weavers are celebrated as the prophets of the coming revolution in Prussia. In the decades that followed, German literature was inundated with poetry, novels, and dramas about the weavers, the most well-known being Gerhart Hauptmann's play *Die Weber* (The Weavers).

Even today the controversy among historians about the Silesian uprising has not quietened down. This event has been particularly important in historiography and interpreted in three different, opposing ways. According to one interpretation, the revolt represented the 'first major class struggle by German workers' and 'the dawning of the labour movement in Germany';[3] for another, it exemplified a hunger riot that evolved out of the sheer desperation of the workers; and for a third interpretation, the uprising was a storming of the machines to protest against industrialisation. These rival interpretations, whose competing natures can only be fully understood in the context of the East-West conflict within Germany, need to be revised in light of new sources and new insights into the history of the labour movement.

Not until the demise of the GDR was it possible for researchers to examine the original source material housed in East German archives. These documents had been locked away for decades because the event, having been declared a key occurrence in the history of the German labour movement, was highly important in legitimising the East German state.[4] Now, the revolt can be interpreted entirely on the basis of verified information found in the rediscovered files about the situation and the motives of the Silesian weavers. Four significant points must be reconsidered in interpreting the weaver uprising. First, the revolt was not perpetrated by the poorest of the poor, but by weavers who feared that they would lose their albeit meagre income and fall into abject poverty. Second, the protest was not directed against industrial machinery, but against certain manufacturers, whom the protesters sought to punish. Third, the rebels were organised only in very rudimentary ways. Fourth, the weavers did indeed share a common outlook, although this was not a specifically working-class consciousness. Instead, they shared a general outlook and self-image shaped by their social status and religion, in which the most important values were embodied in village life, a belief in benevolent authority, and social esteem.

These conclusions, which have been verified extensively elsewhere, are based on a more accurate knowledge of wages, of the relationship between cottage workers and textile wholesalers, and of the crisis in the Silesian textile industry. What places the revolt in a new light is, above all, the information this source material gives us about the social environment and the self-image of the insurgents. A close look at the private households shows that the coping strategies adopted by the cottage workers were not dependent solely on economic factors but were also shaped by their perceptions, hopes, and desires. Furthermore, the economic situation of the weavers cannot be discussed simply in terms of their wages. How well they were doing depended also on the composition of their household, the opportunities for extra income and saving, as well as their integration into the daily system of duties and entitlements.

Following a sketch depicting life in Silesian factory villages in 1844, I will describe in detail the ways in which the private and occupational lives of the weavers were intertwined: household and family, informal local networks in the neighbourhood and community, gender-specific networks as well as traditional systems of patronage. With this in mind, we will then turn our attention to the strategies used by the weavers to maintain or improve their situation, namely their decision to protest violently (at least in 1844) and their decision not to pursue organised representation of their interests (for decades).

The Silesian factory villages in 1844

Peterswaldau and Langenbielau, the scene of the 1844 revolt, were among the largest of the old 'factory villages' in Prussia (see map 3.1). Densely populated and inhabited primarily by textile workers,[5] these two villages specialised almost exclusively in cotton weaving.[6] The large commercial businesses – Zwanziger and Sons in Peterswaldau and the brothers Friedrich and Wilhelm Dierig in neighboring Langenbielau – employed together more than 12,000 textile workers (most of them weavers) as cottage workers.[7] For quite a while, these major entrepreneurs had been scouting the countryside and recruiting weavers from the surrounding communities and districts. In both villages there were also various smaller factories employing several hundred employees, as well as numerous master weavers who employed a handful of men to run just a few cotton looms.[8]

These so-called 'factories' were enterprises that still produced within the framework of an early industrial *Verlagssystem* or 'putting-out' system. The entrepreneur handed his yarn to the weavers, who produced the desired cloth at home on their own looms at the negotiated price. The cottage workers were paid for the fabric they produced, and the *Verleger*, or merchant-wholesalers, sold the cotton, which was bleached later (and sometimes coloured) and dressed, on domestic and especially foreign markets. In a formal sense, the weavers were self-employed; they owned the means of production and only obtained the raw materials from the merchant-wholesaler. However, such independent self-employment existed in theory only. In practice, cottage workers lived in constant dependency on the merchant-wholesaler. Whenever the price for cloth fell, the losses were passed on to the weavers in the form of wage cuts. An overabundance of labour and a shortage of capital on the part of the workers meant that the merchant capitalists were in a position to dictate almost at will the level of wages and the working conditions.

Beginning in the early nineteenth century when the crisis in the Silesian textile industry started, cottage workers became increasingly vulnerable to the drawbacks of the proto-industrial putting-out system.[9] As the bottom slowly dropped out of the price of traditional Silesian linen, many weavers went into debt because they were forced to pay exorbitant prices to rent their looms and to buy yarn on credit, and had to accept drastic wage cuts at the same time. Although there was great technological advancement in weaving looms at the

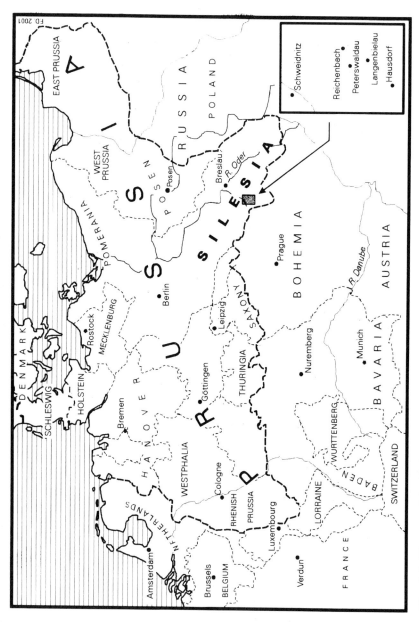

Map 3.1 *The scene of the Silesian weavers' revolt, 1844*

time, the weavers could not profit from this because they did not have the capital to invest in new looms, and the manufacturers were not willing to invest in a means of production that belonged to the cottage workers. As a result, more and more weavers worked ever longer hours, produced goods of increasingly poorer quality, and earned less and less income, while the price for Silesian cloth plunged. The pressure of overproduction 'did not result in unemployment, but in a devaluation of … each individual workplace'.[10]

The demise of the linen industry caused thousands of weavers, such as in Peterswaldau and Langenbielau, to turn to cotton weaving, which was more in demand. Then, around 1840, the cotton market also experienced profit losses, and the merchant-wholesalers paid less for their goods. Now, cotton weavers had to fear that they would share the fate of the spinners and linen weavers and be robbed of their living. Sources from the 1840s reveal the significant divergence in levels of income and property between linen and cotton workers. Whereas the linen weavers were suffering from 'horrific destitution', the cotton workers were earning 'albeit low weekly wages, but there is … always work for them, and they can count on continuous employment'.[11]

Such was life for the weavers in 1844 when the revolt erupted against the Silesian textile merchant-wholesalers. The perpetrators of the uprising were the cotton weavers, not the starving linen weavers, as the Prussian public wrongly assumed at the time.[12] The protesting cotton weavers had good reason to fear that they too would be dragged down into the depths of destitution, because in the Silesian factory villages, communal poor relief existed 'only on paper'. One reason for this was that both Peterswaldau and Langenbielau were owned completely by an aristocratic landowner. Specifically, this meant that the administration, police, courts, and poor relief were dependent on the discretion of the aristocracy. Rich entrepreneurs were required to pay 'only an entirely insignificant proportion' of their wealth in taxes,[13] while the landowners still continued to collect traditional tributes from their subjects, the cotton workers. In 1844, Silesian weavers and spinners were required as a rule to pay a ground rent; some also had to pay a spinning and weaving rent or to render additional personal services (*Handdiensttage*). In addition, there were school fees for each child and protection tributes – one of the highest and most controversial feudal tributes, which was no longer being collected in Peterswaldau.[14] Therefore, the weavers were being exploited both by the merchant they worked for and by the landowner on whose property they lived. In general, no institutionalised protection against poverty existed.

In order to cope with this situation, the Silesian cotton weavers developed an array of strategies, of which violent protest was only a rarely used one. Most of these strategies aimed to plait daily life into a braid of domestic and local relationships, which I intend to reconstruct in detail here. Naturally there are gaps in our understanding of these interrelations because even the most specific, extensive testimony by the defendants and witnesses recorded by the courts gives us only a peek at the private lives of these people. Family relations and income were always mentioned merely in passing and in other contexts, but some evidence does emerge.

Household and Family

The first and most important environment in which the cottage worker was integrated was the household in which this person lived. In addition to the traditional family, there were many other forms of shared households, as the court records suggest. For example, a forty-five-year-old man named Karl Wilhelm lived in his own cottage 'in Upper-Bielau, earns a living as a weaver, is married, hard-working and decent, and has four children'. Other defendants, such as Anton Rabe or Gottlieb Frisch, boarded at the homes of peasants or weavers. Often a son still lived with his father, and sometimes the father was sitting in a poorhouse while the son and his family lived elsewhere as lodgers.[15]

It can be presumed that nearly half of the insurgents brought before the court were married. When one takes into account the average age (namely 29) of the men whose marital status was indicated in court records, then the percentage of married weavers can be presumed to be even higher.[16] More than half of the married or divorced offenders had children.[17] Most likely, illegitimate births were not rare. It was expressly recorded in three cases that the accused had been an illegitimate child.[18]

In the homes of weavers working in the proto-industrial putting-out system, children represented both a burden and a blessing. Since the entire family was involved in the production process, which took place in the living quarters, some of the necessary tasks such as spinning and spooling yarn could be done by the children as soon as they were old enough. The children of cottage workers usually worked instead of attending school, which required costly fees for each child.[19] Descriptions of the workplace from this era depict the man at the weaving loom, while his wife does preparatory work for him: 'In addition to spooling yarn for her husband, the weaver's wife can earn at best an additional 6 silver *Groschen* each week through spinning. This extra income falls away if the woman has small children in her care. Among the weavers of coarse cotton cloth, the wife can earn nothing on the side because she is too busy with the work she needs to do to help her husband'.[20] In this sense, a weaver's family was not only a private institution, but also represented an economic unit, to which each member had to contribute and in which the division of labour was gender-specific.

For a family with four children, 'of whom the youngest is five and the oldest nine years old', the weekly income in 1844 'for hard work and industriousness' amounted to one and a half to two *Talers*. Although it is difficult to determine the exact amount of wages, one fact is clear: the weaving of coarse cotton fabric, which required no special skills and therefore was done by 'the majority of the local weavers', earned them an average of at least a *Taler* and several silver *Groschen* each week.[21] However, the wages of the various textile contracts deviated greatly, depending on the weaver's qualifications, the quality of the product, and the marketing and wage strategy of the manufacturer;[22] and naturally there were worlds of difference between the master weaver, a 'small manufacturer' who owned several looms, and the journeyman weaver, who only rented his means of production.[23]

A weaver's household depended on each and every silver *Groschen* to augment the ever uncertain and endangered income from cotton weaving. In the sources, comments made in passing indicate the ways and byways of earning additional income. If the weaver was one of the fortunate few to own land, then supplementary income could be earned in farming. Of the ninety-seven male weavers arrested and listed as imprisoned in Schweidnitz, only two were noted as being '*Häusler*' or cottagers. The records show that, more commonly, weaving was combined with other types of work, often a temporary stint as a field-worker, brickyard worker, tailor, mason, or artillerist.[24] These side jobs reflect just how attractive weaving was for people who had previously worked in other occupations. In Silesia, as everywhere, weaving represented a suitable component in the mixed economy employing the rural lower classes of the early industrial period because, firstly, the large trade businesses were always looking for workers; secondly, access to the weaving profession had not been controlled by a guild or governmental authority for a long time;[25] thirdly, the work required neither a great deal of training nor a workshop; and fourthly, a weaving loom was quickly purchased or at least rented.[26]

Another source of income was to rent to boarders. Children were also sent into the streets to beg.[27] Last but not least, the wives and children of weavers resorted to stealing fruit and wood from the manor lord's forest. Even several of the men charged with participating in the riots had already been convicted of stealing wood. Relations between the 'uncompromising' foresters working for the manor lord and the poor developed into a 'deadly animosity', which all too often ended in violent confrontation, reported the district administrator.[28]

The expenses of a weaver's household can only be outlined. The modest wages earned by weaving and spinning had to pay for the rent, food, heating, clothing, taxes and the manor lord's tributes. Naturally, 'the dwellings and the primary necessities of life are expensive in the overpopulated factory villages'.[29] In Peterswaldau and Langenbielau, people lived in very close quarters, often in crowded households or as boarders. Food – chiefly potatoes, flour, and vegetables – was more expensive in these two places than elsewhere. Many households depended on credit to an extraordinary degree: 'This life financed by borrowing is astounding. The miller, the baker, the brewer, the flax merchant, the yarn merchant; they all lend to these poor people, who often have nothing to mortgage but their own two hands'.[30] The few cents remaining in a poor man's pocket, if any, were often spent on whatever inexpensive amusements there were. In 1844, eleven pubs and eight liquor stores operated in Langenbielau alone. On Sundays, dances were held in three to four different music halls.[31] The liquor consumption was high in this area, and the influence of alcohol was one factor affecting the behaviour of many of the rioters.[32]

Many weavers attempted to bring their household budgets back into balance by moving to the outlying areas. They lived in the smaller neighbouring villages and brought their goods by foot to the merchants. As a Langenbielau school teacher testified in court in 1844, these people were 'able to work now for the low pay rate … because housing and heating are about half as costly in those places'.[33] This strategy of survival enraged the cottage workers who remained in the factory villages, and they directed their anger at the workers who did not belong to the village. As a report from January 1844 on the events in a Neu-Bielau inn conveys: 'several weavers ... discussed the bleak times and that the Langenbielau manufacturers gave the most and best work to non-local weavers and that the servants of the manufacturers received gifts from the non-local weavers, so that they would prefer them later'.[34]

In 1844, the cotton weavers already feared that they were teetering on the edge of destitution. Yet contrary to the linen weavers, they usually possessed sparse but sufficiently furnished dwellings. This is documented by reports from various sources. A government commissioner, who visited the region follow-ing the riots, noted after his trip that he had seen, 'in general, suitable dwellings, adequate domestic furnishings, ample bedding, clothing and food supplies'. Shortly before the riots erupted, the representative from a charity organisation had inspected the factory villages of Lower Silesia: 'In the hous-ing that I was told belonged to the poorest, I found nearly everywhere sound beds, solid dwellings, and people who were not dressed poorly'. Similarly, two commissioners, sent to the mountain villages by the king in the summer of 1844, reported that there were sufficient furnishings and feather beds in the homes of the weavers. In their investigation, they extensively interviewed tax collectors, mayors, innkeepers, pastors, manufacturers, and workers.[35]

The Schweidnitz prison report, which gives a description resembling a police profile of each of the one hundred and twelve accused incarcerated there, offers us another clear glimpse of the clothing, footwear, even physical condition of the rioters. Of these one hundred and twelve men, only two were described as 'corpulent', one hundred and eight as 'stocky', 'thin', or 'slight', and again only two as 'frail'. With few exceptions, the arrested men were dressed well in clothing made from all sorts of often colourful and patterned material (these weavers rarely produced such patterned cloth themselves; they purchased it). Nearly all of the prisoners owned short or long leather boots, whereas twelve ran about barefoot.[36]

This last fact points to distinct social differences among the protesting weavers – as do all the other reports describing the households of weavers. As has already been mentioned, the situation of the Silesian cottage workers was determined only in part by the wages they were paid and could vary consid-erably from worker to worker. Granted, the majority of the protesters were probably facing a precarious economic existence, a continual drop in wages, and a daily struggle to survive. Still, distinct differences existed: wage levels varied widely, depending on the quality of both the loom and the product and on the manufacturer buying the goods. Important was whether rent was col-lected or paid, the loom was owned or rented, the yarn purchased on credit, or even if additional looms were rented out to others. The number of mouths to be fed in a family and the number of family members sharing the workload also played important roles. A family's financial situation was also burdened if there were young children or one partner succumbed to alcoholism. Critical was also the level of tributes to be paid to the manor lord, which varied from village to village and from family to family. Farming appears to have been rarely a source of additional income. More often, weavers pursued seasonal work of various types and chose to move to smaller villages. The poorest of the weavers also relied on borrowing, begging, and the stealing of wood and berries in order to survive.

The Tapestry of Local Relations

Of interest here are not only the strategies employed by individual households to improve their economic situation but also the collective strategies, meaning primarily those involving the entire village, to cope with the economic pressure bearing upon its inhabitants. Integration into the village community was just as vital to the weaver as were ties to family and household. Cottage workers thought in local terms; it was important for the village to stick together against outsiders; and the social hierarchy in the village community was the most influential factor affecting the weavers' general outlook.

Down through the ages, solidarity and community membership had been entwined. Only members of the community were entitled to claim poor relief. That is why the rioters felt justified in attacking manufacturers who were employing outside weavers.[37] If one was a member of the community, he was also obligated in the eyes of the others to contribute to the common financial burden. However, in the Silesian factory villages, the major entrepreneurs had been able largely to evade the community taxes and that enraged not only the cottage workers. During the protest in Langenbielau, the bourgeoisie and the peasants living there were thoroughly 'disinclined to defend the manufacturers against the brutal attacks' and felt the profit-seeking capitalists had deserved the punishment they were getting. An anonymous letter sent to Pastor Gaup from someone in Langenbielau complained that the wealthy merchant-wholesalers had built themselves up to be 'kings' in contempt of the community. 'Once he has earned his thousands, he defies the town and says, I am going to close my business, I am going to buy myself a place somewhere or do whatever I like'. Therefore, the villagers sympathized with the rioters, as is demonstrated by the laxity of many of the village magistrates (*Gerichtsscholzen*) in arresting the rioters and the later refusal of town residents to provide the factories with guards.[38]

The behaviour of the weavers during the revolt also illustrates the local horizons of their thoughts and actions. The Peterswaldau community was the centre from which the protest began, and the unrest spread as protesters used the social networks of their neighbourhoods to recruit others. The weavers from Lower Peterswaldau first gathered there, then marched together to Upper Peterswaldau, went from house to house, and 'picked up the weavers living there'. Certain men, such as Karl Müller and Friedrich Wilhelm Geburtig, went from dwelling to dwelling and persuaded others they knew to join.[39] The first day of the three-day protest was an entirely local event; both the rioters and their targeted victims were all located in Peterswaldau, where the pastor still had a great deal of influence over the situation.[40]

The song the weavers sang over and over during the uprising was called '*Das Blutgericht*', a song using allusions to the Last Judgment and violent (*Blut*, bloody) imagery to protest and lament the fate of the weavers at the hands of the textile merchants. The song clearly emphasized the local character of the event. It begins with the line 'here in this place judgment is being passed' and repeats in the verses that follow the word 'here' six times.[41] Four Peterwaldau manufacturers are referred to by name and their offences described in detail from the rich food they eat to the liveried servants who work for them. The story of the song takes place at a spot known to every weaver in the village, namely in the *Ausgeberei*, where the clerks of the merchant-wholesaler distributed work and paid for the fabric produced. When Karl Marx called '*Das Blutgericht*' a 'bold outcry' that transcended the local context by 'not once mentioning hearth, factory, or district', he was expressing a bit of wishful thinking.[42] The weavers of Peterswaldau and Langenbielau were concerned only with what was going on in their own backyard and no farther. This is why the cottage workers also did not perceive their work as being dependent on economic forces outside their immediate region. They saw only merchants, who paid them higher or lower wages, and compared these with the 'previously received' wage levels.[43] No reference to market forces, the English competition, or the introduction of machinery is made in either the song '*Das Blutgericht*' or in the petition of pardon for convicted rebels that was written in 1845.

In the village there were several centrally located places where the weavers usually met, even during the three-day uprising. The first of these was the church, since the local pastor enjoyed the trust of his parish. The cottage workers hoped that he would champion their cause against the entrepreneurs, which he did indeed do. In the factory villages, the pastors usually used 'the pulpit to admonish the rich factory owners' that 'they should be Christian enough to share their wealth with the poor suffering weavers whose fate had been placed in their hands and to refrain from mistreating their fellow human beings'.[44] The clergymen Schneider and Knittel in Peterswaldau addressed the merchant family Zwanziger directly from the pulpit, telling the family members to 'consider whether they had acquired their property legally' or had become rich by the 'sweat of the poor'.[45] The churchmen mediated in local conflicts between entrepreneurs and workers.

Another important place in the village was the Silesian 'Kretscham' or pub. Court records note that 'gatherings' of weavers were held in various pubs, namely in the Kretscham in Neubielau, the 'Brandweinschänke Thiel' and in the local court Kretscham.[46] Another traditional meeting place was the so-called 'Kapellenberg' at the edge of Peterswaldau. On the evening of 3 June 1844, 'several weavers, all young lads' met at these 'popular strolling grounds'. Their decision to insult the merchant Zwanziger by singing together the protest song '*Das Blutgericht*' was the spark that lit the fires of violent protest the very next day.[47]

The fact that young men made up the core of the protesters indicates how gender-specific the tapestry of local relations was. Male weavers apparently met in groups at specific places; therefore, the behavioural patterns formed there influenced greatly the choice of a strategy from the strategies of improvement available. All reports on gatherings in pubs and wage negotiations refer exclusively to male weavers, just as the courts only prosecuted and convicted men. On the one hand, such gender specificity can be attributed to the prevailing view of the authorities in which only men were considered capable of active protest and public behaviour. On the other hand, it is likely that roles were indeed distinguished on a gender basis in both the daily strategy to survive as well as in protest behaviour.

The reports on the uprising make it fair to assume that within the inner circle of protesters a mode of behaviour predominated that emphasized masculinity. These men referred to each other as 'brother', calling 'Come on brothers, we're off to Fellmann', or 'Come on brothers, we'll destroy everything', or 'Every weaver into the streets! Come on brothers, we have *all* been abused by the manufacturers'.[48] One indication of the gender-specific rituals involved can be seen in the quasi-military behaviour of the rebels. On 4 June, a troop of them marched in military formation to Zwanziger's factory, and the next day they marched again, in step and carrying a flag, to Langenbielau. One insurgent leader 'went to the head … and waved a pole around as if he wanted to command', while another wanted 'to hit any man on the head who tried to desert'.[49] The witnesses questioned later in court often testified that the male perpetrators used violent and obscene language. Merchants and yarn distributors were 'thoroughly' cursed as 'devils' and 'damned beasts', and the weaver Liebich boasted: 'The damned idiots should have their bellies ripped open and their guts strewn all over the street'.[50]

The women, who were indeed at the protest, assumed another role. They watched, divided the confiscated goods among themselves, and carried these off. When the factory of Friedrich Dierig was stormed, the men threw yarn out the windows 'into the arms of women who carried it away'.[51] The women participated the most on the third day of the protest in smaller assaults on an *Ausgeberei*, the yarn distribution shop, and a local police station, where confiscated booty from the looting of the factories was being stored. Indicative of the gender roles during the riots is that the 'mob consisting of fewer men and more children and women' in Leutmannsdorf was led by men and only 'the men and boys … were armed with sticks'.[52] Even without any input by authorities, the participation in public protest – whether verbal, armed, or violent – was something which male weavers were meant to do, whereas the women were to concentrate on gathering up valuable goods. In this way, the protest behaviour of the weavers reflected their behaviour in daily life, where women were to perform chiefly supportive tasks – such as spooling and spinning for their husbands, caring for small children, or collecting wild berries.

Strategies of Survival, Collective Protest, and the Ideal of Self-employment

The glimpses into the private lives of the Silesian weavers presented here have given us insights into various types of households, the differences in income, the composition of the family and gender-specific roles, local ties and community commitment. These insights will now be considered in connection with the strategies these people chose to protect and improve their existence.

Only by linking survival strategies with knowledge about the private background and moral norms of the weavers can we evaluate the impact of private factors on the phenomenon of collective protest.

Violent protest was used in 1844 by a certain group of cottage workers – those on the edge of destitution. As has been shown here, the people who rioted were those who still had something to lose, not the starving spinners and linen weavers or those weavers who enjoyed a secure job as a skilled worker in a factory. On the contrary, the skilled workers actually defended the factories in which they worked against the storm of protest.[53] This fact corresponds with the findings of recent research: 'Certainly those who protested the hardest and most often were not those who had the least materially but those social groups whose existential base could, to a certain degree, be considered secure'.[54]

Why, then, did this group resort to collective bargaining by riot[55] in June 1844? And why didn't these people organise themselves into labour organisations later? The answers to these questions can only become clear when we examine the concept of traditional self-employment and link it to the household situation and the village community. It is necessary here to look closely at this idea, which represented the crux of the overall outlook and opinion of (male) weavers.

Observers at the time noted repeatedly that cottage workers clung to their own weaving hut, regardless of how much they were then forced to go into debt.[56] Also, they refused to change occupations even as wages began to drop. Very few turned to 'rural day labour' and the large landowners in the region complained that 'domestic servants were always switching to weaving'. The regional appellate judges in Breslau surmised that weaving had become so popular among the poor in the area because 'the work required a minimum of strenuous physical labour and offered a more independent, freer life'.[57] And the judges were right. The road-building project near Langenbielau ordered by the king even suffered from labour shortages in 1844–45. Weavers let it be known that they preferred low-earning outwork to unfamiliar construction work.[58]

The reasons weavers felt this way are not difficult to understand. Work as a field-worker or a roadway construction worker was only temporary and seasonal. More importantly, the life as a farmhand was unattractive because it did not permit a man to establish his own household, to marry or have a family; it reduced him instead to a member of his employer's family with nearly no rights. Yet since the eighteenth century, the position of the artisan in Silesia offered a person a strong measure of independence. He was bound to no guild, owned his own loom, was not dependent on wages, and was free to negotiate a price for his wares with a merchant. This independence, this measure of self-employment became extraordinarily attractive. The fact that this independence had dwindled over time to little more than an ideal, that economic exigencies had forced the cottage weavers to become dependent on the merchants, was something weavers banished from their thoughts to a large extent. To be a self-employed master weaver was apparently the wish of those men who considered themselves to be the providers of their families. Their aim was to provide the 'necessities of life … for us and ours' through 'hard work'.[59] It is interesting that of the ninety-seven weavers arrested following the riots, only nine called themselves 'journeymen weavers'. The other eighty-eight claimed to be self-employed masters.[60]

The ideal of self-employment, which in this sense mirrored the male gender role, influenced the living strategies in many respects. Social esteem in village life was based on the idea of self-employment. The relations between manufacturer and cottage worker were significantly influenced by the idea, as was the attitude of the weavers toward authority and collective interest representation.

Let us examine first the relations with the textile manufacturers. Cottage workers had a very clear idea of what belonged to them and what belonged to the manufacturers. They stormed the mills because they were outraged at the infringement of what they considered to be justified norms. They felt they were right to resort to violence. The values they held were reflected in the grievances they expressed: first, the manufacturer was obligated to pay the weaver prices that adequately reflected the quality of the goods; second, being self-employed, the weaver had the right to be treated politely and with social respect; third, the factory owner could own and earn more than the weaver, but they were both on the same rung of the social ladder. The factory owner could not outwardly claim to have achieved a higher social status through, for example, conspicuous luxury. Fourth, every member of the community, including the factory owners, was to maintain the solidarity among the local population, and this excluded giving priority to workers from the outside when hiring.

The entrepreneurs in Peterswaldau and Langenbielau who were attacked in 1844 had violated these norms many times. The weavers, who considered themselves to be self-employed and thus the merchants' equals, were angered by the 'scorn and ridicule' of the merchants and the 'licenses' they took, first and foremost the entrepreneur Zwanziger.[61] One of the 'main reasons for the hate directed against Zwanziger's business', surmised the regional appeals court, was that 'he had treated the weavers so rudely and brutally'.[62] That the workers found Zwanziger's behaviour arrogant can be explained by the fact that he 'had himself been a simple weaver at one time' and had accumulated a fortune of 220,000 *Taler* in a short span of time. About four weeks before the uprising, the Zwanziger family moved into its second luxurious house, and family members even 'bragged about the amount that the construction had cost them'. Such a display of expanding wealth for all to see adversely affected those struggling with poverty, especially because – in the words of the court – 'there are still many weavers who considered the elder Zwanziger and his family to be their equals'.[63]

The rioters accused the factory owner of living 'luxuriously, gluttonously, and wastefully'.[64] They clearly complained in their protest song that the 'cocky' manufacturer had overstepped the bounds of his social status. The main focus of the song is on the merchant who has recently come into wealth and tries to place himself above the others in the village: his 'domestics' and 'tutors', 'stately carriages' and 'palaces' ('with doors, windows magnificently wide, appearing almost majestic') were labelled arrogant. In order to justify their criticism, the weavers referred to earlier times: 'to the times, twenty years ago' when such derision against the social order would not have been conceivable.[65]

The weavers were still interpreting relations in the terms of pre-industrial textile manufacturing. In their eyes, the merchant-wholesalers were their business partners and therefore obliged to act according to the traditional social norms. It seemed appropriate to engage amicably in a discussion with the merchants to persuade them to increase wages. Wage negotiations had preceded the weaver revolt of 1844. A delegation had been elected to talk to Zwanziger, but was then refused admittance.[66] On the whole, manufacturers enjoyed a certain trust, even respect, among cottage workers as long as they did what was expected of them. This is illustrated very distinctly by the way the weavers behaved during the revolt. Although they destroyed the houses belonging to the hated Zwanziger, leaving little but bare walls standing, they cheered his neighbour, the entrepreneur Wagenknecht: 'Long live Mr Wagenknecht. He didn't pay us too little'. The rioters treated the entrepreneurs they admired and those they despised differently. Money was accepted as compensation from merchants who generally paid the weavers well (such as the merchant Ernst), whereas money was not accepted from otherwise miserly firms like Zwanziger and Hilbert & Andritzky.[67] Apparently the weavers were not at all inclined to label all textile manufacturers as class enemies – a result of their perception of themselves as 'self-employed'.

The cottage weavers also assumed that they still had a rightful claim to their established status as master artisans, and that this must be obvious to the authorities. In this vein, they appealed to various authorities from whom they expected paternalistic assistance and support for their concerns. Thus they turned to the pastor (as mentioned above), the manor lord, and the district administrator (*Landrat*). It was common for textile workers to express their concerns in the form of petitions; and indeed, the 1844 riots were also preceded by petitions to the district administrator, the provincial diet, and the king, the last of which were sent in 1843 and in January 1844. However, the officials had disappointed the Silesian weavers by brushing aside or dismissing their demands for wage increases and the firing of workers in the Langenbielau factories who were from outside the village.[68] Despite this disappointment, the weavers still expressed a degree of trust in the authorities during the violent unrest. Whenever representatives from the government appeared at the mills under siege, the workers showed their respect: 'The district administrator … entered the buildings with the magistrate where the destruction was in full swing; rioters tipped their hats and made room for him to pass wherever he went'. To one aristocratic landowner, who had promised the angry crowd 'that I will report your misery directly to the King himself', the people in the crowd replied: 'We are not rebels, but loyal subjects of the King and all authority …'.[69] It is truly amazing that the three-day-long unrest in the Silesian hills was never directed against the manor lords, although the majority of Junkers had neglected their traditional obligations to care for their subjects.[70] Yet, the weavers apparently still believed in the 'benevolent authority' who would take them seriously because they were self-employed.

In summary, the specific findings that can be stated here about the strategies of protest and survival exhibited by the Silesian weavers only apply to the male weavers, to their attitudes and behaviour, of which we have been able to learn a great deal. Generally, all cotton weavers were threatened with poverty. Wage losses were putting all households in a precarious financial situation. Nevertheless, the degree of poverty varied greatly, since it also depended on numerous factors that had nothing to do with wages. In this situation, each and every person feared for his position in the village hierarchy, for his social esteem. Therefore the weavers used similar strategies to maintain or improve their own position. Certain individual options – such as a change in occupation or migration beyond the neighbouring villages – were not open to them because such options would have contradicted well-established traditions involving integration into the village community and the ideal of artisan self-employment. Other strategies were being used all the time but held out little hope of mastering the increasing severity of the crisis affecting the Silesian textile industry in the 1840s. They included attempts to compensate for wage cuts by working more and involving more family members in production, by saving, by borrowing, and by stealing wood and wild berries. Only a few weavers were in a position to earn a side income by renting out rooms or working a small piece of land.

Faced with such a situation, the cottage workers resorted to various collective strategies. At first, knowing they could count on the support of the village, they protested against the employment of outside weavers and the behaviour of the merchants. (When young lads sang a mocking song every evening about the rich merchant, they were attempting to pillory him symbolically before the entire village.) Then the weavers placed their hopes in the pastor and in talks with the merchant, in order to defuse the wage issue. Finally, they appealed to the state authorities by petitioning as high as to the king. Only as a last resort did they choose the path of violent protest.

The weavers' ultimate decision to storm the mills together was an understandable one. Since negotiation, mediation, and appeal had proven fruitless, violent protest represented a strong measure by which to force the authorities 'up there' to act. In this way, the members of a social group whose shared esteem had been diminished were demanding to have their claims to individual 'self-employment' upheld. The weavers were not so wrong to calculate that violent protest would improve wages and thus their situation. In the short term, their strategy was successful: the entrepreneurs raised their wages after the riots;[71] the village community supported the insurgents to a large extent; the Prussian state ordered more road construction in the area as an employment measure; the bourgeois charity organisations collected on behalf of the weavers, and the clergymen attempted for the most part to exonerate the defendants in the courtroom (the sentences handed down were relatively mild). The tactic of 'collective bargaining by riot' had indeed paid off in the case of the Silesian weavers' revolt.

After all other household and collective strategies failed, the storming of the mills appeared to the Silesian weavers to be the last suitable and promising means. An organised representation of interests was inconceivable for them because, on the one hand, this contradicted the principle of self-employment and thus the greatest goal of these cottage workers, namely to feel like master artisans. This self-employment mentality, which sprang out of the desire to determine one's own fate without a loss of esteem, countered the assimilation into a class collective and misled the weavers into believing that the manufacturers were business equals. On the other hand, the realities of their situation prevented them from organising into a collective, namely the distinct differences in income and the isolated working conditions within the context of family. There were also the additional factors of their religious piety and respect for authority, so that their illusions of help from above prevailed over any steps toward collective organisation.

In the long run, the limited coping repertoire described here led the cotton workers up a blind alley. By the 1890s, masses of textile workers were still living in alarming poverty in the Silesian hills and attempting vainly to keep abreast with the largely mechanised competition. They earned considerably less than factory workers and worked longer days with no protection or social insurance; and they no longer had the strength to protest, as they had in 1844.

Translation: Dona Geyer

Notes

1. For a detailed description of the events that took place from 4–6 June 1844, and a presentation of interpretations of the revolt in literature and historiography, see: Christina von Hodenberg, *Aufstand der Weber. Die Revolte von 1844 und ihr Aufstieg zum Mythos*, Bonn, 1997. I would like to thank Dr Michael Spehr (Frankfurt) for his numerous suggestions.
2. On the debate in the press, see Christina von Hodenberg, 'Mit dem Rotstift gegen die soziale Frage. Die preußische Pressezensur und der schlesische Weberstand 1844', *Forschungen zur Brandenburgischen und Preußischen Geschichte*, Neue Folge 9 (1999): 91–122.
3. Helmut Bleiber, 'Die Krise des aristokratisch-monarchischen Regimes und das Heranreifen einer revolutionären Situation', in *Deutsche Geschichte*, vol. 4, eds Walter Schmidt et al., Berlin-Ost/ Köln 1984, 252. Jacques Droz, *Der deutsche Sozialismus, vol. II: Der utopische Sozialismus bis 1848*, Frankfurt a.M., 1974, 231.
4. The court, police, and ministerial files pertaining to the revolt have been available again since 1990. See Hodenberg, *Aufstand*, 16f.
5. See Heinrich Waldmann, 'Unruhen unter den schlesischen Webern 1793–1844' (Ph.D. diss. manuscript, Halle, 1990) 86f.
6. More than fourfifths of the weaving looms in Peterswaldau produced cotton cloth. See Fritz Hoenow, 'Chronik von Langenbielau' (1931), in *Weber-Revolte 1844*, eds Lutz Kroneberg and Rolf Schloesser, Cologne, 1980, 562.
7. From the general report sent by Commissioner Kehler after the uprising (on 18 June 1844) to the Breslau government. Geheimes Staatsarchiv Preußischer Kulturbesitz Berlin-Dahlem (GStAPK), I. HA, Rep. 77 tit. 507 no. 6, vol. 2, folio 70.
8. In 1844, Langenbielau had 138 small 'factories' and 23 large ones (Veit Valentin, *Geschichte der deutschen Revolution von 1848–1849*, vol. 1, reprint, Cologne 1970, 55). See Waldmann, 'Unruhen', 89f.
9. The causes for the demise of the textile industry have been described often, therefore I will mention here only two key factors, namely the dependency on exports in an unstable market and the superiority of the English and Irish competition. See Gustav Schmoller, *Zur Geschichte der deutschen Kleingewerbe im 19. Jahrhundert*, reprint Hildesheim, 1975, 543ff.; Friedrich Wilhelm von Reden, *Erwerbs- und Verkehrsstatistik des Königstaats Preußen*, Abt. III, Darmstadt, 1853, 1602f.; Alfred Zimmerman, *Blüthe und Verfall des Leinengewerbes in Schlesien*, second edition, Oldenburg and Leipzig, 1892, 286 ff. See also the in-depth regional studies in Karl Ditt and Sidney Pollard, eds, *Von der Heimarbeit in die Fabrik*, Paderborn, 1992.

10. Wolfgang Köllmann, 'Bevölkerung und Arbeitskräftepotential in Deutschland 1815–1865', in *Bevölkerung in der industriellen Revolution*, ed. Wolfgang Köllmann, Göttingen, 1974, 79.

11. Alexander Schneer, *Ueber die Noth der Leinen-Arbeiter in Schlesien und die Mittel ihr abzuhelfen. Ein Bericht an das Comité des Vereins zur Abhilfe der Noth unter den Webern und Spinnern in Schlesien, unter Benutzung der amtlichen Quellen des Königl. Ober-Präsidii und des Königl. Provincial-Steuer-Directorats von Schlesien*, Berlin, 1844, 39, cf. p. 33.

12. Censorship of the press and the written, closed court trials in Prussia caused this misinterpretation of the events by the public. See Hodenberg, *Aufstand*, 70ff.

13. Quote on poor relief taken from Schneer, *Noth*, 33. The quote on taxes taken from a report, dated 8 December 1845, by Minister of Justice Uhden on the community charter of Langenbielau, GStAPK Rep. 89, no. 14701, n.p. See also the report, dated 5 November 1845, by the state ministry on the same topic, ibid.

14. The rate of this feudal duty for the cotton weavers in Peterswaldau and Langenbielau cannot be precisely reconstructed because the examples cited by Schneer (*Noth*, 45 ff.) refer exclusively to linen weaver communities in other districts of Silesia. See Waldmann, 'Unruhen', 87, 92.

15. According to the personal data on the defendants Karl Wilhelm, August Hübner, Joseph Bruschwitz, Gottlob Rohleder, and August Winkler recorded in the court sentencing of the rebellious weavers dated 31 August 1844, handed down by the *Kriminalsenat* of the Breslau *Oberlandesgericht*, the regional appellate court (GStAPK I. HA, Rep. 84a no. 9904, folios 89–254, here folios 191, 196, 135, 213, 196).

16. Rarely do the court records indicate the marital status of the convicted. Court records indicate for only nineteen of the thirty-five sentenced perpetrators in Langenbielau whether these men had a wife and children – while the first sixteen cases contain no such information. Of these nineteen perpetrators, nine were married, one divorced. Five men, all younger than thirty, are noted as being unmarried. No information is given on three very young weavers (19–21), court sentence, ibid., folios 188 ff. Additional information can be derived from a list of those arrested who were incarcerated in the Schweidnitz prison. Of the 122 men, thirty-four were married, forty-four were not married, thirty-four were not specified (average age 28.9). See GStAPK I. HA, Rep. 84a no. 9905, folios 38–68.

17. Of the ten (once) married defendants listed in note 18, three had one child, two had two children, one had three and another four children, and no information was listed for three of them.

18. Cf. Court sentence (fn. 15), folios 137, 144, 207.

19. See Schneer, *Noth*, 78–80.

20. Testimony of the merchant Wagenknecht from Peterswaldau, Court sentence (fn. 15), folio 102. See the comment by the merchant Winter (ibid.) on the reduced wages for 'ordinary cloth (*Parchent*)': 'This even included the spooling by the wife'.

21. Taken from Wagenknecht's testimony (ibid.), as well as from Schneer, *Noth*, 39 f. See also Hodenberg, *Aufstand*, 57 f.

22. See the general report by Kehler (fn. 7), folios 69 ff.

23. For more on the 'rich' weavers, see Josef Mooser, 'Maschinensturm und Assoziation. Wirtschaftliche und politische Mentalitäten der Spinner und Weber in der Krise des Leinengewerbes in Ravensberg, 1840–1870', in *Heimarbeit*, eds Ditt and Pollard, 290–356, here 316, 321. The merchant Zwanziger, whose wage cuts sparked the uprising, paid the worst wages, traded in the most substandard goods and had a reputation for fraudulent deals. See the testimonies of the merchants Wagenknecht and Winter (fn. 20) and the report, dated 8 July 1844, by the Breslau regional appellate judge Count Rittberg and submitted to the Minister of Justice, GStAPK I. HA, Rep. 84a, no. 9904, folio 29.

24. Cf. Court sentence (fn. 15), folios 112, 159, 231, as well as the prisoner list (fn. 16).

25. On the demise of the weavers' guild, see Waldmann, 'Unruhen', 15 f.

26. See Michael Mitterauer, 'Lebensformen und Lebensverhältnisse ländlicher Unterschichten', in *Familie und Arbeitsteilung*, ed. Michael Mitterauer, Vienna, 1992, 39, 50 ff.

27. Taken from the court opinion handed down at the sentencing (fn. 15), folio 95: 'The cases are not rare in which in many families the children of even the diligent weaver must beg'.

28. On 11 July 1844, the district administrator of the Reichenbach District, von Prittwitz-Gaffron, reported on the forester working in the neighboring village of Peiskersdorf: 'He was especially hated for the exaggerated severity with which he confronted women and children

he found looking for strawberries and other wild berries in the woods, trampled the fruit they
had collected, broke their bowls, and chased them off'. (GStAPK I. HA, Rep. 89 no. 15132,
folio 111 f.) On the previous convictions, see folios 241 and 247 in Court sentence (fn. 15).

29. From the court opinion handed down at the sentencing (fn. 15), folio 95.
30. Schneer, *Noth*, 39.
31. See Waldmann, 'Unruhen', 90 ff.
32. See Court sentence (fn. 15), folios 96 f., 115, 168, 203.
33. Testimony of Luschwitz, ibid., folio 103.
34. Ibid., folio 96.
35. Kehler's general report (fn. 7), folio 72. In addition, see Schneer, *Noth*, 41; Waldmann,
    'Unruhen', 126 f.
36. Prisoner list from 9 June 1844 (fn. 16).
37. As protest research has shown, the pattern of 'locals against outsiders' was not uncharacteris-
    tic for riots of this sort. See Manfred Gailus and Heinrich Volkmann, 'Nahrungsmangel,
    Hunger und Protest', in *Der Kampf um das tägliche Brot*, eds Manfred Gailus and Heinrich
    Volkmann, Opladen, 1994, 17.
38. General report by the assessor Kehler (fn. 7), folios 33, 79 f., 85. Anonymous letter, found
    in Langenbielau on 21 June 1844, printed in: Hodenberg, *Aufstand*, 256 f. See also the
    report by the district magistrate (Landrat) on the uprising, dated 8 June 1844, GStAPK I.
    HA, Rep. 89 no. 15132, folio 19.
39. Court sentence (fn. 15), folios 112, 125, 132.
40. While the buildings of the manufacturer Zwanziger were attacked on the afternoon of 4 June,
    the Peterswaldau pastor Knittel 'urged the rioters to stop', which got them to lay down their
    clubs and leave the grounds temporarily: Court sentence (fn. 15), folios 114 f.
41. The weavers' song 'Das Blutgericht', printed in Hodenberg, *Aufstand*, 238–40.
42. Karl Marx, 'Kritische Randglossen zu dem Artikel "Der König von Preußen und die Sozial-
    reform. Von einem Preußen"' (1844), in Karl Marx and Friedrich Engels, *Werke*, ed. by the
    Institut für Marxismus-Leninismus beim ZK der SED, 7.A., Berlin, 1970, vol. 1, 392–409,
    here 404.
43. Quoted from the convicted weavers' petition for pardon, 5 February 1845, printed in
    Hodenberg, *Aufstand*, 254 f.
44. The president of the Kriminalsenat of the Regional Appellate Court, Graf Rittberg, on 8 July
    1844, to the Prussian Minister of Justice Mühler, GstAK I. HA, Rep. 84a no. 9904, folio 31.
45. General report by Kehler (fn. 7), folio 74.
46. See the report of the Kriminalsenat of the Regional Appellate Court, 5 August 1844,
    GStAPK I. HA, Rep. 84a no. 9904, folio 47, as well as the court sentence (fn. 15), folios 97,
    203.
47. Court sentence (fn. 15), folio 111.
48. According to the testimony of defendants Knappe, Blättner, Scholz and Franke, ibid., folios
    222, 178, 184, 172.
49. Ibid., folios 222, 134 (testimony of the weavers Geisler and Franke).
50. Ibid., folios 186, 195, 216, 237.
51. Ibid., folio 195. See also the general report by Kehler (fn. 7), folio 40: The crowd that col-
    lected in the street in front of the buildings belonging to the merchant Zwanziger, 'consist-
    ing in part of women and children', was reported to have destroyed yarn and looted.
52. From a report by the president of the province of Silesia, Merckel, 9 June 1844, and submit-
    ted to the Prussian king: GStAPK I. HA, Rep. 89 no. 15123, folio 4; report of the govern-
    ment commissioner v. Kehler from Leutmannsdorf to the Breslau government, 11 June 1844,
    ibid., folio 79. Similar evidence is in the general report by Kehler (fn. 7), folio 54. See also
    the court sentence (fn. 15), folios 229 ff. and 237 ff.
53. One can find this front between factory and cottage workers in other disturbances of the period.
    In Iserlohn in 1840 and in Aachen in 1830, the factory employees defended their workplaces
    against attackers, among whom the tone was set by self-employed artisans and home workers.
    See Michael Spehr, *Maschinensturm: Protest und Widerstand gegen technische Neuerungen am
    Anfang der Industrialisierung*, Münster, 2000.

54. Hans-Gerhard Husung, *Protest und Repression im Vormärz. Norddeutschland zwischen Restauration und Revolution*, Göttingen, 1983, 221, see also 214. On the protest of the spinners that did not occur, see also Mooser, 'Maschinenstürmer', 300.
55. On this term, see Eric J. Hobsbawm, 'The Machine Breakers', *Past and Present* 1 (1952) 59 ff., 66 f.
56. See Kehler's general report (fn. 7), folio 71.
57. From the court sentence (fn. 15), folio 96; testimony by Pastor Seifert, ibid., folio 105.
58. The daily wage in road construction was about 5–6 silver Groschen and thus more than a weaver's wage, according to the report by the financial administrator Oesterreich (Waldmann, 'Unruhen', 126).
59. Quotes taken from the convicted weavers' petition for pardon (fn. 43), 254.
60. Count was taken from the Schweidnitz prisoner report (fn. 16).
61. 'Das Blutgericht', verses 8, 17. In the convicted weavers' petition for pardon from 5 Feb. 1845, reference is made to the 'most revolting … scorn and ridicule' (reprinted in Hodenberg, *Aufstand*, 254 f.)
62. When the weaver Rogel, who took part in the uprising, was asked by the judge 'why he rebelled', he emphasised the rude behaviour of the merchants above all else: 'You see, I work for Röhrich, and if you arrive just a few minutes too late with some goods, they were mean and threw us out. That had to make you mad, since you hadn't even been paid well to begin with'. From the court sentence (fn. 15), folios 100, 103.
63. Waldmann, 'Unruhen', 88. From the court sentence (fn. 15), folio 100.
64. From the petition for pardon (fn. 43).
65. 'Das Blutgericht' (fn. 41).
66. Court sentence (fn. 15), folio 113.
67. Ibid., folios 113, 114 f., 116f. Two verses of the anonymous protest song deal with the 'good' manufacturers in town who would prefer to treat the poor well and fairly, but are forced by the business practices of their competitors to reduce wages: 'Sind ja noch welche, die der Schmerz / Der armen Leut beweget / In deren Busen auch ein Herz / Voll Mitgefühles schläget / Die müßen von der Zeit gedrängt / Auch in das Gleis einlenken, / Und euerm Beispiel eingedenk / Sich in jedem Lohn einschränken' (fn. 41).
68. See the report from the Breslau Regional Appellate Court, 5 August 1844, GStAPK I. HA, Rep. 84a no. 9904, folio 47; as well as Hodenberg, *Aufstand*, 64.
69. Report of the Regional Appellate Court judge, Count Rittberg, to the Justice Minister, 8 July 1844, GStAPK Rep. 84a, no. 9904, folio 30. Count L. Pfeil-Burghauß, 'Das Vorspiel zum Drama: "Die Weber"', *Deutsche Revue* 22 (1897): 178.
70. A report by the ministry of domestic affairs emphasized that the 'bitterness' of the Silesian weavers was at least 'not directed against the manor lords'. Bodelschwingh, 24 July 1844, to the king, GStAPK Rep. 89 no. 15132, folio 104.
71. See Kehler's general report (fn. 7), folio 79.

Bibliography

Bleiber, H. 'Die Krise des aristokratisch-monarchischen Regimes und das Heranreifen einer revolutionären Situation', in *Deutsche Geschichte*, vol. 4, eds W. Schmidt et al. Berlin-Ost and Köln, 1984.

Ditt, K., and Pollard, S. eds. *Von der Heimarbeit in die Fabrik*. Paderborn, 1992.

Droz, J. *Der deutsche Sozialismus, vol. II: Der utopische Sozialismus bis 1848*. Frankfurt a.M., 1974.

Hodenberg, C. von, *Aufstand der Weber. Die Revolte von 1844 und ihr Aufstieg zum Mythos*. Bonn, 1997.

———. 'Mit dem Rotstift gegen die soziale Frage. Die preußische Pressezensur und der schlesische Weberstand 1844', *Forschungen zur Brandenburgischen und Preußischen Geschichte*, Neue Folge 9 (1999): 91–122.

Gailus, M. and Volkmann, H. 'Nahrungsmangel, Hunger und Protest', in *Der Kampf um das tägliche Brot*, eds M. Gailus and H. Volkmann. Opladen, 1994.

Hobsbawm, E.J. 'The Machine Breakers', *Past and Present* vol. 1 (1952).

Hoenow, F. 'Chronik von Langenbielau' (1931), in *Weber-Revolte 1844*, eds L.Kroneberg and R. Schloesser. Cologne, 1980.

Husung, H.-G. *Protest und Repression im Vormärz. Norddeutschland zwischen Restauration und Revolution*. Göttingen, 1983.

Köllmann, W. 'Bevölkerung und Arbeitskräftepotential in Deutschland 1815–1865', in *Bevölkerung in der industriellen Revolution*, ed. W. Köllmann. Göttingen, 1974.

Mitterauer, M. 'Lebensformen und Lebensverhältnisse ländlicher Unterschichten', in *Familie und Arbeitsteilung*, ed. M. Mitterauer. Vienna, 1992.

Marx, K. 'Kritische Randglossen zu dem Artikel "Der König von Preußen und die Sozialreform. Von einem Preußen"' (1844), in K. Marx and F. Engels, *Werke*, edited by the Institut für Marxismus-Leninismus beim ZK der SED, 7.A. Berlin, 1970, vol. 1, 392–409.

Mooser, J. 'Maschinensturm und Assoziation. Wirtschaftliche und politische Mentalitäten der Spinner und Weber in der Krise des Leinengewerbes in Ravernsberg, 1840–1870', in *Heimarbeit*, eds Ditt and Pollard, 290–356.

Pfeil-Burghauß, Count L. 'Das Vorspiel zum Drama: "Die Weber"', *Deutsche Revue* vol. 22 (1897).

Reden, F.W. von, *Erwerbs- und Verkehrsstatistik des Königstaats Preußen*, Abt. III. Darmstadt, 1853.

Schmoller, G. *Zur Geschichte der deutschen Kleingewerbe im 19. Jahrhundert*. Reprint Hildesheim, 1975.

Schneer, A. *Ueber die Noth der Leinen-Arbeiter in Schlesien und die Mittel ihr abzuhelfen. Ein Bericht an das Comité des Vereins zur Abhilfe der Noth unter den Webern und Spinnern in Schlesien, unter Benutzung der amtlichen Quellen des Königl. Ober-Präsidii und des Königl. Provincial-Steuer-Directorats von Schlesien*. Berlin, 1844.

Spehr, M. *Maschinensturm: Protest und Widerstand gegen technische Neuerungen am Anfang der Industrialisierung*, Münster, 2000.

Valentin, V. *Geschichte der deutschen Revolution von 1848–1849*, vol. 1, reprint. Cologne 1970.

Waldmann, H. 'Unruhen unter den schlesischen Webern 1793–1844', Ph.D. diss. manuscript, Halle, 1990.

Zimmerman, A. *Blüthe und Verfall des Leinengewerbes in Schlesien*, second edition. Oldenburg and Leipzig, 1892.

CHAPTER 4

THE CASE OF CLARINNA STRINGER

STRATEGIC OPTIONS AND THE HOUSEHOLD ECONOMY IN LATE NINETEENTH-CENTURY AUSTRALIA

Bruce Scates

In the winter of 1892 Clarinna Stringer was starving.[1] Her husband's death had left her alone to care for four children; to make ends meet she took in a little washing and sold wood from her backyard in Tyne Street, Carlton. Throughout the summer she had called regularly on the ladies of Melbourne's Benevolent Society; their irregular three-shilling cards for rations were a sensitive barometer of a failing household economy. Normally, the winter months would signal some modest improvement in the family fortunes. As the bitter June winds whipped through Melbourne even the poorest needed wood to warm their families; but 1892 was one of the worst years of a decade-long depression. The building boom was long over and even fuel became a luxury in budgets stretched to breaking-point. That April Mrs Stringer, 'an old case', was refused relief by the local charity; with two grown-up sons to help her, other families were deemed more deserving. By June, she was well behind with the rent and the bailiffs came to confiscate what need or self-denial had kept from pawning.

What followed was an explosion of anger, pain and frustration. Having failed to beat back the bailiff's on her own, Clarinna Stringer ran to the courtyard of Trades Hall where hundreds of unemployed assembled daily. Amongst them were the Salvage Corps, a quasi anarchist collective determined to do battle with the bailiffs and 'salvage' goods and furniture confiscated in lieu of arrears. The arrival of the Salvage Corps put the bailiffs to flight; within a matter of minutes Stringer's furniture, bedding, clothing and 'even the stock in the woodyard' were loaded onto a cart and wheeled off down the street. By that time, its escort numbered 300, a measure of the solidarity amongst those hard-pressed to pay their rent. Unfortunately for Stringer, the party was intercepted by the police and her goods redirected to the premises of Robert Wilson, a local auctioneer. By five o'clock the crowd had reassembled, the proprietor and a 'garrison of four' barricading themselves in the Station Street shop. Mr Wilson had 'no doubt of his ability to withstand the siege'. Steel shutters sealed windows at the front of the building, and a row of iron bars protected either flank; but Wilson, noted the Argus:

> soon found he had miscalculated the temper of the mob. Nor had he considered that the newly tarred road in front of his shop offered an opportunity too tempting to resist. A volley of stones rained upon the walls from the front, smashing most of the windows and under the cover of this brisk fuselage, the 'salvage corps' advanced briskly to the attack and flung themselves on the beleaguered stronghold.[2]

Wilson was rescued by timely intervention from the police, the 'vigorous use of batons' ending what the Argus called the 'rule of the mob'.[3]

There are moments in history, E.P. Thompson once remarked, that are like a lightning strike: in an instant they illuminate the social conditions of their time. The riot in Tyne Street is one such moment. In a single afternoon it mobilized an entire community: friends, neighbours, workmates, families, all shared what John Bohstedt has called 'a praxis of common experience and perception', their poverty threw them together while their collective action drew its strength from 'networks ... and relationships that already existed'.[4] Of course, at one level the story of Clarinna Stringer is quite exceptional. Few women of her generation left so vivid a record of their struggle; fewer still succeeded in mobilising an entire community in support of their cause. But the dilemma which faced Mrs Stringer was (and remains) universal: how, in the absence of a male breadwinner, were their families to survive? The male wage had never been reliable. Well before the depression of the 1890s men had failed as providers; quite apart from death, illness and desertion, unemployment and underemployment were a feature of their working lives. The causes, nature and extent of male unemployment have been the subject of considerable historical inquiry.[5] The focus on this paper is on a very different kind of economy, a 'household economy' which operated irrespective of trade and industry or the vagaries of a man's weekly wage. At its centre were women like Mrs Stringer: their 'strategies for survival' determined if families remain united or divided, if their children were fed, clothed and sheltered, if they 'managed' or if they starved.[6]

Women's formal earnings were a poor substitute for the loss of a man's income. In the nineteenth century they occupied the periphery of the paid economy, working long hours at 'unskilled' jobs for very little pay. Even so, their contribution was crucial to the family's survival. In this 'regime of economic insecurity', meagre earnings 'tipped the balance against destitution for a day, a week, sometimes a year'.[7] The onset of the depression made that balance more precarious still. Many families, which turned to charity or pleaded for the remittance of their school fees, existed solely on the labour of wife and child. Women took in washing and sewing, struggling to 'knock out a living' with mangle or pin.[8] Those with space to spare would sometimes take in boarders, others 'went out' as charwomen, offering their services for payment in cash and kind.[9] The streets, like the home, provided income of a sort. Women, 'pitiable' in their appearance, accosted visitors to the city 'till well into the night': many carried 'babies in their arms' pleading with passers -by to purchase flowers, matches or soap. Street trade like this was usually 'a disguised form of begging'; and often it was a front for prostitution. The most successful flower-seller was usually the prettiest: she made far more by selling her sexuality as well.[10]

Whether her labour was respectable or otherwise, whether it was in the home, the street or the factory, a number of factors limited a woman's ability to provide. Women's work, as Jane Lewis, Bettina Bradbury and Eileen Boris have noted, is 'structured' by her family; paid labour has always to be balanced (as Mrs Stringer's situation again suggests) with the unpaid labour of caring for children and home. This was as true of work attempted within the home as of that taken outside. Mrs Somerville, a character from William Lane's fictional recreation of nineteenth century Sydney, endured the thankless, 'ceaseless' toil of every outworker. On a 'busy' day she might put in eighteen hours at her machine; but her labour was broken and distracted by children and by chores. Mrs Somerville was a seamstress but she was also a mother. All day long a child clung to her breast.[11] What to do with the children was an even greater problem for those who worked 'away'. Lucy Edwards, 'an honest hard-working woman', averaged a pound a week in 1893, just enough to keep a family of five alive. To earn it she left two children in the care of an 'adopted' nine-year-old 'sister' and hurried the others off to school. That same year her youngest son was found 'wandering' the streets of Sydney. He was sent to the *Vernon*, the converted hulk which served as both home and prison for 'uncontrollable' boys. Others took their children with them. Charwomen carried babies in their baskets, 'female beggars' kept their families by their side. The separation of work and home, however, was never easy to assail. Domestic servants were usually employed on the condition they were unencumbered; ironically the 'encumbrance' was sometimes a master's child.[12]

Domestic responsibilities were but one of the many handicaps a female breadwinner faced. Women's work, then as today, was the least 'skilled' and the poorest paid. Most of it was an extension of her (unpaid) labour in the home; male employers did not pay well for washing, cleaning and sewing; such services were extracted without payment from daughters, mothers and wives. Moreover, women workers were dispersed and disorganised. Denied the benefits of trade unionism, they were unable to achieve a fair or even a uniform rate of pay. Charring is a typical example. At one pound a week Mrs Edwards was doing well. Mary Graham, a woman of five years experience, averaged six shillings, hardly 'enough' to get by. Indeed, most of women's occupations offered at best 'a poor living'. Mrs Kelly, a washerwoman in inner-city Sydney, 'work[ed] all day yet her earnings were barely sufficient to clothe her family and pay the rent'. Mrs Elliot, widow and mother to three dependent children, was cheated by her employers and did not get paid at all. Even when women took on the role of surrogate wives or parents their efforts were poorly rewarded. Mrs Wilcox's boarder brought in 8 shillings; each week she fell short of the fourteen shillings' rent. Those who worked in factories did little better, their rates of pay averaging half that of a man's.[13]

Prostitution was probably the only work which paid – but it had its costs as well. Women were exposed to the dangers of male violence, pregnancy and disease: many became addicted to alcohol, some to laudanum and opium as well. Once discovered, these women were outcast from society, labelled 'deviant' by the authorities and denied access to charitable aid; and ironically the one line of work which could provide for their families often meant their families were taken away. James Cronan was sent to the *Vernon* on 9 February 1891. He had been 'found' by the police a few days earlier, 'play[ing] in the same room' where women immorally conducted themselves' with men. His mother protested frantically as Cronan was led away, 'crying he was her baby and should be given back'. Mrs Cronan, too, was forcibly removed from the court.[14]

Prostitution differed from other women's industries in more ways than one: even in the depressed 1890s a prostitute's services were always in demand. In other trades, unemployment and underemployment crippled a woman's capacity to earn. Washerwomen complained of a 'bad run' of work, charwomen that there was not enough cleaning to be found. Moreover, more competed for work than ever before. The streets were filled with hawkers of every kind, 'old and young, tainted and untainted', offering goods no one wanted to buy. In a sense Mrs Stringer's woodyard was a symbol of this failed economy: even in the depths of Melbourne's winter none could afford to buy.[15]

It was not just Mrs Stringer's labour which maintained the woodyard. Children, as Barry Reay's study has suggested, were 'the lynchpin' of the domestic economy: their labour was necessary to keep these fragile family enterprises afloat in hard times. Mrs Stringer's eldest boy performed (in may ways) the functions of his absent father. 'Men's work' it may have seemed but within this domestic economy chopping and carting wood were tasks that often fell to children and wives. By the same token help in the home was necessary to free their parents for more remunerative labour. The eldest children were just as likely to be child minders: at the age of eleven Oswald Marshall's mother 'went out all day' to make a few shillings from charring. George was left at home 'to mind his brother and the baby'. Children also participated in the more formal economy. Even before their schooling was over, girls and boys took their place in workshops and factories. It was poorly paid work (averaging a few shillings weekly) and with little prospect of advancement, but in the collective economic unit of the labouring household every member who could brought in a wage.[16]

Beyond this formal economy functioned what Ellen Ross has called an 'intermediate economy' of street trade and scavenging, dealing and theft. 'All day and half the night' children peddled papers and oranges, pilfered food and clothing and scavenged the suburbs for paper and glass. The entries in juvenile offender records abound with Dickenesque characters: 'cunning', 'thievish', and nimble-fingered lads initiated into a culture of working-class crime. Other skills, however, could prove just as saleable. Brian Newry made his living by 'grinning' 'outside public houses … putting my legs around my neck and all that'. Pretty young girls sold flowers and matches while those with a deformity or affliction pleaded, sang or begged. Many worked for fear of punishment. Charles Blackburn's mother beat him if he 'went home without money': his working day of selling papers, gambling and thieving began at five in the morning and ended late at night. Hunger, too, made just as hard a task master; at the age of ten Frederick Hoflick was brought before the bench 'charged with stealing a quantity of pears, turnips and potatoes'. There were seven children in the family and both mother and father were without work.[17]

Like a woman's earnings a child's were seldom enough to keep a family alive. Much of this work was done on a commission basis. John Lorrimor, sent to the *Vernon* when his mother was imprisoned for vagrancy, 'sold flowers for a woman in Oxford Street [and] made four or five shillings a day'. Of this he kept but eight pence. Albert Anderson 'used to get odd jobs all around' but was usually paid in 'tucker' rather than wages. And however poor the pay, work was not always easy to find. 'I have three can work', Mrs Cummins pleaded, 'but they can't get it to do'. Finally getting work and keeping it were two entirely different matters. 'I could always get plenty of work and live like a gentleman' a new boy on the *Vernon* declared; but his case history told a different story. 'I was a "nigger boy" at Martin chambers … got 10 shillings a week – drove a butter cart for 15/6 but they "went bung"'. Unsuccessful at selling papers, James Monaghan was left 'sulky and defiant'. Protesting he was a stowaway from America, he was brought in penniless from the Domain, a park where the homeless sought shelter and soap box orators discussed the politics of the day. Monaghan's intermittent labour was characteristic of the patterns of the juvenile economy. Children like him floated with the debris of the colonial economy, cheated, exploited, 'knocked about' then dismissed without pay.[18]

As both Mrs Cummins and Mrs Stringer's experience suggests, rising levels of unemployment also affected the cycle of the family economy. In the past, working-class families were at their most vulnerable when the children were young, when the crucial ratio between breadwinner and dependants was at its worst. Only when children had grown could they contribute directly to the family economy, their wages usually increasing with age. The depression, however, turned an asset into a liability: young wage earners, like their parents, were no longer able to find work. The Walsh family in Collingwood was typical of many. When the father lost his labouring job in April 1892, they made do for a time on the earnings of his son, a plasterer, and his daughter, a tailoress. By July, they were all out of work and their modest savings spent. Charity was all that was left.[19]

Raising revenue by her own and her children's labour was one way that Mrs Stringer coped with the loss of a male breadwinner; another related strategy was making do with less. Income (whatever the source) was only a facet of the family economy. 'Expenditure and distribution' as Barry Reay has argued 'were just as important [and] labour history should be as much about budgeting as the male wage'. Food was the major item of expenditure in the weekly budget: as such it was the area in which most of the 'daily economies and sacrifices' were necessarily to be made. Bread was the staple of the working-class diet, although low in nutritional value it kept hunger at bay. Its embellishment with jams and pickles was often the only element of variety in an otherwise monotonous and debilitating diet. And this most humble of foods was also the most versatile. Mixed with milk and a little sugar it served as a hasty pudding, toasted, ground and stirred into boiling water it could pass as a substitute for tea. Fruit, vegetables and meat were much more difficult to come by; scavenged at markets, shops and 'dust tips' or scratched out from narrow gardens in vacant lots and backyards. Such resourcefulness was vital in feeding hungry families. Out of work and 'laid up with illness' Hartly Brown told police his children would have starved if not for his wife's labours in the garden. '[I]t is heart rendering to see me lying here and can do nothing for myself and look at my poor wife and children ... living on potatoes and salt three times a day ... they are nearly all done'.[20] Food that was purchased (on the other hand) was likely to be old, damaged or adulterated. The radical journalist William Lane described the 'greasy, dusty, grimy shops' where daily the poor bought what little they could afford: 'lean scraggy' meat cut from 'ancient oxen', 'mouldy dried fruits', 'discoloured tinned goods' and 'specks', the damaged, half-rotten fruit 'sold as a feast to th[e] poor'. Of course, stolen food was the cheapest of all. In the bitter winter of 1893, a butcher chased a man from his shop in Balmain. The stranger had 'seized a sheep's pluck, which chanced to be the first thing in the shape of meat which came to hand'. Pursuing police followed him to 'a miserable looking house' in the poorest part of the town; entering it 'a horrible scene of destitution and misery opened to their view. The room was utterly devoid of furniture and there was no fire, while the family were seated with their backs to the walls tearing the raw pluck to pieces and devouring it'. Finally, food and for that matter everything else that came into the household, was made to go further than ever before. Meals were 'spun out' with broths, bread and dripping, clothing was patched and repatched, shoes sewn together, even tea leaves dried, strained and dried again. In each case women assumed management of the household economy, negotiating patterns of survival in the absence of a male wage; and in each case they mastered the arithmetic of poverty. In the nineteenth century it was called 'scheming', the reluctant economies, calculated risks, and ingenious strategies which kept starvation at bay.[21]

In the arithmetic of poverty, credit (as Mrs Stringer found to her cost) was the hardest equation of all. Deciding who to pay and when and how determined the viability of budgets on 'the knife edge between sufficiency and want'. Every creditor was carefully evaluated, landlord, baker and grocer stretched to the limit of patience or goodwill. Families, friends and neighbours were also called upon: the humblest offering of flour or tea bound giver and receiver alike in a complex web of reciprocity. In the case of the pawnshop, raising revenue and making do with less went hand in hand. Regular visits could defer the day the bailiff visited: a shilling here and there bought both time and the means to make ends meet. Indeed, the pawnshop, always a feature of working-class economies, was essential to the domestic economy of the unemployed: its grudging and careful use gives many insights into the priorities of the poor. First went 'jewellery', crockery and furniture; poverty left no room for sentiment or comfort. Women sold wedding rings to buy boots for their children, homes were 'stripped of everything' simply 'to get bread'. Last to be sold was the mangle or the sewing machine. Some saw in them the promise of future self-reliance; all prized them as a symbol of a family's self-respect. Even the Charity Organisation Society, a society not known for its sympathy for the poor, was moved by the self-denial of many unemployed. Case no. 6248 consisted of a married couple and five children, 'starving in one of the suburbs'. The officer found them 'late in the evening … the woman and children lying on the floor with a few old sacks to cover them, no food, and children existing on what they could beg'. Families like this one had sold all they could and huddled together for security and warmth. Often such visitors followed 'their' family to the pawnshop, redeeming the overcoats, blankets and baby clothes the cold, sick and hungry could no longer spare.[22]

Well before these meagre resources were exhausted women like Mrs Stringer 'went without'. Applicants to the Benevolent Society were often described as 'malnourished' while visitors to the homes of the poor found grown men and women 'wasting away'. Parents such as these gave what little they had to their children, 'starving themselves in order to feed their [young]'. Edward Kenny, father of nine, divided his meagre ration from the Labour Bureau amongst the mouths of sick and hungry children. Within a matter of days he had 'nothing to give them but water, water, for the eleven nights I watched by their sides on the floor'. Kenny's own hunger was compounded by exhaustion; by night he watched over his children, by day he was 'done up from walking to find work'. Dull times for Kenny were 'starving times': it seemed he and his family had been left 'to die for want'. In Amelia Edwards' case there were not even the rations of the Labour Bureau to rely on. Barely literate and in a hand shaking with hunger and anxiety she addressed her letter 'to the government of new south wals': 'i ham sorrey to tell you that i am in want of some tucker [food] we havenot has much worke for thi year'. Amelia Edwards' husband was away 'some war else' looking for employment; she was left penniless with six children in the house 'an what we are goen to duo i dwo not know'. 'We ar very bad' she concluded, 'so i … hope ther weel be some tucker sent'.[23]

Hunger and illness often went together. The homes of the unemployed, one schoolmaster noted, were places of 'much sickness'. Young and old alike caught cold through want of clothing; poor meals and very few of them lowered resistance to disease. The Bingham family in Redfern, Sydney, was typical of many. The father, a butcher by trade, 'earned very little', the mother, 'by washing' brought in a little more. On a combined income of around ten shillings a week they struggled to support a family of six children. One child died of inflammation of the lungs, a complication of influenza. Another contracted pleurisy and 'friends in the country took him away'. A third child was hospitalised with an unspecified complaint; given rates of infant recovery he was unlikely to return.[24]

Clearly when a family's consumption could be reduced no further, the logical alternative was to reduce the size of the family itself. The best option was to leave the children with friends or relations: as Tamara Hareven's study of the American experience established, the wider and closer a community or family, the less 'margin of insecurity for the poor'. Family structures in Australia (as Mrs Stringers' experience again suggests), however, were neither as strong nor as extensive as they were in North America or for that matter Europe. Many European families had emigrated en masse to the United States, transplanting the ties of the old world to the new. The Australian family, by contrast, was 'born modern' and our experience of immigration was on a smaller and arguably more individualistic scale. The fortunate might have a mother or aunt or cousin to call on. Many, as one applicant for relief put it, 'had no one at all'.[25] For these the Benevolent Asylums established in the major cities were the next best option. Often mother and child were admitted together, discharging themselves to the husband as soon as he found work. But other arrangements were not uncommon. Harriett Berin apologised for the 'disgraceful' state of her children, starving, 'almost naked' and physically unable to attend school: she 'hope[d] the gentleman will think no bad of m'. 'i never had a panny in the ous' she went on to explain 'so i turned to and took in washing to support my children but i cud not manage it i am not strong anuf'. The only option, as she saw it, was to 'place the children in your asylum' and seek employment in Sydney. Then at least they would not hunger and she 'could see them sometimes'. For others visits were not so easy. Like Harriet Berin, Ester Hill's husband was away in parts unknown looking for work; she too was 'not able to work [and] even if I could get it the children are too young to look after the baby'. Ester's home, like Harriet's, 'was void of furniture [and] filthy'; she too appealed to the state to take in her four children 'as i cannot see them starve'. The difference was that Ester had turned to prostitution in a bid to support her failing household. Charity workers would 'do nothing for her' and instead of the support of the local asylum her children were despatched for adoption over a thousand miles from her home. Men too were parted from their families. Widowed husbands 'unemployed and unable to provide shelter' traded their paternity for irregular payments to the State Children's Department. Actions such as these were not hardly individual choices: they were dictated by a labour market in which production and reproduction, earning a living and caring for children were set so rigidly apart.[26]

Other ways of reducing a family's size were well beyond the control of charity or the law. Infants were found abandoned in doorways, parks and graveyards. Most were wrapped securely, some with a note proclaiming their name. Clearly their discovery was intended: the mothers of such children could simply not afford another mouth to feed;[27] and many mouths were silenced altogether. Throughout the depression, levels of infanticide continued to rise. Parents dropped, knocked or smothered their bundles, deaths easily excused as an accident in a Coroner's Court.[28] Annie Walsh was a typical example. Refusing her application for assistance, male officials of the Charity Organisation Society claimed she had 'murdered' her infant and 'hoodwinked the police'. One wonders how she (or her family) were expected to survive.[29] Baby farming was a less painful option, though the end result was often the same. At its best, baby farming offered an extended form of child care. Children could be boarded out in hard times and reunited with their family when things 'came good'; but such reunions were uncommon. The life cycle of a working-class family meant that many months would pass before a mother could afford to reclaim her infant. By that time it had often perished. Infant mortality rates were alarmingly high in the nineteenth century, and separation from a nursing and watchful mother narrowed the chances of survival even more. Then there was the farmer's own interests to consider. A young and growing child ate into an already small commission; an early 'accidental' death saved trouble and expense. Women who resorted to the use of baby farmers were loudly condemned by contemporaries. Miss Goldspink's case is typical of many. A tailoress and unmarried mother, she earned as little as ten shillings a week; and to get even that, it was necessary to farm the baby out. When charity workers found her, the nine-month-old child was 'nearly dying'. Miss Goldspink, they concluded, 'was very heartless to the infant'. All charity offered to Miss Goldspink was a sermon on the virtues of motherhood and a pittance of relief.[30]

Charity, no less than scavenging or 'scheming' was, as Ellen Ross remarked, a 'neighbourhood resource' for the poor. It was an option Mrs Stringer had explored and exhausted long before she turned to the unions for assistance; nor is that surprising. In late nineteenth-century Australia, the union movement was very much a male institution. It was not just that men made up virtually all of its membership; with very few exceptions, men's interests (and privileges) were 'encoded' in the language ritual and policy of the early labour movement.[31] Charity, on the other hand, purported to provide for women when men had failed them: deserted wives, workless widows and fallen women were very much the focus of philanthropy. However, as Mrs Stringer's case again suggests, not all women were eligible for assistance: distinguishing between the deserving and the undeserving poor was axiomatic to the success of colonial charity. Mrs Berkenshire of Carlton, Victoria, was one of the deserving. Her husband had died very recently, leaving her alone to care for three children. In a moment of sympathy she confided in her visitor that she had never married, 'she seemed ashamed and cried of speaking of it', Mrs O'Connell gratefully recorded. Berkenshire was industrious, 'always at home … working at a machine'. Defiant of her poverty and mindful of her motherhood, she kept her house and children tidy. Even in these lean times Mrs Berkenshire 'appeared to wish to do well'. She was well treated by the ladies of the Benevolent Society.[32] Others found it harder to be, or to appear to be, deserving. The easiest case to disqualify were those of 'imposition'. Women unable to produce a rent receipt or reluctant to enter service were struck off the lists without a moment's hesitation; and whilst a home was expected to be clean, visitors kept an eye out for every sign of luxury. Mrs Loop could not be poor, one visitor reported, because she sat down to 'a good tea' and 'a comfortable fire'. Another case was suspended the moment butter was set down on the table.[33] Visitors were equally vigilant in the cause of sexual morality. One unemployed widow was cut off when her landlady complained that she had been out all night 'and came back next day' bringing a disreputable-looking man with her. And somehow clean minds were associated with clean bodies. The 'dirty' and the 'idle, thriftless, brawling and noisy people' were amongst the first to feel the want of charity.[34]

Charity's primary endeavour then was not so much to assist the poor as to remodel patterns of behaviour. Women were required to conform to a stereotype of femininity fashioned in the late nineteenth century: they were to be clean and caring, honest and homely, sober and spiritual. Expectations such as these overrode even the most elementary considerations of a family's survival. In May 1890, Mrs Rumison (unemployed and deserted) was reprimanded for allowing her daughter to work in a factory: relief would be discontinued if she would not find her 'a proper place in service'. That same year Jane Norton was warned 'of the impropriety of allowing a man to reside in her house'. Ironically, taking in a lodger was probably Mrs Norton's last hope of a respectable wage.[35]

Eventually even the most 'deserving' were deserted. As the depression deepened neither the state nor the voluntary agencies it subsidised made genuine provision for the growing number of workless. Ironically, the first casualties in what one historian has called a 'charity crisis' were the principles on which philanthropy was founded.[36] For all the talk of the sanctity of family life, homes were broken up the moment they became economically unviable. Men were sent off to find work, women 'removed to the country' and children surrendered to the asylum.[37] The economies practised by charity were equally drastic. In September 1892, the Melbourne Ladies Benevolent Society resolved that bread alone be given to the workless. A fortnight later, with funds and volunteers exhausted, the society refused to take on any new cases.[38] Sydney's Benevolent Society reached a similar resolution. Relief to the unemployed was cut and cut again; even the sugar ration was reduced, a cruel petty economy. Finally, when the depression was at its deepest, the society repudiated all responsibility for the 'unemployed'. Workless men and women were turned away with their families only to come back again as broken and malnourished men, deserted wives and abandoned children. Only then could their poverty compel assistance.[39]

The riot in Tyne Street raises one final theme for this paper: the relationship between unemployment and political protest, the household and collective action. Collective responses to unemployment were as many and as various as the individual stratagems which maintained the household economy. They too were shaped by age, gender and family structure as well as the wider determinants of the labour market. And just as labour history has privileged the male wage economy in studying the working-class household, it has (with few exceptions) focused on formal public and male-dominated forms of protest. For all their failings and limitations, the Labour Party and the trade union movement have come to institutionalise working-class resistance in this period; we know much less about short lived inchoate, and community-based forms of popular protest, the politics of the street as opposed to those of union or parliament.

The link between the household and collective action is nowhere better demonstrated than in a gender analysis of unemployed protest. A sparse historiography seems overwhelmingly male in its focus. In almost every instance, it is men who march on parliamentary buildings, men who form the deputations and men who receive them. Moreover, the men of the 1890s have become what Marilyn Lake has called 'neutered historical constructs': we examine their class, their politics, never their gender;[40] and yet the rhetoric of manhood dominates the discourse of this period, transcending political boundaries. Disappointed by the failure of mass demonstrations, agitators claimed the unemployed had 'lost their manhood': a man would fight for the right to work, a weakling beg bread from charity. Conservatives used much the same language to draw a different conclusion. The distinguishing feature of 'A MAN', one explained, was his steady self-reliance: 'A MAN' did not expect the state to provide for him, let alone his wife and children. Both conceptions of masculinity had one thing in common: the assumption that men alone were breadwinners and providers. Men would not 'go to the country to die', an angry deputation told Victoria's Premier, 'if their wives and children [were left to] starve [in the city]'.[41]

The lament of failed breadwinners was the refrain of almost every demonstration. Indeed, some of the most powerful symbols of protest were the symbols of defeated manhood. Men marched with shovels through the streets of the city, declaring not just their willingness to work but also the masculine prerogative to toil. The demonstrations themselves were an attempt to recover the camaraderie of the workplace. A man's waking hours were mostly spent in the company of men: work meant more than wages, it provided a sense of identity, a source of social orientation. In this light the decision to march the streets 'in military formation' was more than a gesture to threaten the authorities. Likening themselves to soldiers celebrated, as Elizabeth Faue's study suggests, 'an ideal of male martyrdom, a romanticisation of violence rooted in metaphors of struggle'. Banded together, men hoped to retrieve a sense of purpose and order.[42]

The mass character of such demonstrations generated rituals and symbols common to the urban crowd. Throughout the 1890s, the unemployed staged a series of mock trials and executions. In Sydney, an effigy of Premier Parkes was burnt to the ground, the cry of 'Cut off his head' rising from the incendiaries. In Victoria, J.B. Patterson was executed as Minister of Works and later as the Premier, his head and bell toper falling to the 'groans and execrations' of the crowd. Such episodes demonstrate what one contemporary called 'the theatricality' of Melbourne's unemployed, but they are also evidence of the enduring traditions of popular protest. From the 1860s effigies had been used to entertain the crowd and satirise the authorities; they looked back to a still older tradition, what E.P. Thompson has called 'the theatre and counter theatre of plebeian demonstration'.[43] It was a tradition which could ennoble the smallest and most desperate of protests. In Sydney, workless men marched with loaves of bread impaled on their banners, a conscious reference (contemporaries noted) to the 'excesses' of the French revolution. In Surry Hills hungry men toppled a bakers' cart and distributed its contents to the starving. And it was a theatre, as Thompson suggests, which drew its strength from the subversion of established authority. By 1893, 'agitators' had 'captured' the very symbols of colonial rule: slogans reading 'Anarchy is Liberty' and 'Read News from Nowhere' hung from the Queen's statue in Chancellery Square. The call for an Australian republic rang out from these citadels of British imperialism.[44]

At first glance the pattern of women's protest seems very different. More often than not, charity was the principal site of their struggle. While men gathered in the streets to demand work from the government, women argued over rations in an equally unrelenting battle to feed their families. Many complained at the size and quality of their orders, demanding oatmeal, tinned milk and other such 'luxuries' for sick and malnourished children. Others cheated charity, refusing to declare what little work they had found and (in one remarkable instance) wheeling 'a double perambulator … full of groceries and meat' from one rations depot to another. Countless were reprimanded for 'discourtesy' or refused to 'have their things inquired into'. The price of such 'insolence' was the cold, hunger and sickness that attended suspension of an order. On occasions such as these, women defied the deference and dependency on which philanthropy was founded. Mary Kelly applied for assistance 'under the influence of drink', flouting her improvidence. Another woman tore up her inquiry card and announced that she 'would not be treated like a pauper'.[45]

Women's protest also took on a collective and very public dimension. In September 1892, police noted the effect three female orators had upon a crowd gathered outside St Paul's Cathedral. Each 'portrayed cases of poverty', indicting the failure of church, state and charity to provide for the needy. Their audience numbered sixhundred people, at least fifty of whom were women. Marches through the city streets attracted even greater numbers. In May 1892, a procession of Melbourne's wives and mothers marched on the city's parliamentary buildings. Many carried babes in arms, the public and private spheres blurring in their protest. All pleaded for work for their 'husbands and sons', the men on whom these women were ultimately dependent. All asserted their citizenship in a country where citizenship was denied them.[46]

Demonstrations like this one also recall a rich tradition of protest. As early as the eighteenth century mothers in Europe had marched their families through the streets, their protest 'a sort of militant extension of women's duties'. This radicalisation of domestic duties, the link between household and politics, was equally apparent in Australia. Women sewed banners and embroidered slogans, turning their domestic skills to the purposes of radical iconography. Then they carried them through the streets, marching alongside men in torchlit procession. Their behaviour echoes what E.P. Thompson has called the 'moral economy' of plebeian demonstration. In pre-industrial societies moral economy was manifest in the bread riot: violence often broke out when the price of bread rose above an affordable level and women (traditionally the arbiters of the domestic economy) played an important role in such protest. A similar moral economy motivated the women of colonial society. All believed their menfolk had a right to work, all knew that when that right was refused they would be the ones to care for broken husbands and hungry children. Protest was a product of their domestic responsibilities; but women's protest, as the Tyne Street riot again suggests, was much more than a simple assertion of traditional duties. Domesticity, as Jane Rendell has noted, 'could both limit and broaden horizons', enforcing women's traditional place in the home but challenging accepted notions of passivity and ignorance as well. Defiant, and unruly, contemptuous of police, landlord and charity, Clarinna Stringer embodied just such a challenge.[47]

It is tempting to see women's role in the unemployed agitation as a powerful resurgence of pre-industrial patterns of protest. Indeed several historians have questioned the 'static typology' which divides modern from pre-industrial protest, the former centred on such male-dominated structures as political party and trade unions, the latter on the women-centred spheres of neighbourhood and community. Certainly such typologies are of limited value in understanding Australian popular protest in the 1890s. One is struck by the continuity of traditions: the self-conscious use of certain words, symbols and gestures (what Charles Tilly calls 'the vocabulary of protest') and the community basis of such collective action.[48] Having said that, there were also crucial elements which distinguished women's (and men's) protest from that of preceding generations. The women of nineteenth-century Melbourne demanded work as much as bread. More importantly, they demanded work for themselves as well as for their husbands, besieging the Labour Bureau and asserting their 'right' to register. Turned away, they paraded the city in protest. In June 1892, a 'female assemblage' numbering more than four hundred streamed along Russell Street, 'tapping rather heavily with their umbrellas at the glass windows and doors ... of (Melbourne's) Chinese laundries'. The Chinese they passed en route were 'loudly groaned at', their establishments competing with a traditionally female industry. Here we see what Ann Curthoys has called 'the intersection of class, race and gender', all shaping the nature of popular protest.[49] Even more importantly, the incident emphasises the value women placed upon their paid as well as their unpaid labour. When women protested they did so not just as wives and mothers, as 'moral beings', but also as workers: paid workers on whom their families depended. Their 'economic citizenship' (as John Bohstedt calls it) was crucial to their radicalism. Finally, these women benefited from what Judith Smart has called 'a culture of unionisation', a willingness to organise along political as well as less formal community lines and challenge exiting social structures. The bread riot was a spontaneous rebellion; though its participants followed a certain protocol of protest, their ideology was often vague and their objectives limited. The same could not be said of the women of nineteenth-century Australia. Literate and articulate, versed in the discourse of first-wave feminism, many joined the ranks of radical societies. Others lent their support to an autonomous women's movement. Launching the Brazilian League from the banks of the Yarra, Mrs Brazil claimed it 'would do more [for women] than any [other] society'.

In women's protest, indeed in the unemployed agitation generally, we thus see a fusion of the old and the new: it was at once practical and ideological in orientation, spontaneous and ritualised, 'social' and 'political'. At its centre, though, was the imperative to preserve and strengthen the household economy, the domestic and political world of Mrs Clarinna Stringer.[50]

Notes

1. I thank Rae Frances and all the participants at the Living Strategies Workshop (Amsterdam 1997) for their comments on this paper. The research for this paper was made possible (in part) by a grant from the Australian Research Council.

2. Melbourne Ladies Benevolent Society Minutes (MLBS Minutes) January-April 1892, State Library of Victoria, Ms 124148 3207; *Herald*, 17 June 1892; *Carlton Gazette*, *Argus*, *Age*, 17 June 1892.

3. *Australasian*, *Argus*, 18 June 1892.

4. J. Bohstedt, *Riots and Community Politics in England and Wales 1790–1810*, Cambridge, MA, 1983, 23; see also L.A. Tilly and C. Tilly, eds, *Class Conflict and Collective Action*, London, 1981, 47, C. Calhoun, *The Question of Class Struggle: The Foundations of Popular Radicalism in the Industrial Revolution*, Oxford, 1982, ch. 8.

5. S. Fitzgerald, *Rising Damp: Sydney 1870–90*, Melbourne, 1987, 210–13; M. Howard, 'Unemployment before 1890' (MA thesis, University of Melbourne, 1979) 22–37; J. Lee and C. Fahey, 'Boom for Whom? Some Developments in the Australian Labour Market, 1870–1891', *Labour History*, no. 50 (May 1986): 1–27; Ray Markey, *The Making of the Labor Party in New South Wales 1880–1900*, Kensington, 1988, 37–50.

6. D. Vincent, *Poor Citizens: The State and the Poor in Twentieth Century Britain*, London, 1991, 4. For a companion study focusing on the domestic economy (and social protest) in strike time see Bruce Scates, 'Gender, Household and Community Politics: the 1890 Maritime Strike in Australia and Aoteroa/New Zealand', *Labour history*, no. 61 (November 1991): 70–87.

7. Tamara Hareven, *Family Time and Industrial Time. The Relationship between the Family and Work in a New England Industrial Community*, Cambridge, 1982, 208; Anne O'Brien, 'The poor in New South Wales, 1880–1918' (PhD thesis, University of Sydney, 1982) 50.

8. For representative case histories see Mrs Levers, 24 November 1892, Melbourne City Mission Minutes, University of Melbourne Archives; Mrs Sanders, 24 March 1892, MLBS Minutes; Mrs Morrison, 25 June 1894, Saint Vincent de Paul (St. V. de P.) (St. Bedes) Minutes, Mitchell Library, Ms 2984, 19 (20).

9. Case of Mrs Wilcox, 29 July 1894, St. V. de P. (St. Bedes) Minutes; case of Mrs Murray, 18 October 1896, ibid., (Ashfield) Minutes. There is an extensive literature on the role boarding played in the family economy; it has yet to be examined fully in Australia; see, for instance, John Modell and Tamara K. Hareven, 'Urbanisation and the Malleable Household: Boarding and Lodging in American Families', *Journal of Marriage and the Family* 35 (1973): 467–79; Bettina Bradbury, *Working Families: Age, Gender and Daily Survival in Industrialising Montreal*, Toronto, 1993, 175–81; Richard Harris, 'The Flexible House: The Housing Backlog and the Persistance of Lodging, 1891–1951', *Social Science History* 18 (1994): 31–51.

10. Charity Organisation Society (COS), Annual Report for the Year Ended 30 June 1897, Melbourne, 9, 20; case of Mrs Kelly, 5 June 1895, St. V. de P. (St. Bedes) Minutes.

11. Jane Lewis, ed., *Woman's Welfare, Women's Rights*, London 1983, 8; Bettina Bradbury, 'Women and Wage Labour in a Period of Transition: Montreal, 1861–1881', *Histoire Sociale-Social History*, no. 33 (mai-May 1984): 115–31; E. Boris, *Home to Work: Motherhood and the politics of industrial housework in the United States,* Cambridge, 1994; William Lane, *The Workingman's Paradise: An Australian Labour Novel* (1892; reprint Sydney, 1980) 9.

12. Case of Ernst Henry Edwards, 13 December 1893, Vernon Admission Book, New South Wales State Archives, (NSWSA) 8/1744; COS, Annual Report ... for the Year Ended 30 June 1897, Melbourne, 1897, 20; Raelene Frances and Bruce Scates, *Women at Work in Australia from the Gold Rushes to World War II*, Melbourne, 1993, ch. 2; S. Swain and R. Howe, *Single Mothers and their Children: Disposal, Punishment and Survival in Australia*, Melbourne, 1995, 17–19.

13. Case of Michael Holland, 21 January 1891, Vernon Admission book; Case of Mrs Kelly and Mrs Wilcox, 10 August 1895, 29 July 1894, St. V. de P. (St. Bedes) Minutes; J. Lee, 'A Redivision of Labour: Victoria's Wages Boards in Action 1896–1903', *Historical Studies* 22, no. 88 (1987): 352–72; for the most useful study of women's factory labour Raelene Frances, *The Politics of Work. Gender and Labour in Victoria, 1880–1939*, Cambridge, UK, 1993.

14. R.F. Davidson (Frances), 'Prostitution in Perth and Fremantle and on the Eastern Goldfields 1895–September 1939'(MA thesis, University of West Australia, 1980), ch. 5. Frances' observations are equally germane to the eastern colonies, see M. Arnot, 'Prostitution and the State in Victoria, 1890–1914' (MA thesis, University of Melbourne, 1987); Hilary Golder and Judith Allen, 'Prostitution in New South Wales 1870–1930: Restructuring an Industry', *Refractory Girl*, December 1979, 17–24; also R. Frances, 'The history of female prostitution in Australia', in *Sex Work and Sex Workers in Australia*, eds Roberta Perkins at al., Sydney, 1994, 27–52. For case studies, see minutes of the Female Refuge Society, Sydney, Mitchell Library; case of James Cronan, 9 February 1891, Vernon Admission Book.

15. Case of Mrs Kelly, 23 June 1895, St. V. de P. (St. Bedes) Minutes, Case of Mrs Pinto, 12 July 1892, MLBS Minutes; Charity Organisation Society, Annual Report for the Year Ended 30 June 1897, Melbourne, 1897, 20.

16. For a suggestive discussion of the neglect of the household economy see Graeme Donald Snooks, *Portrait of the Family in the Total Economy. A Study in Longrun Dynamics, Australia 1788–1990*, Cambridge, UK, 1994; also K. Alford's review of the same, *Labour History*, no. 67 (November 1994): 169–71; Barry Reay, *Microhistories: demography, society, and culture in rural England, 1800–1930*, Cambridge, 1996, 113; Case of Oswald Marshall, 7 October 1893; Ernst Henry Edwards, 13 December 1893; Alexander McDougall, 2 September 1894; William Gough, 7 August 1894, Vernon Admission Books; Hareven, *Family Time and Industrial Time*, 189; Ann Larson, *Growing up in Melbourne*, Canberra, 1995, ch. 4.

17. E. Ross, 'Survival Networks: Women's' Neighbourhood Sharing in London before World War One', *History Workshop Journal*, No.15 (Spring 1983): 6; *Sunday Telegraph*, 18 June 1892; Case of Michael Holland, Brian Newry, Frederick Hoflick; 21 January 1891, 5 January 1892, 14 February 1894, Vernon Admission Books; for 'grinning' see Reay, *Microhistories*, 105; Lane, *The Workingman's Paradise*, 37–8, Case of Mrs Sanders, 24 March 1891, MLBS Minutes.

18. Case of John Lorrimor (or McIntosh), Albert Anderson, James Monaghan, Fred Putney, 28 May 1894, 9 May 1894, 25 December 1893, 22 September 1893, Vernon Admission Books; Letter: Mrs William Cummins to Office of Public Instruction, Redfern, 29 May 1899, Redfern School Files, NSWSA, 5/174/50; for suggestive studies of the role of child labour and hawking see John Bullen, 'Hidden Workers: Child Labour and the Family Economy in Late Nineteenth Century Ontario', *Labour/Le Travail*, no.18 (1986): 163–87; John Benson, 'Hawking and Peddling in Canada, 1867–1914', *Histoire Sociale/Social History*, no.57 (May 1985).

19. MLBS Minutes, 2 June, 12 July 1892; A. Davin, 'When is a Child not a Child?', in *Politics of Everyday Life*, eds H. Corr and L. Jamieson, London, 1990, 39.

20. B. Reay, *Microhistories*, 120; O. Hufton, 'Women in Revolution', *Past and Present* 53 (November 1971): 92; Eve Hostettler, 'Making Do': Domestic Life Amongst East Anglican Labourers, 1980–1910', in *Our Work, Our Lives, Our Words*, eds L. Davidoff and B. Westover, London, 1986, 39; Bettina Bradbury, 'Pigs, Cows and Boarders: Non Wage Forms of Survival among Montreal Families, 1861–1891', *Labour/ Le Travail*, no. 14 (1984): 9–46; Case of 'a poor woman living in Foster Street, Leichhardt', 9 May 1892, St. V. de P. (St. Aloysius Boys' Home); Hartly Brown to 'Benevolent Osilam Sydney', 1 March 1894, Colonial Secretary Inward Letters, (hereafter CSIL), Box 5/6193, 94.4832, NSWSA.

21. Lane, *Workingman's Paradise*, 15–17; 'Shocking Cases of Starvation', *Daily Telegraph*, 14 July 1893; Case of Mrs Stirling and Mrs Coles, 2 September 1896, 4 October 1892, NSWBS House Committee Minutes; cases of Mesdames Fitzpatrick and Deny, 20 September 1896, 16 June 1895, St. V. de P. (Ashfield; St. Bedes) Minutes; J.W. Scott and L.A. Tilly, 'Women's work and the family in nineteenth-century Europe', in *The Economics of Women and Work,* ed. A.H. Amsden, Harmondsworth, 1980, 103; Reay, *Microhistories*, 104.

22. P. Johnson, *Saving and Spending: The Working-class Economy in Britain 1870–1939*, Oxford, 1985, 176; for a comparable American study see M. Tebbutt, *Making Ends Meet: Pawnbroking and Working-Class Credit*, New York, 1983; Case of Mrs Chisholm and Mrs Holder, 20 May, 22 July 1894, St. V. de P. (St. Bedes) Minutes; *Argus*, July 1893; Case of Mrs Broadfall, 13 October 1891, NSWBS Minutes; Charity Organisation Society, Annual Report for the Year Ended 30 June 1894, Melbourne 1894, p. 39; Case of Mrs Shields, Dobon and Mc Bride, 22 March, 9, 24 August 1892, MLBS Minutes.

23. Cases of Ellen Hobson and Mrs Stirling, 27 June 1893, 2 September 1896, NSWBS House Committee Minutes; Case of Mrs Walsh, 11 August 1891, MLBS Minutes; *Brunswick Reformer*, 13 February 1892; Edward Kenny to George Dibbs, 22 November 1893, CSIL, Box 5/6160, 93.15567; Amelia Edwards to 'the government of new south wals', undated, CSIL, Box 6180, 93.12370.

24. Case of William John Bingham, Application for Exemption, 30 September 1898, Redfern School File; see also the case of Mrs Holmes, 10 September 1891, MLBS Minutes.

25. Hareven, *Family Time, Industrial Time*, 209; P. Grimshaw, 'Women and the Family in Australian History Reply to The Real Matilda', *Historical Studies* 18 (1979): 415; See for instance J.A. Kelly to Colonial Secretary, 17 July 1893, CSIL, Box 5/6143, 93.9527.

26. Unsigned, undated letter by Harriet Berin appended to Police Report, CSIL, Box 5/6094, 92.14252; Ester Hill to Mr Ferguson, 8 October 1894, CSIL, Box 5/6234, 94.17870; Entry for Joanna, Alfred, Margaret and Elsie Water, 27 October 1892, Benevolent Society of New South Wales (BSNSW) Inmates' Journal.

27. See foundling entries for 18 November 1892, 9 June 1893, BSNSW Inmates' Journal.

28. New South Wales Police Gazette; see also Judith Allen, 'Octavius Beale Reconsidered', in *What Rough Beast? The State and Social Order in Australian History*, ed. Sydney Labour History Group, Sydney, 1982, 120.

29. Charity Organisation Society, 'Minutes', 19 January 1892.

30. Frances and Scates, *Women at Work*, ch. 5; Kathy Laster, 'Frances Knorr: She Killed Babies Didn't She', in *Doubletime: Women in Victoria, 150 Years*, eds Marilyn Lake and Farley Kelly, Ringwood, 1985, 148–57; Case of Miss Goldspink, 8 March 1891, MLBS Minutes.

31. Ellen Ross, 'Hungry Children: Housewives and London Charity', in *The Uses of Charity; The Poor on Relief in the Nineteenth-century Metropolis*, ed. P. Mandler, Philadelphia, 1990, 166; J. Scott, *Gender and the Politics of History*, New York, 1988, 3; for the challenge to masculinist politics see Bruce Scates, *A New Australia: Citizenship, Radicalism and the First Republic*, Cambridge, 1997, chs 3 and 6.

32. Case of Mrs Berkenshire, 2 December 1892, MLBS Minutes.

33. Case of Mrs Loop, 21 October 1890, MLBS Minutes; case of Mrs Grant, 20 May 1894, St. V. de P. (St. Bedes).

34. Cases of Mesdame Harten and Lynch, 24 March, 3 November 1891, MLBS Minutes.

35. Cases of Mesdames Rumieson and Norton, BSNSW House Committee Minutes, 13 May, 16 September 1890.

36. Richard Kennedy, *Charity Warfare. The Charity Organization Society in Colonial Melbourne*, Melbourne, 1985, 150.

37. B. Scates, 'A Struggle for Survival: Unemployment and the Unemployed Agitation in Late Nineteenth-Century Melbourne', *Australian Historical Studies* 24, no. 94 (April 1990): 60–1; Case of Mrs Roberts, 2 June 1895, St. V. de P. (St. Bedes) Minutes; *Brunswick Reformer*, 3 July 1892.

38. MLBS Minutes, 6, 20 September 1890.

39. BSNSW House Committee Minutes, 8 June 1896, 7 March 1897; 22 March 1892; 13 July 1897.

40. See John Hirst, 'Keeping Colonial History Colonial: The Hartz Thesis Revisited', *Historical Studies* 21, no. 82 (April 1984); Marilyn Lake, 'The Politics of Respectability: Identifying the Masculinist Context', *Historical Studies* 22, no. 86 (1986): 117–18.

41. *Workman*, 17 April 1897; COS, Annual Report 1892, Melbourne, 1892. For the importance of the family wage in mobilizing class struggle, see M. May, 'Bread Before Roses: American Workingmen, Labour Unions and the Family Wage', in *Women, Work and Protest*, ed. R. Milkman, Boston 1985, 1–21; and in an Australian context, A. Curthoys, *For and Against Feminism*, Sydney 1988, 112–28; Petition by village settlers, Kooweerup, Report of the Printing Committee, VPP, 1896, vol. 1, no. 1.

42. Report Constable Wardley, 16, 23 June 1892; *Age*, 26 May 1892; S.A. Rosa, *The Unemployed Agitation*, Melbourne, 1891, 11–30, E. Faue, *Community of Suffering and Struggle: Women, Men and the Labour Movement in Minneapolis, 1915–1945*, London 1991, 71; E. Faue, 'The Dynamo of Change: Gender and Solidarity in the American Labour Movement in the 1940's', *Gender and History* 1, no. 2 (Summer 1989): 140.

43. *Truth*, 17 May 1891; *Argus*, 20 June 1890, 14 August 1890; B. Dober, 'The Unemployed in England 1880–1914' (MA thesis, Melbourne University 1982) 124–31; E.P. Thompson, 'Patrician Society, Plebeian Culture', *Journal of Social History* 2, no. 4 (1974): 401.
44. *Melbourne Herald*, 16 June 1892; *Truth*, 31 May 1891; *Workman*, 13 June 1891; *Worker*, 7 January 1893.
45. Case of Mesdames Corsett, Ellis, Gallagher and Kelly, BSNSW House Committee Minutes, 10, 27 November 1891; 15 September 1891; 24 April 1894; Charity Organisation Society, Annual Report for the Year Ended 30 June 1889, Melbourne 1889, 14–15.
46. Report by Constable Geelan, 4 September 1892, Victorian Police Records, Victorian Public Records Office, Series 936; Speech by William Maloney, Victorian Parliamentary Debates, Legislative Assembly, 31 May 1892.
47. Barbara Taylor, '"The Men are as Bad as their Masters ..." Socialism, Feminism and Sexual Antagonism in the London Tailoring Trade in the 1830s', in *Sex and Class in Women's History*, eds J.L. Newton at al., London and Boston, 1983, 200; Victorian Police Records Wardley, 16 June 1892; E.P. Thompson, 'The Moral Economy of the English Crowd', *Past and Present* 19, no. 50 (February 1971): 79; Jane Rendall, *The Origins of Modern Feminism: Women in Three Western Societies, Britain, France and the United States 1780–1860*, New York, 1984, 90–1.
48. See, for instance, R. Holton, 'The Crowd in History: Some Problems of Theory and Method', *Social History* 3, no.2 (May 1978): 22; also M. Harrison, *Crowds and History. Mass Phenomena in English Towns, 1790–1835*, Cambridge, UK, 1988, ch. 1; Tilly and Tilly, eds, *Class Conflict*, 37; also C. Tilly and L.A. Tilly, eds, *From Mobilisation to Revolution*, Reading MA, 1978, 171; for an Australian perspective see Bruce Scates, 'Mobilising Manhood: Gender and the Great Strike in Australia and Aoteroa /New Zealand', *Gender and History* 9, no. 2 (August 1997): 285–309.
49. Reports by Constables Geelan and Wardley, 1, 15 June, 4 September 1892, Victorian Police Records; Ann Curthoys, review of J. Allen, 'Sex and Secrets: Crimes Involving Australian Women Since 1880', in *Australian Historical Studies,* no. 95 (October 1990): 306. For a recent and revealing study of the 'profound racial cleavages' in working class communities see Peter Baskerville and Eric W. Sager, *Unwilling Idlers: The Urban Unemployed and Their Families in Late Victorian Canada*, Toronto, 1998, 104–11.
50. M. Blewett, *Men, Women and Work: Class, Gender and Protest in the New England Shoe Industry, 1780–1910*, Chicago, 1988, 87; John Bohstedt, 'Gender, Household and Community Politics: Women in English Riots 1790–1810', *Past and Present* 36, no. 120 (1988): 95; Judith Smart, 'Feminism, Food and the Fair Price', *Labour History* 25, no. 50 (may 1986): 13–31.

Bibliography

Allen, J. 'Octavius Beale Reconsidered', in *What Rough Beast*, ed. Sydney Labour History Group. Sydney, 1982.

Alford, K. review of G. Snooks, *Portrait of the Family in the Total Economy*, Cambridge, 1994 in *Labour History*, vol. 33, no. 67 (November 1994): 169–71.

Arnot, M. 'Prostitution and the state in Victoria, 1890–1914', MA thesis. University of Melbourne, 1987.

Baskerville, P. and Sager, E.W. *Unwilling Idlers: The Urban Unemployed and Their Families in Late Victorian Canada*. Toronto, 1998.

Benson, J. 'Hawking and Peddling in Canada, 1867–1914', *Histoire Sociale/Social History*, no. 57 (mai-May 1985).

Blewett, M. *Men, Women and Work: Class Gender and Protest in the New England Shoe Industry, 1780–1910*. Chicago, 1988.

Bohstedt, J. *Riots and Community Politics in England and Wales 1790–1810*. Cambridge, MA, 1983.

———. 'Gender, Household and Community Politics: Women in English Riots 1790–1810', *Past and Present*, vol. 36, no. 120 (1988).

Boris, E. *Home to Work: Motherhood and the politics of industrial housework in the United States*. Cambridge, UK, 1994.

Bradbury, B. 'Pigs, Cows and Boarders: Non Wage Forms of Survival among Montreal Families, 1861–1891', *Labour/ Le Travail*, no. 14 (1984): 9–46.

———. 'Women and Wage Labour in a Period of Transition: Montreal, 1861–1881', *Histoire Sociale/Social History*, no.33 (mai-May 1984): 115–31.

———. *Working Families: Age, Gender and Daily Survival in Industrialising Montreal*. Toronto, 1993.

Bullen, J. 'Hidden Workers: Child Labour and the Family Economy in Late Nineteenth Century Ontario', *Labour/Le Travail*, no. 18 (1986): 163–87.

Calhoun, C. *The Question of Class Struggle: The Foundations of Popular Radicalism in the Industrial Revolution*. Oxford,1982.

Curthoys, A. *For and Against Feminism*. Sydney, 1988.

———. Review of J. Allen, *Sex and Secrets* in *Australian Historical Studies*, no. 95 (October 1990).

Davidson, R.F. 'Prostitution in Perth and Fremantle and on the Eastern Goldfields 1895 – September 1939', MA thesis. University of West Australia, 1980.

Davin, A. 'When is a Child not a Child?', in *Politics of Everyday Life*, eds H. Corr and L. Jamieson. London, 1990.

Dober, D. 'The Unemployed in England 1880–1914', MA thesis. University of Melbourne, 1982.

Faue, E. *Community of Suffering and Struggle: Women, Men and the Labour Movement in Minneapolis, 1915–1945*. London, 1991.

———. 'The Dynamo of Change: Gender and Solidarity in the American Labour Movement in the 1940's', *Gender and History* vol. 1, no. 2 (Summer 1989).

Fitzgerald, S. *Rising Damp: Sydney 1870–90*. Melbourne, 1987.

Frances, R. *The Politics of Work. Gender and Labour in Victoria, 180–1939*. Cambridge, UK, 1993.

Frances, R. and Scates, B. *Women at Work in Australia from the Gold Rushes to World War II*. Melbourne, 1993.

Frances, R. 'The History of Female Prostitution in Australia', in *Sex Work and Sex Workers in Australia*, eds R. Perkins et al. Sydney, 1994, 27–52.

Golder, H., and Allen, J. 'Prostitution in New South Wales 1870–1930: Restructuring an Industry', *Refractory Girl* (December 1979): 17–24.

Grimshaw, P. 'Women and the Family in Australian History Reply to The Real Matilda', *Historical Studies* vol. 18 (1979).

Hareven, T. *Family Time and Industrial Time. The Relationship between the Family and Work in a New England Industrial Community*. Cambridge, UK, 1982.

Harris, R. 'The Flexible House: The Housing Backlog and the Persistance of Lodging, 1891–1951', *Social Science History* vol.18 (1994): 31–51.

Harrison, M. *Crowds and History. Mass Phenomena in English Towns, 1790–1835*. Cambridge, UK, 1988.

Hirst, J. 'Keeping Colonial History Colonial: The Hartz Thesis Revisited', *Historical Studies* vol.21, no. 82 (April 1984).

Holton, R. 'The Crowd in History: Some Problems of Theory and Method', *Social History* vol.3, no.2 (May 1978).

Hostettler, E. '"Making Do": Domestic Life Amongst East Anglican Labourers, 1980–1910', in *Our Work, Our Lives, Our Words*, eds L. Davidoff and B. Westover. London, 1986.

Howard, M. 'Unemployment before 1890', MA thesis. University of Melbourne, 1979.

Hufton, O. 'Women in Revolution', *Past and Present* 53 (November 1971).

Johnson, P. *Saving and Spending: the Working-class Economy in Britain 1870–1939*. Oxford, 1985.

Kennedy, R. *Charity Warfare. The Charity Organization Society in Colonial Melbourne*. Melbourne, 1985.

Lake, M. 'The Politics of Respectability: Identifying the Masculinist Context', *Historical Studies* vol. 22, no. 86 (1986).

Lane, W. *The Workingman's Paradise: An Australian Labour Novel* (1892; reprint Sydney, 1980).

Larson, A. *Growing up in Melbourne*. Canberra, 1995.

Laster, K. 'Frances Knorr: She Killed Babies Didn't She', in *Doubletime: Women in Victoria, 150 Years*, eds M. Lake and F. Kelly. Ringwood, 1985, 148–57.

Lee, J. and Fahey, C. 'Boom for Whom? Some Developments in the Australian Labour Market, 1870–1891', *Labour History*, no. 50 (May 1986): 1–27.

Lee, J. 'A Redivision of Labour: Victoria's Wages Boards in Action 1896–1903', *Historical Studies* vol. 22, no. 88 (1987): 352–72.

Lewis, J., ed. *Woman's Welfare, Women's Rights*. London, 1983.

Markey, R. *The Making of the Labor Party in New South Wales 1880–1900*. Kensington, 1988.

May, M. 'Bread Before Roses: American Workingmen, Labour Unions and the Family Wage', in *Women, Work and Protest*, ed. R. Milkman. Boston, 1985, 1–21.

Modell, J. and Hareven, T.K. 'Urbanisation and the Malleable Household: Boarding and Lodging in American Families', *Journal of Marriage and the Family* vol. 35 (1973): 467–79.

O'Brien, A. 'The Poor in New South Wales, 1880–1918', PhD thesis. University of Sydney, 1982.

Reay, B. *Microhistories: Demography, Society, and Culture in Rural England, 1800–1930*. Cambridge, 1996.

Rendall, J. *The Origins of Modern Feminism: Women in Three Western Societies, Britain, France and the United States 1780–1860*. New York, 1984.

Rosa, S.A. *The Unemployed Agitation*. Melbourne, 1891.

Ross, E. 'Survival Networks: Women's' Neighbourhood Sharing in London before World War One', *History Workshop Journal*, no.15 (Spring 1983).

———. 'Hungry Children: Housewives and London Charity', in *The Uses of Charity; The Poor on Relief in the Nineteenth-century Metropolis*, ed. P. Mandler. Philadelphia, 1990.

Scates, B. 'A Struggle for Survival: Unemployment and the Unemployed Agitation in late nineteenth century Melbourne', *Australian Historical Studies* vol. 24, no. 94 (April 1990).

———. 'Gender, Household and Community Politics: the 1890 Maritime Strike in Australia and Aoteroa/New Zealand', *Labour History*, no. 61 (November 1991): 70–87.

———. 'Mobilising Manhood: Gender and the Great Strike in Australia and Aoteroa /New Zealand', *Gender and History* vol. 9, no. 2 (August 1997): 285–309.

———. *A New Australia: Citizenship, Radicalism and the First Republic*. Cambridge, 1997.

Scott, J.W., and Tilly, L.A. 'Women's Work and the Family in Nineteenth-Century Europe', in *The Economics of Women and Work*, ed. A.H. Amsden. Harmondsworth, 1980.

Scott, J. *Gender and the Politics of History*. New York, 1988.

Smart, J. 'Feminism, Food and the Fair Price', *Labour History*, no. 50 (May 1986): 13–31.

Snooks, G.D. *Portrait of the Family in the Total Economy. A Study in Longrun Dynamics, Australia 1788–1990*. Cambridge, UK, 1994.

Swain, S. and Howe, R. *Single Mothers and their Children: Disposal, Punishment and Survival in Australia*. Melbourne, 1995.

Sydney History Group, ed. *What Rough Beast? The State and Social Order in Australian history*. Sydney, 1982.

Taylor, B. "'The Men are as Bad as Their Masters ...'" Socialism, Feminism and Sexual Antagonism in the London Tailoring Trade in the 1830s', in *Sex and Class in Women's History*, eds J.L. Newton et al. London and Boston, 1983.

Tebbutt, M. *Making Ends Meet: Pawnbroking and Working-Class Credit*. New York, 1983.

Thompson, E.P. 'The Moral Economy of the English Crowd', *Past and Present* vol. 19, no.50 (February 1971).

———. 'Patrician Society, Plebeian Culture', *Journal of Social History* vol. 2, no. 4 (1974).

Tilly, C., and L.A. Tilly, eds. *From Mobilisation to Revolution*. Reading, MA, 1978.

Tilly, L.A., and Tilly, C., eds. *Class Conflict and Collective Action*. London, 1981.

Vincent, D. *Poor Citizens: The State and the Poor in Twentieth Century Britain*. London, 1991.

CHAPTER 5

FAMILY AND UNIONISATION IN THE BRICKLAYING TRADE IN TURN-OF-THE-CENTURY MADRID

Justin Byrne

This article traces the connections between the household structures, economies and strategies of the bricklayers in Madrid and the development of unionism in the trade from the turn of the century to the First World War.[1] The research on which this paper is based is focused, as its title suggests, on the world of productive relations, work, workplace organisation, and labour relations rather than on the bricklayers' domestic lives.[2] In at least two crucial respects therefore, it differs from the empirical and theoretical focus of most of those writings on the connections between family and household on the one hand, and collective organisation and action on the other. Firstly, insofar as the research is not explicitly centred on issues relating to family social relations. Secondly, in that it is devoted to an exclusively male occupation and organisation, when analysis of these issues has largely focused on groups of female workers, or industries employing both men and women. Both factors help explain why many of the ideas and arguments presented here are necessarily rather tentative: in theoretical terms, because they may require refinement in the light of a better understanding of the complexity of the issues at stake in the analysis of the family and household as economic and social units; in empirical terms, because the family, household, and gender tend to be less visible in male worlds such as that of the building trades, and hence leave fewer traces in the sources.[3]

Nonetheless, even workplace-centred research, on a group of all male workers cannot ignore these themes. Work and workplace organisation cannot be understood in isolation from the workers' social world outside the factory or building site gate, as there is no firm boundary between the two. We must go beyond the false dichotomy of public and private in order to consider how the two have interacted in labour's history.[4] In this respect, the family and household constitute the obvious place to start, as they are crucial dimensions of all workers' lives, in physical, economic, social as well as ideological terms. Moreover, the family is a crucial nexus between the individual and society. As this article confirms, knowledge of the bricklayers' domestic worlds permits a better understanding of how and why they organised, and the goals they pursued both as workers and men. It is important to emphasise the question of gender. On the one hand, looking at labour organisation and protest from a household perspective brings to the fore the role of other family members, and above all women, in sustaining the bricklayers' households and the social networks on which unionism rested. On the other, it highlights the question of the bricklayers' own gender identity, and the way in which this shaped – and was shaped by – their collective organisation and action.

The Building Industry in Madrid

A village when it was made capital of Spain in 1562, Madrid grew erratically over the course of the next two hundred and fifty years, but much more consistently during the nineteenth century, its population rising from around 200,000 in 1800 to some 540,000 at the end of the century. It developed as the centre of the court, the state, and later business, rather than as an industrial city. Despite some modest industrial expansion and diversification in the second half of the century, the 1900 census returns show that almost 50 percent of the active population was still employed in the tertiary sector – above all in domestic service, commerce, and the administration – while the secondary sector accounted for only some 25 percent of the total workforce. Within this narrow industrial base, from the mid-nineteenth century onwards, the building industry was the 'nerve centre of the economy', driven by the demand for public buildings from a centralising state, premises fit for the businesses this attracted, and housing for the capital's growing population.[5] According to the first comprehensive industrial survey of the city in 1905, building towered over all other branches of the secondary sector except clothing, accounting for some 16 percent of the recorded industrial population. With so many other industries – metal, wood and transport – dependent on it, 'the industrial production of Madrid was determined by the construction cycle, the rhythm of the workshop subordinated to that of the building site'. The importance of the industry to the economy of the city was summed up by the *El Imparcial* newspaper in 1913: 'when the building industry goes well, everything goes well'.[6]

It was, however, a very unreliable basis on which to build an economy. As the 1905 industrial survey of the city put it, 'in Madrid building is carried out in bursts .... It is not done normally or steadily. Either there are a multitude of sites and entire neighbourhoods built at once, or there is an almost complete lack of work'.[7] The latter was all too common. After booming in the 1840s and 1850s, the industry slumped dramatically in 1866 before enjoying a brief revival at the end of the following decade. When this ended in 1883, building entered another deep recession which would continue virtually unabated for over twenty years. After a number of particularly bleak years in the mid-1900s, activity began to pick up in 1909. This brief phase of expansion peaked in 1914, before almost coming to a standstill during the First World War, when the economic disruption caused by the European conflict virtually paralysed the sector. One of the principal characteristics of the sector, and of the lives of those who depended on it, therefore, was instability.[8]

Within this context of instability, the building industry was marked by both continuity and profound changes in its structure, organisation and internal dynamics. As most historians have noted, building remained a very traditional sector in terms of working methods and techniques, the materials used, the division of labour, and the predominance of the small unit of production. In 1905, the 15,500 building workers and 869 employers in Madrid were classified into twenty-nine different trades, many of which comprised just a few small masters, each employing an equally small number of men. However, the second half of the nineteenth century also saw major transformations in the sector, above all springing from the consolidation of a new form of carrying out building work, general contracting, and the appearance of the new figure of the general contractor. These were essentially capitalist middlemen who acted as intermediaries between the investor and producer, subcontracting work to the masters of the specialist trades for a fixed price and often supplying the materials too. In most trades, general contracting fundamentally undermined the autonomy of the traditional independent master artisan, but in bricklaying it spelt their death knell, as the general contractors took on this themselves, hiring foremen to supervise the work of the bricklayers they employed directly. According to the municipal census, in 1884 there were 512 master bricklayers in Madrid. In the 1905 survey, the category of 'master bricklayer' had disappeared to be replaced by a much smaller group of 120 'master surveyors, master builders, and all those who carry out building work following agreement with the owner'. These aggregate figures inevitably hide the real heterogeneity of enterprises in the trade, which would always include small jobbing bricklayers and the self-employed. Nonetheless, they do reflect the major organisational change taking place in the industry at the end of the nineteenth century, and the rapid process of concentration in the bricklaying trade, where in 1905 these 120 employers were said to occupy some 11,000 workers.[9]

This estimate coincides with others given at the end of the nineteenth and beginning of the twentieth century, which signal the existence of between ten and twelve thousand men – and they were all men – working in the trade. The vagueness of the figures reflects the diffuse contours and permeable boundaries of the trade, the fluctuations in the numbers actually employed at any one time, and the weak occupational identity of workers who were among the least skilled, prestigious and lowest paid in the city. According to union sources, by 1904, journeymen accounted for only 10 percent of those working in the trade, the remaining 90 percent being classified as bricklayers' assistants and labourers or general labourers. While the small minority of skilled journeymen bricklayers and their assistants appear to have generally identified themselves, and been identified, as such, many of those employed as bricklayers or general labourers were much more loosely tied to the trade. The main source of demand for unskilled labour in the city, the bricklaying trade was often the temporary home to thousands of labourers, men who according to the union carried out 'tasks which required neither art nor skill'. Often forced to change occupation, many of these would have identified with the labourer Pablo Sánz, injured in a work accident in 1905, who was classified in the municipal census as a 'day labourer' (*jornalero*), and whose place of work was 'where he can be of use' (*dondé vale*). In fact, only a small minority of those working in the trade at any one time figured in the census as bricklayers. In 1915, when *El Trabajo* claimed a membership of over 7,000, only 1,796 bricklayers were registered in the municipal census.[10]

In line with *El Trabajo's* exceptionally broad and inclusive definition of its constituency – which included the general and bricklayers' labourers, and not, as was more often the case elsewhere, just the more skilled workers – the 'trade' will be understood in this article to encompass all those working as 'bricklayers' in whatever capacity. The census returns highlight the difficulties facing any attempt to identify this ill-defined, heterogeneous, and fluctuating group of workers within the city, as well as the obstacles to quantitative analysis. Hence, the interpretation presented here is largely based on qualitative sources such as social surveys, the labour press, and daily newspapers that covered events in the trade. Reports of work accidents have proved especially useful in this respect. In particular, frequent reference will be made here to an exceptionally tragic accident which took place in April 1905, when the roof of the III Reservoir, a huge underground water tank being built in the north of the city collapsed, leaving thirty dead and another sixty injured. In the absence of harder data, the wealth of material generated by this and other accidents provides extremely valuable insights into the bricklayers' family and household structure and strategies, into a social world that would otherwise remain hidden from history.[11]

Collective Organisation

It was only at the very turn of the century that the bricklayers would show any inclination or capacity to organise as a trade. Before then, even within the paltry record of protest, and above all, organisation of the incipient Spanish labour movement, the bricklayers are notable for their limited mobilisation. Various anarchist-, Socialist-, and small master-inspired attempts were made to organise the trade after 1870, but none enjoyed anything but the most fleeting success; nor did the half dozen recorded strikes during the second half of the nineteenth century. All the known conflicts involved only small numbers of workers, usually on just one site, and in most cases ended in the dismissal or return to work in defeat of the strikers. The only form of protest in which the bricklayers did play a prominent role was in the 'job riots' that were a regular feature of Madrid winters. Then, along with other unemployed workers, they would demand public building to ease the endemic 'work crisis' in the city and stave off starvation. The authorities, ever anxious to avert the threat to public order, would often hand out a few more chits entitling the recipients to a day's work building or repairing the city's streets, but these protests hardly constituted an effective means of securing meaningful improvements in the workers' situation. The bricklayers obviously faced the same obstacles that prevented most other workers from mobilising: the hostility of employers and state repression; a highly unfavourable labour market; and a preoccupation with day-to-day survival that hindered the type of longer-term thinking and investments required for strike action, and above all organisation. Moreover, an exceptionally large, fluid and lowly trade, the bricklayers also showed no signs of the strong trade identity, culture, sense of purpose and future, which proved such crucial organisational resources for some other groups of workers.[12]

Yet, at the very end of the 1890s, the Socialist-led bricklayers' union *El Trabajo* suddenly erupted on the scene with unprecedented and exceptional force. Founded in 1886, the union had never enjoyed any real presence in the trade, surviving in the mid-1890s as a merely token force of just three or four dozen members. Yet just a few years later *El Trabajo* was one of the largest unions in the city and the country as a whole. The union's fortunes began to change in 1897, its membership rising from just thirty-three to one hundred during the course of the year. A further three-fold rise in membership during 1898 was followed by even faster growth over the following twelve months: the 326 members of the union in January 1899 had risen to over seven hundred in June, eight hundred at the beginning of July, 940 two weeks later, and 1,321 by mid-November. During the final six weeks of the year the union's membership almost doubled again. On 1 January 1900, *El Trabajo* claimed a membership of nearly 2,500 or some 25 percent of all workers in the trade. *El Trabajo's* sudden and spectacular growth at the turn of the century opened a new period in the history of the bricklayers of Madrid. Moderate growth in 1901 and 1902 was followed by another dramatic rise in membership in 1903, as by the end of the year the union had a membership of over five thousand. After hovering around this figure for a number of years, *El Trabajo* entered a steadier phase of expansion at the end of the decade. Consequently, on the eve of the 1911 general lockout that put an end to this almost uninterrupted period of consolidation, the union could boast a membership of over nine thousand, that is, three-quarters of the estimated workforce in the trade.[13]

El Trabajo's numerical expansion was matched by the development of what was, for the labour movement of the day, an exceptionally effective union machine. The union's organisational drive included the consolidation of a network of site delegates, paid dues collectors and administrative officials, specialised subcommittees, and a powerful executive, as well as the development of a strong organisational culture. The union's strength made it a formidable force in the workplace. May 1900 saw *El Trabajo's* first official strike, and two months later the union signed the first written *bases del trabajo* or minimum working conditions for union members. Over the course of the following decade, with, or more often without strike action, *El Trabajo* was able to secure wage increases, hours reductions, overtime restrictions and other work rules, as well as a virtual monopoly of work in the trade. The union also provided its members with mutual insurance cover and gave them access to a number of other services, not least the facilities of the *Casa del Pueblo* belonging to the Socialist-led union federation, the *Unión General de Trabajadores* (UGT). More intangibly, *El Trabajo* endowed the bricklayers with a distinctive identity within Madrid's emerging working class. It was largely thanks to the strength of their collective organisation that the bricklayers would come to epitomise the insubordinate, militant male proletarian in the city.

How does a knowledge of the bricklayers' household structure, economy and strategies contribute to our understanding of the sudden growth and subsequent consolidation of *El Trabajo* at the turn of the century, and the distinctive strength and character of unionism in the trade over the course of the next decade and beyond? Obviously, family and household are only part of the story, and their incorporation into it cannot take place at the expense of ignoring another, if not the crucial sphere for determining the proclivity and character of labour organisation: work. Indeed, it is precisely by focusing our attention on the complex, multidimensional and two-directional interrelations between these two spheres of workers' lives – home and work – that the analysis of households can deepen our understanding of the history of labour.

In the case of the bricklayers, the workers' domestic lives can be seen to have been a crucial factor in shaping the development of unionisation in at least three respects. First, in so far as their families and households contributed to the dense web of interlocking social networks on which *El Trabajo's* growth and consolidation rested. Second, in the way that the bricklayers' household situation, and the particularly acute insecurity of their lives, shaped the character of their collective organisation, its structure, demands, and development. Finally, it will be argued, the bricklayers' inability to fulfil the role of respectable, male breadwinners and heads of family encouraged them to cultivate their image as rough, tough, defiant men, and trade unionists, as a positive source of gender pride and identity.

Households and Social Networks

Workplace-household interaction is particularly important, firstly, for our understanding of the dynamics behind the remarkably rapid growth of the union at the very end of the century, when dozens and later hundreds of workers joined the union each week. This it should be emphasised, was not an isolated phenomenon. On the one hand, the growth of *El Trabajo* was just one drop in the massive tide of social mobilisation of all kinds that marked Spain's *fin de siècle* crisis, and sent membership of anarchist, socialist and non-aligned unions soaring all over Spain, not least in Madrid. On the other, as in other periods of rapid union growth, it was not unusual for entire groups of workers to join unions en masse. Among the Madrid building trades of the day, this would be the case of the plasterers, tilers and stonemasons, virtually all of whom organised in the space of just a few weeks. When the initiative was taken, recruitment was easy in these small trades, in which workers shared a strong trade culture and identity founded on their possession of skill and, in some cases, recent experiences of organisation. In the case of the stonemasons at least, these bonds were further underpinned by their common roots in the north of the country. With these and other building trades at the forefront of union organisation at the turn of the century, the city's building sites clearly constituted a hive of collective organisation and action. The bricklayers could hardly have remained immune from the new social climate in the workplace, as workers in other trades joined up and downed tools to press their demands. As union propagandists themselves emphasised, the gains won by other building workers showed the bricklayers what could be achieved through collective organisation. Equally, the geometric growth of *El Trabajo* in the autumn and winter of 1899 probably reflects the operation of another close occupational network, the bricklayers' gang, all the workers in which would often have signed up together. However, among such a large, heterogeneous, and fluid group as the bricklayers, many of whom were only loosely tied to the trade and had previously displayed little sense of occupational identity, both the sudden upsurge of organisation in 1898–99, and the subsequent solidity of the union, is better understood by incorporating other explanatory factors. In particular, *El Trabajo's* rapid and lasting growth appears to have been built on the dense social network, or web of intertwined social networks, in which the bricklayers and their families were enmeshed through their household structures, economies and strategies.[14]

By the mid-nineteenth century, stem families appear to have been common in Spain only in the Pyrenean region in the north, while elsewhere in Spain the nuclear family was the norm. This was certainly the case in central Spain and in the capital Madrid, where the nuclear family of three if not just two generations, was the model for all social classes, and defined the households of many of its inhabitants. While this was also true of the bricklayers, in comparison to at least some other industrial workers in Spain they appear to have been more likely to live in non-nuclear households, to have connections with more than one, and to pass through a series of household structures over the course of their lives. Although quantitative and comparative data is not available, everything suggests that the variety of household structures was a characteristic feature of the workers in the trade.[15]

This at least is suggested by the accounts of the domestic situation of the victims in the accident in the III Reservoir in 1905. These reports show, alongside the nuclear family, large numbers of workers living in a wide range of very different household structures: single men sharing with married siblings or other relatives; others living as what would appear to be lodgers in the homes of non-kin; and one case of two married couples sharing the same dwelling, a situation apparently due to a prolonged period of unemployment affecting one of the families involved. None of these arrangements appears to have been unusual for workers in the trade. Rather, they were strategies of income and expenditure pooling that were common among the city's popular classes more generally. This was a consequence of the relatively high cost of accommodation in a city whose population was growing much faster than the housing stock. It also reflected the use of the home as a resource to supplement the family's income or to be traded for services. The social reformers propagating working-class domesticity and respectability, and the representative of the labour movement who denounced the impossibility of workers achieving this, agreed in their analysis of the consequences of this intermingling of the family and non-family members: physically and morally dangerous overcrowding, a lack of intimacy and privacy, and in essence, the absence of a clear division between the public and private spheres in either a physical or social sense. For many of the bricklayers therefore, the independent nuclear household, while perhaps an aspiration, was beyond their reach for much of their lives, an impossibility or perhaps simply not a priority given the very real limitations of their households budgets.[16]

The most common type of non-nuclear household was one in which the bricklayers lived as, or had living with them, lodgers who were also relatives. It would have been easier to incorporate, and tolerate these unmarried brothers and cousins in the enforced intimacy of the home. The prevalence of this type of arrangement reflected two important aspects of the workforce in the trade, firstly the importance of kin networks, and secondly, and tied in with this, the fact that so many workers in the trade – a full two-thirds of those working on the III Reservoir – were more or less recent migrants to the city. Here, the weak demand for unskilled labour in the primary or manufacturing sectors heightened the importance of two, gender specific, sectors of the labour market. For women, the majority of migrants for much of the period, this meant incorporation into the ranks of the fifty to sixty thousand domestic servants employed in the capital. For male migrants to the city, building was the most likely source of work; and within the industry, the numerical weight of the bricklaying trade and its ever increasing demand for unskilled labour meant that, for much of the nineteenth and twentieth centuries, 'a period as a bricklayers' labourer has often been the first step in the city life of the peasant migrant'.[17]

Kinship, therefore, was a crucial factor disturbing the model of the nuclear family household for the workers in the trade. In the case of migrants, the move to the city would have been decided within the context of the peasant family economy and often seen as a way of contributing to it. This was illustrated by reports that at least two of the workers on the III Reservoir had been saving money in order to support parents living outside Madrid.[18] Family ties outside the city could mean not only obligations (as in the case of those supporting aged parents financially), but also that some workers were only temporary migrants to the capital, or at least considered themselves as such. Even for those who planned to settle in the city permanently, returning to their household of origin could offer a last resort in time of crisis; both in the mid-1880s, and again during the terrible slump in the sector during the First World War, thousands of building workers were said to have returned to their home villages.[19] Family and kin networks stretched from the countryside into the city. Many of those working on the III Reservoir had followed other members of the family, and particularly siblings, to Madrid, and were living with them. The existence of kin already established in the city eased entry and integration into the new, and apparently hostile, urban world. Immediate and extended family could provide accommodation on arrival and frequently for years afterwards, information about job opportunities and a pre-established network of social relations.[20]

Just as household intersected with kin, so did both with broader personal communities. These could be formed by fellow migrants from the same area of the country, *paisanos* who tended to live together along the roads which had carried them in, and could take them out of the city, presumably drawn there by convenience but also by the desire to maintain or establish social ties with their community of origin.[21] Nevertheless, crucially, unlike in many other places, neither migrants in general nor the bricklayers in particular lived in regional ghettos, or apart from native-born *madrileños*. Rather, by the turn of the century, the bricklayers tended to live in geographically heterogeneous, but increasingly socially homogenous quarters of the city. The municipal census shows that they could be found in the poorest, least healthy, and least literate parts of the old centre, and above all in the mushrooming suburbs on the outskirts, the social space which would see the emergence of the first specifically working-class communities, culture and identity in the city.[22]

Here, the bricklayers and their families lived in cramped, overcrowded houses, within sight and sound of their neighbours, a situation that further blurred the distinctions between private and public. Domestic chores, such as washing and drying clothes or collecting water from the pump, not only brought their inhabitants into frequent contact in the *patios* and passageways, but also made cooperation inevitable. The distribution of tasks such as cleaning the stairwell or the collective toilets required more formal agreement. Physical proximity and contact did not automatically imply mutual sympathy.[23] However, the intense personal relations of the inhabitants of these houses, many of whom depended on the same industry for their livelihood, shared similar social and material conditions, perspectives and concerns, also favoured the development of collective identities and manifestations of solidarity. At times of crisis, these could make the difference between the survival and break-up of the household, between the life and death of its members. In 1905, the family of one victim of the III Reservoir was said to live from 'the charity of the poor neighbours and pawning all they could', while the baby daughter of another victim, with her mother in a state of shock, 'lives thanks to the charity of the female neighbours of the house as her mother has been left without milk'.[24] Female solidarity at the time of this accident was not restricted to the home. *El Liberal* reported that, after forcing a woman to stop selling water to the rescue workers, 'the poor women of the quarter of Vallehermosa have given a great example of humanity. They have spent the little money they have on jugs and glasses and have given out water free to the workers and soldiers working in the Reservoir'.[25] Women from the same area would then go on to play a prominent role in the two days of street protests and riots that followed. This was a familiar pattern. On numerous occasions, work accidents and the funerals of victims provoked angry reactions from the women who congregated outside the site of the incident. And when at the turn of the century *El Trabajo* converted the funerals for accident victims into formal protests against the unsafe working conditions in the trade, women attending or watching the march would take command of the coffin and confront the police who barred their way.[26]

These incidents point to the widely recognised importance of the women's role in maintaining kin and neighbourhood networks and social relations. They also tend to bear out an argument which Temma Kaplan has convincingly made on the basis of evidence from urban Spain in this period, namely that working-class women's role in, and responsibility for, maintaining the family and preserving life, gives rise to a specifically 'female consciousness', primarily expressed through informal solidarity and action of this type, and which 'sometimes has revolutionary consequences insofar as it politicises the networks of everyday life'.[27]

All this is relevant to an understanding of the rapid upsurge and consolidation of unionism in the trade from the turn of the century onwards. By then, out of choice or necessity, most workers in the trade lived in essentially working-class quarters in the city, in which occupational, kin and personal communities frequently overlapped. Here the bricklayers would be less likely to be discouraged or prevented from joining the union by the pull of what Snow et al. label 'countervailing networks'. Above all in the suburbs, the bricklayers were less likely to feel the pressures of their ferociously anti-union employers or the Catholic Church, which had virtually given up the battle for the hearts and minds of the urban working classes during the nineteenth century. In contrast, here union organisers could and did tap into a dense web of mutually reinforcing networks and channels of information and social pressure. During 1898 and 1899, *El Trabajo* launched a major recruitment drive, later remembered by employers as a turning-point in the union's history. This primarily consisted of frequent, often monthly, propaganda meetings. For the first time, these were not only held in the UGT's union headquarters in the centre of Madrid, but also in outlying suburbs, and in villages situated well beyond the city limits. As the reports in *El Socialista* show, these meetings were an enormous success, ending as they did with dozens, when not hundreds, of workers signing up on the spot. Refusal to do so would have often meant disregarding the example, and presumably exhortations of other members of the household, relatives, neighbours, as well as work mates.[28]

As the union grew during the first decade of the century, family, kin, and neighbourhood networks continued to pull the bricklayers into the union, and ensure that they remained in there. The intermeshing of these social relations and solidarities was visibly manifested on May Day, when columns of bricklayers and their wives would gather in the different suburbs before marching together to the start of the labour day parade in the centre of the city. Equally, at the end of the decade, the complaints voiced by members of the minority Catholic bricklayers' union, who claimed that they were boycotted by their neighbours, is indicative of the way local community networks underpinned union loyalties. By then, the overwhelming majority of bricklayers in the city had incorporated union membership into their repertoire of household strategies, and clearly expected others to do likewise.[29]

The Logic of Union Organisation and Action

Built on, rather than replacing, existing social networks and the strategies of household survival which these encompassed, from the turn of the century onwards union organisation enabled the bricklayers for the first time to engage in collective action to improve the terms and conditions of what was not merely a central dimension of their daily lives but also one of the most important factors shaping the living standards, status, and life opportunities of their families: their work.

The evolution of the trade during the second half of the century had certainly increased the incentives for workplace collective action, by limiting the potential for other types of strategies. The emergence of a new breed of business-minded and larger employers, general contractors who were physically and socially distant from the workplace, meant that paternalist-type relations and patronage were even less prevalent than they had ever been. The consolidation of general contracting also signified that the start-up costs of the independent master increased significantly, and self-employment meant seeking a living on the insecure fringes of the industry doing small jobs and repair work. Within the ranks of the employed, as traditional skill ratios were diluted, only a small minority of workers could aspire to climb the traditional trade ladder leading to journeyman status, and pay. According to contemporary calculations, in 1899 only the journeymen in the trade would have been able to maintain a family of four on their daily wage, as the very 'sticky', customary wage rates of the nineteenth century had been hit by the constant, and in the late 1890s, increasingly rapid inflation, putting saving or investing in a small house out of the reach of most.[30] Moreover, even for this relatively privileged minority of journeymen, bricklaying offered little in terms of security or respectability. Heavy, dirty, comparatively poorly paid, unskilled, and insecure work, bricklaying was towards the bottom of the social hierarchy of trades. It was not just that complaints about undignified treatment by employers abounded at the end of the century, but that in 1892 even a lowly tailor could describe the bricklayers as that 'miserable class of men despised by all'.[31]

If incentives for collective action had long existed, the late 1890s did bring more obvious changes in both the costs of labour protest and in the resources that made this possible. Triggered by Spain's defeat in Cuba and the Philippines at the hands of the United States in 1898, the crisis of the authority of the Restoration state weakened its resolve and capacity to maintain the fierce clampdown on labour seen during the war years, and was soon followed by the first half-hearted moves to combine repression of labour with its incorporation into the polity. At the same time, the widespread and multiform social mobilisation which followed the 'Disaster of 1898' generated increased resources for unionisation. The bricklayers could learn and benefit from the information, experiences and organisational resources generated by workers in other trades, who flocked into the unions in the city at the very end of the century and struck to secure wage increases, reductions in hours, and other gains.[32]

Like their counterparts in other trades, the bricklayers would do so under the direction of the small group of Socialist activists who by 1900 were well established as *the* union organisers in the city. In fact, from 1900 onwards, *El Trabajo* would be one of the prime exponents of the cautious, pragmatic model of labour organisation and strategy advocated by the Socialist-led UGT union federation. This 'management unionism' was based on moderation in the presentation of demands, a willingness to compromise to facilitate negotiations with employers and secure the mediation of the state, and the exercise of restraint in the use of the 'double-edged sword' of strike action. Confrontation with employers, if not a last resort, was certainly best avoided even from a position of strength, that is, when the labour market was favourable and the organisation could count on a well-stocked strike fund and a large and disciplined membership.[33] This was the strategy *El Trabajo* put into practice after 1900, when it first negotiated a collective agreement with the general contractors in the *Sociedad General de Aparejadores y Contratistas de Obras* (SCA). Backed-up by constant, but tightly controlled and limited strike action, this process would be repeated in 1906 and 1907, only to come to an abrupt halt in the 1911, when the employers responded to the union's demands for negotiations by successfully calling a two-month general lockout that crippled the union for almost a decade. Before then, given the model of unionism put into practice by *El Trabajo*, the union's numerical expansion, and steadily increasing power in the workplace was inevitably based on the development of an exceptionally powerful union machine, in which strong leadership from the top was accompanied by increasingly tight rules and sanctions for those who broke them at the bottom. In this way, *El Trabajo* practised something akin to the 'authoritarian' unionism that David Montgomery described in the building industry in the United States in the same period, 'characterised by unity, increasingly strident rules and quasi-military discipline'.[34] As was the case with its US counterparts, the authoritarianism of *El Trabajo* was also demonstrated by the way in which the union enforced the closed shop. In 1902, the union decided that all bricklayers working on sites where its members were employed had to be members of the union. This appears to have been the main factor behind the rise of over 25 percent in its membership during the course of that year. While the union's grip on the labour market slackened during the middle of the decade, by the end of the 1900s it appears to have been firmly established on most sites in the city.[35] A solution to the freerider problem and a vital cornerstone of the union's power, *El Trabajo* did not hesitate to employ intimidation, strike action and, when necessary, violence to defend and extend its monopoly of work and worker representation in the city. As the loss of a quarter of its membership in the six months after the end of the 1911 lockout would confirm, the closed shop was an increasingly important constraint on those debating whether to join the organisation, and one which during the first decade of the century would have been enough to persuade many to join.

By then, however, the benefits of collective organisation and action would have been more than apparent to the bricklayers and their households. Although, as we shall see, 'all the reasonable and licit means that further the object of this society' included household- and state-centred activity, the union's statutes leave no doubt that its fundamental sphere of action was the workplace. The four specific means to be used to achieve the union's overall goal of 'improving the moral and material condition of its members' were 'by procuring that the wages are sufficient to cover its members needs', 'by ensuring that the working day is not excessive', 'by preventing owners, masters and foremen from abusing the dignity of the members', and 'by procuring, adequately in function of the resistance offered by the owners and master builders, that they adopt and maintain the gains that exist at work in the present and which might be obtained in the future, as well as the minimum conditions in wages and hours established'.[36] Two points should be emphasised here. First, the notion of morality and justice expressed in the union's use of the terms 'sufficient', 'excessive', and 'dignity'. As Marcel van der Linden rightly highlights, these point to the meaningful orientations running behind individuals' actions, as well as to traditional, customary notions of work and labour relations which certainly played a role in the bricklayers' collective action.[37] Nonetheless, they were also highly abstract concepts, the precise meaning of which could vary according to circumstance, depending on what the market could bear or employers be forced to accept. In fact, market sensitivity would be one of the distinguishing features of *El Trabajo*, just as it was of the UGT as a whole during this period. A second important point is the emphasis placed on wages, hours, and dignity. The union did struggle, and with considerable success for a wide range of demands both in and beyond the workplace, but these three issues were quite clearly fundamental to the union's objectives. The collective *bases del trabajo* agreements signed in 1900, 1902 and 1907 were essentially limited to issues of hours and wages, while strikes in defence of the dignity of the workers or their union would be a constant during the first decade of the century. These issues, therefore, can be explored to gain a better understanding of the motivations of the bricklayers and their households, and how this fitted in with other strategies they deployed. They also reveal the bricklayers' priorities, and one of the driving forces behind their collective action, namely the search, within, the structural constraints of their situation, for increased security for themselves and their families, as well as for dignity for the union man.

The importance attached to wages is hardly surprising given the subsistence existence of the workers in the trade. Contemporary archetypal working-class family budgets show that the structure of consumption scarcely changed during the fifty years after 1870. Food consistently accounted for an estimated 60–75 percent of the family budget and allowed only the simplest of diets, based on potatoes and pulses, which according to medical specialists of the time was insufficient to meet the calorie requirements of a working bricklayer. Despite living in the cheapest areas of the city, housing accounted for the second largest item – around 20 percent of the total – on the family budget. Another 10 percent went on clothes, leaving, at most, a 10 percent margin for other expenses.[38] For the vast majority of workers in the trade, even this subsistence level of family consumption could not be financed by their wages alone. Skilled and semi-skilled single bricklayers, or married men without dependent children, would have enjoyed a surplus of varying amounts when in work, but even when employed, unskilled labourers would have struggled to survive. The archetypal family budget for a family of two adults and two children produced by the secretary of *El Trabajo*, Nicolás González in 1904 showed that all but the 10 percent of journeymen in the trade would have faced a daily deficit, even when in work. He estimated that, for a bricklayer's assistant, this would have amounted to 0.57 pesetas, or 14 percent of the total budget 'without taking into account that the worker smokes, drinks and or faces some extraordinary expense; if the assistants have a deficit when they work, what is it like for the two categories of labourers?' In strictly financial terms, the answer according to González's own calculations was an average shortfall of 1.65 pesetas or just over 40 percent of their daily expenditure.[39] Six years later, figures published by the French sociologist André Marvaud show that even a journeyman in work every day of the year except Sundays, Christmas Day and 1 May, would have earned some 10 pesetas less than the 1,418.80 pesetas which Marvaud estimated were the total expenses of a family during the course of a year. Other workers in the trade, with similar expenses but lower wages, would have faced an annual deficit of between 174 pesetas (assistants) and 548 pesetas (general labourers).[40]

A decade of union action, therefore, apparently produced scant change and, if anything, deterioration, in the purchasing power of the bricklayers' wage packet. This was despite the fact that between 1900 and 1907, the union won increases in the minimum hourly wage rates of 20 percent or more for all the categories of workers, with the largest increases going to the semi- and unskilled workers who made up the bulk of the workforce and union membership. With prices in Madrid relatively stable during this period, these increases would have brought a sizeable improvement in real wage rates and, when work was available, in their incomes. However, the impact of these wage rises on the bricklayers' wage packet was substantially offset by the major reduction in working hours, which were cut from an average across the year of ten hours a day at the end of the nineteenth century, to nine and a half in 1900, nine in 1902 and eight and a half in 1906. In contrast to employers, although in common with many trade workers elsewhere, the bricklayers showed a consistent preference for reductions in hours over wage rises. This was exemplified by their outright rejection in 1906–07 of the SCA's offer of a one peseta increase in their daily wage rate for a longer working day, as well as by their insistent pursuit of overtime restrictions, which culminated in their imposition of an unwritten, emergency-only overtime rule in 1908. Again in 1911, the bricklayers' opposition to overtime working would be a major bone of contention with employers.[41]

While certainly not exceptional, the bricklayers determined struggle for hours reductions was nonetheless striking given their wages levels. It might be attributed to the existence among the bricklayers of a more modern, instrumental view of their work of the type Peter Stearns identifies as developing in the later nineteenth century, 'in which full pleasure in work was abandoned as unattainable … and better conditions were sought in compensation', and which was parallelled by the rise of a new lifestyle and leisure culture.[42] Equally, as the union maintained, it may have been motivated by the bricklayers' desire to spend more time with their families and on educating themselves.[43] In practice, however, the struggle for shorter hours was mainly inspired by more immediate considerations, and above all by the fundamental problem of unemployment. The reserve army of labour which existed in the city and trade itself meant that chronic unemployment was the norm and full employment unknown even in good years. In 1904, union sources estimated that unemployment in the industry never normally fell below 3 percent, and averaged some 12 percent over the course of the year. If, as the union maintained, most bricklayers only worked an average of two hundred and forty days a year, their real earnings over the course of the year were some 20 percent below the figure obtained by extrapolating from hourly or daily wage rates. Through reductions in hours, the workers sought to combat unemployment, which threatened the collective unity of the trade, and hence their ability to win and maintain other improvements. More immediately, shorter hours and overtime bans constituted an attempt to distribute work more evenly over the year, and among the men. That is over and above higher wages, the bricklayers sought to guarantee a wage itself, thereby reducing the insecurity of their work and income, and it shall be suggested below, alleviating the constant threat this posed to their masculinity.[44]

Whatever the long-term advantages of doing so, the bricklayers' immediate capacity to sacrifice income for reductions in hours reflected the fact that only a very small minority of them were the sole providers for their households. While their wage levels were important, and the bricklayers pursued pay increases vigorously, in practice their earnings alone did not define the limits of the household budget, which also depended on the contribution of other members of the unit. This was something that was rarely mentioned at the time, and which has received all too little attention subsequently. As exemplified by the budget presented by the secretary of *El Trabajo* workers quoted above, the labour movement's demands for the family wage emphasised the dire living conditions of the working class without explaining how families with a permanent budgetary deficit survived. The figure of the male breadwinner which lurked directly behind *El Trabajo's* demands for wage rise in the name of 'fathers of the family', has also hung over the work of many economic and social historians too. Excessively reliant on official statistics and other gendered sources, and working within the culturally determined definitions of work, they have had little to say about the family or household economy nor about the informal sectors of the economy in which probably the majority of children, and above all women worked. Yet an increasing body of research shows that while the ideal of the male breadwinner spread very widely across nineteenth- and twentieth-century industrialised economies, in many countries and sectors it remained just that, an ideal to be aspired to but rarely achieved. Whether in the formal economy, or more frequently in informal sectors, other members of the working-class household, and above all women, played a vital role in balancing its budget, both in monetary form and by providing goods and services. This was certainly the case in late nineteenth- and early twentieth-century Spain, where Angélique Janssens has recently noted, there is a growing body of evidence revealing the inadequacy of the male-breadwinner model for large groups of the working population.[45] Moreover, as was the case elsewhere the figure of the male breadwinner was particularly elusive in sectors in which work was poorly paid, casual, and/or subject to seasonal or cyclical fluctuations. In these contexts, Pat Hudson and W.R. Lee have written, 'most married women were obliged to seek work in the non-formal economy. Wives were forced to supplement family income because of a persistent and serious economic need'.[46]

That this was the case of the bricklayers in Madrid was implicitly or explicitly assumed in the budgets compiled by social commentators of the period, and amply confirmed by the other, frustratingly sparse accounts of the domestic situation of workers in the trade. Again, the catastrophe of the III Reservoir in April 1905 is particularly revealing in this respect. A large proportion of the victims lived in households in which various members contributed to what we must assume was its collective economy. This was the case of both skilled and unskilled workers, and could include members of different generations within the family. Elderly parents, siblings and workers' children earned money by various means, including working as *porteros* (caretakers), midwives, domestic servants or seamstresses. Most frequently of all, the bricklayers' wives, whether legal or common law, earned some money to help sustain the family. Given the very limited opportunities that existed for female employment in the formal economy in Madrid, their work was generally just as, if not even more insecure than, that of their husbands. Many women supported their families by offering services that they carried out within their own home, further dissolving the supposedly rigid separation between the public and private spheres. Frequently a continuation of their own, unpaid, domestic work, work of this type had the advantage of being compatible with their obligations in the household, and for mothers, with child care. This was the case of those who provided lodgings for single men, took in sewing, or provided wet-nursing and child-minding services. Others were employed as *porteros*. Work also took bricklayers' wives outside the home. Numerous examples exist of bricklayers' wives serving or cleaning in other people's houses, or working as washerwomen. Other women engaged in different forms of commerce, such as *traperas* or rag pickers, that most traditional of women's occupations in the city, or selling vegetables. Judging by contemporary descriptions, the scale of these operations was often very small, reminiscent of the penny capitalism described by Elizabeth Roberts.[47]

Earning cash incomes was not the only way in which women helped balance the household budget. Numerous other strategies were deployed to provide the goods and services it required. In the suburbs and villages around Madrid, the possibility of keeping a few chickens or even a small kitchen garden with which to supplement the domestic economy was, perhaps, a factor that attracted bricklayers to these areas. Clothes making would also have been frequent. By the end of the century, the Singer sewing-machine, paid for in weekly instalments, was one of the few items of technology in the more prosperous working-class home. Women were also responsible for attempting to balance the family budget, providing a nutritious diet within the limitations imposed by the family income, and if necessary going without food to make ends meet. When economies such as these failed to balance the budget, it was also women who had to buy food on tick, who arranged to pay off the loans invariably required for major purchases, or who visited the pawn shop. Again this was a task that formed part of women's responsibilities as the holder of the household's purse-strings, if not the manager of its economy.[48]

Low and above all irregular wages, which meant that in the all-too-frequent periods of unemployment women would have been the main if not sole providers, were not the only threat to the survival of the bricklayers' households. Another, crucial source of insecurity in their lives was the high risk of injury or death that was a distinctive feature of building work. Although no official work accident statistics are available before 1903 all the evidence suggests that intensified competition, productivist pressures, deskilling, the use of shoddy materials and methods, and the insufficient, and above all inadequately enforced safety regulations, sent up accident rates at the end of the nineteenth century. The incomplete official accident statistics produced after 1904 show that the construction industry continued to suffer a high and rising proportion of the workplace accidents in the city, and that perhaps as many as 10–20 percent of the workforce had an accident each year. As the *El Imparcial* newspaper commented on the death of a bricklayer who had fallen from unsafe scaffolding in 1906, 'the incident reported above occurs daily. The name varies, the site varies, the height of the plank which breaks or falls varies, but essentially the case is repeated every day'.[49]

A constant complaint and concern of workers and those who tried to organise them in the 1880s and 1890s, the high and apparently increasing accident rate was at the very centre of *El Trabajo's* activities from the end of the century onwards. This was one area in which the enterprise was not the focus of the union's collective action, which centred instead, firstly on the state, and secondly on the household. While employers were held directly responsible for accidents, the state was blamed for allowing accidents to take place, by failing to enact or implement effective safety legislation, as well as for not providing relief for the victims. In 1899–1900 and again in 1913–14, *El Trabajo* launched major campaigns in demand for tighter safety regulations, and above all, inspection and enforcement. These involved the union mobilising the bricklayers on the streets and by the end of the period, labour's representatives in the parastatal *Instituto de Reformas Sociales* (IRS), a body set up in 1903 to analyse and make proposals on social issues. This second campaign did bear fruit, as inspection was intensified and new legislation introduced. Paradoxically, while the authorities' reluctance and incapacity to guarantee workers' safety fuelled the bricklayers' hostility towards the state, work accidents appear to have accentuated *El Trabajo's* commitment to working with it. Experience showed that only the state had the resources and authority to force employers to provide good working conditions and compensation to accident victims and their families.

The latter were the focus of *El Trabajo's* second, and even more significant response to the risk of work accidents: the introduction in 1899 of mutual 'aid for accident victims, invalids and the families of members killed in the future'.[50] This represented a qualitatively new development for the workers in the trade. Informal on-site collections for accident victims aside, there was no record of mutualist activity in the trade, or of bricklayers belonging to the occupationally mixed aid societies that operated in the city. The expense involved would have put it beyond the reach of most workers in the trade, while the particular dangers of their work would have made them an unattractive risk for the societies themselves. *El Trabajo's* initiative also represented a major innovation in the Socialist-led labour movement. Although the Socialists' hostility to mutual aid, seen as a distraction if not an obstacle to labour and political mobilisation, was weakening by the end of the century, very few unions in the capital had created mutual aid societies. Moreover, membership of those that did exist was optional and their activities organically and financially separate from those of the union itself. *El Trabajo*, in contrast, was the first union to establish mutual aid as an integral and obligatory dimension of union membership and organisation, pioneering what would come to be known as the '*base múltiple*' or 'multiple subscription' system of union organisation which from the end of the first decade of the century onwards, would slowly be taken up by the UGT as a whole.[51]

Michel Ralle has suggested that the introduction of welfare benefits was the key factor behind the rapid growth of the organisation at the turn of the century. In doing so, he echoes an argument made at the time by those calling on the UGT as a whole to adopt this model of unionism. In practice, however, the causal relationship between the two developments is rather less clear. On the one hand, the upward tendency in the union's membership was already perceptible before the creation of the aid section, and other smaller trades achieved similar or higher levels of unionisation in the same period without introducing mutual aid. On the other hand, it seems unlikely that, in the absence of any previous experience of formal mutual aid, and before they had tangible evidence that the system actually worked, workers would have seen this mutual insurance as the major attraction of union membership. It is more likely that the bricklayers were driven to organise by the broad range of motivations – notably the promise of higher wages, shorter hours, and improved working conditions – that were swelling the ranks of the labour movement all over Spain at that time. Nonetheless, while the contribution of mutualism to this initial upsurge in the organisation should not be exaggerated, it was certainly a crucial motivation for many workers and their households, and a key factor in the organisational consolidation of *El Trabajo* over the course of the following decade.[52]

The immediate implications of the union's mutual insurance are evident. Those workers who met the strict conditions of entitlement and satisfied the union's inspectors received benefits in case of temporary and permanent incapacity for work, death, and from 1913 an old age pension at the age of fifty-five, or earlier in exceptional cases.[53] Although their real value declined over the course of the decade, the benefits paid were relatively generous. In 1901, when official minimum wage rates in the trade ranged between 2.25 pesetas for general labourers and four pesetas for journeymen, accident victims received two pesetas per working day. Those left incapable of work were paid 1.50 pesetas, later replaced by single one-off payments, 250 pesetas for partial incapacity and thousand pesetas for total incapacity, the equivalent, respectively, of a little over a quarter and a full year's average wages in the trade. The seventy-five pesetas burial benefit was a considerable sum for the time, and would presumably have gone a long way towards meeting the costs this represented. Ever larger number of workers benefited from this dimension of union activities as more and more workers became entitled to make claims. Accident benefit was paid to eighty-nine members of the union in 1901, four hundred and twenty-four in 1906, and eight hundred and seventy in 1910. In 1912, over 11 percent of the union's membership received some form of benefit; by 1922, the union's accounts showed that this figure had risen to 25 percent. The scant protection offered by other forms of insurance meant that the union's mutual aid would often have been the only relief obtained by accident victims and their families. These benefits would have averted much individual hardship in moments of great need and saved many from the indignity of dependence on charity. Although limited in scope and by no means sufficient to provide workers with total economic security, the bricklayers' ambitious attempt to insure workers against the often dramatic consequences that the danger of their work had for them and their families stands out, in both relative and absolute terms, as a major success.[54]

As such, it was one of the most obvious benefits of organisation for both workers themselves and their families. Indeed in bad years for the union, above all after the 1911 lockout, it was one of the few tangible advantages of union membership. Union sources suggest that mutualist activities were particularly attractive to bricklayers' partners, who valued the security which this gave the family and, it was claimed, were otherwise incapable of appreciating the benefits of collective organisation.[55] The union's mutualist provision not only encouraged workers to join the union but, perhaps more importantly, to stay in it, as first they had to earn, and then retain, entitlement to insurance cover: in 1908, accident and funeral benefits were paid out to those who had paid their dues for a year, incapacity pensions after three years, and old age pensions after fifteen years of continuous membership. Initially exempt, by 1908 even the unemployed had to keep up to date with their dues in order not to lose entitlement. Given the acute irregularity of employment, and the considerable cost that union dues represented for bricklayers – in 1909 it was estimated that 5 percent of their annual income went to the organisation – this selective benefit, along with the closed shop, must explain why even when unemployed, as the majority of *El Trabajo* members were in March 1908, they religiously continued to pay their dues.[56] The introduction of the *base múltiple* had other, equally important, implications for the union, contributing to its financial resources, its organisational development and discipline, and the bricklayers' commitment to the union in which they had so much invested. At the same time, the organisation of collective *mutual* insurance, free from outside interference gave the bricklayers a sense of their own capacity to manage their affairs, and to act collectively to improve their situation. In this way, as an integral part of the union's wider project to improve the 'moral and material conditions of the its members', mutualism helped to strengthen the bricklayers' collective organisation and their capacity to win important gains during the first decade of the twentieth century.

Within the panorama of the Spanish labour movement of the day, few unions could match *El Trabajo* in terms of both its organisational development and the gains it brought its members. In the face of a hostile labour market, and in a trade with no recent traditions or experience of labour organisation, the construction of a strong and effective union was a remarkable collective achievement. It testifies to the creative capacity of the bricklayers, and perhaps above all to that of the Socialist activists who led them, adapting an existing model of labour organisation to the peculiar characteristics of the trade. This was reflected in *El Trabajo*'s pioneering development of mutualism, as well as in its adoption of an unusually broad definition of the trade, which encompassed the unskilled general labourers as well as the semi-skilled and skilled workers. This distinctive inclusive strategy – which merits more attention than it has received here – was combined with an 'open' union policy and a hard-won closed shop, which by the mid-1900s was one of the cornerstones of the union's power. However, the union closed shop was as much a consequence as a cause of the bricklayers' support for the organisation, which stemmed above all from the way in which they identified *El Trabajo* as an appropriate vehicle through which to achieve their individual and collective aspirations.

All the evidence suggests that few workers shared their leaders' Socialist ideology or vision of the union as the means to achieve full emancipation in the future. Rather they appear to have been much more interested in the present, in improving their lot in the here and now. This meant many things, but crucially the struggle for a degree of security for themselves and their households. This would explain the undoubted appeal of the selective benefit of accident insurance, as well as the force with which they pursued reductions in hours and overtime restrictions at the expense of higher wages. That the bricklayers were able to reject employer's offers of tempting wage increases in return for longer hours reflects their sense of the collective, but also the fact that so many of the workers were not sole providers, but rather relied on the contribution of other members of the family or household to its collective income. In other words, it is impossible to understand this crucial dimension of the bricklayers' collective organisation and action except in the context of the household and the range of strategies deployed to ensure its survival.

Union Men

Looking at the bricklayers' collective organisation and action from the perspective of the household provides a more socially embedded understanding of the dynamics of *El Trabajo*'s growth and consolidation, its structure, objectives and tactics. Not least, this approach to the study of labour organisation and protest highlights the role women played in maintaining the family in both an economic and broader, social sense, as well as how union organisation rested on, and fitted, into a range of other strategies implemented by different members of the household. This, in turn, draws our attention to the ways in which women were directly involved in the union's activities, attending the union's anniversary meetings each year on 30 April, marching along with their husbands on the May Day parade the following morning, and playing a prominent role in the funeral-protests of workers killed in accidents. Nonetheless, while this type of analysis puts women firmly at the heart of any understanding of the bricklayers' individual and collective living strategies, there is no ignoring the fact that the workers in the trade were all men, or that *El Trabajo* was an exclusively male organisation. In fact, the adoption of a household perspective necessarily focuses our attention on questions of gender, and the existence of distinct and potentially conflicting gender identities and interests within and beyond the home. Given the limitations of the sources, what follows is necessarily a rather tentative attempt to examine these issues, by looking at the nature of the bricklayers' gender identity, and the way this shaped, and was shaped by, their labour organisation and protest.

One of their key sources of identity, and not least gender identity, bricklaying was particularly tightly gendered both objectively and as a social construct. The building site was an exclusively male preserve, as was the culture of the trade. Employers and men related to each other as such. While on Sundays workers may have gone to the countryside to picnic with their families, the after-work and pay-day drinking sessions for which the bricklayers were notorious would usually have been an exclusively male affair. Moreover, within the socially constructed notions of male and female, masculine and feminine work, bricklaying was in many senses particularly masculine. In terms of the polarities identified by David Morgan – dangerous and less dangerous, heavy and light, dirty and clean, skilled and unskilled – and which contemporary evidence suggests would have made sense to the bricklayers, the danger, duress, and dirtiness of their work offered firm grounds for the development of an unproblematic masculine identity. Reports that the bricklayers developed a 'false sense of bravery' in the face of the risks of their work, and that 'fear' was a 'forbidden word' among the workers in the trade, as well as the elegies to the bricklayers' plaster-coated smock and blistered hands published in the union paper in the 1920s suggest that they would have had little difficulty in elaborating a gender identity founded on their physical resistance and readiness to face danger.[57]

However, in other respects, bricklaying was less readily identifiable with recognisable masculine traits. It was, firstly, far removed from the masculine pole of the skill continuum, as the bricklayers were towards the bottom of the socially constructed skill hierarchy of the urban trades, and in contrast to most, very few could claim skilled status. The absence of women workers in the industry did not prevent workers from expressing their loss of skill in gendered terms. This was illustrated by the way in which in 1906 the painters denounced that the declining standard of work in the trade meant that even women could do it. The disappearance of formal apprenticeship, and the employment of boys to do work previously reserved for adults, represented more tangible challenges to the bricklayers' masculinity, disturbing the connection between work, skill and manhood.[58]

The bricklayers' masculinity was also thrown into question by the difficulties they faced in fulfilling the role of the family breadwinner. Women and other family members made a fundamental contribution to the household budget, and would often have maintained it during the frequent spells of unemployment which were a central element of the bricklayers' experience of 'work'. All too frequently, the ideal of the dutiful husband who returned home on Saturday afternoon to hand over his weeks' wage packet to his wife would have been just that. Yet the ideal existed, and constituted an essential element not just of the dominant bourgeois moral universe but also of that of the labour movement and working-class world. Workers' economic demands were justified in terms of their need to fulfil their obligations as male providers and 'heads of family'. This was an argument designed to appeal to bourgeois sensibilities, but also a reflection of an aspiration that formed an essential element of their gender consciousness. Mary Nash has recently shown the growing importance in nineteenth century Spain, as elsewhere, of the 'cult of domesticity', noting that 'despite the generalised reality of women's paid work and their decisive contribution to the family economy', workers also assumed this discourse, and along with it, the idea that women's place was in the home.[59] The reality of most male workers' growing reliance on women's economic support to maintain the family conditioned the labour movement's attitude to the sexual division of labour and spheres. Yet although female work outside the home was not opposed outright, in both Socialist and anarchist thinking it had to be subordinated materially to that of the male until it would be made unnecessary, as reform or revolution would create the conditions for male workers to fulfil their masculine obligations. According to *El Trabajo* secretary, Cipriano Rubio, the duties of their sex included guiding and providing for their womenfolk. Otherwise, women's inherent moral and intellectual weakness meant that if exposed to the abuses of the bourgeoisie, they would be unable to resist the false salvation of religious belief, or worse still, prostitution.[60] Women's work was not only opposed because it was seen as a threat to male employment and working conditions, but also because it threatened men's patriarchal domination of the home. The workers' manifesto from 1868 opposing the employment of women quoted by Nash probably reflected many men's thinking throughout this period: 'another disadvantage is that these women, recruited and preferred in the place of men workers, whether as wives, sisters, or daughters, it is certainly easy to see their pride and dominance with respect to their father, husbands or brothers, and from this, the insults, slanders, disrespect, the charges of being good-for-nothing and lazy made against people who they would otherwise love and respect'.[61] It is tempting to wonder how power relationships within the home would have been affected by unemployment if, as John Tosh has argued was the case more generally, this 'compromised their [workers'] masculine self-respect (including their ability to demand respect from women)'.[62] In this sense, it is easy to imagine that the bricklayer who handed over his wage packet to his wife would have been in a very different position from his colleague who had to ask for some cash to go and buy a drink. Although we do not know his precise motivations, the behaviour of the bricklayer and anarchist leader Cipriano Mera in the 1920s does suggest that his incapacity to act as the sole provider was a source of frustration. Forced to depend on his wife during frequent periods of unemployment, on finding work he immediately took his wife from work and back into the home where she could devote herself to 'her tasks', needless to say, domestic and feminine.[63] The gender implications of unemployment might also help explain *El Trabajo's* clear 'ordering of preferences' in its demands, whereby the union was prepared to forgo wage increases in return for reductions in hours that would spread work over time and among the men. This would be a reasonable response of men for whom 'loss of masculine self-respect was as much an occupational hazard as loss of income'.[64]

In this light, it can be suggested that the physical dangers, duress and roughness of the bricklayers' work, their relatively low-skill status, and the difficulties they encountered in fulfilling the role of providers, conditioned 'the range of masculinities that could legitimately be deployed'.[65] In this way, unable to appeal to the notions of skill, security or respectability as dimensions of their masculinity, the bricklayers elaborated a gender identity based on other physical, psychological and sexual traits considered typically masculine: physical stamina and toughness, a bawdy and ever-unsatisfied heterosexual sexuality, and a nonchalant indifference to both the dangers of their work and the vicissitudes of life more generally. Although we should be wary of confusing social representations with reality, the figure of the dirty, irresponsible, hard-drinking, indolent bricklayer in many a popular song or theatrical piece of the time was surely, if only to be comprehensible to his audience, somehow rooted in reality. This is also suggested by the way that *El Trabajo* sought to distance itself from this image, propagating a form of the 'domesticated manhood' espoused by trade leaders elsewhere in this period, but which in the case of the bricklayers at least appeared to have had little appeal to their members. Although not meant as such, is it possible that when the railway workers' leader Trifón Gómez called the bricklayers of Madrid the 'roughest of men' they took it as a compliment?[66]

It can also be suggested that the bricklayers' sense of masculinity reinforced their identity, organisation and action as workers and as a trade, and that this in turn, bolstered their gender identity. *El Trabajo* constantly evoked the importance of 'manliness', both as a motivation for action and as a quality that made this possible. The union's demands were expressed in gendered terms, wage rises called for in the name of 'fathers of families', and a strike justified on the grounds that the employer 'refused to treat his workers as men with dignity'. Equally, as elsewhere in the nineteenth century, the strength of organised labour was held to depend on the manliness of the individual workers: on the eve of the 1911 lockout, the bricklayers were told that 'commitment' and 'manliness' were all that was needed to win the impending confrontation with employers. Here too, we find that manliness demanded fraternity and solidarity with fellow men, whether this involved ensuring a respectful attendance at a dead colleague's funeral, or following collectively established rules and work practices. In 1909, for example, *El Trabajo* justified the action taken against what was seen as a yellow Catholic bricklayers' union, *La Verdad,* on the grounds that its members could not 'work with those workers who betray the cause of their own brothers and stimulate disorganisation and the loss of gains won through perseverance'. The readiness to face and use violence was a further requisite of this gender ideology. Accordingly, to fall in defence of the union and one's workmates was the ultimate expression of manliness; Francisco Oliva, an *El Trabajo* member killed while picketing a site in 1907, was remembered a decade later as having 'demonstrated exemplary manliness'.[67] In this way, it might be suggested that the bricklayers' well-deserved reputation as the most organised, militant and until 1911 at least, successful trade in the city was a source of gender pride and identity that they would have been reluctant to relinquish: defence of the union was defence of their masculinity.

In this sense, and just to point to an area that requires further research, could it be argued that while inspired by the needs of the family as a whole, the strength of the bricklayers' organisational drive was also inspired by the bricklayers' determination to defend their patriarchal authority in the home? At least, this, along with the intermingling of class and gender identities, is suggested by an incident recorded by Arturo Barea, who as a young bank clerk was harangued by a Madrid bricklayer for the bank employees' failure to organise, and to hence emulate the gains won by *El Trabajo*: 'Of course, to be able to eat has cost us good strikes and good hidings from the police and security guards. But you lot, the gentlemen, how are you going to go on strike, or go with your white collars to the Puerta del Sol to get a beating? I am telling you, that is all you deserve, for cuckolds'.[68]

Conclusions

This brief and in many respects rather speculative attempt to explore the interconnections between the bricklayers' family and household situations and the unusual strength and character of unionism in the trade has focused on three areas in which research in this field can deepen our understanding of labour history.

In the first place, an analysis of workers' family and households, and the varied strategies they deployed, offers a way of identifying and exploring the web of social networks in which they were immersed and which contributed to shape their life opportunities, identities and aspirations. In the case of the bricklayers, it has been argued that in the working-class quarters in which they lived, their family, kin, and personal communities were interwoven, thereby facilitating the spread and consolidation of unionism. At the same time, there is little evidence that many workers in the trade were discouraged or prevented from organising by countervailing social networks or ties, such as those formed around ethnic, religious, or political affiliations and ties. When attempting to account for the proclivity of different groups of workers to organise, or explain why some members of a particular occupational grouping do and others do not, it would seem useful to consider how their decision is influenced by the full range of networks that make up their social worlds. The family is not only one of the most important of these networks, but also one through which they were connected with others, both directly and through other members of the household. In the case of the all-male bricklayers, the role of women in maintaining and developing local personal communities, and probably kin networks too, cannot be ignored, as it would be if research were focused exclusively on the workplace.

Looking at collective organisation and action from the perspective of the family and household should help, secondly, to explain the different character of workers' demands and strategies deployed to obtain these. In the case of the bricklayers, this is perhaps most evident with respect to their willingness and capacity to sacrifice wage demands in return for shorter hours, and, it was hoped, more regular work. This, it has been argued here, is only comprehensible within the context of their collective household economies, to which other family members and, above all their partners, made a vital contribution. Recent research tends to suggest that, as is certainly the case in Spain, the male-breadwinner family has historically been much rarer than once thought, and that almost everywhere, a large proportion of working-class women continued to contribute to the family budget after forming a family. However, the opportunities for female income-generating, the importance of their contribution to the family budget, and the attitude to women's work of those who depended on it, have all varied significantly over time and place, making it a more-or-less viable and attractive option for workers and their families. This suggests that, when considering why some workers mobilise and for what, it is necessary not only to consider the whole range of strategies open to them and the others members of their households, but also the extent to which these strategies were considered desirable or acceptable in economic, social and cultural terms.

Finally, the family and household are crucial spheres in which gender identities are defined and gender relations played out. In the case of the bricklayers, it has been argued that the dangers, duress and unreliability of their work, and the difficulties they experienced in basing their masculinity on claims to skilled status or that of the male provider, encouraged the bricklayers to develop a distinctive rough proletarian masculinity. Besides physical toughness and a certain indifference to the vicissitudes of life, this appears to have favoured their collective action and organisation, in so far as unionism came to be strongly identified with the masculine values of bravery, defiance and fraternal solidarity. The possible implications of this for power relations within the family have merely been hinted at here, but would constitute – sources permitting – another fruitful area for research. In this way, therefore, the adoption of a household approach to labour history might offer a way of achieving the long-heralded, but much more rarely achieved, integration of class and gender in the analysis of working-class and labour movement formation.

Notes

1. I would like to thank Bridget Byrne, Andrew Richards, Paul Rigg and Rickard Sandell, as well as all the participants in the workshop 'From family strategies to collective action', held at the International Institute of Social History in May 1999, for their suggestions and comments on an earlier draft of this paper.
2. This paper is based on research carried out for my doctoral thesis, 'Work, organisation and conflict: the bricklayers of Madrid, c.1870–1914' (European University Institute, Florence, 1998). A full analysis of the issues raised in this paper is to be found there, along with the appropriate bibliography and references.

3. For the centrality of gender in the formation of the working class and the labour movement, see for example, the editor's introduction to A. Baron, ed., *Work Engendered. Toward a New History of American Labour*, Ithaca, 1991, 1–46; and K. Canning, 'Gender and the Politics of Class Formation: Rethinking German Labour History', *American Historical Review* 97, no. 3 (1992): 736–68.

4. See among others, S. Rose, 'Gender and Labor History', *International Review of Social History* 38 Supplement (1993) 145–62.

5. J.L. García Delgado, 'La economía de Madrid en el marco de la industrialización española', in *Pautas regionales de la industrialización española*, eds A. Carreras et al., Barcelona, 1990, 220–56, in particular 237.

6. A. Bahamonde Magro and A. Fernández García, 'La transformación de la economía', in *Historia de Madrid*, ed. A. Fernández García, Madrid, 1995, 515–48, in particular 517; *El Imparcial*, 23 January 1913.

7. Ministerio de Fomento, *Memoria acerca del estado de la industria en la provincia de Madrid en el año 1905*, Madrid, 1907, 147.

8. A. Gomez Mendoza, 'La industria de la construcción residencial: Madrid 1820/1935', *Moneda y Credito*, 177, 1986, 53–81.

9. J. Jimeno Aguis, *Madrid su población, natalidad y mortalidad*, Madrid, 1886, 37; and Ministerio de Fomento, *Memoria acerca del estado de la industria... 1905*, 146–47.

10. *El Imparcial*, 26 August 1904; Archivo de la Villa de Madrid, *Padrón* (Municipal census) *de 1905*, Vol. 391, f.139577; Ayuntamiento de Madrid, *Datos obtenidos del empadronamiento general de habitantes de deciembre de 1915*, Madrid, 1917, 86.

11. The accident in the III Reservoir is analysed more fully in my unpublished paper 'From microhistory to the large processes: the collapse of the III Reservoir of the Canal Isabel II, Madrid April 1905'.

12. For recent overviews in English of the early development of the Spanish labour movement, see in particular P. Heywood, 'The Labour Movement in Spain before 1914', in *Labour and Socialist Movements in Europe before 1914*, ed. D. Geary, London, 1989, 231–65; S. Castillo, 'Spain' in *The formation of labour movements. An international perspective*, eds M. van der Linden and J. Rojahn, Leiden, 1990, 209–69; and A. Smith 'Spain' in *The Force of Labour. The Western European Labour Movement and the Working Class in the Twentieth Century*, eds S. Berger and D. Broughton, Oxford 1995, 171–208. For union organisation in the bricklaying trade, see Byrne, *Work, organisation and conflict*, ch. 5.

13. *El Socialista*, 22 April, 26 June 1898, 10 February, 9 June, 4 August, 6 October, 15 and 29 December 1899; *El Trabajo*, September 1930, November 1932.

14. Sociological research on both historical and contemporary cases has highlighted the importance of social networks in explaining the recruitment patterns of social movements. The seminal article by D.A. Snow, L.A. Zurcher Jr and S. Ekland-Olson, 'Social Networks and Social Movements: A Microstructural Approach to Differential Recruitment', *American Sociological Review* 45 (1980): 787–801, shows that the social networks in which individuals are embedded constitute a key factor for recruitment to social movements. In particular, they argue that the probability of being recruited into a particular movement is largely a function of two conditions: 'links to one or more movement members through a pre-existing or emergent interpersonal tie'; and the absence of 'countervailing networks', that is, alternative networks which compete for individuals' time, energy or loyalties. Among the numerous studies developing this line of analysis, Roger V. Gould's work on the Paris Commune, and Peter Hedström's study of the spatial diffusion of Swedish trade unions between 1890 and 1940 are also of particular interest. V. Gould, 'Multiple Networks and Mobilization in the Paris Commune, 1871', *American Sociological Review* 56 (1991): 716–29, stresses that successful mobilisation depended not on the sheer number of ties, but on the interplay between links created by the insurgent organisation and pre-existing social networks rooted in Parisian neighbourhoods. He found that those members of the National Guard enlisted in their respective neighbourhood-based units resisted longer than their counterparts in city-wide volunteer battalions, a finding which he convincingly relates to this intermeshing of multiple networks, with their corresponding ties and solidarities. P. Hedström, 'Contagious Collectivities: On the Spatial Diffusion of Swedish Trade Unions, 1890–1940', *American*

Journal of Sociology, vol. 99, no.5 (1994): 1157–79, goes deeper into the workings of social networks, to explain why they are of importance for recruitment into social movements. He stresses the way in which the decision of an individual to join a movement is influenced by the other actors in his/her social network. This is because, on the one hand, the individual's decision to participate is based on a comparison of costs and benefits, which vary in accordance with the number of other people who have already joined the movement; on the other, because existing social networks constitute a particularly important source of information about the movement. He insists, finally, on the importance of contagion in mobilisation efforts, concluding that 'spatial properties and network densities are likely to influence considerably both the speed of mobilization process and the success of a movement in organising the relevant population'.

15. For the prevalence of the nuclear family, see D. Reher and E. Camps, 'Las economías familiares dentro de un contexto histórico comparado', *Revista Española de Investigaciones Sociológicos* 55, 1991, 65–91.

16. For examples of non-nuclear families, see *El Imparcial* 8, 12 April 1905; *El Liberal* 8, 14, 15 April 1905; and Archivo de la Villa de Madrid, *Padrón* (Municipal census) *de 1905*, Vol 83, f.300053; M. Pérez-Ledesma, 'El miedo de los acomodados y la moral de los obreros', in *Otras visiones de España*, P. Folguera, ed., Madrid, 1993, 27–64.

17. J. Ruiz Almansa, 'La población de Madrid: su evolución y crecimiento durante el presente siglo (1900–1945)', *Revista Internacional de Sociología* 15–16 (1946): 389–411, in particular 403–6; J.Mª. Sanz García, *Madrid, ¿capital del capital español?*, Madrid, 1975, 146.

18. For the rural household dynamics of migration to the city, see Reher and Camps, 'Las economías familiares dentro de un contexto histórico comparado', 78; D.S. Reher, *Familia, población y sociedad en la provincia de Cuenca. 1700–1900*, Madrid, 1998, 14; C. Borderías, 'Emigración y trayectorias sociales femininas', *Historia Social*, 17 (1993): 75–94; *El Liberal*, 13, 18, 29 April 1905.

19. Jimeno Aguis, *Madrid: su población, natalidad y mortalidad*, 10; *La Construcción Moderna*, 30 January 1916.

20. *El Imparcial*, 12 April 1905; *El Liberal*, 15, 13, 27 April 1905.

21. For examples of recent work emphasising the importance of migration networks, see M.P. Hanagan, 'Labor History and the New Migration History: A Review Essay', *International Labor and Working-Class History* 54 (1998): 57–80.

22. Ayuntamiento de Madrid, *Datos obtenidos del empadronamiento general de habitantes de deciembre de 1915, 45–55*, the first published results of the municipal census to give the occupational breakdown of the 100 administrative quarters of the city.

23. Jaques Valdour who stayed in a house in the Calle Toledo on the eve of the First World War gave a graphic description of the tension that this lack of intimacy could generate; see J. Valdour, *L'ouvrier espagnol. Observations vécues*, Paris, 1919, part II, 264.

24. *El Liberal*, 15 April 1905.

25. *El Liberal*, 9 April 1905.

26. For a fuller treatment of these trade funerals, see J. Byrne,'"Nuestro pan de cada día": accidentes de trabajo y repuesta de los albañiles de Madrid en el cambio del siglo', in *Medicina social y clase obrera en España*, eds R. Huertas and R. Campos, Madrid, 1992, vol.1, 21–49.

27. T. Kaplan, 'Female consciousness and collective action: The case of Barcelona,1910–1918', *Signs* 7, no.3 (1982): 454–566, in particular 545.

28. This recruitment drive can be followed in the pages of *El Socialista,* 1897–1899.

29. See *El Imparcial*, 2 May 1911; *El Eco del Pueblo*, 15 August 1910.

30. *El Socialista*, 8 December 1899.

31. Union Obrera del Gremio de Albañiles de Madrid, *Meeting celebrado por la Unión Obrera de Albañiles de Madrid el miércoles 20 de abril de 1892, presidido por el compañero José Adrados Migallón*, Madrid, 1892, 87.

32. See the magisterial study of the social mobilisation provoked by this crisis of legitimacy by C. Serrano, *Le tour du peuple. Crisis nationale, mouvements populaire et populisme en Espagne (1890–1910)*, Madrid, 1987.

33. For UGT unionism in this period, see the references given in note 11, and S. Castillo, *Historia de la UGT. Vol. I, Hacia la mayoría de edad. 1888–1914*, Madrid, 1998.

34. D. Montgomery, *The Fall of the House of Labour: The Workplace, the State, and American Labor Activism*, Cambridge, 1979, 295.

35. As a member of *El Trabajo's* Executive Committee explained in 1907, 'we have such a degree of perfection that the union has a delegate in every site, so that when a new worker comes he must show his membership card. And if he is not in our union? He can join, but until he does, he does not work'; see *La Paz Social*, August 1907, 266.

36. Article 1 of *El Trabajo, Reglamento de la Sociedad de Obreros Albañiles 'El Trabajo' aprobado en junta general de 9 de agosto de 1888 y reformado en junta general de 13 de enero de 1908*, Madrid, El Trabajo, 1909, 3.

37. M. van der Linden, 'Connecting Household History and Labour History', *International Review of Social History*, Supplement I, 1993, 163–73, in particular 165–67.

38. See, for example, the bricklayers' family budgets given in *El Socialista*, 8 December 1899, *El Imparcial*, 26 August 1904, and A. Marvaud, *La cuestión social en España*, Madrid, 1975, with an introduction by J.Mª Borrás and J.J. Castillo; see also, E. Ballesteros Doncel, '¡Vivir al límite! Diferencias entre el salario monetario y el presupuesto familiar, siglos XIX y XX', in *El trabajo a través de la historia*, ed. S. Castillo, Madrid, 1996, 359–66.

39. *El Imparcial*, 26 August 1904.

40. Marvaud, *La cuestión social en España*, 126–28, 154–55; Calculations based on official wage rates in the trade between 1907 and 1911, contained in Sociedad de Obreros Albañiles 'El Trabajo', *Memoria acerca del 'lock-out' que comenzó en 17 de abril y concluyó en 17 de junio de 1911*, Madrid, El Trabajo, 1911, 32–3.

41. Labour relations in the trade are studied in detail in Byrne, 'Work, organisation and conflict', Chs 6 and 7.

42. P. Stearns, 'The Limits of Labour Protest', in *The Industrial Revolution and Work in Nineteenth Century Europe*, ed. L.R. Berlanstein, London, 1992, 127–47, in particular 133.

43. See for example, *El Socialista*, 4 May, 13 June 1900.

44. J.J. Morato, 'La vida obrera en Madrid', *Nuestro Tiempo* III, May 1903, 542–3; *El Heraldo de Madrid*, 2 April 1904.

45. A. Janssens, 'The Rise and Decline of the Male Breadwinner Family? An Overview of the Debate', *International Review of Social History* 42 Supplement 5 (1997): 1–23, in particular 8. In this respect, David Reher and Enriquetta Camps would be unwise to attempt to generalise for urban Spain as a whole from the experience of what was in many respects an exceptional enterprise, a textile factory in the Catalan town of Sabadell. There, relatively high and stable wages, and limited employment opportunities for married women, may have meant that most wives left work shortly after marriage, but this would certainly not seem to have been the case in many other places, or for the wives of many other workers. See Reher and Camps, 'Las economías familiares', 73, and Ballesteros '¡Vivir al limite!'.

46. See the editors' introduction to P. Hudson and W.R. Lee, eds, *Women's Work and the Family Economy in Historical Perspective*, Manchester, 1990, 2–47, in particular 30.

47. Morato in 1903, and Marvaud in 1910, based their estimations on a family in which both parents and one child were working, Morato, 'La vida obrera', 546–59; Marvaud, *La cuestión social en España*, 154; it is significant that even the wife of Fernando Fermín, a journeyman bricklayer and one of the best paid workers on the site (4.5 pesetas a day), used to serve in various houses, *El Liberal*, 14 April 1905. For other examples of working members of brick-layers' households, *El Liberal*, 12 13, 14, 15 April 1905; *El Imparcial* 18 January 1913; *El Imparcial*, 11 August 1906; 18 January 1913; *El Socialista*, 4 February 1914; *El Heraldo de Madrid*, 11 August 1907, *El Imparcial* 12 August 1907; F. Largo Caballero, *Mis recuerdos*, Mexico City, 1976, 29; see E.A.M. Roberts, 'Women's Strategies 1890–1940', in *Labour and Love. Women's Experience of Home and Family, 1850–1940*, ed. J. Lewis, Oxford, 1986, 223–47, in particular 231–35.

48. *El Heraldo de Madrid*, 26 August 1904; Morato's bricklayer's budget was based on the assumption that 'the *leisured* members of the family' were assigned less food than that given to the active member, *El Socialista*, 8 December 1899. For the very frequent resort to credit and pawn shops see Comisión de Reformas Sociales, *Información oral y escrita publicada de 1889 a 1893*, Madrid, Ministerio de Trabajo y Seguridad Social, fascimile edition with an introduction by Santiago Castillo, 1985, I, 35, 55, 102, 108–9, 226; *El Liberal*, 15 April

1905, and the unpublished interviews that Pilar Folguera carried out for her study of daily life in Madrid in the 1920s, *Vida cotidiana en Madrid*, Madrid 1987.

49. *El Imparcial*, 23 August 1906. For a fuller account of the causes of workplace accidents and an analysis of the bricklayers' response to them, see Byrne, "Nuestro pan de cada día".

50. Sociedad de Obreros Albañiles *El Trabajo, Reglamento...1908*, 24.

51. E. Sánchez de Madariaga, 'De la "caridad fraternal" al "socorro mutuo": Las hermandades de socorro de Madrid en el siglo XVIII', in *Solidaridad desde abajo. Trabajadores y socorros mutuos en la España contemporánea*, ed. S. Castillo, Madrid, 1994, 31–50, in particular 44. In the same volume, see also the editor's introduction, M. Ralle, 'La función de protección mutualista en la construcción de una identidad obrera (1870–1910)', 423–36; and S. González-Gómez, 'La cotización sindical a 'base múltiple', puerta de integración del mutualismo obrero en el primer sindicalismo madrileño', 437–46.

52. M. Ralle, 'La cultura política del primer socialismo español', in *El socialismo en España. Desde la fundación del PSOE hasta 1975*, ed. S. Juliá, Madrid, 1986, 55–85, in particular 83.

53. *El Socialista*, 17 February 1905, 3 February, 1914; *Nueva Era* 1902, 98; The regulations of the union's aid section can be found in Sociedad de Obreros Albañiles 'El Trabajo', *Reglamento...1908*, 24–32.

54. *El Socialista*, 1 December 1913, 31 December 1923.

55. L. Fernández and A. López Baeza, *Manual del obrero asociado*. Madrid, 1919, 160–62.

56. *El Heraldo de Madrid*, 18 December 1909.

57. D. Morgan, *Discovering Men*, London, 1992, especially ch. 2; see for example, *El Socialista*, 12 May 1914, 14 April 1905.

58. *Boletín de la Sociedad de Maestros Pintores de Madrid*, 5 (September 1905).

59. M. Nash, 'Identidad cultural de género, discurso de la domesticidad y la definición del trabajo de las mujeres en la España del siglo XIX', in *Historia de las mujeres*, eds G. Duby and M. Perrot, Madrid, 1993, 385–97, in particular 388–9. See also, K. McClelland, 'Some thoughts on Masculinity and the "Representative Artisan" in Britain, 1850–1880', *Gender & History* 1, no. 2 (1989): 164–77.

60. A. Duarte, 'Entre el mito y la realidad. Barcelona 1902', in *Ayer* 4 (1991): 147–68, in particular 153–5; Rubio in *La Nueva Era*, 1 (1901).

61. Nash, 'Identidad de género', 589–90; it should, however, be emphasised, as David Morgan has done, that the role of the provider and notions of sacrifice and responsibility perhaps are, and have been, less tightly gendered than often thought, Morgan, *Discovering Men*, 90–1.

62. J. Tosh, 'What should Historians do with Masculinity? Reflections on Nineteenth-century Britain', *History Workshop Journal* no. 38 (1994): 179–202, in particular 190.

63. J. Llach, *Cipriano Mera: un anarquista en la guerra de España*, Barcelona, 1976, 19; see also Morgan, *Discovering Men*, 90–1.

64. Tosh, 'What should Historians do with Masculinity?', 193.

65. Morgan, *Discovering Men*, 97.

66. See for example, the representation of the bricklayers in '*El Lockout*' (1919), reprinted in S. Salaün, *El cuplé (1900–1936)*, Madrid, 1990, 281; J. de Lucio, *La chapuza del sofá*, Madrid, 1923; in A. Casero, *Consolar al triste*, Madrid, 1915; *El Trabajo*, February 1923; *El Socialista*, 2 May 1922; Tosh, 'What should Historians do with Masculinity?', 193.

67. *El Heraldo de Madrid*, 12 September 1904, 23 April 1911; *El Socialista*, 1 June 1917.

68. Arturo Barea, *La Forja*, Madrid, 1941, 240.

Bibliography

Bahamonde Magro, A., and Fernández García, A., 'La transformación de la economía' in *Historia de Madrid*, ed. A. Fernández García. Madrid, 1995, 515–48.

Ballesteros Doncel, E. '¡Vivir al límite! Diferencias entre el salario monetario y el presupuesto familiar, siglos XIX y XX', in *El trabajo a través de la historia*, ed. S. Castillo. Madrid, 1996, 359–66.

Barea, A. *La Forja*. Madrid, 1941.

Baron, A., ed. *Work Engendered. Toward a New History of American Labour.* Ithaca, 1991.

Byrne, J. "Nuestro pan de cada día': accidentes de trabajo y repuesta de los albañiles de Madrid en el cambio del siglo', in *Medicina social y clase obrera en España. vol. 1*, eds R. Huertas and R. Campos. Madrid, 1992, 21–49.

———. 'Work, organisation and conflict: the bricklayers of Madrid, c.1870–1914' (doctoral thesis, European University Institute, Florence, 1998).

———. 'From microhistory to the large processes: the collapse of the III Reservoir of the Canal Isabel II, Madrid April 1905' (unpublished paper).

Canning, K. 'Gender and the Politics of Class Formation: Rethinking German Labour History, *American Historical Review* vol.97, no. 3 (1992): 736–68.

Casero, A. *Consolar al triste*. Madrid, 1915.

Castillo, S. 'Spain', in *The formation of labour movements. An international perspective*, eds M. van der Linden and J. Rojahn. Leiden, 1990, 209–69.

———. *Historia de la UGT. Vol. I, Hacia la mayoría de edad. 1888–1914*. Madrid, 1998.

Duarte, A. 'Entre el mito y la realidad. Barcelona 1902', *Ayer* vol. 4 (1991): 147–68.

Fernández, L., and López Baeza, A. *Manual del obrero asociado*. Madrid, 1919.

Folguera, P. *Vida cotidiana en Madrid*. Madrid, 1987.

García Delgado, J.L. 'La economía de Madrid en el marco de la industrialización española', in *Pautas regionales de la industrialización española,* eds A. Carreras et al. Barcelona, 1990, 220–56.

Gomez Mendoza, A. 'La industria de la construcción residencial: Madrid 1820/1935', *Moneda y Credito*, 177 (1986): 53–81.

González-Gómez, S., 'La cotización sindical a 'base múltiple', puerta de integración del mutualismo obrero en el primer sindicalismo madrileño', in *Solidaridad desde abajo. Trabajadores y socorros mutuos en la España contemporánea*, ed. S. Castillo. Madrid, 1994, 437–46.

Gould, V. 'Multiple Networks and Mobilization in the Paris Commune, 1871', *American Sociological Review* vol. 56 (1991): 716–29.

Hanagan, M.P. 'Labor History and the New Migration History: A Review Essay', *International Labor and Working-Class History* vol.54 (1998): 57–80.

Hedström, P. 'Contagious Collectivities: On the Spatial Diffusion of Swedish Trade Unions, 1890–1940', *American Journal of Sociology* vol. 99, no.5 (1994): 1157–79.

Heywood, P. 'The Labour Movement in Spain before 1914', in *Labour and Socialist Movements in Europe before 1914,* ed. D. Geary. London, 1989, 231–65.

Hudson, P. and Lee, W.R., eds. *Women's Work and the Family Economy in Historical Perspective*. Manchester, 1990.

Janssens, A. 'The Rise and Decline of the Male Breadwinner Family? An Overview of the Debate', *International Review of Social History* vol. 42 Supplement 5 (1997): 1–23.

Jimeno Aguis, J. *Madrid su población, natalidad y mortalidad*. Madrid, 1886.

Kaplan, T. 'Female Consciousness and Collective Action: The case of Barcelona,1910–1918', *Signs* vol.7, no.3 (1982): 454–566.

Largo Caballero, F. *Mis recuerdos*. Mexico City, 1976.

Linden, M. van der, 'Connecting Household History and Labour History', *International Review of Social History*, Supplement I (1993): 163–73.

Llach, J. *Cipriano Mera: un anarquista en la guerra de España*. Barcelona, 1976.

Lucio, J. de, *La chapuza del sofá*. Madrid, 1923.

Marvaud, A. *La cuestión social en España*. Madrid, 1975.

McClelland, K. 'Some Thoughts on Masculinity and the "Representative Artisan" in Britain, 1850–1880', *Gender & History* vol 1, no. 2 (1989): 164–77.

Montgomery, D. *The Fall of the House of Labour. The Workplace, the State, and American Labor Activism*. Cambridge, 1979.

Morato, J.J. 'La vida obrera en Madrid', *Nuestro Tiempo* vol. 3 (May 1903).

Morgan, D. *Discovering Men*. London, 1992.

Nash, M. 'Identidad cultural de género, discurso de la domesticidad y la definición del trabajo de las mujeres en la España del siglo XIX', in *Historia de las mujeres*, eds G. Duby and M. Perrot. Madrid, 1993, 385–97.

Pérez-Ledesma, M. 'El miedo de los acomodados y la moral de los obreros', in *Otras visiones de España*, P. Folguera, ed. Madrid, 1993, 27–64.

Ralle, M. 'La cultura política del primer socialismo español', in *El socialismo en España. Desde la fundación del PSOE hasta 1975*, ed. S. Juliá. Madrid, 1986, 55–85.

———. 'La función de protección mutualista en la construcción de una identidad obrera (1870–1910)' in *Solidaridad desde abajo. Trabajadores y socorros mutuos en la España contemporánea*, ed. S. Castillo. Madrid, 1994, 423–436.

Reher, D.S. *Familia, publación y sociedad en la provincia de Cuenca. 1700–1900*. Madrid, 1998.

Reher, D.S. and Camps, E. 'Las economías familiares dentro de un contexto histórico comparado', *Revista Española de Investigaciones Sociológicos* vol. 55 (1991): 65–91.

Roberts, E.A.M. 'Women's Strategies 1890–1940', in *Labour and Love. Women's Experience of Home and Family, 1850–1940*, ed. J. Lewis. Oxford, 1986, 223–47.

Rose, S. 'Gender and Labor History', *International Review of Social History* vol. 38 Supplement (1993): 145–62.

Ruiz Almansa, J. 'La población de Madrid: su evolución y crecimiento durante el presente siglo (1900–1945)', *Revista Internacional de Sociología* vol.15–16 (1946): 389–411.

Salaün, S. *El cuplé (1900–1936)*. Madrid, 1990.

Sánchez de Madariaga, E. 'De la 'caridad fraternal' al 'socorro mutuo': Las hermandades de socorro de Madrid en el siglo XVIII', in *Solidaridad desde abajo. Trabajadores y socorros mutuos en la España contemporánea*, ed. S. Castillo. Madrid, 1994, 31–50.

Sanz García, J.Mª. *Madrid, ¿capital del capital español?* Madrid, 1975.

Serrano, C. *Le tour du peuple. Crisis nationale, mouvements populaire et populisme en Espagne (1890–1910)*. Madrid, 1987.

Smith. A. 'Spain', in *The Force of Labour. The Western European Labour Movement and the Working Class in the Twentieth Century*, eds S. Berger and D. Broughton. Oxford 1995, 171–208.

Snow, D. A., Zurcher, Jr, L.A., and Ekland-Olson, S. 'Social Networks and Social Movements: A Microstructural Approach to Differential Recruitment', *American Sociological Review* vol.45 (1980): 787–801.

Stearns, P. 'The Limits of Labour Protest', in *The Industrial Revolution and Work in Nineteenth Century Europe*, ed. L.R. Berlanstein. London, 1992, 127–47.

Tosh, J. 'What should Historians do with Masculinity? Reflections on Nineteenth-century Britain', *History Workshop Journal*, no. 38 (1994): 179–202.

Valdour, J. *L'ouvrier espagnol. Observations vécues*. Paris, 1919, part II.

CHAPTER 6

'WHO WILL LOOK AFTER THE KIDDIES?'

HOUSEHOLDS AND COLLECTIVE ACTION DURING THE DUBLIN LOCKOUT, 1913

Theresa Moriarty

The Dublin lockout of 1913 ranks internationally among the foremost industrial disputes in the years before the First World War. It began in August 1913 and lasted for six months. The dispute arose over the right of men to be members of the Irish Transport and General Workers' Union (ITGWU), a trade union of only four years standing, formed as an Irish breakaway from British headquarters of the National Union of Dock Labourers, and led by the charismatic figure of James Larkin.[1]

The lockout began on Tuesday 26 August among men working for the Dublin United Tramway Company, in one of the busiest weeks of the Irish social season, at the start of the popular and prestigious annual Horse Show Week of the Royal Dublin Society. They were protesting at being asked to sign a pledge that they would cease to be members of the ITGWU. Drivers and conductors told the passengers to get off, pinned up their union badges and stepped down from their vehicles, blocking the city routes with abandoned trams. The tramcar drivers' challenge to join a union of their own choosing was the prologue to a lockout that was to engulf the whole city, throwing 25,000 or more women, men and children out of work, halting all trade in the city. The public protagonists of the long drawn-out dispute assembled in the first week. Striking drivers were summonsed to court for abandoning their trams. Those still working were attacked. Angry crowds spilled onto the streets to listen to defiant speeches. Police baton charges chased strikers and passers-by along the Liffey quays beside the new ITGWU offices in Liberty Hall. Police reinforcements were called in to Dublin from the country. Larkin was arrested for sedition, imprisoned, then released on bail. A protest meeting for the Sunday afternoon, in Dublin's main thoroughfare was banned by the authorities. When Larkin, smuggled into O'Connell Street in disguise, began to address the crowds, the listeners were batoned off the street by the police. Rioting broke out throughout the city, lasting into the night as police attacked angry crowds, chasing people into, and wrecking, their homes. When the toll of the first week of the lockout was calculated after Dublin's 'Bloody Sunday', hundreds were injured and two men had been killed.

The next morning, when notices appeared in Jacob's biscuit factory that any workers who wore their union badge would be dismissed, three thousand women were locked out, making the city-wide lockout virtually complete. Dublin employers moved quickly to line up behind the leadership of the tram company owner, William Martin Murphy, who headed an extensive Irish and overseas business empire. Four hundred Dublin bosses agreed to demand a signed pledge from their workers renouncing the ITGWU. The employers' undertaking to lockout any worker who refused to sign spread the dispute far beyond the ranks of that union. The lockout spread swiftly by sympathetic strikes, as employers enforced their pledge, or workers refused to handle strike-bound goods, and were then in turn locked out themselves. The arc of the lockout extended to the hinterland of the city, to grain mills along the canals and the market gardens in the county, as farmers' associations locked out their agricultural workers.

The confrontation between Dublin's employers and workers lasted for six months, despite a succession of attempts at conciliation. An effort by the Dublin Lord Mayor to bring the two sides together, the unwieldy industrial relations machinery of a Board of Trade inquiry under Sir George Askwith, the intervention of trade union allies from the British Trade Union Congress, the initiatives of concerned citizens of the Industrial Peace Committee, all were unable to bring the lockout to negotiation or settlement. The Dublin employers' federation refused all terms. The *Times* in London declared Dublin was in 'a state of civil war between labour and capital'.[2]

The 1913 Dublin lockout is more than an episode to view collective action from a family perspective. Its duration and scale demonstrate a moment in which both become inseparable. Unions were forced to improvise family strategies as the dispute lengthened and household members were drawn into the industrial action. One Dublin participant reflected in his autobiography:

> It spread until it was no longer a struggle between certain employers of certain working men. Practically it became a fight to the death between the business men of Ireland and the city of Dublin.[3]

The lockout mobilised accumulated grievances which extended beyond the industrial issues, and combined in a kaleidoscope of discontents, where the pattern constantly shifted and reformed.[4]

Less than half a million people lived in Dublin, ninety thousand of them adult men. An unskilled manual labourer earned around a pound a week, often less (18 shillings). Casual workers' rates are given as twelve to fifteen shillings a week, and could be lower. They were estimated at a government inquiry as more likely to be nine shillings a week. A quarter of all men who worked were manual labourers, unskilled and casual. Weekly wage rates, however, depended on gender, age, health, weather, trade, political loyalties, blacklisting, and the immeasurable and uncontrollable chances of accidents of life and death. Any of these could reduce a family to beggary.

Women were concentrated in a narrow range of industries, as domestic workers, in clothing or food production. Their wage rates were even lower. A report from Dublin during the lockout reported wages that 'are a disgrace to a civilised country':

> two girls were paid 10d for twelve days work and 11d for ten days work.... Two embroideresses in the same firm worked from 8.30 to one o'clock for 1d and 1¹/4d. ... In one factory the girls work fifty hours for 10s. The girl I spoke to had worked there seven years and was twenty-seven years old. No-one earned more at her kind of work than 11s. ... At a paper factory, a girl of twenty who has worked there two years only earns 6s a week, and the forewoman ... only earns 16s a week.[5]

Many of Dublin's women workers were single women, contributing to a household budget. Others were heads of households. Over one thousand tenement households were headed by charwomen.[6] Mary Neal, secretary of the Women's Political and Social Union introduced the circumstances of one woman she met in Dublin to the readers of the British suffragette journal, *Votes for Women:*

> The mother is thirty three years old and has five children. Her husband went to America four years ago, but for the last year she has heard nothing from him, nor has she received any money from him. She earns 7s a week at sack repairing. She spends 1s and 6d on rent, gives 4s.6d to a sister to look after and feed the five children while she is at work, and she pays 2d a week to the Union.[7]

Two years earlier the Irish Women Workers Union had been launched, for women, 'whatever you are or wherever you work', who were excluded previously from Dublin's trade union movement. It was effectively a women's section of the ITGWU, shared premises with it in Liberty Hall, and was headed by James Larkin's younger sister, Delia Larkin.

A Board of Trade survey the previous year had found in Dublin the highest cost of living in the United Kingdom, outside central London, where wages at least had a London weighting to take account of this. Average rents quoted for single rooms were two shillings a week; but they could be much higher. James Connolly, the Belfast organiser of the ITGWU since 1911, said he had paid four shillings for a room for his family in Dublin. In Aungier Street a family paid three shillings and sixpence; in Gardiner Street as much as five shillings.[8] Housing was dire. The most quoted statistic during the lockout was Dublin's 21,000 single tenement rooms counted by the 1911 census (21,433). The city administration admitted that 135,000 people lived in insanitary tenements. Dublin housing statistics counted 87,305 people in 25,822 families lived in the city's 5,322 tenement houses. These were multi-occupied unconverted dwelling-houses of Georgian Dublin, where a single toilet on a landing, or in an outside yard, accommodated the many families who rented rooms from the slum landlords. Dublin tenements were registered in three classes: structurally sound, decayed, and unfit. One third of the population lived in conditions considered to be injurious to physical and moral health.[9] Tenants, and not landlords, were fined for violations of the sanitary laws. Dublin tenements, a London visitor to the Dublin lockout reported, 'have to be seen and smelt to be realised'. Housing conditions proved so ruinous that early in the lockout, two tenements fell into the street on 2 September 1913, 'as though to join the protest', as another writer put it. Seven people were killed in that collapse.

The uncertainties of tenement life were exacerbated by commonplace evictions for non payment of rent. In 1913, it was noted that there was 'a growing population of 30,000 constantly being served with notices to quit', in the city.[10] Dublin tenements were notoriously overcrowded. When the two houses collapsed in Church Street over forty people lived in the sixteen rooms.

Family life in Dublin's 1913 tenements was intensely communal. Life was lived on the stairs, in the hall, and on the steps and streets. Many of the Church Street victims had been standing or sitting in the doorway and street, the housing inquiry heard. Mrs Maguire one of the residents gave evidence, 'I was standing in the hall door of the house, looking at the children playing in the streets. Other women were sitting on the kerb-stone so as to be in the air'.[11] In Sean O'Casey's play, *The Plough and the Stars*, the child, Mollser, dying of tuberculosis, is brought out to sit by the steps of the tenement house to get the warm air:

> Th' sun'll do you all the good in th' world. A few more weeks o' this weather, an' there's no knowin' how well you'll be.[12]

Other aspects of the communal life of the residents of Dublin's overcrowded rooms disturbed the city fathers more. The city councillors were almost indifferent to the tenement dwellers' living conditions, except when:

> I do not think it is in keeping with the decencies of home life to have 10 or 12 families living in one house with an open hall door for all the members of the different families, having different ideas of morality and public conduct, and having the youngsters seeing things that no child ought to see, and with one convenience, with women meeting men going and coming to the same place. For these reasons I think the tenement system is against public morality and decent civilisation.[13]

Moral, rather than material, objections stirred the conscience of Councillor Lorcan Sherlock, Dublin's Lord Mayor, who represented the city's Mountjoy Ward – the 'most congested ward in Dublin'.

The rooms that families lived in were overcrowded; family size was large. 'The average working man had a family of ten children and families of 12 or 15 were quite common', recalled Joseph Quaney. 'Most working class families lived in a single room where the never ending functions of rising, dressing,

cooking, eating and going to bed again were carried out under the most trying conditions'. When the children were still young all these domestic functions would, by custom, be the work of the women of the household. Sickness
stalked these overcrowded rooms. Children fell ill and too often died from a
wide range of infectious diseases in infancy. Whooping cough was then one of
the main killers of children:

> A child lay ill with whooping-cough and was laying exhausted after a paroxysm
> of coughing. Flies were numerous in the room (it was a hot summer) and were
> passing and repassing from the food on the table to the face and body of the
> sick child.[15]

Already overcrowded rooms could still provide a sanctuary for the less fortunate:

> Yet in the midst of such chaos and discomfort, a family would not hesitate to
> take in and give temporary shelter to another family that suddenly lost a bread-
> winner, or was evicted for non payment of rent.[16]

Family life was subject to great material hardship, reinforced by poor diets and
clothing. Children photographed in the street are seldom shod. Lack of decent
clothing could make the difference between a job or unemployment. House
furnishings were pathetically few. Dublin tenement homes were almost entirely
without bric-à-brac or personal clutter. There were often only the bare essen-
tials of furniture and crockery. The pawnbroker had an important role in the
household economy. One observer wrote: 'From inquiries that I made some
years ago I ascertained in a single year, 2,866,084 tickets were issued in the city
of Dublin'.[17] Household members sought recourse from the privations of
home life in pubs and in the streets. The Honorary Treasurer of the National
Society for the Prevention of Cruelty to Children (NSPCC), told the housing
inquiry, 'In no city in these islands with which I am acquainted have the children such a freedom, I might say such possession of the streets, as Dublin'.[18]
Drink was regularly cited as one of Dublin's hazards. The conviviality of the
public house was a refuge from overcrowded rooms, and even more of a necessity when men's wages were paid out there, as they were by custom.
    The poverty and hardship of Dublin tenement life was mediated in most
households by the women. The grounds for selecting tenants by the Corporation included family 'respectability' as well as the ability to pay the high
rents. A family could be deemed unsuitable, 'if they didn't keep their places
clean, and if I think their general appearance is not proper for Christians'.
Asked to define such unsuitability further, this official explained:

> Suppose I go into a place at one o'clock and see the breakfast things on the table
> and the ashes in the grate – then I think they are unsuitable.[19]

The customary arbiter of the 'different ideas of cleanliness and public conduct', noted by the Lord Mayor's moral anxiety, was the woman of the household. John Cooke of the NSPCC placed his own value on feminised skills
within the privations of the household setting:

The woman left to herself in a single room with her children has no chance of cultivating any of the graces of life. She too quickly, as a rule, loses any she ever had. The little of a useful kind she was ever taught she forgets or has no chance of putting into practice. In all the rooms I visited I saw no woman with a needle in her fingers, while there was plenty of tatters on her own and children's garments for the use of it and thread. Even were she inclined to cook, little could be done with the fireplace, while the shelf, if not entirely bare, has seldom anything better than the materials for a poor tea. Under such conditions of living, under such uncertainty of means of livelihood among large numbers, and with the drink habit so strong, it is very easy to account for the squalor and uncleanliness and general untidiness in the slum areas of the city.[20]

Different domestic skills, earning capacity, help from other family members, and even personal taste could determine the difference between survival or going under. However, the poverty of a family was not always determined by a wage earner's rate of pay. Dillon, the Corporation official, explained how domestic arbitration could break down:

Husbands do not give their wives sufficient money. I know a tradesman earning 36 shillings a week and all he gives his wife is 21/- for herself and six children. The woman hides the husband's failings and if you send a letter to him it is stopped by the wife.[21]

The patriarchy of family life was buttressed by necessity. Where there were absolute dependants on a weekly income, then a wage earner, or father would receive the priority for clothes and food. 'Dip in the dip, and leave the herring for your father', was not a childhood rhyme, but a family maxim. Women might determine a family living quarters in yet another way. In one street Corporation officials found:

no respectable woman would go there, because as you are probably aware it is the worst district in the city. It is full of brothels … respectable people felt there would be a certain amount of contamination taking a house in a place like that; not only that, but experience proved that their daughters were liable to gross insult going in and out.[22]

As the employers' challenge to the members of the ITGWU lengthened into weeks and the autumn months of 1913 women and children at the heart of Dublin families became the focus of the struggle. Family strategies and industrial collective action fused as the lockout spread. In early October, James Connolly described this process in the Scottish socialist weekly, *Forward*:

I heard of one case where a labourer was asked to sign the agreement forswearing the Irish Transport and General Workers' Union, and he told his employer, a small capitalist builder, that he refused to sign. The employer, knowing the man's circumstances, reminded him that he had a wife and six children who would be starving within a week. The reply of this humble labourer rose to the heights of sublimity. 'It is true, sir', he said, 'they will starve; but I would rather see them go out one by one in their coffins than that I should disgrace them by signing that'. And with head erect he walked out to share hunger and privation with his loved ones. Hunger, privation – and honour.[23]

Family strategies deployed by the employer in the industrial struggle are acknowledged by both worker and organiser as the cost of their collective action. The dispute over the right of men to be in a union of their choice disappeared from the rhetoric, and was transformed into a passionate articulation on behalf of workers' dependants.

Some of those further afield, who were anxious to lend their support to Dublin, faced a less extreme dilemma than Connolly's building labourer, as they weighed their own disputes in the balance of the Dublin lockout. In England a strike was pending in the Salford docks, where one of the ships booked to transport food to Dublin was waiting:

> The men were obviously struggling between their desire to help the women and children of Dublin and their fear of breaking the solidarity of their own movement in Salford. No one was willing to unload the vessel, but we felt bound to insist it being done. As is always the case, the better side of the men came uppermost in the end and the women and children won.[24]

The most familiar image throughout the lockout is of a suffering mother of starving children. Sir William Orpen, the painter, immortalised this picture of locked out Dublin. Speakers referred repeatedly to the lockout as, an 'attempt to starve our women and children'. A pen portrait of those who waited for food at Liberty Hall evokes:

> The stoic suffering on the face of a mother who is herself too ill to come out, and yet had to wait her turn for food, and then with white lips, and face drawn with suffering makes her way home, a loaf under her shawl, a jug of coffee in her shaking hand, a baby on her arms, a kiddie tugging at her skirts.[25]

The Liberty Hall unions had, since their formation, a strong commitment to their membership beyond the requirements of union business. James Larkin and his sister shared a broad outlook on the part that the union should play in their members' lives. Both staunchly teetotal, the Larkins established Liberty Hall as a venue with a programme of activities for their members' imaginations and talents. Through the work of Delia Larkin in particular, an elocution class started, a choir, and a theatre group, which would inspire the young talent of Sean O'Casey. For the women workers, deprived by convention of public gatherings, she organised a Sunday afternoon discussion group, weekly socials, annual outings and new year dances. Liberty Hall hosted one act plays at Christmas, and St Patrick's Day concerts. A fife and drum band, and then an Irish pipe band were started.

Their most ambitious project opened only weeks ahead of the lockout. A large house and three acres at Croydon Park were rented by the ITGWU, beyond the city limits, as a recreation centre for the union members and families. It was officially opened on 3 August 1913 with a Grand Temperance Fête and Children's Carnival. In Liberty Hall the unions maintained an intimate relationship with their members. James Larkin described Croydon Park to a Liverpool audience, as a place, 'where no-one is allowed in who is not either in that union, or a wife of a worker .... We make our family life focus around the union'.[26] Family members could appeal to Liberty Hall about the conduct of a union member in their household. Barney Conway, Larkin's life-long friend, told James Larkin's biographer, Emmet Larkin [no relation], how, 'The women would often come to Larkin and complain about their husbands' drinking. Larkin would see to it that the wives and children received first con-sideration, and after that the men could do what they liked'. Emmet Larkin cites Larkin's temperance as the foundation for the 'loyalty of workers' wives' to Larkin and, by inference, to the union itself:

> More than one drunken docker went head down the steps of Liberty Hall with Larkin as the propelling force .... Larkin became their moral policeman.[27]

The lockout was conducted as a highly personalised struggle between James Larkin and William Martin Murphy, and in the verbal contest between both sides allegiance was affirmed in these terms. At evictions, in school strikes, at street demonstrations and even in the courts, Larkin's name was invoked by protesters to demonstrate their defiance.

Help was sought from British trade unions. They responded quickly. Two food ships, SS Hare and the Fraternity, arrived in Dublin in early October. British unions and supporters sent money to a central fund launched by the Trade Union Congress (TUC) in London, which purchased the food from the Co-operative stores for shipping and sent money directly to Dublin. Its report a year later commented, 'it can safely be asserted that on no previous occasion had an appeal issued in the name of organised Labour met with such sponta-neous, continued and magnificent support'. When this contribution was counted £93,500 had been disbursed by this fund, from the end of Septem-ber to the beginning of February. Fourteen weekly grants of a thousand pounds came from the Miners' Federation alone.[28] At Liberty Hall the food was distributed in 'pucks', bags of supplies to members' families. Kitchens were opened in the basement making meals daily. Domestic skills were mobilised in this effort as locked-out tramway workers cooked meals with 'a number of locked-out women and girls, as well as by the daughters of locked-out workers'. The *Daily Herald* described:

> Orders for the food coming by the food ship are distributed there in the upper rooms, while in the basement meals are always being cooked and distributed to the mothers and children who come with tin cans and jugs for stew or cocoa and carry away under ragged shawls big loaves baked at the Co-op bakery. Every pas-sage and landing is crowded with patient people, none of who go empty away, for the organisation as far as one can see is perfect.[29]

This effort was assisted by a 'Ladies Committee', headed by Delia Larkin, which drew on energies of women who were outside the trade union move-ment, had never participated in any form of industrial action or even entered a trade union office. Most of these women came from the ranks of the suffrage movement, whose newspaper, the *Irish Citizen*, appealed to their readers' sympathies for the strikers.

A bolder scheme was advanced in London. Socialist feminists, moved by James Larkin's appeal for help, proposed to bring Dublin children to British sympathisers' homes for the duration of the dispute. As Dora Montefiore remembered:

> When Larkin had finished speaking I wrote out a slip of paper and passed it across to him, asking him if a plan like this which had already been carried out by Belgian comrades, and in the Lawrence strike, in the United States, could be arranged by the Daily Herald League, would it have his blessing.[30]

Larkin assented immediately. This was publicised in the daily socialist newspaper, the *Daily Herald*, as an appeal to the women members of the Daily Herald League, an association of local groups of Socialists. The response from distant households to Montefiore's question, 'Who will look after the kiddies?', was instantaneous. Within days, three hundred homes were on offer.

In Dublin the strike committee had given the scheme its blessing, and reports in the sympathetic press suggest it was taken up enthusiastically. The spontaneity of the consent was not as instinctive as this suggests. The removal of children from the scene of industrial conflict to be looked after in the homes of sympathisers elsewhere, improvised on, and combined traditional family strategies with contemporary industrial practice. It was a course of action already familiar to industrial syndicalists before the First World War, and eagerly adopted in a number of the long drawn-out disputes that characterise this period. In 1913 such a plan had been organised during the Belgian general strike in April, and in May by silkworkers on strike at Paterson New Jersey. But, as Dora Montefiore's memory attested, its best-known example was in the US Lawrence textile strike of 1912.

The Industrial Workers of the World organiser, Elizabeth Gurley Flynn, remembered the proposal first came from the strikers, 'that we adopt a method used successfully in Europe – to send the children out of Lawrence to be cared for in other cities'.[31] There the brutal attack by state troopers and police on forty Lawrence children attempting to board a train for Philadelphia had led to public outrage and an inquiry, which turned the fortunes of the strike to success. In 1913 the departure of Paterson children to 'strike mothers' in New York was symbolically staged on May Day and so integral to the story of the strike, the evacuation of the children was dramatised as an episode in the pageant performed by the strikers in Madison Square Gardens that summer. In London the treasurer of the 1913 Dublin Kiddies' Fund was Frances Greville, Countess of Warwick, who had prepared sympathetic homes for children during the London dock strike in 1912.

The children's plan built on established household practice where family and friends frequently took in children, to relieve others in crisis. In both British and Dublin working class households such informal fostering was a recognised custom of family life, and where children had relatives in the countryside, as Dublin households frequently had, they might often be sent to stay there. Support in industrial disputes is more traditionally mediated through trade union organisation and action, such as the TUC fund and the food ships. The appeal to take Dublin children into their homes touched faraway household members of trade unionists and socialists, in which family and community response coincided, and offered both a direct participation in events, and even to shape them, rather than to watch as sympathetic, but passive observers. Those unable to take children were urged to send clothing through the Co-operative movement.

Meetings with the wives of the locked-out workers were held in Liberty Hall on Monday 20 October, where the three women delegates from Britain outlined the plan for the children. Dora Montefiore, who led the group, reported back in the *Daily Herald*:

> Last night the mothers' meeting in one of the largest rooms in Liberty Hall was a sight none of us will ever forget. Miss Larkin told me it was 'the surprise of my life'. The meeting of mothers and babies overflowed, blocking the stairs and struggling out into the street. We gave our message from the workers of England to the wives of Dublin.

She recalled in her autobiography:

> As a result Miss Grace Neal was kept busy Tuesday and Wednesday entering the names of mothers who were anxious to take advantage of our offer. The passage leading to our room was blocked from morning till evening with women and children. We tried to let them in only one at a time, but each time the door opened the crush was so great that often two or three mothers forced their way in. We rejected many who were not the wives of strikers, or locked-out men, and we told them in all instances to go away and make quite sure that the fathers of the children wished them to leave.[32]

Writing this some years after the events in Dublin, Dora Montefiore had reason to stress the organisational care in implementing the plan to bring the children out of Dublin, and the parents' support for it.

The Roman Catholic Archbishop of Dublin denounced the plan in the press. His letter 'to the mothers of Dublin' touched deep wells of anxiety. Although he did not use the word 'proselytism' in his letter, its absence resonated in other phrases he employed in his address. 'Have they abandoned their faith? … the plain duty of every Catholic mother … they can no longer be held worth of the name …'. He admonished Dublin mothers for being prepared to send away their children, 'without security of any kind that those to whom the poor children are to be handed over are Catholics, or indeed people of any faith at all'. Days of melodramatic scenes followed, as the children were prepared to travel and crowds were mobilised to oppose this. At the baths where the first group were being washed and dressed, at the rail stations, shipping berths and the streets round Liberty Hall, crowds milled through the city in demonstration and counter-demonstration, dockers fought to get the children through, priests confronted parents, hymns were sung, slogans shouted and Dora Montefiore and Lucille Rand were arrested and charged with kidnapping. When one group of twenty children succeeded in getting away on the Liverpool boat, they were held by police on their arrival until their fathers' permissions were checked out, on the request of local priests.

As the week unfolded the Dublin streets became a contested territory between the supporters of the scheme, and their opponents, led by the Ancient Order of Hibernians, a Catholic nationalist organisation. Dublin was deeply divided. Prominent figures of Dublin's intellectual and political circles took strong public positions for and against the plan. James Connolly wrote at the end of October that, 'we have never been enthusiastic towards the scheme'. James Larkin insisted later it had been the finest tactical error ever made in the workers' struggle. The children were stopped from travelling. Only a mother and her five children, taken independently of the Herald League initiative, to the home of the suffragette, Emmeline Pethick Lawrence, and the group of children who travelled to Liverpool succeeded in leaving Dublin.

These events had been played out in relief against the background of the industrial issues, which were being contested through a voluntary conciliation council and a government commission. Yet it was the unravelling of the plan for the children on which the lockout turned and Dublin divided. It was precisely where household strategies and collective action combined that such passions were aroused. This marked out the territory where differing household strategies could not be accommodated as interdependent or complementary, and could no longer be reconciled or negotiated. At its most simple, the welcome for a plan to help starving children chafed against loyalties to the Catholic Church and its agents within private and public arenas.

It is worth noting that for all the collective support given to Dublin households during the lockout, family strategies were also deployed to oppose it. It has already been noted that the Archbishop's appeal was made directly to Catholic mothers in the city, and their religious duty confounded with their concern for their families. Yet in law only the fathers' permission to let children travel was recognised. A division between parents was played up in the opposition press. On the first day of the fracas when mothers were questioned, they, 'with one exception, not only protested against allowing the children to go but expressed their vehement opposition to it'. Whilst the supporters claimed mothers and fathers still came to register their children to travel, 'despite the ecclesiastical frowns', the *Irish Catholic*, owned by William Martin Murphy, reported reaction to a priest's challenge, 'Will you send your children to England?':

> There were some murmurs of dissent among a body of men present, but the women were unanimous against sending their children away.[33]

The archbishop returned to the lockout in a public statement at the Dublin convention of the St. Vincent de Paul in Dublin, the leading Roman Catholic charity in the city, to which press reporters had been invited. There he spoke once again of the deportation of 'our Catholic children to England', to homes 'unfit as guardians of Catholic children', but his public opposition to the scheme, he went on to explain was not based, 'exclusively upon that highly objectionable feature of it':

The fantastic policy, as I have called it of spending money in taking the children away for what I hear is called a holiday can do no real good. It can have but one permanent result, and that surely is the very reverse of a beneficent one. It will but make them discontented with the poor homes to which they will sooner or later return.[34]

Delia Larkin visited the children in Liverpool, in an effort to reassure their parents and report in the union paper on their schooling, religious instruction and church attendance. In a passage that also contrasts the children's change of circumstances, she wrote:

The house they are staying at is beautifully situated, having a large field at the back belonging to it were the children can play. Their bedrooms are beautifully arranged and airy; their beds comfortable and warm. Each child is supplied with night attire, and they are being taught the healthy habit of changing all their day clothes when going to bed and putting on their night clothes. They are also taught the clean and healthy habit of taking bath; as a matter of fact they are living as human beings should live.[35]

The following week, in a face-saving statement, the end of the plan to send children away was formally announced:

In view of the bad weather now prevailing along the coast, it will be wise not to expose the Transport Workers' children to long and rough sea passages and they will therefore use the money to give free breakfasts ….

It was planned to provide 250 children with a daily meal before school, under a notice that stated, 'The English workers invite the Dublin children to breakfast', so as to, 'differentiate between the comradely action of fellow workers and the charity doles of clericals and bourgeoisie'.[36]

Some weeks earlier, in late September, an editorial in the Irish women's suffrage newspaper, the *Irish Citizen*, had remarked:

Ireland is not yet accustomed to labour struggles; and the organisation of food supplies for the suffering women and children, which is promptly attended to on the occurrence of disputes in Great Britain, has never been undertaken here on a large scale.[37]

By the end of the year, the *Daily Herald* reported:

The work has grown to such proportions that five rooms in Liberty Hall are set aside for the various activities in connection with the administration of the Fund… . Employed in various categories are the locked out and victimised girls unionists; while a tram-way man cooks the daily dinners for the mothers, and another transport worker prepares the 3,000 children's breakfasts.[38]

In other rooms women stitched clothing and stored the clothes and boots for daily distribution. At the end of the lockout in February 1914, the organisers reported that between 12 November to 28 February the breakfast room had fed three thousand children every morning, and '2,907 children and 150 maternity cases' had been dressed. From 12 December they began to provide dinner for nursing mothers. The effort had twenty-two staff to help, which included visits to families at home.[39]

The events of the 1913 lockout were played out in a year of contested futures for Ireland. The promise of self-government in a Home Rule parliament had heightened Ireland's political culture and divided alliances into two contending camps. The months of long conflict between employer and worker had eclipsed the constitutional issues and suggested an alternative to the political prospects of both the nationalist and unionist blocs. In the outburst of conflicting loyalties in the lockout sensational and unbidden anxieties were articulated in emotional appeals, not only to religious obligation or against proselytising. White slavery, kidnapping, anti-Semitism and sexual misconduct were all invoked. George Bernard Shaw told a London meeting that it was being said in Dublin that parents wanted to be rid of their children to misbehave sexually. The archbishop of Dublin's secretary called up alarming transgressions and precedents in the behaviour he noticed on Dublin streets:

> The women and even young girls were simply barbarian maniacs, yelling and practically threatening the police and trammel them with their fists. I could only compare it to the French revolution.[40]

Even those who were removed from the cockpit of the struggle were touched by the ripples of the Dublin lockout. The Pankhurst leadership of the Women's Political and Social Union divided over Sylvia Pankhurst's attendance at the London rally, which, by the account of her sister Christabel and her mother, Emmeline, broke the political neutrality and compromised the independence of the British women's suffrage movement. For syndicalists like the Industrial Workers of the World (IWW), Dublin was engaging with their own conventions of struggle. Bill Haywood, the IWW organiser, joined James Larkin on his crusade through British cities. Haywood travelled to Dublin telling the afternoon meeting outside Liberty Hall, 'its the happiest day of his life to be with them'.[41] Inside Liberty Hall Haywood recalls he was impressed to see the familiar letters IWW. 'I learned later that these letters stood for "Irish Women Workers"'. He returned to speak at a programme of meetings with Larkin in Britain, before he returned to the US.[42] Elizabeth Gurley Flynn told the New York Civic Forum in a report, 'The Truth about the Paterson Strike', only days before the dispute in Dublin ended:

> In Ireland today there is a wonderful strike going on and they are standing by it beautifully ....[43]

The closedown of Dublin's trade and industry in the deadlock between employers and workers turned the union on a course that transformed household strategies of survival into collective action. The precarious household economies of Dublin workers survived on the margins of subsistence. Their need forced the embattled union to devise an ambitious programme to support their members and their dependants. It combined traditional trade union appeals for funds with communal effort to feed the city's starving families. The opening of Liberty Hall as a strike kitchen placed the union headquarters at the centre of family survival. The scale and duration of the Dublin 1913 lockout made it essential to employ household-based strategies in the union's collective action. It was not a project entirely of its own choosing. It was achieved by igniting a cauldron of discontents and extending the mobilisation far beyond the ranks of its members. Family loyalty survived as an enduring trait of Dublin trade unionism, maintained most characteristically as a Larkinite legacy. Whilst this inheritance was shaped by later events, its origins remain in the struggles and sacrifices of the 1913 lockout. The vast undertaking and the responsibilities that the children's plan acknowledged in industrial disputes did not translate into any permanent organisational commitment by Dublin trade unionism to household participation in industrial action. Strike pay remained the enduring trade union contribution, rather than the mobilisation of family dependants. Community or neighbourly support survived as a private, not a public resource. The children's plan had not been unique to the Dublin lockout. It was an expression of a formal relationship between members, their households and the labour movement, which all too often remains invisible and unorganised during industrial disputes. The socialists of the time embraced this in the word *solidarity*.

Notes

1. Emmet Larkin, *James Larkin, Irish Labour Leader, 1876–1947*, London, 1965, remains the standard biography. Donal Nevin, ed., *James Larkin: Lion of the Fold*, Dublin, 1998, is the most comprehensive treatment of Larkin's life and legacy.
2. Quoted in Bob Holton, *British Syndicalism, 1900–1914: Myths and Realities*, London, 1976, 189.
3. Jim Phelan, *The Name's Phelan*, Belfast, 1993, 148.
4. The metaphor of the kaleidoscope was used by Sean O'Casey in his autobiographies to represent the changing events of the lockout.
5. *Votes for Women*, 24 October 1913.
6. In the occupations of heads of families occupying tenement houses in the city 1,195 were listed as charwomen, the largest group registered after 9,542 labourers, *Report of the Departmental Committee appointed by the Local Government Board for Ireland to inquire into the Housing Conditions of the Working Classes in the City of Dublin*, Dublin, 1914, Appendix XXIV, 348. (This report is cited later as *Dublin Housing Inquiry*).
7. *Votes for Women*, 24 October 1913.
8. *Daily Herald*, 3 November 1913.
9. Arnold Wright, *Disturbed Dublin: the Story of the Great Strike of 1913–14*, London, 1914.
10. *Dublin Housing Inquiry, (Minutes of Evidence)*, 28.
11. Curriculum Development Unit, *Divided City: Portrait of Dublin 1913*, Dublin, 1978, 38.
12. Sean O'Casey, *Three Plays*, London, 1969, 180.
13. *Dublin Housing Inquiry*, 6.
14. Joseph Quaney, *A Penny to Nelson's Pillar*, Portlaw, 1971, 189.
15. D.A. Chart, 'Unskilled Labour in Dublin: Its Housing and Living Conditions', *Irish Social and Statistical Bulletin*, Part 4, 1914, 168.
16. Quaney, *A Penny to Nelson's Pillar*, 189.
17. Quoted in Curriculum Development Unit, *Divided City*, 47.
18. John Cooke, *Dublin Housing Inquiry (Minutes of Evidence)*, 102.
19. Patrick Dillon, Assistant Superintendent of Dwellings, *Dublin Housing Inquiry*, 37.

20. John Cooke, *Dublin Housing Inquiry (Minutes of evidence)*, 102.
21. Patrick Dillon, *Dublin Housing Inquiry (Minutes of evidence)*, 38–9.
22. Edmund Eyre, City Treasurer, *Dublin Housing Inquiry*, 29.
23. James Connolly, 'Glorious Dublin', in *The Workers' Republic*, ed. Desmond Ryan, Dublin, 1951, 123.
24. Harry Gosling, *Up and Down Stream*, London, 1927; quoted in Ken Coates and Tony Topham, *The History of the Transport and General Workers' Union*, Oxford, 1991, volume 1, part II, 474.
25. *Daily Herald*, 20 October 1913.
26. *Liverpool Daily Post and Mercury*, 2 December 1913, quoted in Holton, *British Syndicalism 1900–1914*, 188.
27. Larkin, *James Larkin*, 163.
28. TUC Parliamentary Committee, *Dublin Food Fund. Statement of Accounts and Complete List of Grants, Donations, Collections and Personal Contributions*, London, Co-op Printing Society, 1914. The bulk of the money, almost £63,000, was paid to the Co-op for food and clothing brought by the food ships to Dublin.
29. *Daily Herald*, 20 October 1913.
30. Dora B. Montefiore, *From a Victorian to a Modern*, London, 1927, 156.
31. Elizabeth Gurley Flynn, *I Speak My Own Piece: Autobiography of 'The Rebel Girl'*, New York, 1955, 26.
32. Montefiore, *From a Victorian to a Modern*, 160.
33. *Irish Catholic*, 25 October 1913.
34. *Freeman's Journal*, 28 October 1913.
35. *Irish Worker*, 8 November 1913.
36. *Daily Herald*, 14 November 1913.
37. *Irish Citizen*, 27 September 1913.
38. *Daily Herald*, 24 December 1913.
39. *Irish Worker*, 4 March 1914.
40. Curran to Walsh, 28 August, 1913, Dublin Diocesan Archives, Walsh Papers, 1913, 377/5.
41. *Freeman's Journal*, 1 December 1913.
42. *Daily Herald*, 2 December 1913.
43. Elizabeth Gurley Flynn, 'The Truth about the Paterson Strike', quoted in *Rebel Voices: An IWW Anthology*, ed. Joyce L. Kornbluh, Ann Arbor, 1964, 221.

Bibliography

Chart, D.A. 'Unskilled labour in Dublin: its housing and living conditions', *Irish Social and Statistical Bulletin*, Part 4 (1914).

Coates, K. and Topham, T. *The History of the Transport and General Workers' Union*, vol.1, part II. Oxford, 1991.

Connolly, J. 'Glorious Dublin', in *The Workers' Republic*, ed. D. Ryan. Dublin, 1951.

Curriculum Development Unit, *Divided City: Portrait of Dublin 1913*. Dublin, 1978.

Flynn, E.G. *I speak my own piece: Autobiography of 'The Rebel Girl*. New York, 1955.

Gosling, H. *Up and Down Stream*. London, 1927.

Holton, B. *British Syndicalism, 1900–1914: Myths and Realities*. London, 1976.

Kornbluh, J.L., *Rebel Voices: An IWW Anthology*. Ann Arbor, 1964.

Larkin, E. *James Larkin, Irish Labour Leader, 1876–1947*. London, 1965.

Montefiore, D.B. *From a Victorian to a Modern*. London, 1927.

Nevin, D., ed. *James Larkin: Lion of the Fold*. Dublin, 1998.

O'Casey, S. *Three Plays*. London, 1969.

Phelan, J. *The Name's Phelan*. Belfast, 1993.

Quaney, J. *A Penny to Nelson's Pillar*. Portlaw, 1971.

Wright, A. *Disturbed Dublin: the Story of the Great Strike of 1913–14*. London, 1914.

CHAPTER 7

FAMILY TIES AND LABOUR ACTIVISM AMONG SILK WORKERS IN NORTHEASTERN PENNSYLVANIA, U.S.A., 1900–1920

Bonnie Stepenoff

Is your daughter so much stronger physically that she is able to work ten to fifteen hours for small pay, when your son works only eight hours (if a member of an organization) and for the best pay that collective bargaining can produce?
United Mine Workers Journal, 11 January 1912.[1]

As a private living strategy[2], working-class families have often sent minors and dependent children out to work. Families as well as employers defined these young people, especially those who were female, as secondary wage earners, who could never do more than supplement the income of the primary, usually male, breadwinner. When male heads of multi-income households embraced public strategies,[3] such as union membership, secondary wage earners often remained in the background, bringing home needed income, but refraining, or being discouraged, from active involvement in labour organisations.

In the anthracite (hard coal) mining region in the northeastern section of the state of Pennsylvania in the eastern United States (see map), thousands of male workers joined the United Mine Workers of America (UMWA) and went out on strike in 1900 and 1902. Miners' daughters, who worked in hundreds of silk mills in the region, emulated their fathers and participated in several strikes in the early twentieth century. Local miners' unions sometimes supported female-led protests, but more often undercut these efforts by portraying the silk workers as waif-like children unable to speak or act on their own behalf. Families encouraged active union membership over long periods of time as a strategy for adult males, struggling to support households, but not for female workers, who were mostly single, young, secondary wage earners contributing to the income of their parents' households.

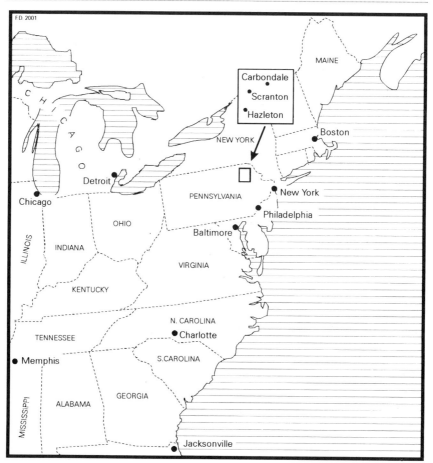

Map 7.1 *The hard-coal region of Pennsylvania, U.S.A.*

Silk mill workers in Pennsylvania's northeastern towns and cities enthusiastically participated in strikes in 1897, 1900–01, and 1907, but in 1920 they
remained largely unorganised. Union silk workers in the neighbouring state of
New Jersey lamented competition from non-union Pennsylvania mills.[4] Orga-
nizers for the Amalgamated Textile Workers of America, founded in 1919,
had success in Paterson, New Jersey, and several other North American textile
centres, but discovered that northeastern Pennsylvania was 'different'.[5] Silk
workers there proved difficult to mobilise for a complex set of reasons involving the nature of the silk industry, but also reflecting the gender, age and family relationships of the workers.

By the 1870s, western European industrialists had mechanised the production of silk thread. In Japan, where silk reeling was a traditional handicraft,
the government and private enterprise recruited girls and young women to
leave their homes and work in western-style factories, producing machine-
reeled silk.[6] Silk reelers in Kofu walked out of the mills in the summer of
1886, protesting wage cuts, long hours, harsh conditions, and favouritism.

Employers locked them out, and the strike ended in defeat.[7] In February 1898, workers struck the silk mill at Tomoku, protesting poor food in boarding houses, a shortened New Year holiday, and Sunday work. Some of the silk reelers' fathers reportedly joined in the week-long protest, but the strike failed.[8] Between 1898 and 1912, Japanese employers tightened their hold on the workers, making it difficult or impossible for them to change jobs, and denying them any autonomous bargaining power.[9]

In the mineral-laden hills of northeastern Pennsylvania, during this time period, manufacturers also recruited girls and young women to work in throwing mills, producing silk thread as well as organzine and tram, the warp and weft of silk fabric. This was a new industry for the region, which possessed unique deposits of anthracite in a rural area close to the urban centres of Philadelphia (Pennsylvania) and New York City. The region's hard coal industry employed only males. Local business leaders eagerly courted a secondary industry that would offer employment to young unmarried women, who would bring wages home to help support parents and siblings. Independent merchants hoped to break the hold of the coal company stores, by developing gainful employment for female workers. Even where company stores did not operate, businessmen hoped to boost sales by encouraging an additional source of family income.[10]

Silk companies built plants in the cities, towns, and villages of the anthracite region expressly to take advantage of the cheap labour of girls and young women. In the 1840s and 1850s, a large number of European manufacturers, labourers, and weavers immigrated and established a thriving silk centre in Paterson, New Jersey, south of New York City.[11] In the mid-1880s, the Knights of Labor organised silk workers there.[12] Rising labour militancy and the introduction of laws against child labour in New Jersey induced entrepreneurs to look elsewhere for new plant locations.[13] Inventions of new machinery made it increasingly possible to employ unskilled labour, especially in the silk throwing (winding or reeling) plants.[14] Lured by cheap fuel and a large supply of labour, manufacturers moved their throwing plants into the hills and valleys of northeastern Pennsylvania.[15] Testifying before a commission of the United States government, silk mill owners acknowledged that their Pennsylvania throwing mills employed a much higher percentage of females and children than their weaving and other plants in Paterson, which relied largely on adult male labour. The silk company executives cited the laxness of child labour laws and the availability of female labour as inducements to setting up for business in Pennsylvania. In addition, they reported that labour troubles in Paterson had caused them to relocate some plants 'so that labour troubles in one place will not control the whole industry'.[16]

Several characteristics of the silk industry discouraged unionisation. A large number of mills and mill owners made it difficult to negotiate settlements that applied uniformly throughout the industry. Operations were highly mobile. The United States never successfully bred silkworms, and manufacturers continued to import the raw material for silk thread, yarn, and cloth from China, Japan, and Italy. Their chief consideration in choosing a location was the availability of labour.[17] Threatened with militant labour action in one locality, owners could easily move some or all of the milling processes to another area.

As previously noted, this was often their motivation for moving from New Jersey to Pennsylvania. In the Pennsylvania mills, a high percentage of female and child labourers appeared to be a deterrent to union militancy.

Despite these conditions, Pennsylvania's silk workers showed a willingness to strike for better wages and shorter hours. As the Japanese silk reelers had demonstrated, gender and youth did not prevent workers from engaging in labour protests. In October 1897, seventy-five silk workers who failed to appear for their shift at the mill in the small town of Avoca sent a letter to the proprietor, demanding a wage increase.[18] On the second day of the walk-out, strikers pelted non-striking operatives with stones and eggs. A mêlée ensued, and the mill owner demanded the arrest of six girls and three boys for rioting.[19] Operations resumed the next day with no increase in wages. If the trouble continued, the owners threatened to move the factory to New Jersey.[20]

Many male workers in the hard coal region – the fathers and brothers of the silk reelers – responded to union organisers and engaged in massive strikes against the anthracite companies in 1900 and 1902. As president of the UMWA, an affiliate of the American Federation of Labor (AFL), John Mitchell united hundreds of thousands of miners and mine labourers, including many recent immigrants, in a challenge to the authority of the owners. From May until the end of October 1902, he held nearly 150,000 miners together in a non-violent strike that threatened to cripple many cities in the eastern United States by creating a fuel crisis. The strike went down in history when President Theodore Roosevelt prevailed upon mine owners to accept arbitration by a special federal board, the Anthracite Coal Strike Commission. In March 1903, the Commission approved a settlement favourable to the miners, and Mitchell became a hero.[21]

The elderly, tough-talking, Mary Harris (Mother) Jones, came to Pennsylvania as a UMWA organiser to goad, chide, and encourage the miners in mass protests. She was a brilliant agitator, much more militant than the conservative Mitchell. With fiery rhetoric and a motherly presence, she inspired wives and daughters to get out and make a noise in support of striking breadwinners, but she had a very traditional view of the family. Her goal was to raise miners' wages to a level that would make it possible for them to support female dependants. She conveyed a very mixed message to female wage-earners, even when she offered them her support. While she regarded miners as strong and able to stand up for themselves, she often portrayed female textile workers as the helpless victims of capitalistic greed.[22]

Within this context of miners' activism, female silk hands became militant in the winter and spring of 1900–01.[23] At least one manufacturer viewed their protests as a 'sympathy strike' resulting from 'the labour troubles in the coal business in October'[24] but the silk mill girls showed a strong desire to take action on their own behalf. In December 1900, young workers walked out of the Klots mill in Carbondale, a small city in the northern section of the anthracite coalfields. Men from various unions in the city met with Klots management and, at first, urged the strikers to settle. A committee of strikers protested, saying the men who claimed to represent them 'knew nothing about silk, the way it's spun, the frames, the crates, or anything connected with it'.[25]

Several UMWA locals agreed to put pressure on their members to allow their children to join in the silk strike.[26] A delegation of strikers attended a miners' union meeting in Jermyn, a town near Carbondale, and asked the men to place pressure on the parents of silk workers.[27] With support from their fathers, silk workers in Carbondale remained off the job, and the strike extended to other communities.

By February 1901, the strike had spread to Scranton, the largest city in the hard coal region, where 2,800 workers walked out of four mills.[28] The local newspaper reported that some of the protesters joined a branch of the Silk Weavers of America and others joined a local of the Textile Workers. With a hint of admiration, the reporter noted that 'To organize the silk workers is a difficult task, as the bulk of the girls are from 12 to 16 years of age and are very enthusiastic'.[29]

At a mass meeting in Scranton on 18 February 1901, Mother Jones gave a rousing speech, declaring that, 'The girls were living under a system of robbery and demoralisation of body and soul'.[30] Her words echoed those of many who crusaded against child labour and insisted that factory work posed a threat to the moral development of children. In subsequent statements, she condemned lax enforcement of child labour laws in Pennsylvania. She also blamed parents, especially immigrants, for allowing their children to work and even filing false affidavits concerning their children's ages.[31] An editorial in the Scranton newspaper took up the issue and argued that if child labour were not available, adult workers would fill the jobs at 'adult wages'. [32]

Mother Jones apparently played a crucial role in bringing the strike to an end. At her urging, the strikers accepted a negotiated settlement.[33] By the end of April, most mill owners had agreed to an 8 to 10 percent wage increase on timed work, some small increases in piece rates, a half-holiday with pay on Saturdays in summer, and some improvements in working conditions, including seats for workers on their dinner breaks.[34] To celebrate the modest victory, Mother Jones led a parade of little girls accompanied by boys who belonged to the newsboys and bootblacks unions, drawing attention to the issue of child labour.[35] Two years later, in 1903, she led a pathetic march of young textile workers from Philadelphia, Pennsylvania, to Sagamore Hill at Oyster Bay, Long Island, New York, to impress vacationing President Roosevelt with the need for reform.[36]

In the winter of 1902–03, the hearings of the Anthracite Coal Strike Commission brought national attention to the hard lives of the silk mill girls. Clarence Darrow, who represented striking anthracite miners, called their daughters to the stand in support of the UMWA demand for higher wages. Girls of twelve and thirteen testified that they worked ten and twelve-hour shifts in the silk mill to add to the income of miners' families. Some of the girls worked night shifts, and few attended school. Darrow argued eloquently that the fathers' inadequate wages made their children easy prey for greedy entrepreneurs seeking a cheap labour force.[37]

Writing for *McClure's Magazine* in 1903, Francis H. Nichols observed the behaviour of working-class children in the anthracite region, where every child of ten could remember two great strikes.[38] Nichols commented intriguingly, though disapprovingly, on their tendency to imitate the behaviour of their militant fathers. He wrote about young boys who spent their days working in the coal breakers, picking slate from the mined coal, and their free time in make-shift union halls, listening to speeches and learning to picket. Interestingly, he also observed young girls, who held down jobs in the silk mills, dressing up for union meetings and learning the language of labour militancy.[39] As a middle-class social critic, he found this behaviour shocking. Especially ironic, in his view, was the fact that schoolhouses often served as union halls.[40] In his view, boys and girls should have been enrolled in those schools, learning solid American values, not lurking around after hours, learning radical dogma; but he had come to the region during a period of labour protest.

The successful conclusion of the great Anthracite Coal Strike left a mixed legacy in northeastern Pennsylvania. Mitchell's leadership helped the miners to maintain solidarity for six months of privation and fear. His willingness to negotiate with business and government leaders resulted in well-publicised hearings and an arbitrated settlement favourable to the miners. The UMWA became entrenched in the region, and Mitchell became a legend. However, he was a very ambivalent labour hero, who hated strikes and proved all too willing to mingle with wealthy capitalists. He lost the union presidency in 1908, and many staunch unionists condemned his affiliation with an alliance of business leaders called the National Civic Federation (NCF). Personally, he sank into alcoholism and obscurity.[41] Still, he remained an icon in Pennsylvania's hard coal region, where John Mitchell Day became an annual holiday, on which miners and their families relived the victory parades of 1900 and 1902.[42]

Some silk workers continued to emulate the miners in strident labour protests. In spring 1903, two hundred workers, mostly girls, struck the Empire mill in Simpson.[43] As in the 1900–01 strike, UMWA locals offered support and advice that resulted in a negotiated settlement. The Scranton newspaper reported that UMWA representatives attended a meeting of the mill employees, noting, as follows:

> Henry Collins, of the executive committee of the United Mine Workers; Stephen Reap, of Olyphant, a member of the district committee; James Heenan, president of local No. 36, and Thomas Callahan, president of the Central Labour union, were present at the meeting and the settlement of the strike is due in large measure to the advice and good offices of these men.[44]

Management conceded employees' demands for a bi-weekly pay-packet and a half-holiday on Saturdays, but offered no pay raises. The local newspaper reported that the mill's employees joined the United Textile Workers (UTW), a union established in 1901 and affiliated with the AFL.[45]

Strikes erupted in Pennsylvania's silk mills in the summer of 1907. By the end of July about two thousand young labourers had walked out of mills in Scranton, including the Sauquoit, Renard, and Harvey mills. The *Scranton Republican* reported that most of the strikers were boys and girls between twelve and sixteen years of age. Apparently, girls were in the forefront of the walk-out, as the newspaper recounted on 25 July 1907, 'The girls who are leading the movement for an eight-hour day are advising their fellow workers to maintain the strictest order'. Workers at the Sauquoit mill in Scranton demanded a reduction in the length of shifts, which typically began at seven in the morning and ended at six in the evening with only a half hour off for dinner.[46]

As more and more workers walked out of mills in Scranton, Avoca, Dunmore, Forrest City, Olyphant, and other cities and towns, the UTW sent organisers to the region.[47] By early August, five thousand strikers packed halls, listening to pleas to join the union. Most of the protesters were female, and many embraced the union message, as the local newspaper reported:

> At the meeting yesterday afternoon, one might well be struck with the need of the girls – for girls they were, and more on the order of children than girls even – for a vacation. Peaked face girls in short dresses sat side by side with young ladies robust and strong and seemingly well able to undertake the arduous work of silk weaving, and everyone present was enthusiastic for organization.[48]

In mid-August, the newspapers may have exaggerated in stating that about six thousand workers had joined the UTW, but clearly the union did appeal successfully to the workers, in spite of their gender and youth.[49]

Despite the militancy and independence of the young women, fathers and father figures, including male union leaders, ultimately stepped in to try and settle the strike. Local 808 of the UMWA held a large meeting in Scranton and passed a resolution offering 'moral and financial support to the silk workers' and endorsing a reduction in the hours of labour.[50] A few mill managers agreed to reduce the working week to fifty hours, but other mills held out for the fifty-eight to sixty-hour working week even for children. The UTW sought help from Rt. Revd Monsignor T.F. Coffey, pastor of the St. Rose Church in Carbondale, as an arbitrator.[51] In the end it was impossible even for these male authority figures to win settlements with all the mill owners, many of whom threatened to move their plants out of the region. Gradually, the workers returned to their jobs after striking various bargains with individual mill owners.

The all-out effort of the UTW in Scranton in 1907 yielded disappointing results. Settlements reached by mediation did not narrow the wage differential between Pennsylvania's mills and those in Paterson. Gains in union membership proved short-lived, and Paterson unionists continued to fret about the need to organise Pennsylvania's workers.[52] Faced with union resistance in Paterson, silk manufacturers could threaten to move plants across the state line.

The youth and gender of the workers prompted the United States government to investigate conditions in Pennsylvania's silk industry. A Congressional committee, which began its work in 1907, reported in 1911 that Pennsylvania dominated the silk throwing industry, producing 62 percent of American silk yarn and thread, while New Jersey continued to lead in the production of finished silk fabric.[53] Between 1870 and 1900, the percentage of child labour decreased in New Jersey's silk industry, but increased dramatically in Pennsylvania's mills.[54] In the thirty-six Pennsylvania factories studied, only 9 percent of workers were adult males (over the age of sixteen); 68 percent were adult females, and 23 percent were children.[55] By contrast in Paterson's mills, 39 percent of workers were adult males; 54 percent were adult females, and only 7 percent were children.[56] Of the female workers in Pennsylvania's mills, only 3.3 percent were married; in Paterson, 11.7 percent of the female workers were married.[57] Overwhelmingly, whether they were adults or children, Pennsylvania's silk workers were unmarried females, who were secondary wage earners living in the households of their parents. Wage scales reflected complex divisions by task and skill, but the differential between Pennsylvania and New Jersey was dramatic. Average weekly earnings (based on a fifty-five-hour week) for Paterson's silk workers amounted to $10.66; for Pennsylvania's workers, the average was $5.12.[58]

Journalists and reformers wrote impassioned denunciations of the evils of child labour in the Pennsylvania silk mills. Socialist writer John Spargo excoriated the silk industry for employing child labour in his defamatory book, *The Bitter Cry of the Children*. Like many reformers, Spargo argued that factory labour corrupted young girls and made them prematurely old. Silk making, he wrote, posed health risks for young girls, who had to stand all day in hot, humid mills amid thundering machines.[59] Far worse, in his view, was the moral atmosphere of the mills, where innocent children came into contact with worldly and sometimes predatory adults, who taught them inappropriate language and behaviour.[60]

In 1910, Florence Sanville went under cover and obtained a job in one of the factories. Conditions in the mill were harsh. Workers stood by their machines all day and even had to stand during their dinner breaks. Sanville failed to note any union activity among young female silk operatives, but she commented on the social bonds they formed both in the mill and after working hours. Mill hands gossiped and socialised freely in ways that the strait-laced Sanville found unladylike. Clearly, she believed her young female co-workers would be better off in school, learning proper moral values, while receiving an education that represented their only hope of escaping the drudgery of factory life. The other option was early marriage, which Sanville lamented as the fate of most young girls in the hard coal region.[61]

Perhaps the most eloquent protester against child labour, Edwin Markham, created a sentimental image of frail young girls robbed of their childhood by the necessity of constant mind-numbing toil. In his book *Children in Bondage*, he contrasted the ideal middle-class child in frilly dresses and long flowing curls with the pale exhausted mill girls, who had to tie back their skirts and cut off their curls so they would not get caught in huge, merciless silk-reeling machines.[62] Markham bitterly condemned silk manufacturers for exploiting young girls in the hard coal region. He quoted the manager of a silk-throwing plant in South Bethlehem (in the Lehigh Valley, south of the hard coal region) as saying, 'The coal-fields is the ideal place for a silk-throwing plant. You get rent cheap, and coal cheap, and labour cheap, and parents don't object to having their children work nights'.[63]

The scandalmongers had a valid point. In 1898 there were approximately eighty-eight silk mills in Pennsylvania, employing 20,365 workers, of whom 3,932 (19 percent) were children sixteen years of age or younger.[64] By 1905, more than 150 silk mills employed 26,918 workers, of whom 4,737 (17.6 percent) were children under seventeen.[65] The Pennsylvania State Factory Inspector reported an alarming rate of child labour in the state. An investigation of the state's manufacturing establishments in 1905 revealed that at least 40,000 workers, about 6 percent of the factory workforce, were children aged thirteen to sixteen. Half of these were girls.[66] In the silk industry, the percentage of child labour was three times the state average. Children who had reached the age of thirteen and were literate could legally be employed. However, the factory inspector noted a reckless disregard for child welfare, stating that:

> There are many children employed in gainful occupations who, because of their physical deterioration as a result of this employment, or for physical deficiencies the result of other causes, appear to be of an age less than thirteen.[67]

Yet these children had affidavits signed by their parents, affirming that they were of legal age.

Despite these disturbing conditions, the fact remained that most silk workers were not children, but young women over the age of sixteen. Census data indicated that in 1905 the silk mills of Pennsylvania employed 6,318 males over the age of sixteen, 4,737 male and female children under sixteen, and 15,863 females over the age of sixteen. Adult women comprised about 60 percent of the workforce. Granted, many of these women were very young, and some may have been debilitated by starting work at an earlier, and much too tender, age; but many were, as the Scranton newspaper put it, 'young ladies robust and strong and seemingly well able to undertake the arduous work'.[68]

Whether they were children or adults, most silk workers were secondary wage earners, living in households headed by their fathers. In Paterson, many silk workers were primary breadwinners and heads of households. Only a tiny fraction of Pennsylvania's silk operatives fit this description. Census data and government surveys confirmed the profile of the Pennsylvania silk worker as a young single female, who brought home wages to help support parents and siblings. Close study of payroll records and census data for workers in Carbondale, a typical silk-producing town, confirmed that even silk workers in their twenties and thirties continued to live in the homes of their parents, sometimes helping to support widowed mothers or supplementing the income of disabled fathers. Many lived in households headed by miners or coal mine labourers, whose employment might be sporadic or interrupted by injuries and illness.[69]

Historian John Bodnar described the pattern of life and labour in the hard coal region that shaped the lives of female silk workers. Growing up in a working family in the early twentieth century meant that childhood was a brief interlude followed by early departure from school and immediate entry into the working world. Young workers, both male and female, turned over their earnings to their parents, whose livelihood depended on a the volatile and dangerous mining industry. Support for parents continued at least until marriage, and when fathers were ill or disabled, might go on for a lifetime.[70]

Female silk workers did participate in strikes in the first decade of the twentieth century, but their status as daughters in working families tended to discourage participation in union activities. In order to join in labour protests, these young women needed and sought permission from their fathers. During the great upheavals of 1900 and 1901, committees of silk workers went to meetings of the UMWA, asking miners to put pressure on their union brothers to allow their daughters to walk out of the mills. The miners supported the young women's protests, but silk mill owners viewed them as sympathy strikes inspired by and secondary to the uprising of the anthracite miners.

Strikes originated and led by young single females consistently ended in settlements negotiated by leaders of male unions. Despite her gender, even Mother Jones represented the power and solidarity of a male organisation, the UMWA. When she spoke of female silk operatives, she used language that made them appear weak, vulnerable, and in need of protection from exploitation in the mills. Through her words and actions, she drew attention to the problem of child labour, often seeming to categorise all the silk mill operatives as children. Her priority was always to raise the wages of miners so they could support their daughters, eliminating the need for female wage labour.

In the first two decades of the twentieth century, union efforts to organise Pennsylvania's silk workers had disappointing results, despite the presence of active male unions in the region. In 1912 the *United Mine Workers Journal* reprinted an editorial from *Life and Labour* addressed 'To the Wives of Union Men'. The writer urged these wives and mothers to allow their daughters to join unions. Apparently there was a double standard in working families. According to the editorial:

> Of course, you rather expect your son will eventually join a union because he is in industry to stay, and in order to earn the best wages and working conditions it is to his advantage to join a union!
>
> But what of your daughter? When you send her out for a position you figure she is only working for a few short years (till she marries) and salary is not of much importance.[71]

The writer took issue with this position, which, however, appeared to be the prevailing one among the wives of union men.

Social reformers reinforced the dependent status of silk workers by portraying them as fragile female children, endangered by their very presence in the mills. Even Sanville, who worked with robust young women and observed their feisty independence, depicted factory work as a corrupting influence and urged that girls be removed from that environment. Stereotyping female mill workers as weak, exploited creatures undercut their ability to stand up for themselves, demanding a better deal from employers.

The irony of all this tender concern was that it may have prevented girls and young women from acting to improve appalling conditions in the mills. As the 1912 editorial writer pointed out, frail females often worked longer hours for much lower pay than their male counterparts. Signing herself 'A Union Man's Wife', she wrote:

> Is your daughter so much stronger physically that she is able to work ten to fifteen hours for small pay, when your son works only eight hours (if a member of an organization) and for the best pay that collective bargaining can produce?[72]

Appealing to mothers, she clearly hoped to influence working men to let their daughters join unions. The urgent tone of the editorial indicated that there was strong resistance to the idea of female union membership.

In January 1913, the Industrial Workers of the World (IWW) led a history-making silk strike in Paterson, New Jersey. After an exhilarating victory in the 1912 textile strike in Lawrence, Massachusetts, the IWW had high hopes for success. One of the strike leaders, the 'Rebel Girl', Elizabeth Gurley Flynn, commented on the vicious way Paterson authorities tried to suppress demonstrations, harassing the protestors with police brutality, arrests, and trials.[73] Nevertheless, the IWW persisted with mass meetings, picketing, children's meetings, and even a grand pageant in New York's Madison Square Garden.[74]

With emotions running high, IWW organisers tried hard to recruit Pennsylvania silk workers to their cause. At first, they received some support from the UMWA. Flynn reported going to the anthracite region to mobilise girls who were working for Paterson-based companies. The local miners' union allowed IWW organisers to use their hall. Since many of the girls were miners' daughters, they agreed not to work on Paterson orders.[75] The UTW also sent organisers to Pennsylvania, reporting the creation of nine new local branches in Scranton.[76]

In February, twelve-hundred workers struck the Duplan silk mill in Hazleton, Pennsylvania, embraced the IWW, and linked their action to the Paterson strike.[77] Skilled workers, including loom fixers (machinists) immediately condemned the strike, inflaming the strikers.[78] At first, UMWA locals offered help, but by March they changed their position as the Hazleton community turned against the IWW.[79] At noisy public meetings, the UTW and the IWW battled for the workers' favour. Local police, clergy, business leaders, and union locals backed the UTW.[80] In April, the *United Mine Workers Journal* announced a settlement with Duplan,[81] while the Paterson strike dragged on through the summer.

In other towns and cities in northeastern Pennsylvania, silk workers remained at their tasks. Even the argument that Pennsylvania wages were much lower than those in Paterson failed to mobilise Pennsylvania's operatives. The influence of a strong male union, the UMWA, made it difficult for Pennsylvania girls to rally to the IWW standard. Community leaders, clergymen, and others loudly proclaimed the dangers of the radical Wobblies. Many silk workers were dependents in the households of UMWA members; parental authority would be difficult or impossible for them to defy.

The Paterson strike failed for many reasons, including the fact that Pennsylvania's mills remained in operation. Lack of centralisation in the silk industry meant that Paterson's unionists bargained with hundreds of manufacturers, many of whom had plants in the neighbouring state. Flynn complained that, 'they had a means whereby they could fill a large percentage of their orders unless we were able to strike Pennsylvania simultaneously'.[82] This the IWW could not do. In the end, the Paterson strikers divided into factions and settled disputes on a shop-by-shop basis. But the Pennsylvania mills played an important role in allowing manufacturers to fill their orders throughout a crucial period during which the strike reached a crescendo and then dissolved in disharmony.[83]

Analysing the strike, Flynn made inaccurate generalisations about Pennsylvania's silk workers. Looking back on the IWW's failure to win their support, she wrote, 'And those mills employed women and children, wives and children of union weavers, who didn't need actually to work for a living wage, but worked simply to add to the family income'.[84] With this insensitive remark, she misrepresented the female workers, who were not wives and daughters of weavers, but more often than not, daughters of coal miners and mine labourers. She also devalued their important contribution to the income of their households, which depended on male breadwinners employed in a volatile and dangerous industry. Young women who left school at an early age and brought wages home to parents and siblings rarely were volunteers who 'didn't need actually to work'. However, Flynn expressed a widely held attitude that because they were secondary, not primary breadwinners, they really did not need a 'living wage'.[85]

Two decades of effort by the UTW and the IWW failed to create solidarity or to close the wage gap between New Jersey and Pennsylvania silk workers. Beginning in 1919, the Amalgamated Textile Workers of America (ATWA) tried to bring silk operatives into one big textile union. They had some success in Allentown, Pennsylvania, a large industrial city south of the hard coal region, and in New Jersey. ATWA organisers remarked, however, that Pennsylvania was 'different'.[86] Wages were lower and the working week was longer than in New Jersey, and yet strikes were infrequent, and workers remained resistant to organisation. These local and regional differences, along with rivalry among union organisations, resulted in a failure to win fair treatment for workers in the industry.

What was 'different' about Pennsylvania workers? They were far more likely than their counterparts in Paterson to be young single females living in the households of their parents. Gender and youth did not prevent them from engaging in strikes and protests during the first decade of the twentieth century; but their protests took place in a cultural context that devalued their actions because of their position as daughters in working-class families. Typically, they had to ask permission from their fathers to walk off their jobs. Male unions, especially the UMWA, stepped in to sanction and support, but also to control the outcome of labour actions by young female workers. Organisers – even female organisers – for labour associations marginalised the silk workers by portraying them as weak, exploited children or as voluntary wage earners, whose incomes were not really necessary for family survival. The result was that these workers, who were essential to the silk industry and had a crucial role to play in labour disputes, remained largely outside the union fold.

Notes

1. 'To Wives of Union Men', *United Mine Workers Journal*, 11 January 1912.
2. Marcel van der Linden and Jan Lucassen, *Prolegomena for a Global Labor History*, Amsterdam, 1999, 13. Van der Linden and Lucassen have defined and explained the relationships between private and public living strategies.

3. Ibid.
4. David J. Goldberg, *A Tale of Three Cities: Labor Organization and Protest in Paterson, Passaic, and Lawrence, 1916–1921*, New Brunswick, NJ, 1989, 22.
5. *New Textile Worker*, 14 February 1920.
6. E. Patricia Tsurumi, *Factory Girls: Women in the Thread Mills of Meiji Japan*, Princeton, NJ, 1990, 26.
7. Ibid., 55.
8. Ibid., 56–8.
9. Ibid., 73–4.
10. Harold W. Aurand, 'Diversifying the Economy of the Anthracite Regions, 1880–1900', *Pennsylvania Magazine of History and Biography* 94 (January 1970): 56.
11. L.P. Brockett, *The Silk Industry in America*, New York,1876, 115–29; Richard Dobson Margrave, *The Emigration of Silk Workers from England to the United States in the Nineteenth Century*, New York, 1986, 13–7.
12. Schichiro Matsui, *The History of the Silk Industry in the United States*, New York, 1930, 209.
13. Margrave, *Emigration*, 327–30.
14. Matsui, *History*, 49; Margrave, *Emigration*, 319; Steve Golin, *The Fragile Bridge: Paterson Silk Strike, 1913*, Philadelphia, 1988, 21.
15. United States Industrial Commission. *Report of the Industrial Commission on the Relations and Conditions of Capital and Labor Employed in Manufactures and General Business*, Volume 14 of the Commission's Reports, Washington, DC, 1901, 672.
16. Ibid., 680.
17. Matsui, *History*, 1.
18. *Scranton Republican*, 26 October 1897.
19. Ibid., 28 October 1897.
20. Ibid., 29 October 1897.
21. Robert H. Wiebe, 'The Anthracite Strike of 1902: A Record of Confusion', *Mississippi Valley Historical Review* 48 (September 1961): 229.
22. Mother Jones, 'The Wail of the Children', in *Mother Jones Speaks: Collected Writings and Speeches*, ed. Philip S. Foner, New York, 1983, 100–3.
23. Bonnie Stepenoff, 'Keeping it in the Family: Mother Jones and the Pennsylvania Silk Strike of 1900–1901', *Labor History* 38 (Fall 1997): 432–49.
24. U.S. Industrial Commission, *Report*, 680–1.
25. *Scranton Republican*, 8 December 1900.
26. Ibid., 19 December 1900.
27. Ibid., 21 December 1900.
28. Ibid., 3 February 1901.
29. Ibid., 2 February 1901.
30. Ibid., 19 February 1901.
31. Ibid., 25 February 1901.
32. Ibid., 26 February 1901.
33. Ibid., 27 April 1901.
34. Ibid., 29 April 1901.
35. Ibid., 30 April 1901.
36. C.K. McFarland, 'Crusade for Child Laborers: "Mother" Jones and the March of the Mill Children', *Pennsylvania History* 38 (July 1971): 283–96.
37. Bonnie Stepenoff, 'Child Labor in Pennsylvania's Silk Mills: Protest and Change, 1900–1910', *Pennsylvania History* 59 (April 1992): 109–10. Transcripts of the Anthracite Coal Strike Commission testimony are housed in the Michael J. Kosik Collection, Historical Collections and Archives, Pattee Library, Pennsylvania State University.
38. Francis H. Nichols, 'Children of the Coal Shadow', *McClure's Magazine* 20 (February 1903): 436.
39. Ibid., 442.
40. Ibid.
41. Craig Phelan, *Divided Loyalties: The Public and Private Life of Labor Leader John Mitchell*, Albany, 1994, 314.

42. Bonnie Stepenoff, "'Papa on Parade": Pennsylvania Coal Miners' Daughters and the Silk Worker Strike of 1913', *Labor's Heritage* 7 (Winter 1996): 6–21; William J. Walsh, *The United Mine Workers as a Social Force in the Anthracite Territory*, Washington, 1931, 193.

43. *Scranton Republican*, 7 May 1903.

44. Ibid., 16 May 1903.

45. Ibid.

46. Ibid., 25 July 1907.

47. Ibid., 31 July 1907.

48. Ibid., 2 August 1907.

49. Ibid., 16 August 1907.

50. Ibid.

51. Ibid., 29 September 1907.

52. Goldberg, *Tale of Three Cities*, 21–2.

53. United States Congress, Senate, *Report on Condition of Woman and Child Wage-Earners in the United States*, Volume 4: *The Silk Industry*, Washington, DC, 1911, 17–18.

54. Ibid., 33.

55. Ibid., 43.

56. Ibid., 51.

57. Ibid., 58.

58. Ibid., 163.

59. John Spargo, *The Bitter Cry of the Children*, New York, 1909, 177.

60. Ibid., 181–4.

61. Florence Lucas Sanville, 'Home Life of the Silk-Mill Workers', *Harper's Monthly Magazine* (June 1910): 22–31; Sanville, 'A Woman in the Pennsylvania Silk-Mills', *Harper's Monthly Magazine,* April 1910, 651–61.

62. Edwin Markham, *Children in Bondage,* New York, 1914, 156–7.

63. Ibid., 164.

64. United States Department of Labor, *Bulletin of the Department of Labor* Volume 5, Washington, DC, 1900, 600–1.

65. *Report on Condition*, 43.

66. Pennsylvania State Factory Inspector, *Annual Report*, Official Document Number 15, Harrisburg, Pa., 1905, 5–7.

67. Ibid., 6.

68. *Scranton Republican*, 2 August 1907.

69. Stepenoff, 'Child Labor', 113–19.

70. John Bodnar, 'The Family Economy and Labor Protest in Industrial America', in *Hard Coal, Hard Times*, ed. David L. Salay, Scranton, 1984, 85.

71. *United Mine Workers Journal*, 11 January 1912.

72. Ibid.

73. Elizabeth Gurley Flynn, *Rebel Girl: An Autobiography, 1906–1926*, New York, 1973, 160.

74. Ibid., 165–70.

75. Ibid., 167.

76. *United Mine Workers Journal*, 20 March 1913.

77. Patrick M. Lynch, 'Pennsylvania Anthracite: A Forgotten IWW Venture, 1906–1916' (Master's Thesis, Bloomsburg State College, Bloomsburg, Pennsylvania, 1974) 112.

78. Ibid., 115.

79. Ibid., 116.

80. Ibid., 122–29.

81. *United Mine Workers Journal*, 10 April 1913.

82. Elizabeth Gurley Flynn, 'The Truth about the Paterson Strike', in *Rebel Voices: an I.W.W. Anthology*, ed. Joyce L. Kornbluh, Ann Arbor, 1964, 216.

83. Ibid., 224.

84. Ibid., 216.

85. Ibid.

86. *New Textile Worker*, 14 February 1920.

Bibliography

Aurand, H.W. 'Diversifying the Economy of the Anthracite Regions, 1880–1900', *Pennsylvania Magazine of History and Biography* 94 (January 1970).

Bodnar, J. 'The Family Economy and Labour Protest in Industrial America', in *Hard Coal, Hard Times*, ed. David L. Salay. Scranton, 1984.

Brockett, L.P. *The Silk Industry in America*. New York, 1876.

Flynn, E.G. 'The Truth about the Paterson Strike', in *Rebel Voices: an I.W.W. Anthology*, ed. J.L. Kornbluh. Ann Arbor, 1964.

———. *Rebel Girl: An Autobiography, 1906–1926*. New York, 1973.

Goldberg, D.J. *A Tale of Three Cities: Labour Organization and Protest in Paterson, Passaic, and Lawrence, 1916–1921*. New Brunswick, N.J, 1989.

Golin, S. *The Fragile Bridge: Paterson Silk Strike, 1913*. Philadelphia, 1988.

Linden, M. van der, and Lucassen, J. *Prolegomena for a Global Labour History*. Amsterdam, 1999.

Lynch, P.M. 'Pennsylvania Anthracite: A Forgotten IWW Venture, 1906–1916', Master's Thesis, Bloomsburg State College. Bloomsburg, Pennsylvania, 1974.

Margrave, R.D. *The Emigration of Silk Workers from England to the United States in the Nineteenth Century*. New York, 1986.

Markham, E. *Children in Bondage*. New York, 1914.

Matsui, S. *The History of the Silk Industry in the United States*. New York, 1930.

McFarland, C.K. 'Crusade for Child Labourers: 'Mother' Jones and the March of the Mill Children', *Pennsylvania History* vol. 38 (July 1971): 283–96.

Mother Jones. 'The Wail of the Children', in *Mother Jones Speaks: Collected Writings and Speeches*, ed. Philip S. Foner. New York, 1983.

Nichols, F.H. 'Children of the Coal Shadow', *McClure's Magazine* 20 (February 1903).

Phelan, C. *Divided Loyalties: The Public and Private Life of Labour Leader John Mitchell*. Albany,1994.

Sanville, F.L. 'A Woman in the Pennsylvania Silk-Mills', *Harper's Monthly Magazine* (April 1910): 651–661.

Sanville, F.L. 'Home Life of the Silk-Mill Workers', *Harper's Monthly Magazine* (June 1910): 22–31.

Spargo, J. *The Bitter Cry of the Children*. New York, 1909.

Stepenoff, B. 'Child Labour in Pennsylvania's Silk Mills: Protest and Change, 1900–1910', *Pennsylvania History* vol. 59 (April 1992).

———. '"Papa on Parade": Pennsylvania Coal Miners' Daughters and the Silk Worker Strike of 1913', *Labour's Heritage* vol. 7 (Winter 1996): 6–21.

———. 'Keeping it in the Family: Mother Jones and the Pennsylvania Silk Strike of 1900–1901', *Labour History* vol. 38 (Fall 1997): 432–49.

Tsurumi, E.P. *Factory Girls: Women in the Thread Mills of Meiji Japan*. Princeton, NJ, 1990.

Walsh, W.J. *The United Mine Workers as a Social Force in the Anthracite Territory*. Washington, 1931.

Wiebe, R.H. 'The Anthracite Strike of 1902: A Record of Confusion', *Mississippi Valley Historical Review* vol. 48 (September 1961).

CHAPTER 8

THE TRADE UNION AS SURVIVAL STRATEGY

THE CASE OF AMSTERDAM CONSTRUCTION WORKERS IN THE FIRST QUARTER OF THE TWENTIETH CENTURY

Henk Wals

In 1910 the Amsterdam trade union paper *The Construction Worker* printed the following dialogue between two neighbours:[1]

First Neighbour Woman: So neighbour woman, where are *you* off to with your best things on?
Second Neighbour Woman: To the meeting.
First Neighbour Woman: Huh??
Second Neighbour Woman: That's right – something wrong with that?
First Neighbour Woman: Well that's a good 'un. Last year you cursed your fella out 'til you were blue in the face if he went to the meeting, and now you're going yourself.
Second Neighbour Woman: Yes I did, but can you blame me? He drank like a fish, and when he got back from the meeting he was always three-fourths pie-eyed. Anytime he needed to come up with a fib so he could go soak it up, it was always: I gotta go to the meeting.

The rest of the story can be summed up as follows: the Second Neighbour Woman prevailed on her husband to give up his union membership. The result was that the union's president – 'a proper, noticing fellow' – came to visit and explained the union's purpose to her in painstaking detail. The wife saw the light and promised 'to cut out keeping her man from the union'. The husband gave up his gin and after a while was even elected to the executive board. It was annoying that he was now away from home almost every day, but the Second Neighbour Woman was able to deal with that. The dialogue then ended as follows:

| Second Neighbour Woman: | So now there's a special meeting tonight with a special speaker and you'll see that I don't want to stay behind. I'm far too glad that my man's a union member. |
| First Neighbour Woman: | Well you could knock me over with a feather, what a change. Hey, have a good time. If they go after my man you won't see me holdin' 'im back.[2] |

The dialogue is fictional. It is meant to persuade the spouses of male union members to cease opposing their husbands' union membership. We encounter a number of such attempts in the union press of the early twentieth century. We can draw two conclusions from this fact: (1) women in working-class families did not have a wholly positive attitude towards unions, and (2) women's opinions had an impact on the Amsterdam construction workers' degree of organisation. Further, the sketch reveals a rarely mentioned motive for becoming a union member: the convivial gatherings, from which it was evidently difficult to return home sober.

Interest in trade union membership appears a more complex subject than has often been thought. Most historians of the workers' movement looked for the answer in (Marxist) ideology. One simply became a union member once one had attained a certain level of class consciousness. Non-members were, according to this same logic, *unconscious,* which is often read as apathetic, dull or selfish. There was no other explanation for their behaviour. Instead of contributing to the emancipation of their class they just drudged along, living from hand to mouth, without any perspective for the future. According to this vision the union was an instrument of social change; and the degree of organisation was an expression of workers' inclination to contribute to this change. Protestant unions, which rejected Marxism and class struggle, were thus often not considered to be *real* trade unions.[3] Their leadership was in the hands of the propertied class, which tried in this way to keep the workers away from the socialist workers' movement.

What we miss most of all in this approach is the presumption that workers are autonomous, thinking beings who are supposed to take their fate into their own hands. When workers are called 'class-conscious' in Marxist-orientated historical writings, that really means little more than that they have arrived at the conviction that Marxist theories are correct. When they only have 'trade union consciousness', that means little besides the fact that they have come to believe that they should join a union. The tautological nature of this type of explanation ensures that the considerations and motivations of the people involved are insufficiently illuminated.

Another historiographical problem arises in research into trade union membership, above all in memorial volumes and historical writings produced by the union movement itself. In the course of the twentieth century, unions in a number of countries made substantial achievements. Dutch society for example would have looked quite different if the unions had not made their mark on it. That would not have been possible without a reasonable number of members. Membership was thus extremely sensible, we tend to think with hindsight. There must have been something wrong with the workers who *weren't* members. This helps account for the image of the apathetic, dull worker who failed to join the union out of ignorance or indifference.

On the other hand, the fact that workers genuinely do make conscious, autonomous choices is far from a new insight. Mancur Olson applied rational choice theory, developed in the 1950s, to the workers' movement as early as 1965.[4] Rational choice theory presupposes individuals who act by weighing costs and benefits against each other. People are treated as rational actors inasmuch as they strive for utility maximisation. Collective behaviour is to be explained on the basis of these utility-maximising actions. People will join trade unions, for instance, when they think that they can achieve something through a union that they could not achieve as individuals. However, calculating individuals would *not* join unions if they thought that unions would reach their goals even without their particular membership, so that they could 'freeride'. In this sense the costs of solidarity are constantly weighed against its rewards. A judgement of this kind is at work in strikes, for instance.[5] People can take possible higher wages in the event of a victorious strike into consideration, but also for instance the possible penalties that would result from a defeat, the wages forfeited during the strike, and the prestige gained in colleagues' minds.

This multiplicity of variables highlights a weakness of rational choice theory: the analysis of cost-effectiveness often becomes so complex that making a correct choice comes to seem impossible. In addition the number and character of variables can vary from one individual to the next, and therefore provide a doubtful basis for explaining collective behaviour. Moreover, the presupposition of rational choice theory is open to question: does every individual really strive for utility maximisation? Do people really think in such a rectilinear way? These doubts have made rational choice theory primarily the domain of theorists. Yet its starting-points are not senseless. How rationally people act varies from one person to the next; nobody leads a 100 percent-pure calculating existence; but on the other hand a striving for utility maximisation is basic to many individual and collective decisions.

Other scholars as well have called for more attention to be paid to individuals and their decisions. Anthony Giddens for example posited that people act intentionally, but that does not always mean that they are aware of their own motives or that they have a complete picture of all the conditions in which their actions take place. Thus they know what they are doing, or think they do, but the result of their actions can be more extensive and lie outside their field of vision. The complexity of human interaction increases exponentially with the number of actors involved and the period of time under consideration.[6] Michael Mann made the link between the acting individual and the formation of organisations. He began from the assumption that people must cooperate in order to satisfy major needs and in this way arrive at the formation of sources of ideological, economic, military and political power. Sources of power are thus mixed so as to create networks, in which different actors are dominant at different times.[7] Both of these approaches are applicable to the study of trade unions. People cooperate within them, with the formation of a source of economic power as the most important result; but some members can have other *intentions,* such as taking advantage of the union's insurance coverage, for example.

Marcel van der Linden has advocated seeing the decision whether or not to join a trade union as a household's 'living strategy'. Union membership then forms one of the possibilities in a whole strategic repertory. On the level of an individual household one can think for example of actions such as moving, saving, buying insurance, borrowing money or looking for another job. [8] In addition, there are a number of strategies involving help from outside. Besides joining a social movement organisation, there are mutual support by relatives, personal communities or patronage. Whether people choose to join a social movement organisation depends, according to Van der Linden, above all on two things: the degree of risk associated with participation in an organisation and its actions and the extent to which the 'freerider problem' arises. Van der Linden also urges taking non-organised groups into account. This can deepen our understanding of the motives of organised workers.[9] This is true of course, though the motives of the unorganised are also interesting in and of themselves.

The dialogue at the beginning of this article is a good illustration of the argument for a survival-strategy approach to organisation. The demand for union membership needs to be examined by making connections among the private sphere, work and working-class organisation. As far as I know, there has been scarcely any research done in this field.[10] In this article I shall try to make such a link. Amsterdam construction workers around the turn of the nineteenth and twentieth centuries will serve as a case in point. Within the private sphere the household occupies a central place. In early twentieth century Amsterdam the household almost always consisted of a nuclear family made up of a father and mother and a number of children. I will inquire which factors played a role in the decision whether or not to join a union.

As usual, not many sources have been preserved from the private sphere. Those most directly relevant to households are the files of the Amsterdam poor relief, which I have drawn on. I also make use of various sorts of trade union materials, above all surveys, pamphlets and newspapers. I have searched these sources for forms of expression that can shed light on the judgements that construction workers made in the context of their families. Moreover I analyse the degree of organisation by examining the rise and fall of family-orientated provisions such as private unemployment insurance.

Declining Security and Respectability

A new phenomenon arose in the Amsterdam construction industry in the 1870s. Amsterdam's population grew explosively, and the newcomers needed housing. A great building boom began. Housing was no longer built only for specific clients but for the anonymous housing market as well. Entrepreneurs had whole blocks of dwellings built, which with luck they were subsequently able to sell at a profit. The new entrepreneurs generally built with borrowed money provided by mortgage banks. In this way entrepreneurs without capital launched speculative or shoddy construction projects which were constantly on the verge of bankruptcy.[11]

Of course construction for specific clients continued as well. The old custom was for a client to approach a carpentry or masonry firm. The firm then began to build and was paid according to the number of hours worked. From the builder's point of view therefore speed was not called for; on the contrary. The client usually received a good product, which however cost him more money than necessary. For this reason there was a steady transition in the second half of the nineteenth century, following the pattern set in waterway and road construction, towards the so-called contracting system. Builders could bid to do a specified job for a set amount of money. The client then usually chose the contractor who made the lowest offer. This contractor then committed himself to do the construction for the agreed-upon price. In this way the principle of competition took root in the construction industry.[12]

All this had far-reaching consequences for the construction industry. Due to competition and narrow profit margins, contractors sought to keep costs as low as possible. That had several effects:

- It pushed wages down. Both contractors and private builders had an interest in keeping wages as low as possible. The lower the wages, the better the entrepreneur's chance to survive and earn something.
- On the other hand, the bosses tried to increase their employees' level of production. This took place in two ways: introduction of piecework and tightening of discipline. These methods were sufficient. Workers did in fact work much harder.
- Employers looked for ways to increase efficiency. This led to mechanisation and increased division of labour. Carpentry yards and sweatshops, which produced ready-made building materials, were established. It also became advantageous to separate easy from difficult work, so that less-skilled labour could be paid lower wages. An increasing number of crafts and specialisations thus arose.
- As soon as a project was done, the workers were immediately laid off. Thanks to the connection with the money market, construction also became dependent on the economic conjuncture. Whether construction workers could immediately move on to another project depended on the economic conjuncture. In slow periods this was usually not the case. In 1908 for example, which was an extremely bad year, carpenters averaged 8.3 weeks of unemployment. Painters averaged 8.7 weeks of unemployment and masons as much as 14.4 weeks.[13] The craft groups that worked above all in new construction, such as masons, hod-carriers (who brought stone and masonry up onto the scaffolding) and navvies, mostly had only a loose relationship with the boss. They suffered most from unemployment. Other groups like carpenters and painters not only worked on new construction but also did repair and maintenance work. They were also often permanently employed by a carpentry or painting shop. In their milieu the harsh conditions in private construction were thus felt less.

We can conclude that the new situation, taken as a whole, had two major consequences for the living conditions of workers and their families. First, their livelihoods became less secure. Second, their dignity and respectability came under threat. The first point requires no further explanation, but the second does.

According to Marcel van der Linden, both the need for security and the drive towards dignity and respectability are important incentives for household members.[14] Other writers like Barrington Moore and Alf Lüdtke had pointed out even earlier the importance of respectability in working-class life.[15] According to Francis Fukuyama the desire for respect is one of the basic drives underlying human action. People do not only seek material comfort but also respect and recognition. They consider that they are worthy of respect because they possess a certain worth or dignity. If others act as if they are worthless, if their worth is not acknowledged, then they become angry. It is no accident that we use 'indignation' as a near-synonym for 'anger'.[16]

Workmen founded their dignity in part on their ability to provide for themselves and their families. The better the quality of life they could provide, the more pride they could take.[17] As an Amsterdam carpenter said in 1903: 'I want to be honoured and respected, because I am a man who earns bread for himself and his kin with his own hands'.[18] When unemployment deprived a worker of his ability to provide for his family, his dignity was seriously injured. 'Unemployment has wreaked havoc among us and unfortunately many of our people have given up in the face of it', said a union pamphlet in 1909. '*That's no life for a man*'.[19]

An unemployed construction worker had to go from one construction site to the next to ask bosses for a job. As humiliating as that was in itself, the situation was still more degrading once the family's financial resources were exhausted. This usually happened quite soon, since few families were able to accumulate savings. One study of family budgets in 1917 showed that five out of the forty-three families studied were able to put some money aside.[20] The records of the Amsterdam poor relief also point in the same direction. Using its files, I built up a database of 359 records with data about construction workers who came into contact with it in the period 1900–25.[21] In twelve of these 359 cases the file reported that the family had lived on its savings for a short period before turning to poor relief.

In that case the household had to fall back on a well-known repertory of strategies, such as borrowing money, pawning household goods and buying food on credit. The wife also had to go out to work if she could – at least in the early years of the century; for a married woman to work outside the home was seen increasingly in later years as a humiliation. As a result by the 1920s this strategy was scarcely ever resorted to. It was a question of honour. 'Workers who are prepared … to let their wives work outside the home in order to do some lady's dirty work … are asses who deserve the owners' kicks', said the union newspaper *De Bouwvakarbeider* (The Construction Worker) in 1914.[22] My poor relief database shows that in the years 1907–09 wives went out to work in thirty-four out of a hundred cases; in the years 1915–17 in nine out of a hundred; and in the years 1922–24 in only five out of a hundred. In forty cases the type of work is known: housecleaning in twenty-two cases and often sewing, washing or peddling in the others.

If there was no other way, the family had to appeal for poor relief. This was also a far from uplifting experience; poor relief visitors would seek out relatives to ask if they could contribute to the family's maintenance. Neighbours were asked if the family's conduct was proper. The visitors checked on the family by descending on it at unexpected times – all in return for a dole that barely supported an absolutely minimal living standard. There was thus not much left of the dignity of the family concerned.

Workers' dignity also came under threat at the workplace. For those who had learned their craft well and were proud of it, inferior working practices were abhorrent. Speed was everything in such projects; the builders forced their workmen to do more or less shoddy work. This reduced craftsmen to the level of those who *could* only do shoddy work. Sometimes craftsmen were even at a disadvantage, since there were workers who specialised in shoddy work and could turn it out more quickly than craftsmen could.

In the 1870s, when there was more work than construction workers to do it, the workers could still take all sorts of liberties. 'The very limited influence that bosses had on workmen, who sensed that they were indispensable, led to great disorderliness at work', observed a commission investigating the state of the construction trades in 1898.[23] The workmen had a rather casual attitude towards working hours, for instance. They worked when they wanted to, and thanks to the high wages were evidently able to do so. A hod-carrier told the commission that in the early 1880s some workmen generally worked only three and a half or four days a week.[24] Monday was a day to spend drunk, and during the rest of the week too gin drinking was more the rule than the exception. In the case of jerrybuilding the employer hardly cared how long the workmen worked. They could decide that as they saw fit. If workers worked too little, the boss simply hired more.[25]

However, when in the course of the 1880s conditions in the construction industry got worse, more and more entrepreneurs considered these 'liberties' undesirable. They had to keep a sharper eye on their costs. Those who managed to keep their workers hard at work were at an advantage. This led to disciplinary measures. More and more contractors forbade hard liquor. 'Everyone knows that if they get drunk they're out and don't get to come back', stated a contractor in 1891 to another commission of enquiry. His company had no troubles of this kind. There had been problems in the past, 'but by holding fast to the principle tooth and nail we have pretty much eliminated this evil'.[26]

Where it was not possible to apply the piecework system, workers were less inclined to push themselves harder. In this case other measures were indicated. These usually amounted to stricter rules and intensified supervision. Surveillance was often accompanied with corresponding abusive language. Workmen found this difficult to bear:

> The boss or foreman, who just keeps pushing, for whom the hardest you can tear along is never fast enough. It's all too true that these people see us as machines, as tools without minds or hearts. Or have you never had to endure his

scorn or curses? Perhaps you bore it in silence, but it raged in your gut, or when you came home it burst loose on the heads of your innocent wife and children. Why didn't you give him what he had coming to him and tell him that you just wouldn't be treated this way? Because you knew that he could throw you out anytime and that hunger was lying in wait for you.[27]

This development was thus not conducive to construction workers' self-respect. Neither was the lack of all sorts of facilities on construction sites. Facilities cost money, and many employers therefore decided that they could do without. Eating sheds, drinking water and toilets were especially rare in jerrybuilding. A mason called the lack of toilets on construction sites 'really pathetic, something nasty'. Most workmen did not enjoy 'sitting ashamed behind a board or in a bit of cellar, listening to jeering or immoral talk'. According to one pamphlet they felt they were 'put on a level with beasts'.[28] The absence of toilets was in conflict with ideas of self-respect, particularly in a time when many workmen sought recognition through behaviour in keeping with middle-class norms of civilisation. Fully-fledged citizens simply do not respond to the call of nature under a bridge; and if you are forced to do so then you are not a fully-fledged citizen – that was their feeling.

The lack of drinking water and eating sheds was also experienced as humiliating. Workers had to 'go ask well-disposed people for a little bit of water in a bottle',[29] or try to become friends with an innkeeper.[30] One navvy related that his boss had in fact had a shed built; but the overseer could only use it, if the overseer in fact came to work. 'Seems to me', said the navvy, 'that if a shed can be put there for one man, a hall could be made for 30 men; then we wouldn't be exposed to cold and poverty like this at lunchtime'.[31] The message is clear: eating outdoors was not only unpleasant, but also humiliating.

Not every group of construction workers felt the same kind of threat to their respectability. Workers on new construction had a harder time than workers who also did maintenance and repair work. They were unemployed more often, were often paid by piecework and were 'driven on' by foremen. We may take it that unskilled workmen particularly, like hod-carriers and navvies, risked leading a life pretty much 'devoid of honour'. Carpenters, thanks to their training, expertise and construction responsibilities, had a certain status. In addition they had the prospect of upward mobility. More than a few carpenters became contractors, overseers or draughtsmen.[32] Masons and plasterers also enjoyed some degree of prestige, even if they were considered not very educated.[33] They could in any event earn a reasonable income if they worked hard. The workmen who had to get by on the basis of their muscles alone stood lowest in the hierarchy.

The Rise and Development of Trade Unions

Whereas supply and demand on the labour market for construction workers had formerly been reasonably in balance, now they diverged with each shift in the economic conjuncture. At one moment labour would be scarce; at another moment there would be a surfeit of it. In addition the employers' inclination to push down wages became increasingly, painfully evident. In a case like this 'forming a trust' becomes an obvious solution: joining forces gives the sellers (or renters, if you like) of labour the possibility of obtaining better prices. In this way creating artificial labour scarcity for a company made it possible to drive up the price. In other words, workers had the possibility of winning better conditions of labour by striking or threatening to strike. This tactic required organisation, however, formal or informal. The formal form – the trade union – turned out in the course of time to have advantages.

The trade union was, however, more than a labour-power sellers' trust.[34] Depending on the union concerned, it had at least two other functions. The first was organising resistance. The second was providing insurance: the unions began providing services whose goal was to decrease the insecurity in their members' lives. Two different currents arose in the early twentieth century: the syndicalist current, where the resistance function predominated, and a new, 'modern', social democratic wing, whose goal was above all to advance its members' interests. There were also Protestant and Catholic unions, but they never attained significant numbers in Amsterdam.[35] In any event they were really only distinguished from the social democratic trade unions by their religious backgrounds and their somewhat more restrained attitude in making demands on employers.

The modern unions wanted to be pragmatic, professional and efficient. They considered improving working conditions their foremost task. This could best be achieved through negotiation with employers. They used the strike weapon as a threat in negotiations, but preferred not to resort to it. If it proved necessary, however, the struggle had to be fought to a successful conclusion. For this reason the modern unions formed strike funds, which were meant to enable them to provide members with an income during strikes. Decreasing the insecurity in their members' lives was a second goal. To this end funds were formed that guaranteed members benefits in case of illness, unemployment or death. At the same time insurance served as a means to bind members to the union in order to limit the all-too-great outflow of members.[36] When possible, the modern movement worked with salaried officials and a central leadership. The members were supposed to line up behind their leaders without too much grumbling.

The syndicalist unions were supposed to have different, revolutionary principles. In theory they aimed at a general strike, whose goal was to overthrow the existing society. Afterwards a new society would be established in which the trade unions would own the means of production and organise industry. In order to bring this about workers were supposed to practise by going out on strike often. It was also important for workers to delegate as little power as possible to representatives or officials. While the finer nuances of syndicalist theory will have escaped most members, a spirit of resistance manifestly predominated in the syndicalist unions. They went out on strike whenever they could, in order to win a little ground but also for the sake of the struggle itself. The leadership also left the initiative in the members' hands, as a consequence of the so-called 'direct action tactic'.

Intimidation and violence were not shunned in the syndicalist movement. When in 1905 a contractor let his workers work too long for too low wages, the members of the syndicalist carpenters' union went after him. 'By means of a big chorus of catcalls, including hard words and a few blows, this business … was cleared up'. When another contractor had carpenters working more than fourteen hours a day, union members intervened once more: 'A team of 50 men showed up in the evening, went on site, pulled the boys together and sent the boss into conniptions – with the result that they laid down their tools and from that moment on enforced a nine-hour day'. When a boss wanted to lay off a number of workmen because there was no work for the time being, he was 'soon taken in hand about the matter'.[37]

More of these stories, told with a certain gusto, can be encountered in syndicalist pamphlets and annual reports from this period. Often they have a somewhat macho air about them. Spontaneous actions were very popular, and best of all was showing the boss with the aid of physical force that there were limits to his power. It was a question of self-respect. When social democratic and Christian unions sat down at the bargaining table with employers and treated them with respect, the syndicalists considered that they had already lost the battle, whatever the outcome. Not that the outcome was unimportant, but action itself met a need that was at least as great.

On the whole the syndicalist and social democratic union movements had roughly equivalent numbers of members in Amsterdam. Preferences varied widely by occupational group, however. Groups that found work on a casual basis in new construction felt most attracted to the syndicalist union movement. The casual character of their labour probably played a role in this respect. Negotiations over wage scales were common, while the quality of the piecework that was done was also subject to discussion from time to time. This led to conflicts that could escalate. Furthermore workers had to act quickly in order to improve their working conditions. Their stint on a particular project (and thus their period of employment) was usually soon over. This was conducive to the practice of direct-action strikes of the kind that the syndicalist union movement often resorted to.[38]

The Unorganised

Most Amsterdam construction workers did not join a union. Only around 1920 did unionisation levels temporarily exceed 50 percent in some occupations; after 1920 the level declined once more, as Figure 8.1 shows. While the source only indicates the number of members insured against unemployment, the graph gives a reasonably good picture of total union membership, since almost all unions made participation in their unemployment funds compulsory.

Union membership was clearly not a generally accepted survival strategy. There are at least seven reasons why this was so.

Figure 8.1 *Union members with unemployment insurance as a percentage of the total number of construction workers, 1906–1925*

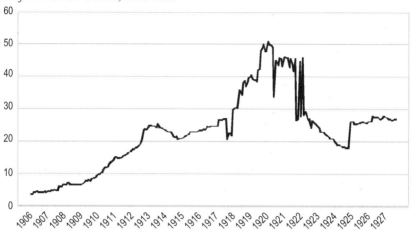

Source: Statistische Maandberichten Amsterdam (Amsterdam Monthly Statistical Reports), 1906–27.

1. People Could Get By without the Union Movement

There was a group of workers to which both historians of the workers' movement and union outreach efforts paid little attention: those who could manage quite well without the union movement. This was a group of workers who always worked hard, had good relations with the boss, and were thus rarely unemployed and earned reasonable wages, above all through piecework. One union paper called them 'eager beavers'. Nonetheless the paper had to admit that this was a fairly large group.[39] *Not* being a union member was part of this group's survival strategies.

2. Distaste For the Union Movement

Union activists were often associated with strikes, riots and other unpleasantness. Workers and their families who went hungry while there was no work because other workers were out on strike did not take kindly to those unions. This was why the social democratic unions rejected syndicalist 'direct-action strikes' as irresponsible. The social democratic carpenters' union Concordia Inter Nos for example observed in 1909 that the union's growth was held back 'by the irresponsible carrying on of a number of fanatics who are busy with "direct action"'.[40]

3. The Union Had Too Little to Offer

There was also a group of workers who simply thought that the union gave them too little for their money. 'It won't make a bit of difference', they would say.[41] Others had a more philosophically based standpoint: 'This is how it's always been and how it'll always be', they thought. 'You have to have masters and servants'.[42] Some workers did join, expecting immediate results; when there was none they were once more nowhere to be seen. 'Perhaps you have been a member for a few weeks or months, but when no mountains of gold landed on your doorstep, you once more deserted the cause', one union scolded the unorganised.[43] The same union had already observed a few years earlier that lack of immediate tangible results had led many workers to abandon the fight.[44]

4. Budgetary Considerations

Benefits were naturally evaluated in relation to costs. The decision whether or not to join the union movement often hinged on the issue of dues. In many construction workers' families union dues were seen as a major stumbling block. This was a problem for unions, at least for the social democratic and confessional ones, since they asked for more dues than the syndicalist unions. 'Most of our fellow tradesmen use the high dues as an argument against joining our union', the social democratic masons' union noted in 1910.[45] When the carpenters' union tried to rouse mechanical woodworkers to enthusiasm for the organisation, most found dues an insuperable obstacle.[46] Four years later the union tried again, this time with more success: employees signed up in a couple of factories. However, when a period of unemployment broke out shortly afterwards, most of the woodworkers turned their backs on the union once more, on the grounds that it was not doing anything for them.[47]

The woodworkers' behaviour is nonetheless understandable. Dues formed a heavy burden on family budgets, above all for members of the organised social democratic unions, certainly in hard times. Membership in the social democratic masons' union, including unemployment insurance, cost the average mason 52 Dutch cents a week in 1910. For the same amount the family could buy a kilo of beef, which was a rare sight on the dinner table in those days. That was ultimately the choice: either join the union, with uncertain benefits situated somewhere in the future, or have meat on the menu several times a week *now.*

Most families lived on the edge of a bare minimum budget. A small alteration in budgetary circumstances could make a great difference. In the framework of the family budget, trade union membership was a highly elastic good. People were sometimes willing to join if they could afford it without too much sacrifice; but if they had to give up other, more essential things, then union membership was quickly given up. Figure 8.1 shows how the economic conjuncture influenced union membership. The crisis during the First World War, the prosperity of the early 1920s, and the harder economic times afterwards can all be read clearly from it.

5. Women's Resistance

The vantage point of the family budget also explains many women's resistance to their spouses' union membership. Thanks to their responsibility for the household, women had to deal with day-to-day budgetary problems more than men. They were thus constantly obliged to make choices. Many women saw more advantage in serving their families wholesome meals, for example, than in waiting for the vague promise of the benefits of trade union membership to materialise.

The union was also responsible for workplace conflicts, which in the short run augured nothing good for the family. If the male breadwinner lost his work, then his wife had to assume that role temporarily. Given that the work that she could get was quite disagreeable and that she was not relieved of her domestic tasks in her own family, she viewed the prospect with dread. Furthermore, as I mentioned earlier, in the course of the twentieth century it became more and more 'shameful' for married women to go out to work.

For these reasons many construction workers' wives had no use for the union. 'Most women are fed up when the dues collector comes by', the social democratic masons' union declared. 'Many a man has to listen then to all sorts of sweet things about the trade union at that time, and it is not rare for this to become an occasion for bickering'.[48] In 1909 the paper *De Bouwvakarbeider* devoted a whole article to the problem, which began as follows:

> It is a well-known fact that very many working class women are very unsympathetic (have no very warm feelings towards) the union movement. They often try by hook or by crook to keep their husbands away from it, or, if their husbands nonetheless become members, to stand in the way of their attending union meetings.[49]

Those meetings were indeed an additional source of friction. In a work week that left extraordinarily little free time as it was, meetings meant that family cares were still more exclusively a burden for the wife, leaving aside the possibility that she might have enjoyed occasionally seeing and speaking with her husband from time to time. There was also an additional consideration. In far too many cases, *De Bouwvakarbeider* mentioned towards the end of 1910, the husband treated the meeting as a sort of day or evening out. He had a few drinks with his friends before or after the meeting, came home tipsy and – if the meeting was on Sunday – left the Sunday meal waiting on the table. 'That is something that the wife as a rule cannot put up with', the paper acknowledged. 'And naturally she blames the union'.[50]

6. Freeriding

In much of the literature 'freeriding' is seen as an important reason for not joining a union,[51] though with doubtful justification. The theme of freeriding is based on the thought that unions were successful and won benefits for the employees. In itself that is not inaccurate; but as I mentioned earlier, a great part of that success could only be demonstrated with hindsight. In the early twentieth century it was by no means clear to the average worker what exactly the unions were winning. Their conditions were not becoming so much better, and even if they were, it was open to question whether the unions deserved the credit for it. The impressive calculations that the social democratic union movement made (the masons' union claimed to have 'earned' Fl742,339.28 in wage increases for its members in the years 1907–12) were often taken with a grain of salt. The same holds true for the great number of victories in labour conflicts about which the syndicalist unions boasted in their propaganda. In other words, many unorganised workers had no great opinion of the union movement's achievements, or were not very attentive to them; but in that case they had little reason to see themselves as 'freeriders'.

A second reason why the importance of the theme of freeriding is often overstated is that it is frequently referred to in trade union sources. There was a special reason for that: from a publicity point of view, characterising all unorganised workers as freeriders was an obvious tactic. It was a way to drive home the value of the union to non-members, and gave members the comforting feeling that their financial sacrifice was not a waste of money.

7. Employers' Resistance

Another theme often found in the literature is that employers fought against trade union membership. In the Amsterdam construction trades, however, that was true only to a quite limited extent. In the 1890s the employers still exercised the expected pressure to prevent their employees from joining unions. Union members could be put on a blacklist and eventually go hungry. Bosses spread insinuations that leading union members were not good at their crafts.[52]

In sources about the first decades of the twentieth century, however, we encounter relatively few traces of employers who put up fierce resistance to trade union membership. Of course there were problems from time to time. Strikers sometimes had a hard time finding work, or tradesmen seen as troublesome were sacked on some pretext or another. However, as soon as it became clear in the 1900s that reaching agreements with the unions was possible, most entrepreneurs no longer saw union membership as a problem. Sometimes just the opposite was the case: in a major lockout in 1909, unorganised workers tended to be locked out by bosses rather than union members working under contract.

The organised

There are three kinds of reasons to join a trade union. The first is that people see concrete, material advantages to membership. Insurance is the most readily apparent, but there can also be the hope of finding work more readily or of winning higher wages in the near future. The second kind of reason is belief in the movement's ideology. Depending on the kind of union, its ideology can include various different ideas. People may think that wage workers need to unite their forces in order to do well in negotiations with employers; but they may also believe that the power of the union will lead to overthrow of the existing society and lay the basis for a new one. In Marxist terms this is the difference between 'trade union consciousness' and 'class consciousness'. The third kind of reason is more emotional. Some workers had an unquenchable desire to *resist* something, whether their boss or authority in general. This desire usually originated in feelings of dissatisfaction, discontent or anger; but the feeling of needing to join a union could also arise for example from a need for a 'cosy nest' or the idea of forming part of a tradition. Naturally the three kinds of reasons are often combined with each other.

Material Considerations

Most workers joined unions because of the material benefits offered by membership. Union insurance policies were the most important attraction among them, particularly unemployment insurance. The unions themselves generally denied this, or kept quiet about it, but sometimes they did acknowledge that benefits constituted the trade union's major attraction for many members. When there was a proposal in the social democratic masons' union in 1909 to establish an unemployment fund, the editors of *De Bouwvakarbeider* were not enthusiastic. 'What was the objective when our Union was established?' they asked. 'Was it to support each other when we go through wretched times, or was it to fight for better working conditions?' The latter was the case, they maintained. If an unemployment fund were set up now, the benefits would become the main reason why many people would join. The union would change from a fighting organisation to a charitable one.[53]

If unemployment insurance really was a significant factor, then that should be visible in higher membership figures after it was introduced or in lower membership figures after it was ended. In fact in a number of cases insurance did have a considerable impact on membership totals:

- In November 1907, before the syndicalist masons' union set up an unemployment fund, it had seventy members. Afterwards its membership quickly rose to one hundred and thirty, an 86 percent increase.[54] The social democratic masons' union created an unemployment fund in March 1910. Branch membership subsequently rose in the second quarter of 1910 from 57 to 116: a remarkable growth, all the more so because the membership of the masons' union in the Netherlands as a whole declined in those months from 1882 to 1776.[55]
- The syndicalist National Federation of Construction Workers was granted the right to a state contribution to the union's unemployment fund on 25 March 1918. In the same year the number of members nation-wide rose from 5803 to 8079, an increase of over 71 percent. The greatest increases were registered in the months April, May, June and July. The increase was approximately three times greater than in the previous year.[56] The Federation itself linked the increase to the unemployment fund.[57]
- Another interesting membership increase took place in a number of unions in 1919. It seems very likely that this increase was related to the so-called Unemployment Insurance Emergency Act, which took effect in November and provided for an extra state contribution to the unions. The unions were accordingly able to pay out benefits 'of an amount sufficient to pay for the necessary maintenance of life of their unemployed members' for at least ninety days.[58] That made such an insurance policy attractive. The law took effect on 3 November 1919.

  The syndicalist construction workers' federation (the National Federation of Construction Workers) had 8,079 members as of January 1919, but its membership rose to 10,749 in November and reached a total of 13,451 in December: a gain of an additional 64 percent. In Amsterdam the totals in January, November and December respectively were 2,801, 3,490 and

4,094, a gain of 46 percent.[59] When the law took effect on 3 November, new members were immediately entitled to benefits. The Federation's office staff worked overtime in order to keep up with the deluge of administrative work; but during 1920 something went wrong. The Federation ran short of cash, and in July and August the state contributions failed to arrive; because many members had also 'pulled back' after roughly three months, there was a real exodus of members in the spring and summer. While there were still 14,066 people on the membership list in April, the total had shrunk to 9,217 in December. In Amsterdam the figures were 4,373 and 3,497.[60] When the extra state contributions ceased on 1 January 1922, the Federation decided to abolish the unemployment fund. The result was a new exodus. At the beginning of 1922 there were still 7,993 members on the books. In December the total had declined to 4,809. In Amsterdam the number of members went down from 3,509 to 2,734. While the Federation's membership explosion in 1918–19 cannot be entirely attributed to people in search of insurance, a substantial part of it can. The almost 3,200 new members in the fourth quarter of 1919 were in any event insurance clients, in the Federation's own opinion.[61]

- The Protestant construction workers' union (Netherlands Christian Construction Labour Union) also increased its membership considerably after November 1919. Membership almost doubled in 1919: there were 5,718 members registered in January, about 8,000 in mid-July and 10,048 in the union's ranks at the end of December. In Amsterdam the Protestant union was never a factor to be reckoned with, but its membership there nonetheless rose from 393 to 550, an increase of almost 40 percent.[62]

- We also see a membership increase in 1919 if we examine a number of the other trade unions in Amsterdam, but a less spectacular increase than in the Protestant construction union and the syndicalist federation. These new members were also lured by the advantageous terms offered by the new unemployment insurance law.[63]

The difference between these trade unions and the syndicalist federation in particular is interesting. Why did most new members in November choose the syndicalist union movement? Presumably because Federation members paid a half-hour's wage per week in dues in 1919 while the social democratic and confessional unions charged at least twice as much.[64] The surge in working-class radicalism around 1920, which some authors think explains the growth of the syndicalist movement, should be examined from another angle in light of Unemployment Insurance Emergency Act.[65] The enormous peak seen in total union membership in 1920 can very likely be attributed to this law. Until now researchers have missed this possible connection.[66]

We feel justified in concluding on the basis of these cases that for a not inconsiderable number of construction workers unemployment insurance was a good reason to join a trade union. The percentage increases after the introduction of insurance, or after an improvement in terms, are considerable. A more exact statement than 'a not inconsiderable number' is unfortunately in general not possible.

Besides unemployment insurance, health and life insurance were probably yet another factor attracting people to unions, although there is little quantitative evidence to be found. Along with these insurance policies, unions also offered other services to their members, such as free legal assistance.

The fact that many members were in search of short-term advantage is apparent from the fairly high membership turnover in most unions. A high turnover rate usually indicates that rational choices are being made.[67] In the years 1910–17 roughly 20 percent of members on average left the social democratic carpenters' union each year.[68] In the social democratic masons' union between 1910 and 1918 the figure was as high as almost 47 percent.[69] Many people joined at moments when a campaign was in progress, for instance when a contract was being negotiated. At such moments there was a great probability of strikes breaking out, and it was agreeable to be able to draw on the unions' strike funds. The social democratic masons' union, for example, initiated action in the spring of 1909 against poor individual contracts. The union leadership foresaw that as soon as the actions had died down a little, hundreds of building-trade workers would leave the union again, mostly by simply failing to pay their dues.[70]

The social democratic carpenters' union, too, had to contend with this phenomenon. In 1912 the leadership observed that as the expiration of the contract was approaching many people were signing up. It predicted however that soon, once the affair was once more temporarily settled, many of the new members would leave again.[71] In fact the union was forced to conclude afterwards that the year 1913 had been rich in new members, but that a high proportion of them had left right away.[72]

One final example of opportunistic membership was revealed at the masons' union's congress in 1909. The decision was taken there that people would have to wait a year after joining before having the right to sick pay. The reason was that there were people who joined exactly as many weeks before 1 December as was required in order to begin drawing sick pay on that date. For many masons and hod-carriers 1 December in particular was often the start of a period of unemployment. When the moment struck they called in sick at the union hall and received benefits. As soon as they had collected their maximum ten weeks of sick pay, they resigned from the union. Then after a while spring arrived and once more work was available.[73]

Ideological Reasons

Only a few workmen joined from purely ideological motives. One may expect that the ideologically committed play an active role in the movement; but the number of active members was slight. Unpaid officials, section heads, dues collectors and recruiters belonged to a very small minority. Other members rarely let themselves be drawn into union activities. Most meetings, for example, were far from well attended. Almost all the annual reports of the social democratic carpenters' union mention this fact. In 1909 an average of sixty-five members, less than a fifth of the membership, attended the business meeting each month. In 1911 the figure was 15 percent. The union paper was read very little.[74]

Organisers of special meetings were also rarely able to congratulate themselves on a high attendance. When the social democratic masons' union organised a public meeting on 29 April 1909, they prepared thoroughly for it. Large posters were pasted up everywhere and manifestos were handed out to thousands of building-trade workers. The result was that on the evening in question fourteen people attended.[75]

Members could also usually not be stimulated to join demonstrations, and certainly not if it required taking a day off work. When a march was held on May Day in 1907 under the slogan 'All out for the eight-hour day', the leadership of the social democratic carpenters' union had to admit to its mortification that there were almost no members present.[76] Most members could not find it in their hearts to sacrifice a day's wages for the march. The same was the case in 1909, but in the evening 'a fairly great number' of members marched behind the banner in the procession.[77] The leaders also had cause for satisfaction in 1911: about a hundred members joined the march.[78] At that moment 735 carpenters were union members. Evidently the leaders were content with a turn-out of fewer than 14 percent of the membership.

In 1913, a peak year for the workers' movement, 250 members of the carpenters' union attended on 'Red Monday', a propaganda gathering for universal suffrage. With a fifth of the members, this was the high point to date in the field of membership activity.[79]

So some members were ready to march in a demonstration now and again, but as soon as something demanded more time or money, people generally disappeared. The leadership had for example invested considerable work in a petition campaign for universal suffrage. Almost everyone was willing to sign immediately, but when members were asked to canvass and donate an hour's wages, there seemed to be extraordinarily little interest.[80]

Members' limited involvement was not a peculiarity of the social democratic union movement. The leadership of the syndicalist construction workers' federation noted that most members considered that they had done their duty in paying in their dues on Saturday.[81] This was a remarkable pronouncement from a union that generally boasted of having primarily conscious workers in its ranks. The syndicalists too had to contend with low turn-outs at their meetings.[82] In 1905 for instance they organised a meeting for each trade in the framework of their campaign for a nine-hour work day. The carpenters' meeting was the best attended: out of the thousands of Amsterdam carpenters, fifty came to take a look.[83] The business meetings also failed to evoke the interest hoped for:

> When members are called out to a business or other meeting they often don't have the time to attend a meeting that one time in a fortnight or a month – it's too much trouble, too cold, too warm, too far, too early, too late; in short they can always find an excuse to miss it.[84]

A further indication of the level of involvement in the union's ranks is the referenda that the syndicalists held from time to time. These usually evoked little interest from the members. When for example the Federation consulted its members in late 1909 about a number of quite important issues, only 369 of the 1,306 members (28.3 percent) returned their ballots.[85]

Emotional Reasons

Still to be examined are the emotional reasons. We must seek these above all in the syndicalist union movement. With their sometimes violent actions, spontaneous direct-action strikes and revolutionary rhetoric, the syndicalist unions more than any others radiated a spirit of resistance. The social democratic and Protestant unions did not. Their propaganda summed up the gains won in a cool, clinical way. They calculated how much money the union had 'earned' in recent years in wage increases, and emphasised their insurance coverage, legal assistance and other practical benefits; but they did not preach revolution and insubordination against the boss. Workers clearly did feel an urge to be insubordinate. Certain groups of construction workers experienced resistance as one of the few means of preserving their self-respect and dignity. As I sketched out earlier, their work and domestic conditions offered few opportunities for this. Unskilled workers, such as hod-carriers and navvies in particular, were forced to lead an existence that was largely 'devoid of honour', at least according to prevailing middle-class norms. More successful groups of construction workers such as carpenters lived increasingly according to these very norms. They reduced their consumption of alcohol, practised birth control, furnished their homes discriminatingly, and abided as much as possible by the principle of the male breadwinner. In short, to the full extent possible they imitated petty bourgeois middle layers of society.

Some of the less successful groups of building-trade workers tried to escape from their lack of honour precisely by rejecting those middle-class norms. The Dutch sociologist Haveman has posited that unskilled workers developed in this way a distinctive culture, both socially and geographically isolated, within which they shaped a life-style of their own.[86] According to his colleague Van Doorn there existed in fact a 'proletarian rear guard' with its own subculture, though he contested the idea that it corresponded exactly to the group of unskilled workers.[87]

The syndicalists' leaning towards militancy was a good fit with this subculture, as did their (impulsive and aggressive) methods of struggle. In the syndicalist union movement the least-skilled, most casually employed groups were in fact prominent. In 1918, 98 percent of the organised navvies were in syndicalist unions, as were 88 percent of the organised hod-carriers.[88] Among the organised masons, 80 percent belonged to the syndicalists.[89] The proportions were reversed among the skilled workers, who generally had more permanent employment. Among carpenters 81 percent belonged to the social democratic unions, and among painters 65 percent.[90] They felt more at home in the 'bourgeois', efficient social democratic movement, which saw little point in deeds of resistance.

A question that could be raised is whether there was a link between the construction workers' origin and trade union membership. Were there for instance groups of migrants who showed a particular preference? Did the transition from countryside to city give rise to a particular mindset (of resistance)? The fact that there were many immigrants in Amsterdam is well known. Most of them arrived in the 1870s. In 1898 a survey established that there were few native-born Amsterdammers among construction workers. Carpenters, for example, often came from the northern provinces of North Holland and Friesland. Masons and navvies by contrast came more often from the southern Netherlands, particularly North Brabant.[91] Over a quarter of a century later, in 1927, approximately two thirds of the carpenters, masons and hod-carriers were native-born Amsterdammers. Only the navvies largely (in 70 percent of cases) originated outside Amsterdam.[92]

This much we know, but we cannot make any connection with the unions: membership records have not been preserved. We can only guess. It is probable that the syndicalist union movement for example counted many former residents of Brabant among its members, given its high percentage of navvies and masons; but this is not certain and in any event is not very significant. I have not been able to find any evidence of a causal relationship between possible rural origins and a militant mindset.

Conclusion

Our initial question was why workers joined or failed to join unions. The household strategies approach has helped to clarify the answers. There were good reasons for Amsterdam construction workers not to join a trade union. Their choice bore little relation to apathy or lack of consciousness and quite a lot to their household budgets: the trade union cost money. Most families gave priority to immediate necessities rather than to what the trade union had to offer in terms of longer-term security, defence of interests or action. From their own point of view they had good reasons for making this choice.

Union actions also gave raise to irritation. Those who launched them were playing with fire, many thought. The construction process formed a chain: first the foundation had to be laid, then piles driven, then the carpentry, then the masonry, and so forth. A few hotheaded workers could thus bring all work to a standstill. Furthermore an action could spread endlessly through charges of scab labour and lockouts. In this way each strike involved a danger of unemployment for countless workers; and an unemployed breadwinner was a painful blow to the whole household.

These two factors help explain why many women in particular were opposed to unions. Managing the household budget was their task in most families. For this reason they rued each day that the messenger came round to collect union dues. It meant that money left the family purse for which they considered they had better uses. During unemployment they had to struggle to make ends meet. Going out to work themselves was one way to do so, though most women saw that increasingly as a shame for them personally.

The urge towards respectability was an important motive in working families' lives, as Marcel van der Linden has rightly observed; but this urge could have different expressions in relation to union membership. In many people's eyes respectability meant being able to live according to the reigning 'bourgeois' system of norms. In practice this meant being able to live on the male breadwinner's wages and having a 'properly' furnished home. It also meant avoiding what middle-class citizens saw as uncontrolled and undesirable behaviour, such as violence, public drunkenness and unmarried cohabitation. A reasonable and above all regular income was a very good means towards this end; but a regular income in particular was not an attainable goal for all building-trade workers. Since construction was organised around the economic conjuncture and specific projects, workers were likely to be without work from time to time.

As Barrington Moore has posited, people wanted at work as elsewhere 'to be treated with ordinary human respect'.[93] That did not always occur. Casual and unskilled labourers in particular had little cause for pride. 'A workman's feeling of honour isn't high when he's not skilled', as one Amsterdam carpenter said in so many words in 1891.[94]

One possibility of nonetheless preserving self-respect was resistance. The syndicalist union movement offered a good opportunity. By means of a direct-action strike, workers could make it clear to the boss that he did not have absolute power over his employees. It was of course possible to strike without a union movement as well, but in practice an organisational link was useful, if only to organise financial support. Casual, unskilled labourers constituted the syndicalist unions' major base of support. They also went out on strike most often. Amsterdam hod-carriers struck more than six times as often as carpenters in the years 1900–25, and navvies almost four times as often.[95]

Skilled tradesmen such as carpenters and painters were more often permanently employed. They worked not only in new construction but also in workshops. These were mostly small undertakings where workmen worked side-by-side with the boss and these conditions created a feeling of connection. This connection and the permanent character of employment explain why these groups of workers went out on strike less often than masons, hod-carriers and navvies, who were only employed on new construction projects. The permanent workers' dignity was under less of a threat; there was less need to resist. The effort to attain a middle class way of life was a more plausible way for these groups to lead an existence worthy of respect.

The social democratic and confessional unions met these groups' needs better than the syndicalists did. Bourgeois virtues *par excellence* like discipline, self-control and civility were high among their priorities. They thus had a base of support in Amsterdam above all among carpenters and painters. Violence was rare in the social democratic union movement, and strikes were avoided if at all possible. They did however meet another need of working-class families, one that in addition fitted well with the thirst for respectability: the longing for security. Most unions offered health, life and above all unemployment insurance. This turned out to be popular. When people did join unions, this was often their most important reason.

In their propaganda the unions often aimed information about their insurance offerings at the woman in the family, assuming that security was something that would appeal to her.[96] This is a convincing argument for the hypothesis that union membership can be seen as a household strategy.

Translated by Peter Drucker

Notes

1. This article is based on my dissertation, *Makers en Stakers. Amsterdamse bouwvakarbeiders en hun bestaansstrategieën in het eerste kwart van de twintigste eeuw* (Builders and Strikers: Amsterdam Construction Workers and Their Survival Strategies in the First Quarter of the Twentieth Century), Amsterdam, 2001.
2. *De Vrouw: Orgaan van den Centrale Bond van Bouwvakarbeiders* (The Woman: Organ of the Central Construction Workers' Union) (n.p., n.d.), 4. Discovered in the 1910 volume of *De Bouwvakarbeider* (The Construction Worker), IISH.
3. Society in the Netherlands was increasingly organised in the early twentieth century according to world-views. Thanks to this 'pillarization' Protestants, Catholics, social democrats and 'revolutionaries' each had their own institutions: political parties, unions, broadcasting companies, etc. Trade unions did not escape from this logic either. Deadly competition reigned at first among the Protestant, Catholic, social democratic and revolutionary trade unions.
4. Mancur Olson, *The Logic of Collective Action: Public Goods and the Theory of Groups*, Cambridge, MA, 1965.
5. An interesting summary of factors can be found in Debra Friedman, 'Why Workers Strike: Individual Decisions and Structural Constraints', in *The Microfoundations of Macrosociology*, ed. Michael Hechter, Philadelphia, 1983, 250–83.
6. Anthony Giddens, *The Constitution of Society: Outline of the Theory of Structuration*, Cambridge, UK, 1984.
7. Michael Mann, *The Sources of Social Power, Volume 1: A History of Power from the Beginning to A.D. 1760*, Cambridge, UK, 1986. An outstanding discussion of both Mann's and Giddens' theories can be found in: Anton Schuurman, 'Mensen maken verschil: Sociale theorie, historische sociologie en geschiedenis' in: *Tijdschrift voor Sociale Geschiedenis* 22, no.2 (1996): 168–204. My short summaries are based on this work.
8. For an exhaustive summary, see Van der Linden's introduction to this anthology.
9. Marcel van der Linden, 'Households and labour movements' in *Economic and Social History in the Netherlands: Family Strategies and Changing Labour Relations* 6, Amsterdam, 1994, 129–44.
10. Van der Linden, 'Households and labour movements', 130. Van der Linden also noted as early as 1994 that 'there has been no effort to establish a systematic link between working-class families and labour movements'.
11. This development can be observed in other countries as well. On England for example see E.W. Cooney, 'The origins of the Victorian Master Builders', in: *Economic History Review* 8 (1955–56): 167–76, and Richard Price, *Masters, Unions and Men: Workcontrol and the Rise of Labour 1830–1914*, Cambridge, UK, 1980.
12. This sketch is based on Jeroen J.C. Sprenger, 'Schets van de bouwnijverheid in Nederland, 19e-20e eeuw', in *Historische Bedrijfsarchieven. Bouwnijverheid en -installatiebedrijven: Een geschiedenis en bronnenoverzicht*, Amsterdam, 1993; A. Knotter, 'De Amsterdamse bouwactiviteit in de 19e eeuw tot ca. 1870: Loonarbeid en trekarbeid op een dubbele arbeidmarkt', *Tijdschrift voor Sociale Geschiedenis* 10 (1984): 123–54; Ad Knotter, *Economische transformatie en stedelijke arbeidsmarkt: Amsterdam in de tweede helft van de negentiende eeuw*, Zwolle, 1991; and J.J. van der Wal, *De economische ontwikkeling van het Bouwbedrijf in Nederland*, Delft, 1943.
13. *Statistische Maandberichten Gemeente Amsterdam*, 1908. These figures are for carpenters affiliated with the carpenters' union Concordia Inter Nos (Concord among Us), the painters affiliated with the painters' union Vooruitgang Zij Ons Doel (May Progress Be Our Goal) and the masons affiliated with the masons' union Door Verbroedering Verbetering (Improvement through Brotherhood).
14. Van der Linden, 'Households and labour movements', 131. Van der Linden adds a third point: the desire for justice, of which the desire for equality is an important part. I am inclined to link this point to the desire for dignity and respectability. Justice, equality, dignity and respectability are related concepts.
15. Alf Lüdtke, *Eigen-Sinn: Fabrikalltag, Arbeitererfahrungen und Politik vom Kaiserreich bis in den Faschismus*, Hamburg, 1993, 147; Barrington Moore Jr, *Injustice: The Social Basis of Obedience and Revolt*, White Plains, NY, 1978, 160.

16. Francis Fukuyama, *The End of History and the Last Man*, New York, 1992, 165.
17. Alf Lüdtke, *Eigen-Sinn*, 147.
18. J.R., *Het lot van den Nederlandschen Timmerman en de weg tot verbetering*, Amsterdam, n.d., 15.
19. *Wat meer dan noodig is: Een woord aan de bouwvakarbeiders te Amsterdam, naar aanleiding van de overeenkomst met de A.P.V. welke 1 mei a.s. van kracht wordt*, n.p., 1909, 15 (my emphasis).
20. Directie van den Arbeid, *Arbeidersbudgets gedurende de crisis*, 's-Gravenhage, 1917.
21. In order to make comparisons possible, I focused on the periods 1907–9 (one hundred records), 1915–17 (one hundred records) and 1922–24 (one hundred and two records), periods of relatively high unemployment. Another 57 records were entered from the remaining periods.
22. *De Bouwvakarbeider*, 2 May 1914, 3.
23. *De toestand der werklieden in de bouwbedrijven te Amsterdam: Rapport uitgebracht door de Commissie van Onderzoek, benoemd door den Gemeenteraad in zijne Vergadering van 30 Juni 1897* (The Situation of Workmen in the Construction Industry in Amsterdam: Report Issued by the Investigating Commission Appointed by the Municipal Council at its Meeting on 30 June 1897), Amsterdam, 1906, 30.
24. 'Résumés der verhooren van Getuigen voor de bouwbedrijven' (Summaries of the Testimony of Witnesses from the Construction Industry), 1897, in *Archief van de Commissie van Onderzoek, benoemd door den Gemeenteraad in zijne Vergadering van 30 Juni 1897* (Archive of the Investigating Commission Appointed by the Municipal Council in its Meeting on 30 June 1897), Amsterdam Municipal Archive no. 5408, 95.
25. *De toestand der werklieden*, 27.
26. *Enquête gehouden door de Staatscommissie benoemd krachtens de wet van 19 januari 1890* (Survey Held by the State Commission Named according to the Law of 19 January 1890) (Staatsblad no 1), Part III, Amsterdam, n.p., n.d., 439.
27. J.R., *Het lot van den Nederlandschen Timmerman*, 6.
28. Ibid., 8.
29. Ibid., 8.
30. *Enquête Staatscommissie 1890*, 376.
31. Ibid., 406.
32. *De toestand der werklieden*, 19. See also the annual reports of Concordia Inter Nos 1913, 14; 1914, 15; 1915, 16; 1916, 9. In 1913 the social democratic carpenters' union lost 368 members, of whom fourteen left because they had become bosses. Five of those who had left were now seconds-in-command, four were overseers and two were draughtsmen. There were thus 24 Concordia members in all who had managed to better their position. In 1914 there were thirteen, in 1915 four and in 1916 nine.
33. *Gedenkboek van den Nederlandschen Aannemersbond 1895–1920*, Bussum, 1920, 243; *Enquête Staatscommissie 1890*, 21, 398.
34. Cf. T. van Tijn, 'A Contribution to the Scientific Study of the History of Trade Unions', *International Review of Social History* 21 (1976): 212–39.
35. In only one field did a confessional current organise more than 10 percent of the workforce, namely among carpenters from 1913 on. Membership totals of the carpenters' branch of Patrimonium (1907–8), the Protestants Christelijke Timmerliedenvereeniging (Protestant Carpenters' Union) (1909–1914), St. Joseph (1907–16), and the carpenters' branch of the Gereformeerd Christelijk Werklieden Verbond (the Reformed Christian Workmen's Alliance 1907) are all based on the Statistische Maandberichten Amsterdam (Amsterdam Monthly Statistical Reports); membership totals of the carpenters' branch of the Nederlandsche Christelijke Bouwarbeiders Bond (Dutch Christian Construction Workers' Union) (1911–16) are based on its annual reports.
36. See also M.H.D. van Leeuwen, 'Trade Unions and the Provision of Welfare in the Netherlands 1910–1960', *Economic History Review* 50 (1997): 764–91.
37. Timmerlieden-Vereeniging "Bewust Streven", Afd. van de Landelijke Federatie van Timmerlieden ("Conscious Striving" Carpenters' Union, Branch of the National Carpenters' Union), *Voor de Amsterdamsche Timmerlieden* (For the Amsterdam Carpenters), Amsterdam, 1906, 29–30.
38. Marcel van der Linden and Wayne Thorpe eds, *Revolutionary Syndicalism: An International Perspective*, Aldershot and Brookfield, 1990, 7–9.

39. *De Bouwvakarbeider*, 23 August 1913, 2.
40. Timmerliedenvereeniging Concordia Inter Nos, *Sluit U aan! Ter toelichting: Waarom C.I.N. een collectieve overeenkomst met de Algemeene Patroonsvereeniging "Tot vaststelling en handhaving van arbeidsvoorwaarden voor de bouwbedrijven te Amsterdam" heeft aangegaan*, n.p., n.d., 1.
41. Centralen Bond van Bouwvakarbeiders in Nederland, *Aan de vruchten kent men den boom*, Amsterdam, 1913, 2.
42. Timmerlieden-vereeniging Bewust Streven, *Voor alle arbeiders en timmerlieden in 't bijzonder*, Amsterdam, 1905, 5.
43. Centralen Bond van Bouwvakarbeiders, *Eigen Schuld...!*, n.p., 1917, 3.
44. *Aan de vruchten kent men den boom*, 1.
45. *De Bouwvakarbeider*, 24 December 1910, 3.
46. Concordia Inter Nos Annual Report for 1913, 38.
47. Concordia Inter Nos Annual Report for 1917, 21–2.
48. *De Vrouw*, 1, from *De Bouwvakarbeider*, 1910, IISH.
49. *De Bouwvakarbeider*, 6 March 1909, 1.
50. Ibid., 24 December 1910, 2.
51. For a bibliography on this subject see: Van der Linden, *Households and Labour Movements*, 143.
52. A. Leusink, *Op hechte fundamenten: Geschiedenis van de Algemene Nederlandse Bouwarbeidersbond*, Amsterdam, 1950, 33.
53. *De Bouwvakarbeider*, 3 April 1909, 2.
54. *De Bouwvakarbeider*, 1 May 1909, 2; *Statistische Maandberichten Amsterdam*, November 1907, 17.
55. Centrale Bond van Bouwvakarbeiders Annual Report, 1910, 17.
56. Landelijke Federatie van Bouwvakarbeiders Annual Report, 1918, 44.
57. Landelijke Federatie van Bouwvakarbeiders in Nederland, *Gedenkboekje uitgegeven ter gelegenheid van het 10-jarig bestaan: 1 Februari 1909–1 Februari 1919*, n.p., n.d., 82.
58. *Handleiding voor gemeentebesturen bij de uitvoering van het werkloosheidsbesluit 1917*, 's-Gravenhage, 1921, 9.
59. Landelijke Federatie van Bouwvakarbeiders Annual Report, 1919, 19.
60. Landelijke Federatie van Bouwvakarbeiders Annual Report, 1920, 77, 82–3, 127–32.
61. Ibid., 82.
62. NCB Annual Report, 1919–1920, 36–7.
63. *Statistische Maandberichten Amsterdam*, 1919. The carpenters' union Concordia Inter Nos saw their wages go up by 7.3 percent over the course of the year; the General Dutch Painters' Union had a 19.1 percent increase; the Central Construction Workers' Union achieved a meager gain of 2.5 percent and the Netherlands Roman Catholic Construction Workers' Union gained only 1.6 percent.
64. Landelijke Federatie van Bouwvakarbeiders Annual Report, 1919, 29. The Central Construction Workers' Union, for example, charged more than an hour's wage in 1917 (Centralen Bond van Bouwvakarbeiders, *Wat de organisatie bracht: Een overzicht over het resultaat van 10 jaar werken*, Amsterdam, n.d., back cover. The Federation on the other hand did impose weekly additional payments on its members during actions (Landelijke Federatie van Bouwvakarbeiders Annual Report, 1920, 83).
65. See e.g. Erik Hansen and Peter A. Prosper Jr, 'The National Arbeids-Secretariat between Two Wars: Revolutionary Syndicalism in the Netherlands, 1919–1940', *Histoire social – Social History* 27 (1981): 205.
66. See e.g. Annette van den Berg, *Trade Union Growth and Decline in the Netherlands*, Amsterdam, 1995, 39–41.
67. Van den Berg, *Trade Union Growth*, 209.
68. Concordia Inter Nos Annual Reports, 1910–17.
69. Centrale Bond van Bouwvakarbeiders Annual Reports, 1910–18. The years 1913 and 1917 are missing.
70. *De Bouwvakarbeider*, 13 November 1909, 3.
71. Concordia Inter Nos Annual Report, 1912, 27.
72. Concordia Inter Nos Annual Report, 1914, 4.

73. *De Bouwvakarbeider*, 22 January 1910, 1.
74. Concordia Inter Nos Annual Reports, 1 September 1908–1 January 1910, 8; 1910, 12; 1911, 16.
75. *Het Bouwvak* (The Building Trade), 1 June 1909, 4.
76. Concordia Inter Nos Annual Report, 1 September 1906–31 August 1907, 11.
77. Concordia Inter Nos Annual Report, 1 September 1908–1 January 1910, 11.
78. Concordia Inter Nos Annual Report, 1911, 19.
79. Concordia Inter Nos Annual Report, 1913, 39.
80. Concordia Inter Nos Annual Report, 1911, 32.
81. Landelijke Federatie van Bouwvakarbeiders in Nederland, *Een ernstig woord aan de leden der Landelijke Federatie van Bouwvakarbeiders*, n.p., 1921, 5.
82. *Het Bouwvak*, 1 June 1909, 4.
83. *Sluit U aan!*, 14.
84. *Een ernstig woord aan de leden der Landelijke Federatie van Bouwvakarbeiders*, 5.
85. *De Bouwvakarbeider*, 11 December 1909, 2.
86. J. Haveman, *De ongeschoolde arbeider: Een sociologische analyse*, Assen, 1952; Jac. A.A. van Doorn, *De proletarische achterhoede: Een sociologische critiek*, Meppel, 1954.
87. Van Doorn, *De proletarische achterhoede*.
88. Membership figures for the hod-carriers' union Ontwaakt door Nieuw Leven (Awakened by New Life) are based on the *Statistische Maandberichten Amsterdam*. Membership figures for the navvies' union Helpt Elkander (Mutual Aid) are based on the National Federation of Construction Workers' annual reports. Membership figures for the Amsterdam branch of the Central Construction Workers' Union are based on its annual reports.
89. Membership figures for the masons' union Door Verbroedering Verbetering in 1907–18 are based for the *Statistische Maandberichten Amsterdam*, and for 1919–20 on the National Federation of Construction Workers' annual reports. Membership figures for the Amsterdam branch of the Central Construction Workers' Union are based on its annual reports.
90. Membership figures for Schildersgezellenvereniging Nieuw Leven (New Life Painters' Fraternal Union) are based on National Federation of Construction Workers' annual reports for 1919–20. Membership figures for Schildersgezellenvereeniging Vooruitgang Zij Ons Doel (May Progress Be Our Goal Painters' Fraternal Union) and the carpenters' union Bewust Streven are based on the *Statistische Maandberichten Amsterdam*. Membership figures of the carpenters' union Concordia Inter Nos are based on the *Maandschriften CBS* (Central Statistical Bureau Monthly Releases).
91. Knotter, *Economische transformatie en stedelijke arbeidsmarkt*, 100–13.
92. *Rapport der Commissie van Onderzoek*, 1927, 76, 78.
93. Moore, *Injustice*, 133.
94. *Enquête Staatscommissie 1890*, 242.
95. Sjaak van der Velden, *Stakingen in Nederland: Arbeidersstrijd 1830–1995*, Amsterdam, 2000, provided on CD-ROM.
96. Landelijke Federatie van Bouwvakarbeiders in Nederland, *Notulen van het derde congres gehouden op 21 en 22 april 1912 te Utrecht*, Amsterdam, n.d., 28.

Bibliography

Berg, A. van den, *Trade Union Growth and Decline in the Netherlands*. Amsterdam, 1995.

Cooney, E.W. 'The Origins of the Victorian Master Builders', in *Economic History Review* vol. 8 (1955–56): 167–76.

Doorn, J.A.A. van, *De proletarische achterhoede: Een sociologische critiek*. Meppel, 1954.

Friedman, D. 'Why Workers Strike: Individual Decisions and Structural Constraints', in *The Microfoundations of Macrosociology*, ed. M. Hechter. Philadelphia, 1983, 250–83.

Fukuyama, F. *The End of History and the Last Man*. New York, 1992.

Giddens, A. *The Constitution of Society: Outline of the Theory of Structuration*. Cambridge, UK, 1984.

Hansen, E., and Prosper Jr, P.A. 'The National Arbeids-Secretariat between Two Wars: Revolutionary Syndicalism in the Netherlands, 1919–1940', *Histoire social – Social History* vol. 27 (1981).

Haveman, J. *De ongeschoolde arbeider: Een sociologische analyse*. Assen, 1952.

Knotter, A. 'De Amsterdamse bouwactiviteit in de 19e eeuw tot ca. 1870: Loonarbeid en trekarbeid op een dubbele arbeidmarkt', *Tijdschrift voor Sociale Geschiedenis* vol. 10 (1984): 123–54.

Knotter, A. *Economische transformatie en stedelijke arbeidsmarkt: Amsterdam in de tweede helft van de negentiende eeuw*. Zwolle, 1991.

Leeuwen, M.H.D. van, 'Trade Unions and the Provision of Welfare in the Netherlands 1910–1960', *Economic History Review* vol. 50 (1997): 764–91.

Leusink, A. *Op hechte fundamenten: Geschiedenis van de Algemene Nederlandse Bouwarbeidersbond*. Amsterdam, 1950.

Linden, M. van der, and Thorpe, W., eds. *Revolutionary Syndicalism: An International Perspective*. Aldershot and Brookfield, 1990.

Linden, M. van der, 'Households and Labour Movements' in *Economic and Social History in the Netherlands: Family Strategies and Changing Labour Relations* 6. Amsterdam, 1994, 129–44.

Lüdtke, A. *Eigen-Sinn: Fabrikalltag, Arbeitererfahrungen und Politik vom Kaiserreich bis in den Faschismus*. Hamburg, 1993.

Mann, M. *The Sources of Social Power, Volume 1: A History of Power from the Beginning to A.D. 1760*. Cambridge, UK, 1986.

Moore Jr., B. *Injustice: The Social Basis of Obedience and Revolt*, White Plains, NY, 1978.

Olson, M. *The Logic of Collective Action: Public Goods and the Theory of Groups*. Cambridge, MA, 1965.

Price, R. *Masters, Unions and Men: Workcontrol and the Rise of Labour 1830–1914*. Cambridge, UK, 1980.

Schuurman, A. 'Mensen maken verschil: Sociale theorie, historische sociologie en geschiedenis' in: *Tijdschrift voor Sociale Geschiedenis* vol. 22, no. 2 (1996): 168–204.

Sprenger, J.J.C. 'Schets van de bouwnijverheid in Nederland, 19e-20e eeuw', in *Historische Bedrijfsarchieven. Bouwnijverheid en -installatiebedrijven: Een geschiedenis en bronnenoverzicht*. Amsterdam, 1993.

Tijn, T. van, 'A Contribution to the Scientific Study of the History of Trade Unions', *International Review of Social History* vol. 21 (1976): 212–39.

Velden, S. van der, *Stakingen in Nederland: Arbeidersstrijd 1830–1995*. Amsterdam, 2000.

Wal, J.J. van der, *De economische ontwikkeling van het Bouwbedrijf in Nederland*. Delft, 1943.

Wals, H. *Makers en Stakers. Amsterdamse bouwvakarbeiders en hun bestaansstrategieën in het eerste kwart van de twintigste eeuw*. Amsterdam, 2001.

CHAPTER 9

HIGH-COST ACTIVISM AND THE WORKER HOUSEHOLD

INTERESTS, COMMITMENT, AND THE COSTS OF REVOLUTIONARY ACTIVISM IN A PHILIPPINE PLANTATION REGION

Rosanne Rutten

Why do poor workers engage in high-cost activism that demands from them and their households considerable material sacrifices and physical risks while the benefits for their households appear relatively small and insecure?[1]

This question struck me when I returned in 1992 to one of the major sugar-cane plantation regions of South-east Asia, the Philippine province of Negros Occidental, where I had done research some fourteen years before.[2] During the first research in 1977–78, I had lived on a plantation ('Hacienda Milagros', a pseudonym) where workers were taking the first steps towards collective action and were forming a local chapter of a labour union, gradually achieving success. Inspired by the theory on household living strategies, I explained the activism of the workers as a sensible strategy to defend and improve the income and living conditions of their households, as they sought to raise wages, improve housing, enforce coverage by the state's social security system and medicare, and safeguard stable employment – though the workers did encounter repression by the planter and police at first. The strategic role of married women in workers' collective protests, I argued, stemmed from their role as managers of the household and keepers of the household budget, a role that was publicly acknowledged and that allowed these women to act as the workers' spokespeople to the planter, police, and other relevant parties. Thus, the relationship between household subsistence interests and social activism seemed clear-cut, the one reinforcing the other.[3]

Things had changed, however, when I revisited Negros Occidental. Many workers of Hacienda Milagros, and a large number in the plantation region at large, had joined or supported a communist guerrilla movement, the CPP-NPA (Communist Party of the Philippines-New People's Army), a movement that counted by 1988 some 24,000 guerrillas nation-wide and controlled or influenced about 20 percent of the country's villages and urban neighbourhoods.[4] Their support declined only in the late 1980s-early 1990s as the government intensified its counter-insurgency activities. Living in Hda. Milagros in 1992, I heard numerous accounts of risks and sacrifices over the past years: men and women neglecting their household duties to become activists, teenaged children leaving home to do unpaid, high-risk work as full-time activists in the movement, married activists parting with their newborn babies in order to continue their full-time work for the revolution, while worker-families that stayed behind were vulnerable to repression either by the military or by guerrilla fighters. Four men of Hda. Milagros had been killed by the government military or paramilitary forces; three of these men were full-time activists of the movement at the time of their death.

All these sacrifices to household interests and family attachments were made with an uncertain outcome in view – and if activists believed in the ultimate victory of the revolutionary movement, they expected it only in the long term. In many cases, moreover, these sacrifices were not accepted by all members of the household, but involved intra-household conflicts. To interpret workers' involvement in this high-risk, high-cost activism as a 'household living strategy', then, would leave much unexplained. Here, I take up this theme to discuss some salient aspects in the ambivalent relationship between worker households and activism.[5]

Poor People's Activism: A Household Strategy?

The household, composed of people who 'share the same cooking pot' and sleep under the same roof, and the family, defined here as family members who live together (two units that overlap to a large extent) are among the primary groups that shape people's interests, responsibilities, and loyalties. To understand why people support and join a social movement some studies have, therefore, looked at the household/family unit for relevant motivating factors. They show a marked difference in analytical focus.

Studies on poor people's movements – in particular labour, peasant, and rural revolutionary movements – tend to focus on the socio-economic unit of the *household*, and perceive the economic (subsistence) interests of the household as the main driving force of collective action. Using the 'household strategies' paradigm, explicitly or not, they view the activist poor primarily as household-providers fighting for a better deal.[6] In contrast, studies on 'new social movements' (movements based on other than material class interests) that show an interest in the domestic circle of activists, tend to deal with the socio-cultural unit of the *family*. They note the importance of the family as a locus of mobilisation, stress the role of identity politics, and employ the 'cultural identity' paradigm. The first body of literature neglects potential shifts in perceived interests and identity, the second neglects the more mundane concerns of household livelihood and household responsibilities, in particular when the activists are relatively well-off.[7]

The household living strategies approach certainly has some merits for the analysis of collective action. In contrast to an earlier view of poor people 'exploding' into protest under the pressure of accumulated material strains,[8] the focus on living strategies has helped to promote a concern for motives, decision-making processes, choice situations, and opportunities. Moreover, the view that social ties (in this case the network of household relations) mediate between individual interests and collective action is a useful correction to some currents in collective-action theory that presuppose more or less atomistic individuals reacting to impersonal forces. In this respect, the household strategies approach connects to studies on micromobilisation which deal with the influence of personal ties on people's decisions to engage in activism.[9] The costs and risks of activism may, as well, become more visible through a focus on household survival. Activism requires contributions in money, goods, and manpower that have to be accommodated somehow by the activists' households, and these costs may set the limits to people's activism. As Eric Hobsbawm noted, 'peasant agitations must stop for the harvest. However militant peasants are, the cycle of their labours shackles them to their fate'.[10] Finally, the notion that activism is part of a household strategy suggests that collective action is but one of several options that poor people consider. Finding out why and when needy persons do opt for activism, and how they combine it with other types of action, may further provide insight into the considerations that motivate or constrain it.[11] Yet a major flaw of the household living strategies approach is the assumption that (poor) people act primarily in the material interest of their household.

Problematic Assumption: A Direct Link between Household Interests and Activism

Studies that view poor people primarily as defenders of the interests of their households tend to assume a direct link between household interests and collective action: poor people take collective action when the subsistence interests of their households are threatened, and/or when their activism is rewarded with tangible benefits to their households, such as access to land, protection, and low-cost credit. However, the notion that household interests are the driving force of poor people's activism entails the risk of 'explaining' activism retrospectively as a household living-strategy without adequate evidence that this is indeed so. This is encouraged by several assumptions that underlie the household living strategies approach:

The Household: Unity of Interests or Conflicting Interests?

Individual and household interests are conflated in many studies on poor people's activism. Statements such as: 'peasants whose survival is in immediate question will recognize the common cause and rise up',[12] equate 'peasants' with peasant householders, assume they act in the interest of their whole household, and neglect to specify whether other household members might object to 'rising up'. Even some studies inspired by rational-choice theory – which explicitly distinguishes between individual and group interests – nevertheless combine individual and household interests into a diffuse category of 'individual' interests, and thereby skirt the issue of a possible conflict of interests between individual and household. When Samuel Popkin notes, 'peasants are self-interested, and that means that they are concerned with individual benefits, not group benefits' when contemplating participation in collective action, then he includes economic benefits for the household under 'individual benefits' and refers to social entities that transcend the household as 'groups'. [13]

However, as Diane Wolf has argued, the assumption of 'household unity and consensus in pursuing one collective goal' ignores 'intrahousehold conflict, inequality, and exploitation and basically views household unity as unproblematic'. Moreover, it assumes that 'individuals within the household sublimate their own wishes to [the] larger goal' of defending the collective good of the household.[14]

Not all people identify equally with the interests of their household. After all, commitment to one's household is culturally and socially produced, and sanctioned through power relations. Its intensity can vary by one's position in the household, incentives, and powers of enforcement.[15] Married women, when socialised as nurturing mothers and caring wives, rewarded when fulfilling these household responsibilities, criticised when not, and involved in social networks that reassert these responsibilities, may feel the most committed to their household and its collective interests. Teenagers, involved in peer-groups that foster commitment to social units other than their families, may feel so the least.

Moreover, household members may disagree about the proper way to defend or improve household interests. Women may try to stop husbands from taking risky actions for fear of losing their husband and breadwinner. Men may consider public activism improper for their wives. An eye for such intrahousehold dynamics may bring into focus, for instance, cases of 'husbands who intervened to prevent their wives' striking', as noted among nineteenth-century French worker households.[16]

Individuals committed to their household may themselves feel torn by such conflicting views. For instance, poor women may perceive that 'revolutionary change would enable them to function better as wives, mothers, and providers', and hence revolutionary activism may arise out of their felt obligations to the household.[17] However, when personal costs of activism clash head-on with daily responsibilities at home, guilt-feelings about neglecting obligations as nurturers or breadwinners – possibly deepened by social ostracism – may prove a powerful deterrent to activism. Such dilemmas, well-known among activists, are sometimes publicly acknowledged. A women's organisation affiliated with a major Salvadoran revolutionary movement, for example, called on women to organise 'without experiencing guilt vis-à-vis the "neglected" roles of mother and wife'.[18]

In short, decisions within households about participating in collective actions often involve conflicts and negotiations. Studying such intrahousehold conflicts can illuminate to what extent the activism of *individual* household members actually reflects a *household* living strategy that is supported and approved of by the household as a whole.

Conversely, intrahousehold or intrafamily conflicts may foster individual support for a social movement. In her study on peasant participation in the national independence war in Zimbabwe, Norma Kriger found, for instance, that gender and generational conflicts motivated women and young men to support the guerrilla movement as a means to improve their position *vis-à-vis* (older) men.[19]

Is the Household the Main Social Unit that Commands People's Loyalty?

The household strategies approach assumes that people feel primarily loyal and responsible towards their own household, and that responsibilities towards other people and social entities take the back seat. This household-centred view of individuals tends to ignore that social ties with people outside the household 'create obligations that may conflict with responsibilities as members of a household'.[20]

Hence, by assuming that poor people turn activist to protect the interests of their household, we may easily neglect other social networks and organisations that may shape their interests, responsibilities, and willingness to engage in collective action. We need to place, therefore, such 'multiple social embeddings' of individuals at the centre of our research: by studying the specific obligations and interests that each set of relations fosters among the people involved, we can explore how these social ties may facilitate or work against participation in collective action.[21]

This approach is apparent in recent studies that deal with the relational basis of 'political identities' and the identity-changes that may result from an involvement in shifting networks.[22] Several earlier studies on peasant collective action, by Joel Migdal and Samuel Popkin among others, likewise argued that peasants' involvement in wider social and political networks (in particular those of social movements) could change their perceived interests and goals,[23] and that shifts in local power relations could foster 'new conceptions of identity and self-worth among the peasantry'.[24] Migdal and Popkin both referred to peasants whose long-term involvement in revolutionary organisations changed their perceived interests from individual and household gains to the collective gains of a much larger population. All these studies clearly counter the notion that people are motivated by one fixed set of single-group interests.

The household is, then, but one of many social entities that may claim the loyalty of individual (potential) activists – albeit a very prominent one. Studies that do take account of the multiple networks in which (potential) activists are involved tend to focus on networks that promote activism.[25] But involvement in diverse networks may also entail competing claims – claims on the individual that may constrain activism. Sets of social relationships can be 'demanding in regard to time, energy, and emotional attachment', and may 'constitute countervailing influences' and commitments 'with respect to alternative networks and lines of action'.[26] As a study on women's participation in a Tennessee union argued, for instance, 'household, corporation, and union, [may] compete with one another for the time and allegiances of individuals and, in so doing, constrain individual decisions to engage in activism'.[27]

Households and social movements may thus compete for the commitment and resources of their members. Social movements try to incorporate supporters in a network of social ties that provide ideological and social sanctions aimed at promoting commitment.[28] Radical or underground movements whose cadres engage in high-risk activism seek to maximise member commitment by trying to monopolise their social networks and isolate them from competing ties.[29] Ties with family members and with spouses or lovers, in particular, entail emotional attachments and responsibilities that may weaken the activists' commitment to the movement and their willingness to take high risks.[30]

Household Strategies

The assumption that poor people act on the basis of 'household strategies' (long-term plans of action for the benefit of the household) may tempt authors to interpret specific actions as the concrete expression of household strategies without concrete evidence that this is so. As Marianne Schmink notes,

> Most studies focus only on the outcome of behavior, presuming that the logic motivating household decisions is revealed in crystallized form by the outcome of those decisions …. The existence or nonexistence of explicit goals and the nature of their content and time frame are questions for empirical research …. If households have no explicit objectives and merely respond to one set of circumstances after another, then the concept of strategy becomes synonymous with the household's history … [and] can lose its meaning to the extent that it becomes *a mere functionalist label applied ex post facto to whatever behavior is found*. [emphasis added][31]

Wolf has rightly argued for replacing the term 'household strategies' with the more neutral term of 'household practices', which 'imputes fewer motives to the actors' and leaves it to researchers to determine empirically to what extent activities of household members are indeed part of household strategies.[32]

Taking Account of Culture

It is often assumed that people shape their household strategies in response to the opportunities and constraints they face. A shift towards social activism is then explained by shifts in material and strategic options. Yet people's living strategies are also cultural and social constructs.[33] People define certain strategies as feasible and desirable, and internalise these definitions through socialisation; such definitions are subject to change. Hence, cultural notions affect how people perceive and weigh their available options. In the Philippine plantation region of Negros Occidental, for instance, social activism gained in respectability among plantation workers as a result of social and ideological changes, as is elaborated further below.

Household Interests Versus High-risk/High-cost Activism

The household living strategies approach cannot adequately explain why people engage in activism that entails high costs and high risks for their households – in particular, full-time participation in a revolutionary guerrilla movement – while providing insecure returns. A common explanation in terms of household interests states that poor people engage in such activism only when they are forced to react to an acute household subsistence crisis or an acute danger to the physical survival of themselves or other household members. In the area of my research, however, these conditions did not apply to many of the workers who had become full-time members of the guerrilla movement. Studies inspired by the rational-choice approach, in contrast, argue that people engage in high-cost activism when the high costs they incur are matched by high rewards.[34] Rewards include material benefits for the activists' households (material goods acquired through collective action, such as land in the case of peasant movements) and, for individual activists, social rewards such as status and power within the activist organisation. These studies tend to ignore, however, that individual rewards may entail household costs: households of individual activists may lose more to the activist cause than they gain, and may bear substantial risks of repression.

In Hacienda Milagros, the material benefits to the households of full-time revolutionaries were minimal compared with the costs. Social and emotional 'benefits' were certainly experienced by household members: respect for the family within the NPA's community network, personal gratification from having a close family member fighting for a just cause, admiration for the activism of a child or sibling, supported by the prevailing revolutionary discourse that stressed the value of sacrifice and martyrdom; but these were overshadowed by costs. Family members were burdened by anguish. They experienced, moreover, the absence of their child or sibling as a material loss and as a missed contribution to household uplift by safer means. Besides, future benefits for the household expected after the movement's victory, including worker ownership of hacienda land, would be reaped by all households supporting the movement regardless of any extra efforts of its members.

In many cases, it was *against* the will of their parents and against the interests of their households at large that sons and daughters decided to engage in the costly activism of full-time revolutionaries. What facilitated their move was their increasing *detachment* from their families, in social and emotional terms. The majority of plantation workers who joined the guerrilla movement as full-timers were young single men and women, who identified less with the immediate interests of their households than their parents and younger siblings and who, in their pre-marriage state, were not yet committed to a new household of their own. It was their relatively weak commitment to their own household that made them, to cite Doug McAdam, 'biographically available' for high-risk activism.[35]

For these activists, new circles of identification (activist peer groups and the revolutionary movement) and a new ideology had been instrumental in refocusing the object of their personal responsibilities and loyalties away from the 'narrow' circle of their household towards the movement and the 'oppressed people' at large. An extreme expression of such redefinitions of personal commitments is the willingness to sacrifice one's life for the common good, to become a 'martyr'. This redefinition of identity is supported by the individual's active network of movement cadres and supporters who form new, influential reference groups.

Martyrdom and household interests seem to fit badly. Truly baffling from the vantage point of the household living-strategies approach is, for instance, the following remark by a Punjabi woman in Canada, 'As for my sons, I'll feel proud if they get killed for a holy cause'.[36] The woman belonged to a Sikh migrant community and supported the movement for an independent Khalistan. Though she and her husband had suffered repression in India, her immediate family was not physically or economically threatened at the time she made the remark. In this immigrant community, families attached honour to the high-risk activism of their members, supported considerable sacrifices by close kin, and shared a commitment to the wider cause of the Sikhs, a commitment reproduced through active ideological work and community-based social control. This shared, family-based commitment apparently resolved the potential conflict between the household and high-risk activism.[37]

Case studies that analyse such socio-cultural processes of identity shifts primarily deal with high-risk activists whose households are economically quite secure, for instance, militant Sikh migrants in Canada, Basque activists of the ETA, Irish supporters of the IRA.[38] Given the common assumption that poor people's activism is, in contrast, driven by household interests and commitments, researchers are ill-equipped to recognise shifts in poor people's perceptions of their life-world and their responsibilities and loyalties in it, in particular when these involve a weakening of identification with their own household.[39]

In the following sections, I discuss and illustrate some of the points argued above by exploring how worker households in a Philippine sugar-cane plantation, Hacienda Milagros, have dealt with the problem of the costs and risks of activism.

Social Activism in the Hacienda Region of Negros Occidental

The province of Negros Occidental, on the Central-Philippine island of Negros, counts several thousand sugarcane haciendas on the vast lowland plain that stretches from the northern tip of the island to the upland frontier some seventy-five miles to the south, flanked on the west by Panay Gulf and on the east by a volcanic mountain range that divides the island in two. Fifteen sugar centrals stand as industrial enclaves in the canefields. The milled sugar is sold on domestic and export markets which firmly link the provincial society with distant commercial centres. The haciendas range in size from about twenty to over a thousand hectares (the majority fall within the twenty to one hundred and fifty hectares range), and are mostly owned by planter families who live in the provincial towns or Manila. Some two hundred thousand wage-dependent workers (women and men) from a total provincial population of 2.2 million, do back-breaking labour in the canefields and survive precariously on low and irregular wages. Permanent workers who live with their families on hacienda premises, and casual workers who live on or near haciendas, plough, weed, and cut the ripe cane, and are joined by migrant cane-cutters in the harvest season.[40]

Personal dependency has long marked the worker-planter tie in Negros Occidental. Organised forms of collective action developed slowly. In the first half of this century, two millenarian movements, followed by several workers' mutual-aid societies (controlled by urban intellectuals and politicians), had a following among hacienda workers in scattered parts of the island, but they did not last long.[41] Planter repression thwarted union efforts in the 1950s and 1960s.

Ironically, it was only after the declaration of martial law in 1972 by then President Ferdinand Marcos that labour unions gradually gained a foothold in haciendas. Facilitating factors were the state's (partial) control of planter violence, and the president's effort to court the worker population by proclaiming new minimum wage laws and welfare measures, and having these widely aired over the media. Moreover, in reaction to the martial-law regime, an increasing number of the provincial Roman Catholic clergy radicalised politically. They started a movement for organising hacienda workers and poor villagers into so-called Basic Christian Communities (BCC), which served not only as communities of worship but also as organisations for collective claim-

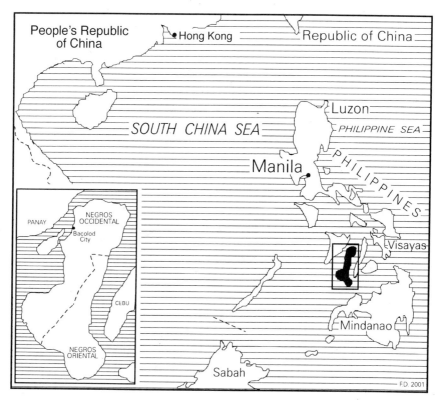

Map. 9.1 *The province of Negros Occidental, Philippines*

making *vis-à-vis* the planters and the state. These BCCs would form the organisational nuclei for many hacienda-based chapters of the new, militant labour union, the National Federation of Sugar Workers (NFSW).

Opportunities for workers' collective action further increased with the expansion across the province of a nationwide revolutionary movement, the CPP-NPA. The CPP-NPA, henceforth called 'NPA', was founded in the national capital region as a Maoist guerrilla movement in 1968–69. In Negros Occidental, student activists established its first rural base in the southern peasant uplands in the early 1970s, and local NPA organisers expanded into the hacienda lowlands in the late 1970s and 1980s.[42] By 1986, some 100,000 peasants and hacienda workers across Negros had joined the NPA's community-based mass organisations, and some 450 guerrilla fighters, recruited from the local population, were fielded across the island, backed up by several thousand community militias.[43] Decline in NPA strength set in as the new government of President Aquino (1986–92) launched a concerted counter-insurgency drive coupled to an amnesty programme, and as the restoration of electoral democracy won middle-class support for the government and strengthened the position of provincial élites. Contributing further to the decline was a split in the revolutionary movement over issues of strategy and leadership.[44]

Hacienda Milagros

Hacienda Milagros is an average-sized sugarcane hacienda (130 hectares) located in the lowlands, with some sixty wage-earning families living and working on its land. The planter lives with his family in the provincial capital, a half-hour jeep-ride away. A resident overseer and two or three foremen make up the local management; they are, together with several drivers of trucks and tractors, the only salaried employees (*empleados*) in the hacienda. The resident workers (men, women, teenagers, and some children) are paid daily or piece-rate wages. Their low and irregular income has long spelled poverty, marked by malnourishment, illnesses like tuberculosis, and low levels of education. Conditions have somewhat improved in the last twenty years, partly brought about by workers' successful collective actions: infant mortality declined, more children are able to attend high school, and several worker and *empleado* families presently own battery-powered television sets. However, the cramped houses lack latrines and electricity, and many families cannot cover basic costs of medicine and education.

Workers of Hda. Milagros took advantage of successive opportunities for organisation and collective action. In varying numbers, they first organised into a BCC in the mid-1970s, then joined a moderate labour union to claim legal benefits (thirteenth month pay), which the planter finally provided after he had locked out several active union members. They subsequently joined the left-wing union NFSW which helped improve labour conditions, and eventually many (though not all) willingly supported the NPA. By the mid-1980s the NPA considered the hacienda a solidly organised community. In this period, the NPA backed up workers' actions for better wages and benefits, while extracting an increasing flow of contributions from the worker households for the benefit of the movement at large. Workers' support for the NPA declined in the late 1980s-early 1990s as counter-insurgency activities intensified and as the movement split into two rival factions.

The Household: a Locus of Conflict and Solidarity

In Hda. Milagros, the people who form a household and need to keep it afloat are members of the nuclear family plus, in several cases, one or two grandparents or a married daughter or son with spouse and child. To a varying extent, they share a single budget and pool their labour and resources; a young couple that lives in may handle its own budget. The culturally prescribed responsibilities of household members are clear enough: the husband as the main income provider should turn over his income to his wife, who controls the household budget and needs to make ends meet. Most women in the hacienda are, by necessity, substantial income-providers as well, but they tend to view their wage labour in the canefields or their work as small-scale traders or laundrywomen as a means of 'helping their husbands'. Children are expected from an early age to help with household chores and later to contribute to household income, and it is primarily their mothers who are responsible for disciplining the children to take up these tasks. These joint responsibilities for household subsistence as well as actual interdependencies are matched by values that promote loyalty, commitment, and emotional attachment to one's immediate family, and hence identification with household interests.

Nevertheless, the actual pooling of labour and income in the household may be a source of conflict and bargaining, locally referred to as 'problems in the household'. Some men refuse to hand over their income to their wife, or 'roam around' with their male friends instead of helping around the house. Some women and men spend a sizeable part of the household budget on alcoholic drinks and gambling. Teenaged children may be unwilling to help in the house or to share their wage earnings as much as their parents expect them to. Given the intensive social life in the hacienda, peers, kin, and neighbours are major competitors to the loyalty, time, and resources of household members.

Household Living Practices in Pre-activist Days

To feed and clothe the members of their household, provide an adequate roof over their heads, and finance the education of their children, is certainly an important goal for married workers of Hda. Milagros, and a major source of daily worries.

In pre-activist days (up to the 1970s) the following repertoire was more or less standard among the workers of Hda. Milagros: during the labour-intensive milling season, men, women, and older children worked as much as possible in the canefields for a wage. The lean season in cane cultivation, with hacienda work budgeted by household, forced workers to fall back on other sources of income: men worked as carpenters in the hacienda or as construction labourers or fish vendors in the provincial capital, Bacolod City. Women sought extra earnings as small-scale traders of foodstuffs, and sold the produce from their kitchen gardens as well as a pig or two and some chickens they were raising throughout the year. Some daughters and sons who worked as household helpers or shop assistants in the city sent monthly remittances home. Efforts to improve living conditions and raise the life chances of the children included sending one or more children through high school (if financially possible) and allowing enterprising children to try their luck in Manila.

Individual efforts and personal ties of assistance were the means by which workers tried to cope with setbacks and improve the living conditions of their household. This included migrating to other haciendas, the upland frontier, or the city, and developing a network of ties with (potential) benefactors. Within the hacienda, good personal relationships with the foremen and overseer were rewarded with better access to light work, house-repair materials, and hacienda credit. Workers' personal networks of kin, ritual kin (through the *compadrazgo* system), friends, and neighbours, extending well beyond the hacienda, also served as conduits of help in hard times, though not in the more organised form of mutual-aid societies. Workers' protests against planter policies (too little rice credit in the lean season, inadequate upkeep of houses, and the like), were limited to complaints to the overseer, either individually or in small groups. Given their personal dependency on the planter and overseer for access to work, credit, and any possible improvement in their households' life chances, avoiding 'trouble' with these powerful figures was a common-sense strategy.

The Period of Labour Activism

Household Interests Promoting Labour Activism

Household subsistence was the focal point of the early labour activism in the hacienda in the 1970s. Workers responded to the mobilising efforts of labour unions that were pressing for the payment of legal wages and benefits. Informed by radio of new labour laws, about half of the women and men of Hda. Milagros formed a union chapter in the mid-1970s and filed a labour case in court to claim their thirteenth month pay. They were eventually successful in court, but at the cost of lockouts and other forms of harassment by the planter. Vulnerable to such planter repression, most workers gave up membership in this union.

Meanwhile, progressive Catholic clergy inspired by Vatican II's call for social justice were likewise mobilising workers by addressing the problems of household subsistence and poverty. The local parish priest and nuns began to organise workers of Hda. Milagros into a BCC to enable them to defend their interests collectively. They appealed to the right of labourers to human dignity and hence their right to secure a decent livelihood for their families, and addressed the married workers as 'fathers' and 'mothers'. For the workers, these were meaningful appeals.

As they joined a left-wing labour union in the late 1970s, the NFSW, labourers of Hda. Milagros continued to stress their familial responsibilities in the collective actions they staged. When they lodged collective complaints against the planter – concerning low piece-wages, poor housing, too little work, low rice credits in the lean season (distributed per household) – they often referred to the need of their families for adequate food and housing. Married women, as managers of their households' finances, were often the spokespersons, sending a powerful message to the planter that they were speaking on behalf of their families.

Household Interests Discouraging Labour Activism: Dealing with Conflicting Interests

Household interests, however, could militate against labour activism. 'If I lose my job, what then? Can the union sustain my family then?' Such concerns with the risks of labour activism were particularly marked during the early days of activism in the hacienda, when the risks of planter repression were real. Households of Milagros were divided. Workers had to chose between two conflicting household interests: striving collectively for better labour and living conditions, or protecting their relatively secure position as permanent workers and possible other 'privileges' such as a favourable access to work and house repairs through friendly ties with the overseer. At first, many households opted for the last and were reluctant to join collective actions – in particular households with close kin ties to the overseer.[45] However, as the planter replaced the local overseer with an outsider (which dissolved workers' kin ties with local management) and as organised workers reaped small successes when the planter gradually turned from repression to accommodation, most of the reluctant workers eventually joined as well.

Subsequently, another friction between household interests and labour activism arose: competition between household and union for the households' manpower and material resources. Workers who participated in a delegation to the planter's house, or in rallies in the city, had to skip a day's work and hence their households lost their day's income. This problem increased as workers got involved, through the union, in a broad left-wing movement that staged numerous rallies in the provincial capital against worker exploitation, discrimination against women, human rights abuses, oil price hikes, and the like. Worker activists sought a solution by means of a system they called 'one undivided part' (*isa ka partida*). They arranged that most work in the hacienda was done in large groups on a piece-wage basis. The wage income was shared equally among all workers in each group, including those worker-members who had to forgo a day's work to participate in collective actions for a collective good. The wage share of these activist workers was called *consumo*, income to cover their households' basic consumption needs.

Activists also addressed household interests in their effort to solve the freerider problem. The selective rewards that the worker-officials of the hacienda-based union chapter were able to supply to active union members concerned primarily resources for the household. Active union members were rewarded, for instance, with privileged access to farmlots (small pieces of land that the planter had 'loaned' cost-free to worker households for subsistence production, as a result of union pressure) and to union-supplied inputs for these farmlots, such as fertiliser on credit. Workers who were unwilling or afraid to support the union, attend its regular meetings in the hacienda, and participate in collective actions, received lengthy home visits by worker-officials who argued that the union was in the best interest of their families. Negative sanctions included social isolation. In this tightly-knit community where families worked, lived, and spent their leisure time together, or at least in close proximity, and where the union became a new focal point of organisation and interaction, not supporting the union meant social marginalisation. It also entailed isolation from the channels of communication of the broad left-wing movement in the region (legal and underground) through which workers were informed, for instance, about impending military patrols in the area.

Increasing Costs: The Period of Revolutionary Activism

The Limits of a Household-interests Approach

Workers' subsequent support for the revolutionary movement NPA consisted of three possible forms. Each consecutive form of support involved more costs and risks: (1) Providing small but regular contributions in cash, rice, and other goods, and regular attendance at left-wing rallies in the city: as the NPA gained control over the hacienda, the NPA demanded such contributions of all households. (2) Taking up the role of a local part-time activist (without remuneration), which demanded considerable investments in time and increased the risks for oneself and one's household. And (3) leaving home and joining the movement as a mobile, full-time activist, in return for a very small allowance (to cover the costs of soap and the like): in Hda. Milagros, thirteen young single women and men, and two married men, took this step to become full-time organisers, guerrilla fighters, medical assistants, and financial officers. Eventually, small allowances for the 'dependants' (children of full-timers) were added, which remained, however, far below subsistence level.

The first type of support for the NPA did appear to be related in a positive and direct sense to the household interests of the workers. Workers of Milagros explained to me that they supported the movement (in the form of regular contributions in cash and kind) in order to safeguard the gains they had achieved through union actions, in particular the gains in the security and improvement of household livelihood. In their view, the guerrilla fighters protected union activists and enhanced the bargaining power of workers, by threatening planters with violent reprisals if they failed to give in to workers' demands or repressed workers' activism. In a considerable number of haciendas, NPA activists burned canefields or tractors of planters unwilling to pay higher wages, and threatened or actually killed overseers who sought to block worker activism. In the absence of a strong state that would protect workers' rights, the workers had, for the first time, a powerful supporter that enhanced their bargaining power considerably.

However, concerning the second and third type of support, conflicts within households and between household members and revolutionary activists revealed considerable tension between the interests of the household, as perceived by some of the household members, and the interests of household members who became activists. Stated simply, parents or spouses of activists felt that the latter acted against the immediate interests of their household. They tried either to dissuade them from their activism (which sometimes involved serious frictions and disputes), or they gradually adopted the latter's view that it was right to sacrifice household interests for the interests of a wider community of the poor. I elaborate these points further below.

How the Movement Tapped the Household for the Revolution

The revolutionary movement sought to tap the household as a reservoir of economic and social resources. Contributions to the NPA were levied by household: a monthly contribution of a small can of rice and two pesos (the cash amount was about one tenth of the daily wage in the mid-1980s); plus occasional contributions, solicited house-to-house, for the meals of visiting NPA fighters, transportation to city-based rallies, or medical emergencies. Besides, hacienda households sheltered and fed organisers and other full-timers deployed in the hacienda or passing through, and those tending small hacienda stores were asked to provide goods such as cigarettes.

Moreover, the movement could profit from the household as a unit of reproduction and care. Since full-timers received only minimal allowances from the movement they tried, whenever possible, to solicit such valuable goods as jackets, shoes, and medicine from their own households, through a network of couriers. As full-timers married and had children in the movement, these children were placed under the care of the household of either the mother's or the father's parents, or otherwise of other trusted households in the full-timers' area of operation.

The household also served as a unit of camouflage and protection for revolutionary activists. Hacienda homes were used as 'fronts' to shelter cadres, hold ideological seminars and local meetings, as well as meetings of revolutionary committees. Operating within and near hacienda homes allowed full-timers to blend into daily routines of household activities whenever military patrols got near.

The Ideological Framing of Household Sacrifices for the Movement

To gain the initial, minimal forms of contributions from hacienda workers, NPA organisers appealed to the household interests of the workers and to their responsibilities as fathers and mothers. In informal talks and seminars, they highlighted the inability of the workers to provide a decent livelihood for their households and to secure a better future for their children which, they said, could only be remedied through organised action under the wings of the revolutionary movement. Thus, they touched a highly sensitive spot among married women and men: the status of married people within the local community, as well as their own sense of self-worth, was closely linked to their performance as parents. In a sense, the organisers appealed to workers to be good mothers and fathers – according to established cultural notions – and to accept the necessary sacrifices that organisation and collective action entailed. Married men were explicitly organised as fathers in a hacienda-based organisation of 'fathers', and married women in an organisation of 'mothers'.

NPA organisers, then, sought to align workers' household interests with the interests of the movement. They partly succeeded in doing so. Backed by the coercive powers of the NPA, and operating through local union networks, labourers of Milagros were successful in gaining from the planter wage increases and the free use of a small part of hacienda land for subsistence agriculture. As some workers put it, 'the NPA will defend us when we have problems with the planter', and 'without the NPA, we will lose our gains and the planter will become despotic again'. Moreover, NPA activists tried to discipline drunkard, quarrelsome, or adulterous spouses, and pressured them, under threats of physical punishment, to act as responsible heads of households.

Concerning part-time and full-time activists, however, the added contributions they were expected to provide to the movement were not balanced by added benefits to their households. Household benefits, actual or expected, accrued to most worker households in the hacienda regardless of whether or not they invested *extra* time and resources in the movement. This posed a problem for NPA organisers: they needed, somehow, to motivate potential activists among the workers to forsake the immediate interests of their household and their concrete responsibilities as household members.

Commitment to one's household or immediate family is, to a large extent, a product of socialisation, an ideology that celebrates and reaffirms such commitment, and real relations of interdependency and interaction that tend to develop and confirm it. On these four fronts – ideology, socialisation, real interdependencies, and regular interaction – the movement introduced alternatives that had the effect of weakening a household's claim on the loyalty of its members, and of shifting – to a varying extent – commitment from the household to the NPA.

NPA organisers introduced a new concept in the hacienda, *personal enteres* (personal interests), a concept with a negative connotation that denoted placing one's personal and family interests before those of the movement and oppressed people at large. It stood in stark contrast to the glorified 'service to the people'. Together with other NPA-introduced terms like *burgis* (denoting the whole complex of bourgeois culture marked by family-based accumulation and power) and *pyudal* (referring to 'feudal', authoritarian personal relations, including relations in the family), the concept was meant to erode that essential Filipino value: the centrality of family interests and loyalties. *Personal enteres* became a catchword among organisers and local activists.

These terms were introduced as part of a large-scale ideological offensive to inspire support for the movement. They fit into the Marxist analysis of society that organisers presented to the workers, an analysis that defined current conditions as unjust, identified the people and structures to blame, suggested that the aggrieved party could do something about it, and set out a path of action.[46] Numerous seminars, as well as songs, dances, and plays enacted by the movement's youth group in the hacienda, all stressed the need to sacrifice for the eventual liberation of 'the oppressed people', and attached honour to such sacrifice. These new perceptions were activated and reproduced within new, NPA-dominated networks and organisations in the hacienda.

One of the largest sacrifices for a household – letting go of a son or daughter who wanted to serve the movement as a full-time revolutionary – was handled delicately by NPA organisers. Strong parental opposition could turn into antagonism toward the movement. High-ranking NPA officials asked parents seriously and solemnly for permission to take their child, focusing on the moral value of sacrifice. They took care to recast familial sacrifice and loss as contributions to future improvement of the family's life chances: they argued that the only way to give their children and grandchildren a truly brighter future (a prime cultural value) was to let their activist child join the movement as a full-timer. Parents who asked about death benefits or allowances in case their child should perish, were told there would be none, but their child would be viewed as a hero, and the workers in the hacienda would stand by the bereaved family. Whatever the sentiments of the parents, they could not force their children to stay. Many youths left against their parents' wishes.

Dealing with Costs: Conflicts in the Household

Apparently, activist workers of Milagros set one clear limit to the costs of their activism: their households should not starve as a result of it. Thus, married workers whose households depended heavily on their income did not leave home to become full-time revolutionaries, unless they were forced to hide from the military. Neither did single youths who were the only ones living with, and caring for, their elderly parents.[47] In such cases, then, responsibility towards the household overruled all other loyalties.

The only married persons who joined the movement as *full-timers* were two men who were targeted by the military because of their part-time activist work for the movement and ran a considerable risk of being killed if they were to stay in the hacienda. Both discussed this decision with their families. As one recounted, 'I asked permission from my wife and parents'. They discussed how their households would survive in their absence, and solutions were sought in soliciting help from their extended families. Perhaps these were the only cases in which activist sacrifices to the household were unequivocally supported by all members of their households.

In the case of teen-aged children or young single men and women who left home to join the movement full-time, conditions were different. They were not targeted by the military; they chose to take this step, within the constraints of their activist peer group, the influence of revolutionary ideology, the recruitment appeals of NPA organisers, and their past careers as part-time activists.

In doing so, many deviated considerably from the 'living strategies' their parents had mapped for them. Some were high-school students at the time they left home to become an underground cadre. Their parents and siblings had borne their schooling costs as an investment in a better future for the children themselves and possibly their siblings, and those investments then came to nothing. Others were workers in the canefields and were needed as income-earners, and possibly also as 'investors' in the schooling of younger siblings. Besides these considerations, awareness of the physical risks to which their child would be exposed clashed with the parents' concerns for improving the life chances of their children. The relative weight of these considerations could vary among parents. Parents who were not actively involved in the NPA organisations in the hacienda, and who felt little affinity with the cause and ideology of the movement, resented their child's NPA career the most. Among parents who were part-time activists in the hacienda and sympathised with their child's convictions, reactions ranged from refusal to consent with a heavy heart.

In contrast with full-timers, *part-time activists* – who remained in the hacienda – were faced with a different set of problems in their households: the majority were married women and men whose busy schedules impinged on their household duties. Such worker-activists included officials of the hacienda-based party-branch (a branch of the underground CPP) and of the organising groups of women, men, and youths, as well as members of the committees on organisation, education, finance, defence, and health care that were eventually established. Their activities involved numerous tasks that were typical of agents in any centralised organisation: holding seminars, attending meetings, writing progress reports, and managing the implementation of programmes handed down by their superiors. Wives complained that their activist husbands failed to do their share in feeding, clothing, and protecting their families. Husbands had similar complaints about their activist wives, as I learned during my field-work:

> The husband of an organiser, not active in the movement himself, began to complain that his wife was helping other people elsewhere but failed to help the people in her own house: since she had cut back on her wage-work in the canefields, her children lacked money for uniforms and other schooling costs. She tried to solve the problem by laying out a commercial vegetable garden in her yard to be tended by her children, but her children were uncooperative and she ended up tending the vegetables herself in the few spare moments she had.

This illustrates a general problem across the movement. 'The more their responsibilities for the movement increased, the more they lacked time for their families', said a former activist in the southern uplands; if they were to shoulder even more responsibilities, 'their families would go hungry'.

The standard solution employed by the NPA was ideological and moral. Leaders of the 'fathers' or 'mothers' would explain to the duped spouses that their activist spouse was working for the *common* good and his or her sacrifices deserved full support. In fact, most activists preferred some form of conjugal activism, in which both spouses were firmly involved in NPA networks, shared the same level of ideological 'awareness', and were equally committed to the movement, though not always equally active. In such cases, spouses of activists tended to accept the latter's obligations to the movement and took over some of their household tasks as well.

Meanwhile, as local part-time activists began to identify with their new roles and responsibilities, their thoughts were more and more with the movement, the 'struggle', their new responsibilities, their superiors in the movement who regularly checked on their performance, and their activist network in the hacienda that began to claim much of their time. In several cases, at least, their growing commitment to the movement and its cause tended to weaken their concern for their own households.

Dealing with Costs: Clashes between Full-time Revolutionaries and their Superiors

The movement expected complete commitment from its full-time activists. To this effect, it sought to minimise competing attachments as much as possible: family visits were curtailed, and longing for loved ones was branded as 'sentimentalism'. Courtship – the first step towards creating a new family of one's own – was strictly regulated, allowed only between partners with an equal level of revolutionary awareness and commitment to the cause, and was expected to culminate in a party marriage that placed commitment to the movement first. In this endeavour, the movement had a valuable asset: the image of the full-timer as a model of selfless dedication to the interests of the poor and to the revolution. This image was very attractive to idealistic youths, and those who went full-time were thoroughly socialised in this new identity, which linked self-sacrifice for the common good to a powerful sense of self-worth. Many full-timers did complain about the strict courtship rules, and many started illicit relations with comrades and were punished with demotion; but apparently these attachments to lovers who were fellow-activists did not considerably weaken their commitment to the movement.

However, new familial responsibilities came into play as full-timers married fellow cadres in the movement and had children. Full-timers were not allowed to form a household with their spouse and newborn baby. After all, 'serving the people' was considered a full-time job that left no room for a family life of one's own. The spouses were often deployed in different areas, and had to leave their own children under the care of their parents or other trusted persons, whom they were allowed to visit only once in a while. Nevertheless, the children's existence activated parental attachments and a sense of parental obligation.

The interests of these activists as full-timers *and* parents began to clash with those of the movement. They felt that the movement provided too little financial assistance for the upkeep of their children. The NPA even cut off the children's allowances when the movement's income (derived from 'voluntary' taxes, extortion, and 'confiscation') declined. Several ex-full-timers whom I interviewed recounted that they experienced this as a form of disrespect for themselves as persons, and for their sacrifice for the movement. Moreover, as their children grew older in their absence, they became even more painfully aware that they were unable to be good parents and they blamed, to a varying extent, the movement's leadership for it.

These problems of family subsistence and familial obligations formed one of the reasons for the *exit* of full-time activists from the movement, often in combination, for instance, with illness or personal conflicts with superiors. This outflow of married full-timers was a region-wide phenomenon and increased in scope as the demographic make-up of the body of full-timers changed towards a larger percentage of married members. For the movement, the outflow became an acute problem when the inflow of new (mostly single) recruits declined – a decline that was due, in particular, to an intensification of counter-insurgency.

Networks and Competing Loyalties

Besides the household/family, other networks and organisations may compete for the loyalty of individuals and may shape their interests and sense of obligations. We should view this as a dynamic process, related to people's involvement in changing social networks. Studies of collective action and social-movement participation have long focused on social ties that facilitate such action and disregarded 'ties that are constraining involvement'.[48] Since 'individuals are embedded in many relationships that may expose the individual to conflicting pressures', we need to study the effects of these 'multiple embeddings' on social activism, as Doug McAdam and Ronnelle Paulsen argue.[49] Take, for instance, the following case:

> In the early 1980s, the household of the overseer of the hacienda that neighbors Hda. Milagros was riven by conflict over the issue of support for the revolutionary movement. The overseer was firmly locked into a patron-client tie with the planter. Feeling a deep personal loyalty towards the planter, he resisted any support for the 'subversive' movement. His wife and daughter, however, got involved in the leftwing network of the local Catholic Church by means of their active membership of a Church-based women's group and the Basic Christian Community (BCC) in the hacienda, and they developed a sympathy for the broad leftwing movement which later focused on the NPA. The daughter became a BCC activist. Based on her experiences, discussions, and contacts with NPA supporters within this leftwing Church network, and her marriage to a radical Church activist, she eventually joined the NPA. This process involved intense conflicts between father and daughter, but the father's opposition was defeated by the growing influence of the NPA in the community.

By the mid-1980s, NPA activists in Hda. Milagros had formed organising groups of women, men, and youth, and numerous NPA committees, which in turn formed new networks that competed with the household for the individual's time, energy, and loyalty. That these community-based NPA organisations were not based on household clusters, but on gender and generation, may have helped to weaken the activist workers' primary loyalty to their household.

The youth group of the NPA was the most successful in redirecting individual loyalties towards the NPA. It acted as a peer-group engaged in 'cultural work', staging revolutionary plays and songs. Many hacienda youths were keen to join, and besides the camaraderie and excitement it offered, their involvement in the youth group increased their commitment to the movement's cause. Members of the youth group were groomed to become activists and eventually full-time NPAs in total service to the movement; the activities of this group were partly intended to move the youths into a peer-group committed to the NPA. Some parents tried to prevent this from happening by refusing to allow their teen-aged children to follow seminars or join the youth group, or by sending them to relatives in Manila when organisers put pressure on their children to join.

New instances of conflicting loyalties developed as the power balance in the area changed in favour of the Philippine army in the late 1980s-early 1990s. A former high-ranking NPA cadre from Milagros was captured by the army in 1988 and, disillusioned by the NPA leadership in the previous years, he began to support the army in its campaign to convince workers to renounce their support for the NPA. In his *anti*-NPA activism in the area – which consisted primarily of ideological work (seminars), helping NPA cadres to exit safely from the movement, and convincing workers to avail themselves of the government services that were offered as part of the counter-insurgency campaign – he could draw on the deep concern of parents to see their NPA-activist children return home safely. He also tried to recruit his nieces and nephews from Milagros into a youth group that staged anti-NPA songs and skits at public gatherings in the area. These girls and boys – too young to have experienced the NPA cultural group that was active in the hacienda before – thought it fun and earned an allowance besides. However, these teenagers were still embedded in a community-based network of the NPA, with several adult women and men of Milagros (some of whom were their relatives) retaining their positions as local NPA activists. These activists noted with concern that the youths were being 'brainwashed' by the military and eventually stopped their participation.

What makes these social ties relevant, then, is whether they foster identification with people or communities other than the household, and thus affect the individuals' perceptions of their responsibilities and commitments towards others.

Controlling Resources to Create Commitment

To create commitment towards a much larger category of people than the household or other primary groups, the NPA depended on a fragile set of interlocking resources, which it developed gradually and lost again to a large extent under the impact of counter-insurgency and political liberalisation. Here I summarise how, in the research area, NPA control over these resources was related to shifts in commitment among the hacienda population.

Through an effective use of violence, the NPA helped to provide household-oriented incentives that encouraged workers' initial support for the revolutionary movement. NPA threats or actual violence initially pressured planters into some concessions to their workers and protected workers, if only for a short period of time, against planter and state repression. These 'goods' served as incentives to convince workers that the movement was taking their subsistence interests seriously. In exchange, most workers were willing to support the NPA in the form of small, regular contributions in cash and kind levied by household. At this stage, their commitments to household and movement were aligned. (Workers unwilling to provide this support experienced another side of NPA control over the means of violence: they were threatened into compliance.)

The ability to supply these household-oriented incentives depended, in turn, on at least four interrelated resources: (1) Relative freedom of movement for mobile NPA guerrilla squads in the hacienda lowlands, facilitated by the terrain that provided cover (sheltered riverbanks and creeks, endless fields of sugar-cane that stood tall at least part of the year, a base area in a forested mountain range at a manageable distance from the lowland haciendas) and local contacts whose houses provided shelter. Until the mid-1980s, NPA cadres in the research area also profited from enemy weakness: planters and municipal police lacked effective means to counter armed NPA presence in haciendas – a presence that each planter had to face individually – and the (para)military concentrated rather on the NPA-controlled uplands where most armed encounters took place. (2) A web of relationships, gradually developed, that linked over a wide area NPA leaders, guerrilla squads, local organisers, and trusted supporters in hacienda communities, providing an effective structure for mobilising support and producing (and distributing) incentives. The community-based NPA network in the hacienda, built on previous union and religious organisations, also incorporated face-to-face relations of kinship, friendship, neighbourhood, and work, and eventually hacienda-born activists who became cadres intensified the links between community and movement organisation. Community social controls, moreover, pressured sceptics into conformity. (3) An ongoing ideological framing of the NPA as 'the army of the people' that 'served the poor', and the enactment of this ideology in real life in the hacienda community by cadres who were trained to behave respectfully towards the workers, helped to organise collective actions with armed NPA backing if necessary, and sought to promote a disciplined family life by punishing such 'vices' as gambling, drinking, and adultery. (4) The NPA's image as the only credible opposition force during the Marcos regime. This helped to generate active or tacit support among NGOs, the middle classes, and even among some planters who resented Marcos's control over the sugar industry. Their support expanded the NPA's room to manoeuvre. Moreover, in some cases at least, the NPA was able to coordinate with NGOs to provide poverty-alleviating assistance in communities that it controlled. There, workers credited the NPA for delivering these household-oriented goods.

A different set of incentives was instrumental in convincing workers to place the interests of the movement and the wide category of 'oppressed poor' *before* the interests of their own household or other primary groups, and so to become dedicated part-time or full-time activists. The following resources of the NPA were central here: (1) A formal social-movement organisation which provided activists with incentives and sanctions that fostered identification with the movement: regular individual assessments on the basis of activity plans and achievement reports, criticism/self-criticism sessions at the level of work teams, a range of sanctions for underperformers, and social and emotional rewards for those who performed well (feelings of personal fulfilment, the satisfaction of contributing to a just cause, praise from close comrades). Commitment to the movement was, moreover, fostered by an emotional attachment to the small NPA work teams to which all activists belonged. (2) An ideology that honoured revolutionary cadres as selfless vanguards who embodied the interests of the 'oppressed poor'. It attached great value to their 'sacrifice for the people', envisaged a just society made possible through this sacrifice, and professed ultimate victory, based on the scientific claims of Marxism. (3) Social ties that carried this message, and personal relations that fostered commitment to it. These were provided by the mobilising networks and the organisational structure of the NPA, including the small activist work teams. (4) A reflection of this 'discourse of sacrifice' in actual relations and events, which would convince activists that the discourse was credible. It was movement policy to honour those who sacrificed for the cause, and to try to create at least within the community of activists the just society it claimed to strive for. Only by demonstrating that it lived up to its image, could the movement attract and maintain the commitment of its activists.

When this fragile edifice fell apart in the research area from the late 1980s onwards, the ability of the NPA to solicit sacrifices and create commitment among hacienda workers declined. Counter-insurgency activities contracted the NPA's room to manoeuvre: as a military detachment was established near Hda. Milagros and paramilitary bands scouted the area – a scenario carried out throughout the hacienda lowlands – teams of guerrilla fighters and political cadres no longer moved as freely from the nearby mountainous uplands to the hacienda lowlands. This restricted the NPA's ability to win concessions from planters and to protect workers. It also disrupted the network of relations between hacienda workers and the NPA organisation, and hence the social channels along which commitment-generating meanings and incentives had been provided. Outside activists avoided the hacienda because of the risks, ideological seminars and cultural shows in the hacienda ceased, and the youth group was disbanded when it came under police surveillance. Disrupted, too, was the routine of activity plans, meetings, and assessments of the NPA's community organisation in the hacienda, hitherto enforced by outside NPA cadres, which had helped to encourage local activists to remain committed to the guerrilla organisation.

For full-time revolutionaries, incentives declined as well. Faith in ultimate victory receded. As the financial resources of the NPA dwindled, full-timers experienced an urgent lack of medical care and a cut in the allowances for their 'dependants', and some felt the NPA leaders did not respect their sacrifices as they should. The NPA saw a decline in its taxable mass base, was unable to maintain previous levels of 'forced taxation' of planters and shopkeepers, and lost support among the province's middle classes with President Aquino's restoration of formal democracy. Moreover, a number of full-timers from Hda. Milagros perceived that ideology and practice began to diverge considerably. Still committed to 'serving the people', they began to doubt whether they were serving the right movement and leaders to do so. Context of this change was the widened democratic space under Aquino, and the subsequent strategy debates among the NPA leadership which culminated in a hardline 'total war' approach after the collapse of a cease-fire agreement in 1987. As NPA leaders in Negros Occidental began to concentrate resources on warfare and the use of terror and less on safeguarding material gains for the poor, a number of leaders and cadres protested that the interests of the poor were sacrificed to the armed struggle, resigned from the movement, and became vocal critics of the NPA. The nation-wide split of the CPP-NPA in 1992–93, which began as policy debates among provincial and national leaders, further lowered full-timers' commitment to the movement. Eventually, the NPA in the province divided into two competing factions, and as conflict and distrust began to mark relations within the small NPA work teams and committees, the NPA's professed image no longer reflected reality. The teams lost their commitment-creating function, and the disarray in the organisation disrupted the system of organisational incentives and sanctions. Many full-timers from my research area resigned and returned home or moved to the city, aided by a government amnesty. Some who remained committed to 'serving the people' and who remained involved in activist networks turned to legal forms of action through labour unions and other social movements.

Defining Social Activism as a Feasible and Expedient Option

Whether workers define social activism as a feasible and suitable option certainly affects their decision to engage in collective action. Workers of Hda. Milagros considered collective action inappropriate in the early 1970s, then gradually came to view it as acceptable, and eventually as downright respectable in the 1980s when the hacienda was under NPA control. This shift in the workers' perception of collective action not only resulted from better opportunities and better chances of success. It was also related to how influential people or institutions defined workers' collective action and broadcast this image for public consumption, and how workers used these images to cope with changing realities.

Up to the early 1970s, the action-repertoire of workers of Hda. Milagros did not include organised collective action. Besides being risky for workers because of their personal dependence on the planter, collective action also ran counter to the perceptions and behavioural dispositions related to patron-clientage that still permeated the hacienda community. This confined workers to presenting careful requests for personal favours.[50] Moreover, the government, in the first years of martial law, easily condemned collective action as 'subversive', a label that some workers adopted. Besides, workers of Milagros were hardly familiar with this strategy at the time, and lacked a social-movement organisation that could provide support.

However, many workers started to consider collective action as an acceptable option by the mid-1970s. Progressive Catholic clergy played a crucial role here. In promoting the organisation of hacienda workers, they presented an ideology that defined collective action as a positive, necessary, and honourable survival strategy, and spread this message by means of seminars, songs, sermons, and religious plays. Moreover, for workers of Milagros who became involved in activist Church networks, these new perceptions, as well as new interdependencies and mobilising interactions, facilitated the development of behavioural dispositions that were conducive to collective protest. The meetings of the newly formed BCC in the hacienda and the first confrontations with the planter provided a training ground for collective claim-making, a training that helped workers to overcome fear and embarrassment when confronting the planter and (other) authorities while maintaining self-control. Consequently, collective action also became workable. The clergy's message of collective action as a *viable* strategy was, however, somewhat contradicted by initial planter repression.

In the 1980s, social activism became a respectable and more or less 'official' activity in the hacienda, supported by a widely disseminated ideology based on Marxist and Maoist thought. The revolutionary movement successfully backed up the collective actions of workers and so made this strategy increasingly viable and rewarding. Eventually the NPA more or less imposed on workers a programme of regular organisation and mobilisation. At the same time, workers who came into conflict with NPA activists and who experienced the more repressive side of the movement, began to perceive their expected participation in the numerous meetings, collective protests, and rallies rather as a duty performed for the NPA than as a valuable strategy to improve their own and their household's life chances. They participated, they said, primarily to avoid being suspected of being unwilling supporters of the movement. Some began to tag these forms of collective action, again, with the negative label 'subversive'.

What are perceived as feasible and desirable living practices, then, can change over time. Such perceptions can also vary among people in the same community, and in the same household, as the following case of a worker household of Milagros illustrates:

Husband and wife were both local part-time activists for the NPA. But for their children they wished another career: the standard model trajectory of a high school education followed by a job in the city. Things turned out differently. One daughter dropped out of high school to become a full-time NPA activist against her parents' wishes. Another became a youth organiser, then was offered an opportunity to become a housemaid in Hong Kong through a relative, but refused in order to stay with her activist boyfriend in Hda. Milagros. Her parents were heartbroken that she let this golden opportunity pass by – an opportunity to earn a substantial salary that could have helped to raise the entire household economically. Meanwhile, a son who had been a guerrilla fighter for some time, skilled in the art of planning ambushes, left the movement and settled in Manila, where he joined a group of men who staged occasional hold-ups when they were in need of money for drinking sprees. His parents condemned the use he made of his revolutionary training.

The tensions and conflicts within this household, then, revealed considerable differences in what household members considered acceptable and desirable options for themselves and others.

Conclusion: The Household as a Composite of Interests and a Moving Target of Analysis

The preceding notes on high-cost activism by poor labourers suggest a way of analysing the link between the household, household interests, and high-cost activism that leaves room for: (1) possible disunity and conflicting interests within the household; (2) changes across time in people's loyalties and commitment towards others, within and outside their households; and (3) changes in people's perceptions of expedient living strategies. Rather than assume that activist workers are motivated by one fixed set of single-group interests – in particular, the material interests of their household – this perspective considers the changing, multiple networks in which people are embedded, and the multiple sets of interests and identities that these social relations may foster. It incorporates in the study of poor people's activism a relational analysis of commitment-formation and identity shifts.

In this light, we should consider the household as a 'moving target of analysis'. Though the expression has earlier been used to indicate shifts in the structure and economics of concrete households,[51] I emphasise here the changes in social attachments and perceptions of household members. As we have seen, mobilisation by a social movement may change the obligations that people feel, the targets of their commitments and attachments, and the living practices they value. Since individual household members are involved in changing social networks (of which the household is but one), we need to consider how these various social ties may compete for their commitment and resources, and how new social ties may reshape their interests and commitments – away from the immediate interests of their household. Awareness of this process can help explain why workers engage in high-cost activism when the benefits to their households appear small and uncertain.[52]

Participation in a social movement and involvement in activism should be viewed as processes as well. Such participation is not based on a single decision to opt for that 'strategy'. Rather, it is 'a processual ... phenomenon', in which 'decisions to participate over time are ... subject to frequent reassessment and renegotiation'.[53] The history of collective action among workers of Hda. Milagros suggests that the prolonged interaction between the workers and the revolutionary movement NPA reshaped relevant networks, loyalties, perceptions, and behavioural repertoires among a considerable number of workers in such a way that they tended to dispose these workers favourably, albeit temporarily, towards high-cost activism.

Notes

1. An earlier version of this article was presented at the Workshop on Living Strategies organised by the International Institute of Social History, Amsterdam, 28–29 November 1997. I wish to thank the workshop participants, as well as Charles Tilly for his brain-teasing questions about my research, John Wiersma for his stimulating theoretical insights and knowledge of Negros Occidental, the Editors of *Theory and Society* for their encouraging comments and, most of all, the workers of Hacienda Milagros who shared with me their experiences. The

research was financed through a grant from the Royal Netherlands Academy of Arts and Sciences. This version appeared also in *Theory and Society* 29 (2000): 215–252.

2. The research in the 1990s concerns the rise and decline of popular support for the revolutionary movement CPP-NPA from the perspective of two communities in Negros Occidental, a lowland sugar-cane plantation and an upland village. This article concentrates on developments in the plantation. It is primarily based on the informal interviews I had with workers, male and female, when I lived there for nine months in 1992 and one month in 1995. Re-establishing old friendships and contacts from my previous field-work in 1977–78, I tried to reconstruct the mobilisation histories of individual persons and families in the context of the plantation community.

3. Rosanne Rutten, *Women Workers of Hacienda Milagros: Wage Labor and Household Subsistence on a Philippine Sugarcane Plantation*, Amsterdam, 1982.

4. Gregg R. Jones, *Red Revolution: Inside the Philippine Guerrilla Movement,* Boulder, 1989, 8. The number of civilian sympathisers and supporters was estimated at 1.7 million people in 1986. By 1993, the number of guerrillas had dropped to an estimated 10,600, and the percentage of NPA-controlled or -influenced villages and urban neighbourhoods had dwindled from 20 to 3 percent. Estimates for 1997 mention 6,790 guerrilla fighters nation-wide, a number that increased again to almost 8,000 by 1999. Alfred W. McCoy, 'Low Intensity Conflict in the Philippines' in *Low Intensity Conflict: Theory and Practice in Central America and South-East Asia,* eds Barry Carr and Elaine McKay, Melbourne, 1988, 61; John McBeth, 'Internal Contradictions: Support for Communists Wanes as Party Splits', *Far Eastern Economic Review,* 26 August 1993; 'Military Slays Four Communist Rebels', Philippine News Agency through the e-mail newslist Balita News, 6 August 1999. On the CPP-NPA, see also Patricio N. Abinales, ed., *The Revolution Falters: The Left in Philippine Politics After 1986,* Ithaca, 1996; William Chapman, *Inside the Philippine Revolution,* New York, 1987; Joel Rocamora, *Breaking Through: The Struggle Within the Communist Party of the Philippines,* Pasig City, Manila, 1994; Mark P. Thompson, 'The Decline of Philippine Communism: A Review Essay', *South East Asia Research,* 6 (1998): 105–29.

5. A more detailed analysis of why and how workers supported the CPP-NPA, which traces the process of mobilisation and demobilisation among workers of Hda. Milagros, can be found in Rosanne Rutten, 'Popular Support for the Revolutionary Movement CPP-NPA: Experiences in a Hacienda in Negros Occidental, 1978–1995', in Abinales, ed., *The Revolution Falters,* 110–53.

6. See e.g., Michael Adas, 'From Avoidance to Confrontation: Peasant Protest in Precolonial and Colonial Southeast Asia', *Comparative Studies in Society and History* 23 (1981): 217–47; James C. Scott, *The Moral Economy of the Peasant: Rebellion and Subsistence in Southeast Asia,* New Haven and London, 1976; Timothy P. Wickham-Crowley, *Exploring Revolution: Essays on Latin American Insurgency and Revolutionary Theory,* Armonk, NY and London, 1991; Ronald Waterbury, 'Non-revolutionary Peasants: Oaxaca Compared to Morelos in the Mexican Revolution', *Comparative Studies in Society and History* 17 (1975): 410–42.

7. See e.g., John D. McCarthy, 'Constraints and Opportunities in Adopting, Adapting, and Inventing', in *Comparative Perspectives on Social Movements: Political Opportunities, Mobilizing Structures, and Cultural Framings,* eds Doug McAdam, John D. McCarthy, and Mayer N. Zald, Cambridge, 1996, 141–2.

8. Rod Aya, *Rethinking Revolutions and Collective Violence: Studies on Concept, Theory and Method,* Amsterdam, 1990, 21–49. For a related critique of the 'spasmodic view' of collective protest, see E.P. Thompson, 'The Moral Economy of the English Crowd in the Eighteenth Century', *Past and Present* 50 (1971): 76–136.

9. See e.g., David A. Snow et al., 'Frame Alignment Processes, Micromobilization, and Movement Participation', *American Sociological Review* 51 (1986): 464–81.

10. E.J. Hobsbawm, 'Peasants and Politics', *Journal of Peasant Studies* 1 (1973/74): 12.

11. Scott, *The Moral Economy of the Peasant,* 194–95; Marcel van der Linden, 'Connecting Household History and Labour History', *International Review of Social History* 38 (1993): 163–73.

12. Waterbury, 'Non-revolutionary Peasants', 440.

13. Samuel Popkin, 'Political Entrepreneurs and Peasant Movements in Vietnam', in *Rationality and Revolution,* ed. Michael Taylor, Cambridge, 1988, 11.

14. Diane L. Wolf, *Factory Daughters: Gender, Household Dynamics, and Rural Industrialization in Java*, Berkeley, 1992, 14–15; and Wolf, 'Daughters, Decisions and Domination: An Empirical and Conceptual Critique of Household Strategies', *Development and Change* 21 (1990): 43–74.

15. Don Kalb, for instance, has shown how a particular employment policy fostered commitment to, and solidarity within, the households of workers in the Philips lightbulb and appliances factories in the Netherlands in the 1920s and 1930s. By rewarding fathers who provided the factory with several hard-working and obedient daughters, and by guaranteeing the subsistence of loyal worker households in lean times, the Philips company promoted intrahousehold interdependence and parental socialisation of children into committed income-earners for their household. Among shoemakers in the same region who laboured under a similar employment regime, daughters cut short their rare participation in a strike when their 'fathers had forcefully reminded [them]. . . that their "irresponsible behaviour" was threatening household incomes'. Don Kalb, *Expanding Class: Power and Everyday Politics in Industrial Communities, The Netherlands, 1850–1950*, Durham and London, 1997, 51, 91.

16. Louise Tilly, 'Paths of Proletarianization: Organization of Production, Sexual Division of Labor, and Women's Collective Action', *Signs* 7 (1981): 416.

17. Carol R. Berkin and Clara M. Lovett, 'Part Two: Introduction', in *Women, War, and Revolution*, eds Carol R. Berkin and Clara M. Lovett, New York, 1980, 82. Linda Lobao made a similar point regarding women and revolutionary activism in Latin America: 'when women have major responsibility for both domestic and nondomestic aspects of family survival, and they perceive government as threatening, they may participate in revolutionary movements, especially if such movements are seen as facilitating these joint roles of mother and wage earner'. Linda Lobao, 'Women in Revolutionary Movements: Changing Patterns of Latin American Guerrilla Struggle', in *Women and Social Protest*, eds Guida West and Rhoda Lois Blumberg, New York and Oxford, 1990, 185.

18. AMES (The Association of Salvadoran Women), 'Participation of Latin American Women in Social and Political Organizations: Reflections of Salvadoran Women', *Monthly Review* 34 (1982): 18–19, quoted in Lobao, 'Women in Revolutionary Movements', 200.

19. Norma J. Kriger, *Zimbabwe's Guerrilla War: Peasant Voices*, Cambridge, 1992.

20. Jane Collins, 'The Household and Relations of Production in Southern Peru', *Comparative Studies in Society and History* 28 (1986): 667.

21. Doug McAdam and Ronnelle Paulsen, 'Specifying the Relationship between Social Ties and Activism', *American Journal of Sociology* 99, 1993, 640, 642.

22. Craig Calhoun, 'The Problem of Identity in Collective Action', in *Macro-Micro Linkages in Sociology*, ed. Joan Huber, Newbury Park, 1991; and Charles Tilly, *Durable Inequality*, Berkeley, 1998, 218.

23. Joel S. Migdal, *Peasants, Politics, and Revolution: Pressures Toward Political and Social Change in the Third World*, Princeton, 1974, 251–2.

24. Popkin, 'Political Entrepreneurs and Peasant Movements in Vietnam', 60.

25. See e.g., Roger V. Gould, 'Multiple Networks and Mobilization in the Paris Commune, 1871', *American Sociological Review* 56 (1991): 716–29.

26. David A. Snow, Louis A. Zurcher, Jr, and Sheldon Ekland-Olson, 'Social Networks and Social Movements: A Microstructural Approach to Differential Recruitment', *American Sociological Review* 45 (1980): 793.

27. Daniel B. Cornfield, Hilquias B. Cavalcanti Filho, Bang Jee Chun, 'Household, Work, and Labor Activism: Gender Differences in the Determinants of Union Membership Participation', *Work and Occupations* 17 (1990): 132.

28. Cf. Michael Hechter, 'The Attainment of Solidarity in Intentional Communities', *Rationality and Society* 2 (1990): 142–55.

29. Cf. Lewis A. Coser, *Greedy Institutions: Patterns of Undivided Commitment*, New York, 1974.

30. Jeff Goodwin, 'The Libidinal Constitution of a High-Risk Social Movement: Affectual Ties and Solidarity in the Huk Rebellion, 1946 to 1954', *American Sociological Review* 62 (1997): 53–69.

31. Marianne Schmink, 'Household Economic Strategies: Review and Research Agenda', *Latin American Research Review* 19 (1984): 95.

32. Wolf, 'Daughters, Decisions, and Domination', 20, 263.
33. Van der Linden, 'Connecting Household History and Labour History', 166.
34. See e.g., Popkin, 'Political Entrepreneurs and Peasant Movements in Vietnam'; and Jeffrey Race, *War Comes to Long An: Revolutionary Conflict in a Vietnamese Province*, Berkeley, 1972.
35. McAdam defines 'biographical availability' as 'the absence of personal constraints that may increase the costs and risks of movement participation, such as full-time employment, marriage, and family responsibilities'. Doug McAdam, 'Recruitment to High-Risk Activism: The Case of Freedom Summer', *American Journal of Sociology* 92 (1986): 70.
36. Cynthia Keppley Mahmood, *Fighting for Faith and Nation: Dialogues with Sikh Militants*, Philadelphia, 1996, 105.
37. Iris Jean-Klein, who studied family and community contexts of Palestinian activists on the West Bank, noted divergent views within the Palestinian family. Once a son had become involved in high-risk activism, the emotionally intimate mother-son bond and competitive father-son relationship fostered, in some cases at least, a cooperative attitude of mothers and an unsupportive stance of fathers, with mothers hiding knowledge of their sons' illicit sorties from their husbands. Though a mother might do her utmost to prevent her son from taking high-risk actions, her social and emotional dependence on him promoted complicity and cooperation once his activist involvement was known to her. In contrast, as sons formed a potential threat to their father's authority in the Palestinian family, an activist son who withstood the hardships of imprisonment and therefore felt entitled to some authority in the house, might encounter protracted opposition from his father. 'Even if and where the senior male member of a household was himself involved in resistant activities ... the emergence of his sons as activists posed a multiplicity of centres of moral authority which competed with each other .... Senior men showed their resistance to the state of affairs in the course of daily household procedures, silently or militantly'. Iris Jean-Klein, 'Palestinian Militancy, Martyrdom and Nationalist Communities in the West Bank during the Intifada', in *Martyrdom and Political Resistance: Essays from Asia and Europe*, ed. Joyce Pettigrew, Amsterdam, 1997, 98.
38. Mahmood, *Fighting for Faith and Nation*; Joseba Zulaika, *Basque Violence: Metaphor and Sacrament*, Reno, 1988; Robert W. White, 'From Peaceful Protest to Guerrilla War: Micromobilization of the Provisional Irish Republican Army', *American Journal of Sociology* 94 (1989): 1277–1302.
39. Exceptions are studies that consider the effects of poor people's involvement in social-movement organisations, e.g. Migdal, *Peasants, Politics, and Revolution*, and Race, *War Comes to Long An*.
40. Relevant studies on the plantation society of Negros Occidental include Filomeno V. Aguilar, Jr, *Clash of Spirits: The History of Power and Sugar Planter Hegemony on a Visayan Island*, Honolulu, 1998; Alan Berlow, *Dead Season: A Story of Murder and Revenge on the Philippine Island of Negros*, New York, 1996; John A. Larkin, *Sugar and the Origins of Modern Philippine Society*, Berkeley and Los Angeles, 1993; Alfred W. McCoy, *Priests on Trial*, Ringwood, Victoria, 1984, and 'The Restoration of Planter Power in La Carlota City', in *From Marcos to Aquino: Local Perspectives on Political Transition in the Philippines*, eds B.J. Kerkvliet and R.B. Mojares, Honolulu, 1991; Niall O'Brien, *Island of Tears, Island of Hope: Living the Gospel in a Revolutionary Situation*, New York and London, 1993; Romana de los Reyes and Sylvia Ma. G. Jopillo, *Pursuing Agrarian Reform in Negros Occidental*, Quezon City, 1991; Rosanne Rutten, 'Courting the Workers' Vote in a Hacienda Region: Rhetoric and Response in the 1992 Philippine Elections', *Pilipinas* 22 (1994): 1–34, and 'Popular Support for the Revolutionary Movement CPP-NPA'.
41. Larkin, *Sugar and the Origins of Modern Philippine Society*, 136–46, 188–93; Alfred W. McCoy, 'Baylan: Animist Religion and Philippine Peasant Ideology', *Philippine Quarterly of Culture and Society* 10 (1982): 141–94; David Sturtevant, *Popular Uprisings in the Philippines 1840–1940*, Ithaca, NY, 1976.
42. Leonardo S. Nicdao, 'History of the Establishment of the CPP/NPA in Negros Occidental', typescript, n.d., 3; Jones, *Red Revolution*, 92–3.
43. Miguel G. Coronel, *Pro-Democracy People's War*, Quezon City, 1991, 658, 660, 665, 669.
44. Negros Occidental counted, in 1998, some three hundred guerrilla fighters belonging to the two rival armies that grew out of the split in the NPA. 'AFP takes all COIN operations vs

NPA', Philippine News Agency through the e-mail newslist Balita News, 11 January 1999. On the decline of the NPA, see Abinales, ed., *The Revolution Falters*, and Thompson, 'The Decline of Philippine Communism'.

45. For a more extensive discussion of this episode, see Rosanne Rutten, 'Class and Kin: Conflicting Loyalties on a Philippine Hacienda', in *Cognation and Social Organization in Southeast Asia*, eds Frans Hüsken and Jeremy Kemp, Leiden, 1991, 183–92.

46. On similar 'collective action frames' which are intended to inspire action, see William A. Gamson, *Talking Politics*, New York, 1992, 7.

47. Ben Kerkvliet made a similar observation in his study of the 'Huk' peasant guerrilla movement in the Philippine region of Central Luzon in the 1940s to 1950s. Speaking of the time when the movement was fighting the Japanese occupation forces, he states, 'villagers believed that every family should have at least one adult male to look after it; consequently many husbands and brothers did not feel free to join [the guerrilla army].' Benedict J. Kerkvliet, *The Huk Rebellion: A Study of Peasant Revolt in the Philippines*, Berkeley, 1977, 68.

48. McAdam and Paulsen, 'Specifying the Relationship Between Social Ties and Activism', 642.

49. Ibid., 640, 642.

50. Cf. 'In Veblenesque terms, there is a trained capacity for handling the world in a particular way, and a trained incapacity for handling it in any other way'. Ulf Hannerz, *Cultural Complexity: Studies in the Social Organization of Meaning*, New York, 1992, 67.

51. Benjamin N.F. White, 'Rural Household Studies in Anthropological Perspective', in *Rural Household Studies in Asia*, eds Hans P. Binswanger et al., Singapore, 1980, 21.

52. The present case of shifts in solidarities among worker-revolutionaries differs from the 'logic of solidarity' found among labour activists in nineteenth century Europe and the United States. The 'logic of solidarity' refers to workers widening their solidarities in the form of strategic coalitions with other classes or class segments on the basis of perceived shared interests, when expedient. The widening solidarities of these workers were all the while firmly anchored to their interests as labourers and breadwinners. In other words, workers' primary commitments to household members and workfloor mates remained at the centre of their expanding concentric circles of solidarity. (Michael Hanagan, *The Logic of Solidarity: Artisans and Industrial Workers in Three French Towns, 1871–1914*, Urbana, 1981, and *Theory and Society, Special Issue on Solidarity Logics* 17 (May 1988), eds Charles Tilly and Michael Hanagan). The present case of Philippine workers who became revolutionary activists shows how wider solidarities may 'detach' committed activists from their interests as householders and labourers, and indicates that those who became the most committed to forming class and cross-class solidarities under the aegis of the revolutionary movement (the young single men and women who became full-timers) were mostly informed by interests other than their interests as household members and workers.

53. Snow et al., 'Frame Alignment Processes, Micromobilization, and Movement Participation', 466–67.

Bibliography

Abinales, P.N., ed. *The Revolution Falters: The Left in Philippine Politics after 1986.* Ithaca, 1996.

Adas, M. 'From Avoidance to Confrontation: Peasant Protest in Precolonial and Colonial Southeast Asia', *Comparative Studies in Society and History* 23 (1981): 217–47.

Aguilar, F.V. Jr, *Clash of Spirits: The History of Power and Sugar Planter Hegemony on a Visayan Island.* Honolulu, 1998.

Aya, R. *Rethinking Revolutions and Collective Violence: Studies on Concept, Theory and Method.* Amsterdam, 1990.

Berkin, C.R., and Lovett, C.M. 'Part Two: Introduction', in *Women, War, and Revolution*, eds C.R. Berkin and C.M. Lovett. New York, 1980.

Berlow, A. *Dead Season: A Story of Murder and Revenge on the Philippine Island of Negros.* New York, 1996.

Calhoun, C. 'The Problem of Identity in Collective Action', in *Macro-Micro Linkages in Sociology*, ed. J. Huber. Newbury Park, 1991.

Chapman, W. *Inside the Philippine Revolution.* New York, 1987.

Collins, J. 'The Household and Relations of Production in Southern Peru', *Comparative Studies in Society and History* 28 (1986).

Cornfield, D.B., Cavalcanti Filho, H.B., and Bang Jee Chun, 'Household, Work, and Labor Activism: Gender Differences in the Determinants of Union Membership Participation', *Work and Occupations* 17 (1990).

Coronel, M.G. *Pro-Democracy People's War.* Quezon City, 1991.

Coser, L.A. *Greedy Institutions: Patterns of Undivided Commitment.* New York, 1974.

Gamson, W.A. *Talking Politics.* New York, 1992.

Goodwin, J. 'The Libidinal Constitution of a High-Risk Social Movement: Affectual Ties and Solidarity in the Huk Rebellion, 1946 to 1954', *American Sociological Review* 62 (1997): 53–69.

Gould, R.V. 'Multiple Networks and Mobilization in the Paris Commune, 1871', *American Sociological Review* 56 (1991): 716–29.

Hanagan, M. *The Logic of Solidarity: Artisans and Industrial Workers in Three French Towns, 1871–1914.* Urbana, 1981.

Hannerz, U. *Cultural Complexity: Studies in the Social Organization of Meaning.* New York, 1992.

Hechter, M. 'The Attainment of Solidarity in Intentional Communities', *Rationality and Society* 2 (1990): 142–55.

Hobsbawm, E.J. 'Peasants and Politics', *Journal of Peasant Studies* 1 (1973/74).

Kerkvliet, B.J. *The Huk Rebellion: A Study of Peasant Revolt in the Philippines.* Berkeley, 1977.

Jean-Klein, I. 'Palestinian Militancy, Martyrdom and Nationalist Communities in the West Bank during the Intifada', in *Martyrdom and Political Resistance: Essays from Asia and Europe*, ed. J. Pettigrew. Amsterdam, 1997.

Larkin, J.A. *Sugar and the Origins of Modern Philippine Society*, Berkeley and Los Angeles, 1993.

Linden, M. van der, 'Connecting Household History and Labour History', *International Review of Social History* 38 (1993): 163–73.

Lobao, L. 'Women in Revolutionary Movements: Changing Patterns of Latin American Guerrilla Struggle', in *Women and Social Protest*, eds G. West and R.L. Blumberg. New York and Oxford, 1990.

Jones, G.R. *Red Revolution: Inside the Philippine Guerrilla Movement.* Boulder, 1989.

Kalb, D. *Expanding Class: Power and Everyday Politics in Industrial Communities, The Netherlands, 1850–1950.* Durham and London, 1997.

Keppley Mahmood, C. *Fighting for Faith and Nation: Dialogues with Sikh Militants.* Philadelphia, 1996.

Kriger, N.J. *Zimbabwe's Guerrilla War: Peasant Voices.* Cambridge, 1992.

McAdam, D. 'Recruitment to High-Risk Activism: The Case of Freedom Summer', *American Journal of Sociology* 92 (1986).

McAdam, D., and Paulsen, R. 'Specifying the Relationship between Social Ties and Activism', *American Journal of Sociology* 99 (1993).

McCarthy, J.D. 'Constraints and Opportunities in Adopting, Adapting, and Inventing', in *Comparative Perspectives on Social Movements: Political Opportunities, Mobilizing Structures, and Cultural Framings*, eds Doug McAdam, John D. McCarthy, and Mayer N. Zald. Cambridge, 1996.

Migdal, J.S. *Peasants, Politics, and Revolution: Pressures Toward Political and Social Change in the Third World*. Princeton, 1974.

McCoy, A.W. 'Baylan: Animist Religion and Philippine Peasant Ideology', *Philippine Quarterly of Culture and Society* vol. 10 (1982): 141–94.

———. *Priests on Trial*. Ringwood, Victoria, 1984.

———. 'Low Intensity Conflict in the Philippines' in *Low Intensity Conflict: Theory and Practice in Central America and South-East Asia*, eds B.Carr and E. McKay. Melbourne, 1988.

———. 'The Restoration of Planter Power in La Carlota City', in *From Marcos to Aquino: Local Perspectives on Political Transition in the Philippines*, eds B.J. Kerkvliet and R.B. Mojares. Honolulu, 1991.

Nicdao, L.S. 'History of the Establishment of the CPP/NPA in Negros Occidental', typescript, n.d.

O'Brien, N. *Island of Tears, Island of Hope: Living the Gospel in a Revolutionary Situation*. New York and London, 1993.

Popkin, S. 'Political Entrepreneurs and Peasant Movements in Vietnam', in *Rationality and Revolution*, ed. M. Taylor. Cambridge, 1988.

Race, J. *War Comes to Long An: Revolutionary Conflict in a Vietnamese Province*. Berkeley, 1972.

Reyes, R. de los, and Jopillo, S.M.G. *Pursuing Agrarian Reform in Negros Occidental*, Quezon City, 1991.

Rocamora, J. *Breaking Through: The Struggle Within the Communist Party of the Philippines*. Pasig City, Manila, 1994.

Rutten, R. *Women Workers of Hacienda Milagros: Wage Labor and Household Subsistence on a Philippine Sugarcane Plantation*. Amsterdam, 1982.

———. 'Class and Kin: Conflicting Loyalties on a Philippine Hacienda', in *Cognation and Social Organization in Southeast Asia*, eds F. Hüsken and J. Kemp. Leiden, 1991, 183–92.

———. 'Courting the Workers' Vote in a Hacienda Region: Rhetoric and Response in the 1992 Philippine Elections', *Pilipinas* 22 (1994): 1–34.

———. 'Popular Support for the Revolutionary Movement CPP-NPA: Experiences in a Hacienda in Negros Occidental, 1978–1995', in Abinales, ed., *The Revolution Falters*, 110–53.

Scott, J.C. *The Moral Economy of the Peasant: Rebellion and Subsistence in Southeast Asia*. New Haven and London, 1976.

Schmink, M. 'Household Economic Strategies: Review and Research Agenda', *Latin American Research Review* 19 (1984).

Snow, D.A., Zurcher Jr., L.A., and Ekland-Olson, S. 'Social Networks and Social Movements: A Microstructural Approach to Differential Recruitment', *American Sociological Review* 45 (1980).

Snow, D.A., et al., 'Frame Alignment Processes, Micromobilization, and Movement Participation', *American Sociological Review* 51 (1986): 464–81.

Sturtevant, D. *Popular Uprisings in the Philippines 1840–1940*. Ithaca, NY, 1976.

Thompson, E.P. 'The Moral Economy of the English Crowd in the Eighteenth Century', *Past and Present* 50 (1971): 76–136.

Thompson, M.P. 'The Decline of Philippine Communism: A Review Essay', *South East Asia Research* 6 (1998): 105–29.

Tilly, C., and Hanagan, M., eds. *Theory and Society, Special Issue on Solidary Logics* 17 (May 1988).

Tilly, C. *Durable Inequality*. Berkeley, 1998.

Tilly, L. 'Paths of Proletarianization: Organization of Production, Sexual Division of Labor, and Women's Collective Action', *Signs* 7 (1981).

Waterbury, R. 'Non-revolutionary Peasants: Oaxaca Compared to Morelos in the Mexican Revolution', *Comparative Studies in Society and History* 17 (1975): 410–42.

White, B.N.F. 'Rural Household Studies in Anthropological Perspective', in *Rural Household Studies in Asia*, eds H.P. Binswanger et al. Singapore, 1980.

White, R.W. 'From Peaceful Protest to Guerrilla War: Micromobilization of the Provisional Irish Republican Army', *American Journal of Sociology* 94 (1989): 1277–1302.

Wolf, D.L. 'Daughters, Decisions and Domination: An Empirical and Conceptual Critique of Household Strategies', *Development and Change* 21 (1990): 43–74.

_____. *Factory Daughters: Gender, Household Dynamics, and Rural Industrialization in Java*. Berkeley, 1992.

Wickham-Crowley, T.P. *Exploring Revolution: Essays on Latin American Insurgency and Revolutionary Theory*. Armonk, NY and London, 1991.

Zulaika, J. *Basque Violence: Metaphor and Sacrament*. Reno, 1988.

CHAPTER 10

RETREAT FROM COLLECTIVE PROTEST

HOUSEHOLD, GENDER, WORK AND POPULAR OPPOSITION IN STALINIST HUNGARY

Mark Pittaway

In mid-December 1951 in an attempt to prevent absenteeism on the days immediately after Christmas the Hungarian government announced that it would end the practice of paying wages before the holiday.[1] Instead, workers would receive their wages on 27 December. This resulted in considerable discontent. In the Ikarus bus plant in Budapest both the union and the party organisation were deluged with complaints. Management and the factory organisation received assurances from the ministry that wages could be paid on 23 December despite the decision. The factory party committee immediately issued a statement to that effect to the discontented workforce. On 23 December payment of wages began to workers on the morning shift. At eleven, however, the ministry intervened to prevent the payments to those scheduled to receive their wages at 1.30 p.m. Management objected, resulting in a dispute between the enterprise and the ministry. Ernö Gerö, second in the Stalinist party leadership and its economic policy supremo, was called on to arbitrate. He ruled that no more of the wages should be paid. By this time it was 3.30 p.m. and some fifteen hundred workers were waiting impatiently. As the decision was announced the fifteen hundred staged an angry demonstration occupying the offices of management and of the factory party organisation. The demonstration was broken up only by the use of force. The ÁVH – the Stalinist secret police – took 156 people into custody for their role in the demonstration.[2]

This demonstration was the largest single act of collective protest by industrial workers in Hungary during much of the period. It was an exceptional event, during the Stalinist years in Hungary, unlike its neighbours, there were no major instances of open popular unrest prior to 1956 – whether strikes, political protests or bread riots.[3] This apparent lack of open collective protest existed alongside considerable poverty, declining standards of living, extreme repression and increasing work intensity across industry. Despite this even open attacks on workers' incomes met with only sporadic opposition.[4]

As collective protest became more sporadic, members of working class households began to centre their activities increasingly on the private sphere. There was a considerable desire on the part of many to seek a relative degree of household self-sufficiency in the production of foodstuffs rather than depend on the unreliable state sector. In mining areas the state began to sponsor a programme of subsidised private house building. This proved to be highly popular simply because a house with a garden offered working class households greater opportunities for producing food independently of the state sector.[5]

In other words, as collective protest declined, industrial workers increasingly began to centre on the private sphere. Why was this so? The seemingly obvious answer of a high degree of political repression initially springs to mind. This undoubtedly played a partial role. Yet this seems to ignore the fact that collective protest was more prevalent in the rest of East-Central Europe than in Hungary, whilst the populations of these other states were subject to a similar degree of political repression. The severe poverty of the Stalinist years provides another plausible explanation. It might be said that this fails to account for the precise dynamics of the retreat from open collective protest that occurred. While poverty and political repression provide part of the solution to our puzzle, the processes that reshaped the boundaries between public and private in Stalinist Hungary were more complex and subtle.

The retreat of open collective protest recast gender relations both within industrial production and the household. Although political scientists and others frequently sought to analyse the occasional explosions of popular protest that periodically characterised socialist societies across the region, there has been little work since 1989 on the nature of the more everyday forms of collective action.[6] There has been virtually nothing on the gender dimensions of such protest – an analytical framework that can reveal much about the shifting boundaries between the household and place of work. In a study of the gender dimensions of resistance and protest in Communist Poland, Padraic Kenney has argued that a gendered division between the public and private spheres played a decisive role in structuring the patterns of mens' and womens' protest.[7]

The argument presented here identifies a clear similarity between gender ideologies in both Poland and Hungary – for the early socialist period at least. The notion of a gendered split between a male public realm and a female private realm permeated society. Despite the superficially egalitarian rhetoric of the labour mobilisation campaigns of the Stalinist regime this notion was reinforced, rather than challenged by the new state.

The argument presented here suggests that working class womens' and mens' experiences of socialist industrialisation created an ideal of social privatisation, and of household self-sufficiency. Increasingly a world of poverty, often insecure wages from the state sector combined with the pervasive shortage in the field of official consumption to transform the state-dominated public realm. This public sphere, for many working class households, became an arena in which needs could not be satisfied. A moral economy developed in which the household strove for autonomy from the state dominated public realm. This was never completely achievable, indeed, in many cases it was completely unachievable. Households, in so far as they were self-sufficient, were so because of the complex linkages between the public and private sphere. The ideological effects of an ideal of social privatisation should not, however, be underestimated – they legitimised a gradual withdrawal, albeit initially prompted by state repression, from forms of public protest in the factory or the community. They did not eliminate popular opposition but served to channel it – in the workplace into more covert forms of resistance such as pilfering that further supported informal economic activities centred on the household.

Such a shift from public to private had important implications for gender relations within both the workplace and the household. While the Stalinist state advocated gender equality at work and expanded female employment, paradoxically women invested more in the maintenance of the household. This was reflected in patterns of collective protest, as well as in survival strategies. Furthermore, male bargaining within the workplace reflected the redrawing of the boundaries between public and private realms. Informal bargaining around wages tended to be underpinned by assumptions that reflected shifting gender relations.

The argument is developed thematically throughout the chapter. The first section deals with the notion of the public and private during the post-war years in Hungary. The second considers the changing patterns of collective protest within the workplace. The third section deals with the realm of consumption, and the fourth with the household.

The Gendered Dimensions of Public and Private in Post-War Hungary

As the Hungarian Workers' Party[8] began to construct the formal institutions of Stalinist dictatorship in Hungary in 1948, the state initiated labour competition in the factories. Labour competition was intended to mobilise workers to increase production. Furthermore, as far as the more idealistic of the builders of the 'new' state were concerned, it was to herald a revolution in production and working class attitudes towards their work. Propagandists reacted with concern at opinion poll evidence, collected in 1948 in the industrial suburbs of the capital, that 37 percent of factory workers' wives did not know whether their husbands participated in the labour competitions. These propagandists recognised that factory workers' wives, however, were concerned with the affairs of the home and their immediate community. They were thus 'separated from the factory, factory work and the labour competition'.[9]

The compilers of opinion poll surveys about the attitudes of household members to changes that were occurring in the factory were revealing the traces of an ideal of a gendered separation of the public and private in industrial Hungary. Urban industrial workers subscribed to an ideal of the male worker as breadwinner and the married wife as manager of the household. These attitudes were reflected in the attitudes of factory committees – which in heavy industry at least – were dominated up until 1949 by the representatives of the skilled, male worker élite. In the Lampart Factory in 1948, women were systematically moved by the committee from the best-paying jobs to lower ones. This was justified on the grounds that the family 'responsibilities' of their male colleagues should be taken into account when distributing work. In the Ganz Shipyards the factory trade union distributed potatoes and other benefits paid in kind only to 'the men and their families', explicitly excluding female labour from direct access to them.[10]

While working class masculinity conferred the role of the breadwinner on male workers, the female role of household management conferred several responsibilities on women. While this included housework, the management of 'house-keeping' money, and shopping for the household[11] it could also lead to the adoption of other forms of unpaid work for the household outside the home itself. During the period of poverty that accompanied post-war reconstruction, many urban households were provided with an allotment on which chickens were kept or vegetables were grown. In many industrial areas it was the wives' of factory workers who worked the allotments while their husbands laboured for wages. Consequently when school holidays arrived, enterprises were deluged for requests from families with children for child care to allow mothers to work on the allotment.[12] Such a division of responsibilities was commonplace in worker-peasant households where the men commuted to work in neighbouring industrial centres, while women assumed the management of the farm.[13] This gender division of household labour could lead to alternative forms of female participation in the public sphere, at least prior to Stalinism. Ethnographer Erzsébet Örszigethy traced the fortunes of a series of worker-peasant households examining the strategies they adopted from the 1920s onwards. The husbands took jobs in the Budapest public transport company. The women took responsibility for the landholdings – given that their means of subsistence were guaranteed they used their landholdings to produce for the market. This enabled them to enter the public sphere as, if only on a small scale, market gardeners.[14]

With the advent of Stalinism, the new state offered a vision of social transformation characterised by sociologist Zsuzsa Gille as 'metallic socialism'.[15] Heavy industry was expanded as Hungary became 'a country of iron, steel and machines'.[16] As elsewhere in Eastern Europe this vision of socialist industrialisation was sharply gendered. It celebrated male productive labour and promoted the development of heavy industry – a sector that largely employed men.[17] As the aims of the First Five-Year Plan were announced, the gendered nature of the vision of social transformation upon which it was based was not lost on many women in industrial areas. They failed to see how an expansion of heavy industry would directly benefit them, preferring instead a plan that raised living standards, improved housing and community services. In Újpest when the plan was popularised, male workers supported the aims of the plan even though some questioned its feasibility. Among women the picture was entirely different. They asked 'why so many construction sites are needed, it would be better to give higher wages'.[18]

Despite the ambivalence of many working class women, the First Five-Year Plan seemed to offer a radical restructuring of gender relations, through opening the doors to full participation in the socialist labour force to women. In 1950 labour planners envisaged introducing 123,000 new women employees into the labour force during the course of the First Five-Year Plan. Of these, 40,000 were to come from the ranks of young women, 43,000 from agriculture and 40,000 from urban households; 54,000 were to go into industry and 22,000 into construction. Of this 76,000, 20,000 were to be directed to the machine industry, and 1,500 to the mines.[19] The National Planning Office pursued an egalitarian policy in the workplace. On training schemes for skilled workers it called for a policy of affirmative action. This policy stipulated that a minimum of 30–50 percent of the training places be filled by young women. [20] To this end it explicitly called for a 'reorganisation of male labour' to facilitate the entrance of women into previously male-dominated occupations. It explicitly instructed enterprises 'not only to place women into occupations that have generally been filled by women, but they have to take the line that women should be directed to every occupation'.[21]

Even this policy – which was not to meet with much success – did not challenge established gender ideologies in so far as they related to the boundaries between public and private. Instead it envisaged 'freeing women from their domestic duties' through the expansion of crèches and day-care centres for children, and the growth of factory and communal eating facilities. Furthermore the regime envisaged the growth in the availability of labour-saving devices such as washing-machines and most ambitiously the industrialisation of housework.[22] Assumptions about a gender division between a male public realm of work and a female private realm formed the backdrop to the retreat from collective protest. Such assumptions were shared by working class men and women themselves and played an important role in structuring their attitudes and actions. In some ways, paradoxically, they were reinforced by the new socialist state.

The Retreat from Collective Protest in the Workplace

Hungary's Stalinist turn heralded a revolution in production. The dependence of the practice of comprehensive economic planning on the application of principles derived from scientific management has been much neglected by those who have analysed it. In the Soviet Union and Eastern Europe its implementation entailed considerable institutional centralisation along with an individualisation of responsibility for the achievement of the production targets it laid down. Hungarian economic planning was characterised by this apparently paradoxical combination of collectivist centralisation and an individualised production regime on the shop floor. The organisation of production, systems of mobilisation and remuneration were explicitly individualised and tied to the goals laid down in the plan.[23]

The institutions that resulted from the introduction of comprehensive economic planning were far from popular. In the workplace industrial workers developed a strictly instrumental attitude towards payment-by-results and labour competition. Workers only participated where direct material benefits resulted.[24] The late 1940s were, fortunately for the new regime, a period in which real wages rose rapidly.[25] When wages did not rise, as with the attempts to increase production norms in 1949, the state met a wave of shop-floor protest from both male and female workers.[26]

In late 1949 work was explicitly individualised with the promotion of individual participation in labour competition and the introduction of the Stakhanovite movement in Hungary. Wages rose, not just of the new Stakhanovites – or outstanding workers – but of the workforce in general. Despite distrust of the new Stakhanovite workers the workforce were generally content as a result of their increased wages.[27] The individualisation of production that central planning entailed was completed with the transformation of the wage system accompanied by a norm revision for the vast majority of the workforce. The first major step was to change the basis on which work was rewarded. A piece-rate system was introduced for the majority of the workforce in March 1950. The central component of the system was that the work done, not the individual worker, was the subject of remuneration. Through this the principle was established that payment should reflect the amount and value of what was produced by a worker as laid out in the plan. Alongside this new system, tighter production norms were to be introduced in Summer 1950.[28]

The introduction of the new norms met with one of the largest waves of worker protest in the post-war period. As early as July before the introduction of the new norms, worker anger took the form of workers ignoring and cold-shouldering union and party officials on the shop-floor. In one Szeged factory a well-organised go-slow was used. In Kecskemét one worker was detained by the secret police for publicly comparing the regime to that of the Nazis. In a neighbouring factory, a norm-setter was physically assaulted. He had argued that their 200 percent fulfilment was the result of the laxness of workers' production norms. In one textile factory the factory committee president stated that a new norm revision would follow if the new norms were systematically overfulfilled. At the Hoffher tractor factory, the electricians broke into the factory on a Sunday and wrecked one of the most expensive machines in protest. The discontent across industry was only defused through the Korea week labour competition campaign in early August, which management organised to allow workers to fulfil the new norms.[29] Despite this the damage had been done and any shaky legitimacy that institutions such as the labour competition possessed had been destroyed.

This was to be made clear to the regime through the pattern of much of the worker protest that emerged. Labour competition was blamed directly by many workers for the norm revision and in many cases the 'heroes of labour' were personally attacked for class treachery. In many Budapest factories angry workers held the Stakhanovites responsible for what had happened. In Kiskunfélegyháza construction workers destroyed a wall built by Stakhanovites after they called workers to a labour competition to overfulfil the new norms. In many cases the pressure that many Stakhanovites experienced forced them to fall back with their workmates and oppose the new norms publicly. One Stakhanovite in the construction industry openly attacked the new norms as being too tight. In the textile industry, at the Magyar Pamutipar cotton factory one Stakhanovite was forced, under pressure from workmates, to make a formal request to the norm office to base norms on average and not Stakhanovite fulfilment.[30]

The state, however, was prepared for labour unrest and showed a willingness to use repressive measures against those who protested. In the United Lighting and Electrics Factory management working in close cooperation with the secret police were able to identify and squash discontent before it grew. Only two workers were sacked for 'oppositional behaviour' in connection with the tightening whilst four were arrested by the secret police for 'spreading rumours' likely to lead to discontent. This policy was replicated right across the country. In one Felsőgálla factory, a worker who publicly stated that only the norms of those workers with fulfilment rates of over 500 percent should be cut was sacked. Management were sometimes able to avoid the intervention of the secret police. In the machine shop of the Tatabánya mines in July a work stoppage was halted after twenty-five minutes simply as a result of management threatening to report those participating to the authorities. Even individual acts of protest and attempts to bargain informally with management over the new norms were dealt with brutally. Attempts by brigades on one western Hungarian construction site to institute a go-slow in order to secure better norms met with police intervention.[31]

Norm revision and reductions in living standards fed a negative solidarity among workers against the state. From 1950 onwards they were united in feeling exploited by a 'bloodsucking government'.[32] This opposition was expressed in the way that workers collaborated to beat factory systems designed to control them. In the Danube Shoe Factory there was a degree of solidarity between all workers when it came to getting poor output past the quality-control systems in the factory. In 1953, the plant newspaper criticised workers on production line 301 for being prepared to accept and pass on without question the poor quality shoes made by other workers.[33] Such forms of solidarity were common across industry and had an important political dimension. Upon his escape to the West in 1953, one former worker in a heavy engineering factory, in answer to the question of why workers collaborated to keep the quality of their work at a low level, or to use more materials than was strictly necessary, answered that 'psychologically the situation was ... that they (the workers) were happy if they could harm the Communist system'.[34]

The culture created by workers' negative solidarity against the state provided a basis for concealed acts of collective protest to continue. Élek Nagy, later a worker's council leader in Csepel during the 1956 Revolution, stated that 'there were a whole series of hidden strikes under Rákosi and then under

Imre Nagy, which were generally caused by wage issues. The norm-setter gave us the time (for a given job). Then a workmate went to complain ... then we decided to organise a "black" strike'.[35] One worker in the Danube Shoe Factory remembered that 'in 1953 there were grumbles about the norms, at one time it came to the workers going out on an unofficial smoke-break to protest. Work stopped for ten minutes. Because the workers didn't want to risk any more, the management simply forgot the incident, and no-one felt the consequences'.[36]

Beneath these forms of concealed collective protest lay another level at which discontent was expressed. Much worker resistance took an 'infrapolitical' form – a form that was concealed from the direct view of those in power and consisted of individual acts such as jokes, persistent rumour-mongering and the expression of anti-regime statements through graffiti.[37] Many of these statements of discontent revealed deep discontent with the low living standards of industrial workers. Young workers from Tatabánya who escaped to the West in 1953 recounted how, under cover of darkness, they would go from the workers' hostels into the town to tear down posters inviting them to produce 'More coal for the homeland', or to 'sign up for peace loans, build a future for your family and your children', and replaced them with their own home-made posters with slogans like 'Long live the Americans!', and 'don't work for such low wages!'.[38] Negative solidarity against the state made widespread theft by workers from their employers possible during the early 1950s. This often provided the basis for participation by workers in informal, sometimes illegal, economic activity beyond the scope of their employment.[39]

Shop-floor opposition to state policy has been characterised as negative solidarity against the state for the reason that it coexisted with an extraordinary decline in solidarity between workers at the point of production. The individualisation of production increased wage differentials between workers – often between workers who had the same job description. Despite the collectivism of regime ideology this individualisation of production was highly visible by late 1950. Furthermore the implementation of the regime's policy of rapid industrialisation led to the emergence of widespread shortages of materials, labour, machinery and tools in Hungarian industry during the early 1950s. Although the precise impact of such shortages varied from sector to sector, enterprise to enterprise and, often workshop to workshop, they decisively reshaped the rhythms of production and the shop-floor experience of industrial labour. The level of earnings became increasingly unpredictable. Industrial workers increasingly began to compete with their workmates for scarce work in order to survive.[40]

This competition was given enormous impetus by informal bargaining between lower management – desperate to meet plan targets in an unpredictable economic environment – and a discontented workforce. Workers in a favourable position within the division of labour of a given plant were able to use their bargaining power to gain advantage manipulating wage systems, or securing preferential access to remunerative work. As the state became concerned about the rapidly declining quality of industrial production, skilled, experienced workers were also able to argue for preferential treatment.[41]

As this occurred older skilled workers, who on the whole had worked prior to 1948, were able to shape the division of power, work and earnings on Hungarian shop-floors. Their opposition to certain consequences of state labour policies pursued during the early years of socialist industrialisation was to play an important part in a phenomenon best characterised as the reproduction of pre-socialist hierarchies in the workforce.[42] The gender implications of this reproduction of hierarchy are of particular interest to us here. As the 1950s progressed, women were increasingly marginalised on the shop-floor, as they enjoyed less countervailing power in informal bargaining than their male colleagues.

This was illustrated most clearly in those sectors like textiles where the workforce was largely female. In textiles the introduction of new norms in 1950s had led to increased work intensity and low wages. A high proportion of the largely female machine operators in the spinning and weaving halls could not make out. In the Magyar Pamutipar, one of the capital's largest textile factories, many of the machine operators complained during 1951 that 'it just isn't possible to maintain this tempo for much longer' and 'it's a wonder that the workers can manage this'. With this high work intensity, in textiles a higher proportion of the workforce failed to make out than almost anywhere else in industry. In July 1951 the proportion of the workforce failing to fulfil their norms in the two spinning shops were 21.7 percent and 46.72 percent, whilst in the weaving shop 31.53 percent of the workers failed to reach 100 percent. In addition the average wages in the factory stood at 645 Ft per month in October 1951. This was well below the industrial average.[43]

Some of the female machine operators did gain preferential treatment. This was not based upon the kinds of informal bargaining seen elsewhere in the economy. In textiles this took place entirely within the boundaries of the labour competition. The management of the Magyar Pamutipar, rather unusually for a large industrial enterprise in 1952, was able to report that 'the norms are firm' – a sign that very little, if any, bargaining over job rates occurred. Among the machine operators in the weaving shops preferential treatment was granted to those workers who operated the most machines simultaneously. The quality of the cotton they received was the best, ensuring that they did not have to cope with the thread snapping. This provoked tension between those who operated eight machines and those who operated sixteen machines. Normally the latter earned twice as much as the former but a decline in the quality of the cotton had led to lower earnings amongst those operating eight machines whilst preferential treatment in the distribution of the raw materials had ensured that those working sixteen machines had stable earnings. Such practices caused complaints; in 1951 one young worker complained that 'there are materials of variable quality. The good quality ones are taken by the "good" workers ... it's easy to work well when you have good materials'.[44]

Among the largely male skilled workers who maintained the machinery; informal bargaining of a kind visible elsewhere was endemic. They were far more willing to resort to the tactics of go-slow and of non-cooperation than their female colleagues in order to secure preferential treatment. Rumours of imminent norm revision were frequently used in order to ensure that at such times the workers did not 'go too fast with their work'. Such strategies were often accompanied by intimidation of norm-setters who complained that 'the maintenance staff were putting pressure' on them. Increasingly as work intensity increased together with the demands on the machinery, male skilled workers were able to translate their relative autonomy, at least when compared with the machine operatives, and management's dependence on them to their advantage. It was this small group of workers that gained countervailing power to bargain informally with management to secure better earnings.[45]

The differential access of male maintenance workers and female machine operators to informal bargaining strategies can to some extent be attributed to the differences in their position within the division of labour in a socialist textile enterprise. What is difficult to explain is the lack of female protest at their subordinate position within the workplace. The changing patterns of collective protest in the textile industry help illustrate the more general problem. There is no evidence that women workers were any less inclined than men to engage in collective protest in the pre-Stalinist period, indeed the reverse is true. Women machine operators in one Budapest plant in 1949 led a two-day strike against the introduction of higher production norms. The strike closed the factory, making it the most serious single strike in the country prior to the outbreak of the 1956 Revolution.[46] In spring 1950 when piece-rate wage systems were introduced across industry, once again female machine operators in textiles were more militant than almost any other group in industry engaging in a series of strikes of several hours right across the capital.[47]

The crushing of worker protest against norm-revision in summer 1950 seems to have represented an even more radical turning-point in textiles than in industry as a whole. Despite a huge increase in work intensity and a large fall in earnings, collective protest disappeared. Increasingly machine operators reacted to their working conditions by giving up and leaving. In 1951 in the Magyar Pamutipar, party officials noticed that 'a large number of workers quit and seek work at factories where they don't have to work Sundays or at night. Neighbouring factories are hiring those that left without permission'. Labour turnover stood at around 18–20 percent over the course of the first five months of the year. Such labour mobility fed an absolute problem of labour shortage, party officials frequently requested the recruitment of more labour while management replied that increasingly it could not be found.[48] Increasingly, married women left the textile industry – machine operators were recruited from the ranks of female school-leavers in rural areas who in turn left the industry when they married.[49]

Where open protest did occur it did not relate to the questions of working conditions or wages, though considerable discontent with both existed. Instead it directly addressed questions of working time, and the attempts of the state to extend it, limiting the time available to women for the management of the household. In textiles the state expanded the number of working days by cutting down the number of public holidays and tentatively introduced seven-day production. This provoked considerable opposition because they attempted to redraw the balance that the largely female workforce made between work in the factory and in the private sphere. These attempts began in 1950. The first step was to force workers to work on the Saturday before Easter. In deference to the moral economy of the machine operators who regarded their Saturday afternoon as one for making preparations for the Easter Sunday holiday, they had been previously allowed the afternoon off. Attempts to make them work the full day were met with vociferous protests throughout the factory and a problem of considerable absenteeism for every year thereafter. The extension of the working week to include Sundays in 1951 was met with similar protests. Though party agitators suspected that this opposition was due to 'religious agitation' they could never prove this. Machine operators saw this measure as an attack on both family and household.[50]

Gendered notions of a split between public and private realms were reshaping collective protest, as much as did state repression. State attempts to extend working time for women and thereby restrict the amount of time to be devoted to the household provoked open protest while reductions in wages and working conditions provoked job-quitting. Furthermore much bargaining over remuneration and work seemed to be deployed by skilled male workers only, and was often at the expense of women. This provoked surprisingly little protest or open complaint. The argument presented here is that this was in part because the formal, state-controlled economy was failing to satisfy the economic needs of Hungarian households. Given that a repressive state had closed off the avenues to collective protest, improvements in wages and incomes could not be achieved through collective action. Severe poverty and shortage in the sphere of consumption fuelled the growth of an ideal of social privatisation that women had more to invest in than men. It is however working-class poverty and the problems of consumption that will be discussed next.

The Economy of Shortage in Everyday Life

Problems with the supply of goods were first noticed in Hungary's mining areas. In Tatabánya the problems began in September 1950 with shortages of sugar that led to workers queuing for supplies. The shops ran out of potatoes, onions and other fresh vegetables. By early October the city council responded by distributing daily supplies from 6 a.m. onwards in the market place.[51] Official organs received complaints about consumers having to queue for sugar, especially from households where both partners worked and as a result were unable to queue, thus forcing them to go without for weeks on end.[52] As far as workers in the VI pit of the mines were concerned the fact 'that workers had to run around after them (groceries)' was a sign that the regime 'continually talks about rising living standards and gives us nothing'. Another stated that living standards were declining because 'on the market there aren't any goods'. The shortages meant that the workers 'only earn salt and paprika now'.[53]

The shortages in towns like Tatabánya were to spread quickly to all industrial areas. As a result 'shortage' became not only a fundamental determinant of life within the sphere of socialist production, but also within consumption.

Shortages fundamentally reinforced the perception that the formal economy was incapable of satisfying material need. The chaos that characterised it shaped the search of many households for a degree of autonomy from it. Despite the fundamental importance of the experience of socialist consumption in shaping popular attitudes to the state, the private and the public, as well as the formal and informal, it has received little attention in critical social scientific investigation of the patterns of everyday life in state socialist societies.[54] Shortages of goods undermined the legitimacy of the regime and called into question for many working class consumers the relationship between work and reward. Problems in the realm of consumption fundamentally reduced the willingness of industrial workers to respond to the work incentives that were designed to improve their performance in the realm of socialist production. The problems of consumption were to create the space for a large parallel economy alongside that of official socialist production that operated autonomously of, whilst not being entirely separate from it.

Labour histories of proletarianisation and industrialisation under capitalist conditions have underlined the role of increased working-class consumption in improving work discipline. More recently historians of scientific management have seen high consumption as having stabilised Fordist production regimes in the capitalist West.[55] The state in early socialist Hungary aimed to mobilise Hungarian society behind its policy of proletarianisation and its individualisation of production relations within factories with the promise of higher consumption. In 1953 in a party propaganda pamphlet the regime made increases in living standards and in consumption central to its appeal. Though it admitted there had been 'difficulties' in the field of food supply, it argued that 'the free market prices of many foodstuffs have fallen and a state of general plenty has been created in the provision of industrial goods'.[56]

The reality of early socialist consumerism in this regard fell short of state intentions or its propaganda. Though the number of shops increased substantially the conditions in them were often inadequate. In Újpest during the course of the 1950s the number of shops selling spices doubled. Between 1951 and 1958 the number of butchers increased from 29 to 40. Despite this, even as late as 1958 officials judged that 'alongside modern and pleasant shops there are those which are old-fashioned and give cause for concern on health grounds'. Furthermore whilst the centre of the district was well provided for, 'goods supply to outlying areas' was 'inadequate',[57] disadvantaging the residents of those parts of the district. In the new town of Sztálinváros, despite its privileged position as far as state investment in services was concerned, similar problems were experienced. In 1954 the local representative of the Ministry of Internal Commerce admitted that 'the development of commerce has been pushed into the background in recent years' and that this had led to poorly designed and often inadequate shopping facilities in the town.[58]

Even though the provision of shops and basic services for consumers in the industrial centres left much to be desired it was at least considerably better than in the surrounding villages from where many workers commuted. In the villages surrounding Tatabánya there was a simple lack of basic facilities and services; a grocer's shop only existed in those villages where a marketing co-operative for agricultural produce had survived the collectivisation drive, though most had a small pub.[59] In rural Zala county, which because of the oil industry, contained a significant number of village-dwelling commuting workers the situation was similar. In 1953 there were thirty-one villages without a shop; of these one had a population of between five hundred and a thousand, whilst the remaining thirty had populations of over under five hundred. As a result some village dwellers were often four kilometres from the nearest shop.[60]

In theory, however, from 1951 onwards working class consumers were able to turn to the 'free markets' where producers sold their goods directly to consumers at market prices. Such a market was created in Sztálinváros in 1952, but was not as widely used as hoped by working class consumers. One official reported that 'in the morning it is the housewives who live locally, after work the workers come down to get necessary things. The real situation is that very few use it'.[61] 'Free markets' suffered from a problem of legitimacy as in many consumers' minds they were often associated with speculation and a poor deal. Many consumers incorrectly referred to the 'free market' as the 'black market' implicitly refusing to recognise its officially tolerated status;[62] and because of the reliance of both state shops and 'free markets' on the state of agricultural production, food supply in both state shops and on the 'free markets' suffered from the same problems. Where agricultural production was of a high quality and quantity the markets tended to be well stocked.[63] In industrial areas they tended to be poor.[64] Furthermore during times of agricultural dearth they tended to be poorly stocked.[65]

At least in urban households, on account of their strict gender division of labour, the working class consumer was often the woman within the household. It was her responsibility to negotiate the problems of food shortages and poor standards of service and design in the shops. This task was often made more difficult by both the acute poverty in many working class households during the early 1950s and the gender division of household income. Poverty and declining living standards were serious problems in the early 1950s. According to trade union figures, real wages were some 16.6 percent lower in 1953 than in 1949. The average income of households living from wages and salaries had fallen by 8 percent over the same period. This was reflected in changing patterns of household expenditure. Groceries accounted for 45.9 percent of the budget of an average household in 1949, a figure that had risen to 58.8 percent by 1953. The share of expenditure on clothing had fallen from 18.2 percent to 10.4 percent. Furthermore the average household's consumption of meat, fat and milk was lower in 1953 than in 1938.[66] These averages concealed the desperate poverty of many households, one young worker who had escaped to the West remembered that many of his neighbours had 'gone every six weeks to give blood to get a supplementary income'.[67] In the early 1950s, the sight of large numbers of people scouring Budapest's rubbish dumps for scraps of food or assorted bric-à-brac to sell was very common.[68]

In addition to this absolute poverty, severe pressure was brought to bear on working class household budgets. In urban households with very few dependants, living standards were low. For larger households the situation was desperate. One miner's wife who fled to the West in 1952, described the problem

of budgeting given the low level of industrial wages and the relatively high
level of prices:

> My husband gave me the whole of his wage to manage the household …. At the
> beginning of the month the mine paid the first instalment that was always about
> 320 Forints, and I had to budget with it so that it would last until the middle of
> the month, when my husband got the second instalment of his monthly pay.
> During that time I only bought the most necessary things, like fat, oil, flour …
> then came the second part … from that with the most basic living standard I
> managed to save 100 to 120 Forints, though that was only done because my
> husband instead of resting did extra shifts … so that sometimes I could buy
> material to make clothes for the children.[69]

Often, however, the husband or male partner refused to give all his earnings over to his wife or partner insisting that he keep sufficient income for
leisure while he expected his wife to maintain the household. Often women
were severely disadvantaged by this distribution of the household budget. An
extreme example of a situation that was by no means uncommon was that of
a young woman who lived with her fiancé in a poor Budapest district. Though
her fiancé was a skilled worker he 'drank and gambled on the horses' which
resulted in her getting '600 or 700 Forints' of the '1100 to 1200 Forints' he
earned monthly, and from this housekeeping allowance he would 'often ask
for money back'. On account of high prices she was often unable to buy food
for herself or afford to heat the flat during the day in winter. She ate only
bread and jam, and stayed in bed simply to keep warm when not out shopping
for the household.[70]

Even where women were able and willing to ease the income problems of
their households by participating in the labour force of the socialist sector, the
burden of homemaking fell upon them. This in a world characterised by
shortage, unresponsiveness and inefficiency was far from an easy task. One
Budapest consumer who did not work described the daily shopping routine
when the supply of food and goods was not interrupted by shortage thus:

> every morning I got up at six and went to the *Tejért* (the dairy shop) to buy nec-
> essary things for breakfast …. I had of course to queue, but at least in the week
> I could buy as much milk as I wanted, or as much as I could afford. It was only
> on Saturday there was a restriction on how much I could buy, just a litre per per-
> son …. I had to buy bread at the *Közért* (general grocery store) … after my fiancé
> had gone to work I would do the shopping for lunch and dinner, by this time
> one did not have to queue.

Consumption was frequently characterised by many small trips to the shops in
the industrial districts simply because 'the wives of workers didn't have
enough money to buy large amounts'.[71]

For working women, especially for those on morning shifts, shopping had
to be done before or immediately after work; and because of the lack of capacity of many of the shops and the frequent late deliveries of many foodstuffs,
there was the problem of queuing. In Sztálinváros in 1952 queues frequently

developed in the morning hours before work and then in the afternoon at the end of the first shift at 2 p.m. It was reportedly common to have to queue for 'hours' whilst the bread was delivered, shelved and distributed. This forced many to wait for up to two hours in the morning and then to wait again in the afternoon before they were able to buy what they wanted.[72]

Commuters from rural areas, even those with no land, were in a less favourable position than consumers in the socialist economy. In rural households where one or more members worked in urban industry the gender division of labour had been modified, with women likely to remain in the village and work in agriculture.[73] In such cases it was the men who would combine their work with shopping for goods that, where a family owned land, could not be cultivated at home, or were generally scarce in the village. This division of labour within a household unit existed both where the men commuted over a long distance returning home only every few weeks, and where the worker commuted on a daily basis. In both instances commuters' consumption habits differed significantly from their urban counterparts, though for different reasons. The major difference was that commuters did not go to the shops frequently, but tended to go infrequently and buy noticeably large amounts. In the case of long-distance commuters this was in order to take large quantities of goods that were scarce in their home villages for their families over the time that they were away. In 1953 in Sztálinváros the long-distance commuters were said to be taking advantage of the favourable supply of meat to the town alongside 'customers who do not work here', causing a run on meat supplies on the day before the free Saturday when they were off work.[74] Those who commuted on a day-to-day basis would buy larger amounts than urban residents for another reason, namely that they would buy for friends and relatives in their home village who did not have any other connection with the urban world. One commuter to the mines in Tatabánya was challenged on the train home by a trade union official as to why he had ten loaves of white bread, and replied that he had been asked to buy them for his neighbours.[75]

Commuting workers' consumption patterns led to accusations that they hoarded goods. This contributed to a climate in which commuters were actively discriminated against. In Tatabánya in 1952 one trade union official instructed the director of the local shop to 'give out the white bread at midday when the buses to the villages depart'. He justified this on the basis that 'the commuters take loaves and loaves of the bread from the town dwellers, the same happens with the flour ... and so hinder our shopping for food'.[76] This kind of discrimination was widespread and led to considerable anger among commuting workers. One village youth described his day-to-day experience of such discrimination stating that in his village 'meat was not available, if someone wanted to buy meat they had to go to town. In the town, if they knew you were from the village and wanted to buy they very unwillingly gave you fat, let alone meat, because it was commonly said, why do the villagers come to the town, when in the village they have plenty of everything'.[77]

The considerable difficulties created by the inadequacy of the state shops and 'free markets' intensified during the periods of extreme food and goods shortage. The experience of this phenomenon had two effects. The first was to encourage working class consumers to resort to a series of measures designed to mitigate the situation. The second was a more long-term process that led to the development of a trend towards reduced dependence on the wage packet from the socialist sector and the goods available in the state shops. This led workers to strive for greater household self-sufficiency. Even the most successful households who tried to become more self-sufficient never managed completely to achieve this objective.

Firstly the various forms of immediate adjustment to shortages which working-class consumers attempted to deploy are examined. The most common response among those with sufficient cash available to them was to buy as many goods as possible when they became available and to hoard them. As a result of the financial constraints on most working class households, it was reportedly those with spare money, who had either an extra source of income or food through land, and were not dependent on their low wages from industry for survival that were able to employ such a strategy. In February 1952, as fat and eggs reappeared in the shops in two counties, it was reported that 'largely villagers' bought up the goods with the intention of hoarding them; from one shop five thousand eggs were sold in two hours.[78] Some families sought to buy as many goods as possible by sending all the family members to queue. In one case in Tatabánya five members of the same family had stood in one queue and had each bought flour.[79] In 1951 rumours of food shortages often provoked waves of panic-buying.[80]

Shortages, buying as much as possible and hoarding significantly reshaped buying patterns amongst those who had the ready cash to do so, and severely disadvantaged those who did not. Food and goods shortages often forced consumers to resort to informal, unofficial and often illegal solutions to their problems. Certain working class consumers were able to secure privileged access to goods through kin and friends who worked in the stores. In February 1953 it was reported that staff in the state shops in Tatabánya were secretly reserving scarce supplies of flour for their friends and relatives.[81] Very little direct evidence exists of bribery, but its existence seems likely given that overcharging by staff in shops, with the staff pocketing the extra, seems to have been a common practice throughout industrial Hungary during the early 1950s.[82]

The other form that informal, unofficial and illegal strategies took was that of buying through the 'black' market. Due to administrative control, access to it could be extremely restricted. Many people came into contact with unofficial economic activity through itinerant sellers from rural areas who would offer food in exchange for used clothes or industrial goods.[83] Given the need for extra cash, working-class consumers themselves sought to exploit shortages in order to supplement their own incomes. In Miskolc in 1951 cases were reported of workers who had bought boots that were in short supply, then selling them illegally for prices higher than those in the state shops.[84]

Households sought a degree of autonomy for the household as a long-term response to the problem of shortages. This strategy was well illustrated by the problem of bread production and consumption in the mining areas. Much state-produced bread was not only frequently late but was of extremely poor quality. As a result of this poor quality, by 1953 working class consumers demanded the freedom and the goods to make the bread themselves. Many miners told a party committee investigating their living conditions that 'they wanted to eat home-made bread, as the factory-made bread was of appalling quality' and demanded that the appropriate flour and yeast be made available in the shops.[85]

Household Autonomy: Ideals and Realities

With the beginning of socialist industrialisation the state became concerned about those it termed *kétlaki* – in other words those workers who were members of households with land and therefore incomes from agriculture. It saw this as a central obstacle to 'new' workers acceptance of socialist work discipline. A campaign was implemented in 1951 and 1952 that had two prongs. The first prong aimed to use propaganda to make the *kétlaki* existence socially unacceptable in the eyes of other workers. Regime propaganda portrayed the worker-peasant existence as detrimental to all of the workers, including the worker-peasants themselves, because it prevented the development of a purely socialist consciousness. In the words of one propaganda booklet, 'the *kétlaki* miner is his own enemy'. Furthermore by concentrating on their own land it was inevitable that they would betray their work colleagues, by undermining the earning possibilities of their workmates by going sick. The second prong was to launch a programme of agitation among the workers to persuade them to sell their land at a favourable price, either to the local council or to join the co-operative.[86] In areas where a worker-peasant lifestyle had deep roots, this campaign engendered considerable opposition from the wives who managed the smallholding while their husbands went to work. Women did not want the land sold, nor did they want to join co-operatives even when their husbands were willing to agree to state demands. From their vantage point as managers of the household they saw land as giving the household a degree of independence from the shortages of the socialised retail sector and the unreliability of their husbands' earnings. In villages in the Zala oilfields wives were said to have threatened their husbands with divorce and suicide if they joined the co-operatives. They had refused to cook for their husbands where they had signed away their land. One oil worker told the authorities what his wife had told him – 'it (the land) is there to help us live, because of it we have not starved, but if it is taken away from us we will (starve)'.[87]

Despite the pressures to which agricultural households were subjected in the early 1950s, in the face of shortage the worker-peasant existence represented an ideal to which many workers, and especially working-class women subscribed.[88] With the limited liberalisation that followed a change of government in 1953 those workers – normally worker-peasants – with sufficient resources to build a private house, did so.[89] The growth of private house construction fed a growing parallel economy as the state sector, – hit by power cuts and shortages – failed to meet the material demands of the population.[90] Materials pilfered from their official workplace formed one major source of construction materials for such houses. A journalist who escaped to the West

in 1956 cynically commented that 'the villages surrounding the "great constructions of socialism" contain the most new peasant cottages, built from
excellent materials, and of sound construction ... of course the material
"removed" from the site of the socialist constructions'.[91]

Household autonomy in early socialist Hungary was premised in the minds
of many upon either the private ownership of land, a family house or access to
some source of income outside an unreliable state sector. The household was
at the centre of an informal economy that grew up in the cracks created by the
malfunctioning of the state sector. The repression and poverty prevalent in the
official realm during the 1950s, led to the creation of a household-centred, par-
tially visible economy. Paradoxically, however, this economy was based on an
interaction between worker experiences of the state sector – both in production
and consumption. It drew on notions that property conferred independence
that were far from unique to Hungary[92] and further reinforced and strengthened them. Not all households, however, were autonomous in any sense –
although those that were relatively less independent of the state sector suffered
the greatest poverty. The differentiation that opened up between working-class
households on the basis of access to resources, other than those provided by the
state, fuelled the spread of an ideal of social privatisation.

For households dependent on wages alone in urban Hungary by the mid-
1950s living conditions were poor. Even according to a poverty line set at a
miserably low level, the National Council of Trade Unions estimated that in
1956 35 percent of households dependent on wages from the state sector
lived in poverty. Among urban households it discovered that the key determinant of poverty was the ratio of earners in a household to dependants. This
left young families – with one earner where the mother could not find any
work – in dire poverty.[93] Low household earnings went together with poor
housing conditions; in 1957 it was still common in industrial towns that 'a
five-member family live in a one room flat'.[94] In such families where incomes
could not be increased through younger family members taking work in
industry, rising prices cut into household incomes during the early 1950s.[95]

The large number of young urban households with children had several
options open to them. The male earner could attempt to increase his income
through moonlighting if the sector in which he worked gave him skills that
could be deployed in the informal economy. Where the worker provided a service the route to an extra income was easy to find. Household electricians' wages
were around Ft 1,000 a month, but they could often make another Ft 400 to
Ft 500 monthly through what one former electrician described as 'black work'.
His employers' – the local housing repair co-operative – charges for repairs
were high and often the electrician could pocket the money for the job by charging the customer lower rates. In one case the customer 'eagerly agreed but after
she had to call the co-operative to say the work hadn't needed doing'.[96]

Access to incomes from 'black work' were not open to everybody and
depended either on the nature of their state job or personal connections. The
second possibility open to a low-paid worker would be to take a second job.
This possibility, however, was circumscribed by legal regulation. These provisions were commonly side-stepped, which led workers to take up secondary

employment unofficially. In 1953 wages amongst railwaymen varied between Ft 420 and Ft 700 monthly. Of these some eight thousand employees failed to earn more than Ft 570. In such cases many workers spent their spare time undertaking additional employment, most commonly informal agricultural work to guarantee a basic standard of living for their families.[97] Access to such informal work was often dependent on contacts secured through workmates in the socialised sector of the economy. This was especially true of casual labour in agriculture during periods of harvest. As early as summer 1951 the local authorities had noticed that the Sztálinváros construction site was being used as an informal labour market to recruit casual labour.[98]

The third possibility for poverty-striken urban families was for other adult household members, normally the wife and mother, to seek work. It was nevertheless difficult for a woman to find work in Hungary during the early 1950s.[99] From 1953 female unemployment was privately recognised as a problem by the authorities, as opportunities for women to enter manual employment were extremely restricted. In Budapest in 1955 and 1956 the labour exchanges reported a problem of finding industrial work for women, leading local authorities to state that there was a problem of hidden unemployment among women, the extent of which 'can only be estimated'.[100]

A fourth option was to spend less by recycling clothes. Bodies such as trade unions noted that 'large families restrict their expenditure on children's clothes through handing them down from the older to younger children'. In doing this, however, they came up against the problems of the poor quality of the clothing sold in Hungarian shops. Mothers were thus forced to 'ensure they remained usable through continual repair and re-stitching, whilst they continued to keep a stock of really inferior clothes'.[101]

Lastly such households could attempt to reduce their expenditures by becoming more self-sufficient. This attempt to shift towards greater self-sufficiency took a number of forms that were generally more open to those who lived in or close to rural areas than to workers in Budapest. Often it led to the theft of certain goods that were in short supply in the socialised chains of shops. This was the case with firewood, of which there was a significant shortage in winter 1952. In areas close to woods and forests this led to a significant problem of the illegal felling of trees. One miner's wife who escaped to the West in 1952 remembered that 'because my husband wasn't a member of the trade union, we didn't get wood' at concessionary prices. That meant 'wood cost 280 Forints for a cubic metre' and anyway was in short supply. Instead they went to the nearby woods to cut wood, which was only possible to do 'on Mondays and Fridays, when no-one was there to look after the wood', because, if caught, they faced a heavy fine.[102] In some rural areas a growing problem of poaching was experienced as many workers in both industry and agriculture illegally hunted to ensure that they acquired an adequate supply of meat.[103] Another sign of this shift was the growth of unofficial fishing. During the early 1950s the state reorganised fishing clubs, placing them under the control of the enterprises and banning those who were not members of a club from buying either fishing tackle or obtaining a fishing licence. The state furthermore ordered anglers to keep a record of every catch so that when their records were inspected, the authorities would be able to see that the angler had caught only the amount of fish that was deemed necessary to feed the family. Yet unofficial fishing was widespread.[104]

Rural dwellers enjoyed considerable advantages over their urban work-mates in pursuing strategies based on household self-sufficiency. At many industrial establishments the expansion of the workforce during the early 1950s had led to many of the rural poor escaping underemployment in their home villages by taking unskilled industrial work. These workers commuted and were able to use their gardens as a buffer against unreliable earnings and chaos in the state sector.[105] Alongside this existed the *kétlaki* phenomenon. This was not unique to the socialist period. The evidence does suggest that it expanded as a result of the parallel pressures of collectivisation campaigns and socialist industrialisation. The first official post-war estimate of the extent of this phenomenon, in 1957, suggested that of households attached to agricultural producer co-operatives 29 percent had permanent, non-seasonal income from wages. Of households that owned family farms, 35 percent had some income from industry.[106]

The expansion of the *kétlaki* lifestyle cannot be understood without some reference to rural communities' experiences of the various strands of Stalinist agricultural policy. From 1948 onward the intensification of 'class war' politics by the state, increases in taxation and compulsory deliveries, as well as the attempts to socialise agriculture transformed rural life. The combination of high taxation of land as well as the sharp increases in compulsory deliveries severely squeezed the incomes of individual landholders by 1951. Even before compulsory deliveries, amounts of goods that had to be sold to the state at fixed prices were levied, taxation of smallholders was high. The son of one remembered that in the early 1950s 'tax under normal circumstances was 250 Forints per month, but in many cases rose to 300 Forints, because if we couldn't give anything to the state it was put into tax'.[107]

Compulsory deliveries were often punitive whilst the arbitrary methods used to enforce them were bitterly resented. One young farmer remembered that the local supervisor of agricultural procurement:

> strictly ensured that the correct amount was collected ... at the latest milk had to be brought to them (the authorities) by quarter past six in the morning. The calculation took place monthly ... the yearly delivery of milk was 660 litres from our first cow, 380 litres from the second one. They didn't take into account that we also used them as beasts of burden and so the poor, tired animals hardly produced any milk on the days we worked with them. For this reason we were happy if a single cup of milk was left for us in a day ....

In response to such pressure many smallholders resorted to the blatant avoidance of regulations.[108]

Taxation and compulsory deliveries had pushed many small farmers close to starvation by late 1952 and early 1953. As a result of compulsory deliveries 'the farmer got less for his produce, than his seed had cost him causing general hunger in western Hungarian villages. The rural population had to wait in long queues for bread and flour, whilst the family who could get hold of half a kilo of flour was delighted'.[109] Living conditions for members of the new agricultural co-operatives were little better. Many were extremely disorganised and their production levels were low. Taxes ate into the low earnings of the agricultural co-operatives. One member of a co-operative remembered that by 1952 'the older members did not have a fillér for pocket money or a cigarette unless their children went out and found some other work'.[110]

Faced with this misery the younger members of many agricultural households were sent out to work. The way this worked was illustrated by the experience of one smallholder family in predominantly rural Tolna county:

> M.K. could not maintain his independence any longer, and his daughter Ilonka went to work for the post office. She helped at home in the morning, and collected and delivered letters in the afternoon. She gave her money to her father, couldn't buy herself clothes from it, and stole food from work so that her mother and younger sister could have something decent to eat.

Often the needs of family members led to changes in the gender division of labour in smallholder households. One escapee from a southwestern Hungarian village stated that 'the women have never worked as much as they do now. Nobody employs anyone else in the village because there aren't applicants, and it's impossible to accept them anyway. Women have to leave the housework to work in the fields'.[111]

It was predominantly poor rural youth that took jobs in industry. The lack of any security of income for the rural poor was the major motivation for such young people. This forced families to send one or more of its young members out to earn a secure income. The household unit could use this as a hedge against the failure of the agricultural producer co-operative to pay out at the end of the year, a bad harvest or a severe tax or compulsory delivery collector. One such worker who took up employment on a large construction site lived on a farm of eight kh (about four hectares); as a result of the farm's inability to guarantee an income for the family he had to go to work. He remembered that 'twice a month he could go home for one and a half days and had to spend half a day of free time travelling. He gave his family 200 Forints of his monthly earnings and had to live from the rest'. In some cases where there was no child of working age it was the head of the household who went to work; 'the private farmers were attached to their small amounts of land and were not willing to enter the co-operative. The majority of private farmers couldn't live from their land and were forced to go and work away. The peasants in general went to the construction sites to get work, the women and children farmed the land'. Many were driven by the notion that for work the wages 'were paid in cash that you receive in your hand. Furthermore in the town they take the effort to provide bread to the people'.[112]

The earliest surveys of the phenomenon from 1957 confirm that those who took up industrial employment came from the ranks of poorer villagers. Of agricultural households with less than one kh[113] of land, 51 percent had one or more family members working in industry, with 15 percent having two or more members. For households with between one and three kh the respective proportions were 37.6 percent and 9.1 percent. Among households with more property the phenomenon was virtually non-existent, of those farming between 20 and 25 kh of land the proportions stood at 8.8 percent and 0.9 percent.[114]

It is important not to idealise the worker-peasant lifestyle. Many households were pushed into it by dire poverty. Furthermore it was premised on a particular configuration of gender and generational relations within the households which were often profoundly exploitative. In a climate of low wages and shortages many of these new worker-peasants refused to accept the demands of their jobs in the socialist sector, when they conflicted with those of the household. This was despite the fact that unauthorised absenteeism was a criminal offence during the early 1950s and offenders were often prosecuted. This concerned many in the party leadership, including Mátyás Rákosi – Hungary's home-grown Stalinist dictator– who stated that 'these workers during the harvest go absent from their factories, and disrupt the rhythm of production. At the same time because of their work in the factory they don't pay enough attention to their land, which shows itself in their production. These *kétlaki* workers, in one go, disrupt industrial and agricultural production'. Many local functionaries shared the views of their leaders and indeed many worker-peasants did strongly defend their way of life. One such worker in one western Hungarian construction enterprise bluntly told his superior that 'the democracy secured for him seven kh of land, and he had to work it. First came his land and second came the factory'. Indeed at harvest time a large number sought to leave the factory to perform agricultural work on their land. In July 1951 in the Mátyás Rákosi Works around two thousand workers asked for unpaid leave to work on their land. In machine manufacture absenteeism was high among these *kétlaki* workers who 'at the beginning of the spring agricultural season leave work for a longer or shorter period or quit completely … during the harvest season labour turnover becomes a mass phenomenon'. Of those that remained employed in industry *kétlaki* workers came to work tired given that in their 'free-time' they had had to perform agricultural labour. Those on the night shift in the oil industry often went to sleep, given the relative lack of supervision, to conserve their strength for work during the day in the fields.[115]

Nevertheless as the weight of taxation and compulsory deliveries lessened after 1953 the members of such households had a degree of independence and countervailing power that was envied by many of their workmates. In the post-1953 period the incomes of individual landholders increased at a faster rate than those of industrial workers. In the Tatabánya coalfields in 1954 officials in the local branch of the state savings bank began to notice that worker-peasants were becoming less dependent on their wages. Increasingly their wages would be left in the bank and not be touched for months on end as they lived from their agricultural incomes and produce. After a reasonable amount had been accumulated it would be spent on consumer goods, or on luxury items like a motorcycle.[116] The relative affluence of worker-peasants fuelled considerable resentment among poorer urban workers who lacked access to alternative sources of food and income.[117]

Conclusion

It has been argued throughout this chapter that industrial workers responded to socialist industrialisation and the consolidation of the Stalinist state in the factories through investing in an ideal of social privatisation. The brief sketch of the fortunes of various kinds of households outlined above demonstrates that all of them were unable to manage from the wages provided by the state sector alone. They sought to some extent to compensate for this. The extent to which they were able to do this was based on whether they could combine wages with some other means of satisfying material need. Some households managed better than others – those split between agriculture and industry were the best placed while the dire poverty of those households entirely dependent on wages demonstrated their disadvantage.

The sources of income on which households drew were very diverse. Their extent is impossible to estimate precisely because of the lack of reliable information. Nevertheless there is evidence of a multiplicity of different sources of income and resources ranging from wages, expanding employment within households, moonlighting, theft, hunting and fishing, growing vegetables, keeping chickens and combining farming with an industrial wage. In years of severe working-class poverty differential access to sources of income not derived simply from the state sector stratified working class households. Furthermore – as the jealousy of worker-peasant incomes attests – all workers were acutely aware of how household circumstance divided them.

The Stalinist state crushed collective expressions of protest, action and organisation. Its vision of creating a class-conscious working class that could be mobilised around the goals of building socialism was not realised either. Instead poverty and shortage forced industrial workers to supplement their incomes and find resources outside the formal state sector in order to survive. Hidden discontent fuelled informal bargaining, legitimised theft from the workplace, absenteeism during the harvest period, and moonlighting. For many industrial workers the state sector became a realm of poverty and shortage where needs could not be satisfied. State repression meant that the public sphere could not be used to express discontent, improve living conditions, or to protest. Shortage in production and consumption created tension between individuals and groups as the discussion of both the particularisation of worker identity and of consumption shows. Poverty was felt to be a household problem, and this drove an ideal of greater social privatisation. The lack of collective protest in Stalinist Hungary was much more, therefore, than simply a response to considerable state repression. The circumstances of socialist industrialisation promoted a withdrawal into the household. Not all, indeed only a minority of households, pursued this strategy with significant success. Yet the fact that some households could mitigate their poverty by combining industrial work with agricultural activity, striving for greater household self-sufficiency, or engaging in informal economic activity did legitimise social privatisation as an ideal. The spread of an ideal of social privatisation as an ideal led to a marked decline in social solidarity.

The subtext of the argument that has been presented here is one that deals with the consequence of socialist industrialisation for gender relations and identities. Given the sharp gendered split between public and private that much gender ideology assumed in Hungary, ideals of social privatisation would have deeply conservative implications. Despite the apparent egalitarianism of the state it never challenged established ideologies of gender directly, but accommodated itself to them. The evidence seems to suggest that women had a deeper investment in ideals of social privatisation, the protection and maintenance of the household than their male workmates. This led to an apparent paradox. Although women were supposed to assume a central role in the socialist labour force according to Stalinist ideology, women were less willing to protest as workers than men. After 1950 they withdrew more substantially from collective protest about workplace issues than male workers. Where they did protest it was about the extension of working time. Women, it would seem, invested more in ideals of social privatisation than men. This was because they coped with the consequences of socialist industrialisation not only as workers but as homemakers and consumers.

It would be an overstatement of the case made here to say that Hungarian society was 'atomised' by the Stalinist state. Such arguments are often premised on a myth of an all-powerful state. The argument presented here suggests that although it prevented collective protest, it did not control social process. In fact, if studies of Stalinism were to focus more on the material world and less on the political, a picture would emerge of a weak state confronting a weak society. The state was repressive but it could not control the shop-floor, nor indeed how people made their living more generally despite attempts to re-shape agricultural production and enforce proletarianisation. The state was confronted by a privatised society – one that, at least until the outbreak of the 1956 Revolution, was characterised by the pursuit of an ideal of household self-sufficiency and independence from the state.

Notes

1. An earlier version of this chapter was presented at the workshop 'From household strategies to collective action', held at the International Institute of Social History, Amsterdam, 28–29 May 1999. It is based on research for Mark Pittaway, 'Industrial Workers, Socialist Industrialisation and the State in Hungary, 1948–1958' (PhD Thesis, Department of Economic and Social History, University of Liverpool, 1998). This research was conducted in Hungary between 1994 and 1997, and was supported by a studentship from the ESRC (Economic and Social Research Council). I would like to thank Nigel Swain, Padraic Kenney, András Tóth, Martha Lampland as well as the participants at the workshop mentioned above for discussions that have shaped the argument of this chapter.
2. Magyar Országos Levéltár, MSZMP Budapesti Bizottság Archiviuma (Hungarian National Archive, Archive of the Budapest Committee of the Hungarian Socialist Workers' Party, hereafter MOL M-Bp.) -95f.4/118ö.e., 81–87.
3. On protest elsewhere in the socialist states during this period, there was substantial working-class protest in the GDR in 1951, see Andrew Port 'When workers rumbled: the Wismut upheaval of August 1951 in East Germany', *Social History* 22, no. 2 (1998): 145–73. In Yugoslavia the Tito regime's attempts to collectivise agriculture met with substantial and violent peasant opposition, see Melissa K. Bokovoy, *Peasants and Communists. Politics and Ideology in the Yugoslav Countryside, 1941–1953*, Pittsburgh, 1998, 134–40. The death of Stalin in 1953 led to substantial open protest in many states, though not in Hungary. In

May tobacco workers in Plovdiv rioted, see R.J. Crampton, *A Short History of Modern Bulgaria*, Cambridge, 1987, 176. In Czechoslovakia there were riots in Plzeň, see Otto Ulc, 'Pilsen: the unknown revolt', *Problems of Communism* 14, no.3 (1965): 46–9. The best-known disturbances that followed Stalin's death were those of 17 June 1953 in the GDR. The best English language account is in Mary Fulbrook, *Anatomy of a Dictatorship: Inside the GDR, 1949–1989*, Oxford and New York, 1995, 177–87.

4. For some examples of sporadic opposition see Politikatörténeti éa Szakszervezeti Levéltár (Archive of Political History and Trade Unions, hereafter PtSzL) A Volt Szakszervezetek Közpönti Levéltár anyaga (Materials of the former Central Archive of the Trade Unions, hereafter SZKL), Szakszervezetek Országos Tanácsa (National Council of Trade Unions, hereafter SZOT), Közgazdasági Osztály (Economics Department, hereafter Közgazdaság)/13d./1952.

5. For the general point see Pittaway *Industrial Workers, Socialist Industrialisation and the State*, 305–9. I explore the case of the meanings the state and mineworkers' families attached to the limited private house building campaigns of the early 1950s in Mark Pittaway, 'Stalinism, Working Class Housing and Individual Autonomy: The Encouragement of Private House Building in Hungary's Mining Areas, 1950–1954' in *Style and Socialism. Modernity and Material Culture in Post-War Eastern Europe*, eds Susan Emily Reid and David Crowley, Oxford, 2000, 49–64.

6. Probably the best overview of such events from the pre-1989 period in English is J.M. Montias, 'Observations on Strikes, Riots and Other Disturbances' in *Blue Collar Workers in Eastern Europe*, eds Jan F. Triska and Charles Gati, London and New York, 1981, 175–87.

7. Padraic Kenney, 'The Gender of Resistance in Communist Poland', *American Historical Review* 104, no. 2 (April 1999): 399–425.

8. Magyar Dolgozók Pártja – created in 1948 as the result of a forced union of Hungary's Social Democratic and Communist Parties, it was to become the ruling party for much of the 1950s. It was dissolved as a result of the 1956 Revolution, and reconstituted as the Magyar Szocialista Munkáspárt (Hungarian Socialist Workers' Party) on 1 November 1956.

.9 Tibor Garai, *A kultúrtényező jelentősége a versenyszellem kialakításában (The Importance of the Factor of Culture in Creating the Mentality of Competition)*, Budapest, 1948, 14–15.

10. PtSzL SZKL A Magyarországi Vas- és Fémmunkások Központi Szövetség iratai (Papers of the Federation of Metalworkers of Hungary, hereafter Vasas)/ 520 d./ 1948; címtelen jelentés (untitled report).

11. Personal Interview with B.P.-né, Dunaújváros, 8 February 1995.

12. For such a request from wives' of Tatabánya mine-workers see MOL Magyar Általános Kőszénbánya Személyzeti Osztály iratai (Papers of the Personnel Department of the Hungarian General Coal-Mining Company) Z254/10cs/38t, 493.

13. For pre-Second World War evidence on the importance of the existence of the worker-peasant household in certain regions of the country see Ferenc Erdei, *Futóhomok (Running Sands)*, Budapest, 1977, 53–4; Zoltán Szabó, *Cifra Nyomorúság. A Cserhát, Mátra, Bükk földje és népe (Poverty Covered with a Superficial Show of Wealth. The Peoples and Lands of the Cserhát, Mátra and Bükk)*, Budapest, 1938, 48–52; useful evidence on the gender dimensions of worker-peasant households in the immediate post-war period is provided in István Markus, 'A Demokrácia Két Éve Martonvásáron (Szociográfiai vázlat) (Two Years of Democracy in Martonvásár (A Social Report))', *Forum*, 1946, 251–61.

14. Erzsébet Örszigethy, *Asszonyok Férfisorban (Women Adopting the Roles of Men)*, Budapest, 1986.

15. Zsuzsa Gille, 'Wastelands in Transition: The Three Waste Regimes in Hungary, 1948–1998' (PhD dissertation, University of California at Santa Cruz, 1999).

16. The phrase is that of Ernö Gerő. See his *A vas, az acél és a gépek országáért (For a country of iron, steel and machines)*, Budapest, 1952.

17. See Kenney, 'The Gender of Resistance', 403–4.

18. MOL M-Bp.-95f.3/55 ö.e., 46–47.

19. MOL Magyar Dolgozók Pártja-Magyar Szocialista Munkáspárt Központi Szervek iratai (Papers of the Central Organs of the Hungarian Workers' Party – Hungarian Socialist Workers' Party, hereafter M-KS-) 276f.116/43ö.e., 15–16.

20. MOL M-KS-276f.116/43ö.e., 17.
21. MOL M-KS-276f.116/43ö.e., 16.
22. The documents contained in the dossier MOL M-KS-276f.116/43ö.e. are full of such plans.
23. Mark Pittaway 'The Social Limits of State Control: Time, the Industrial Wage Relation and Social Identity in Stalinist Hungary, 1948–1953', *Journal of Historical Sociology* 12, no.3 (September 1999): 271–301.
24. Garai, *A kultúrtényező jelentősége*.
25. 'A Magyar Munkásosztály Fejlődése (The Development of the Hungarian Working Class)', 20, Central Statistical Office, unpublished report, Budapest, 1954.
26. MOL M-KS-276f.116/18ö.e.,6.
27. MOL M-KS-276f.116/18ö.e., 22–23.
28. Pittaway 'The Social Limits of State Control', 280–1.
29. MOL M-KS-276f.116cs/19ö.e., 129–30; MOL M-KS-276f.116cs/19ö.e., 220–3; MOL M-KS-276f.116cs/18ö.e., 180–3; MOL M-KS-276f.116cs/18ö.e., 197–9; MOL M-KS-276f.116cs/19ö.e., 1; MOL M-KS-276f.116cs/19ö.e., 5; MOL M-KS- 276f.116cs/19ö.e., 58; MOL M-KS-276f.116cs/19ö.e., 43–5.
30. MOL M-KS-276f.116cs/18ö.e., 180–3; MOL M-KS-276f.116cs/19ö.e., 5; MOL M-KS-276f.116cs/ 40ö.e., 77–82.
31. MOL M-Bp.-95f.4/120ö.e., 214; PtSzL SZKL Komárom Szakszervezetek Megyei Tanácsa (Komárom County Council of Trade Unions, hereafter Komárom SZMT)/42d./1950; *Szakszervezetek Országos Tanácsa Esztergom-Komárom Megye Bizottság, Tatabánya, 1950. augusztus 24. (National Council of Trade Unions Komárom-Esztergom County Committee, Tatabánya, 4 August 1950)*, 1; PtSzL SZKL Komárom SZMT/43d./1950; *Kiértékelés (Evaluation)*, 1; PtSzL SZKL Komárom SZMT/43d./1950; *Szakszervezetek Országos Tanácsa Esztergom-Komárom Megyei Bizottság, Tatabánya, Jelentés, 1950 augusztus 29.(National Council of Trade Unions Komárom-Esztergom County Committee, Tatabánya, Report 29 August 1950)*, 1.
32. This phrase is taken from the response of a worker to the beginning of the New Course, quoted in PtSzL SZKL SZOT Bér-Munkaügy Osztály (Wage-Labour Department, hereafter Bér-Munkaügy)/33d./1953; *Feljegyzés a kormányprogrammal kapcsolatos üzemi tapasztalatokról (Report on factory experiences of the government programme)*, 1.
33. Futószalag (Conveyor Belt), 29 August 1953.
34. Open Society Achive (OSA), Radio Free European Hungarian Research Materials (hereafter RFE Magyar Gy.) Magyar Gy.6/ Item No. 08794/53, 1.
35. Quoted in Gyula Kozák and Adrienne Molnár, eds, *'Szuronyok hegyén nem lehet dolgozni'. Válogatás 1956-os munkástanács-vezetők visszaemlékezéseiből ('It isn't possible to work with a bayonet at your head'. A collection of interviews with 1956 workers' council leaders)*, Budapest, 1994, 13.
36. OSA RFE Magyar Gy.6/ Item No. 3677/56, 2.
37. For a discussion of the whole nature of 'infrapolitical' resistance as a concept see James C. Scott, *Domination and the Arts of Resistance: Hidden Transcripts*, New Haven and London, 1990, especially Ch. 7. For an examination of such kinds of 'resistance' in their Hungarian context see István Rév, 'The Advantages of Being Atomized: How Hungarian Peasants Coped with Collectivisation', *Dissent*, Summer 1987, 335–50.
38. OSA RFE Magyar Gy.6/ Item No. 06687/53, 5.
39. MOL M-Bp.-176f.2/190/6ö.e., 204.
40. For this analysis see Pittaway, 'The Social Limits of State Control', 282–6.
41. Ibid., 291–2.
42. For an in-depth examination of this phenomenon see Mark Pittaway, 'The Reproduction of Hierarchy: Skill, Working Class Culture and the State in Early Socialist Hungary', *Journal of Modern History* (forthcoming).
43. For a more in-depth examination of working conditions in the textile industry in the early 1950s, see Pittaway, *Industrial Workers, Socialist Industrialisation and the State*, 133–43; on the increase in work intensity in the plant over the course of 1951 see *Pamut Újság (Cotton Newspaper)*, 31 January 1952; MOL M-Bp.-143f./14ö.e., 222; MOL M-Bp.-176f.2/236/2ö.e., 247; on low norm fulfilment in early Spring 1951 see *Pamut Újság*, 16

April 1951; for the average worker's wage in the factory in late 1951 see MOL M-Bp.-176f.2/236/4ö.e., 69.

44. MOL M-Bp.-176f.2/236/7ö.e., 151; MOL M-Bp.-95f.3/56ö.e., 101; PtSzL SZKL Textilipari Dolgozók Szakszervezet iratati, 1949–1955 (Papers of the Textile Industry Workers' Union 1949–1955, hereafter Textiles-a)/140d./1949–1955; *Magyar Pamutipar. Jegyzökönyv amely készült 1951. nov 10–én az olvasó teremben megtartott Ü.B. értekezeleten (Magyar Pamutipar. Minutes of a factory committee meeting held in the reading room on 10 November 1951)*, 2.

45. MOL M-Bp.-95f.3/345ö.e.,p.8; MOL M-Bp.-176f.2/236/4ö.e., 268; MOL M-KS-276f.116/40ö.e., 74.

46. For this strike see PtSzL SZKL Textiles-a/129d./1949; *Jelentés a Magyar Textilipar részleges leállásról (Report on the partial production stoppage in the Hungarian Textile Industry)*.

47. MOL M-Bp.-95f.4/2/168/b ö.e., 37.

48. *Pamut Újság*, 2 August 1951; MOL M-Bp.-95f.4/60ö.e., 133; MOL M-Bp.-143f./9ö.e., 308; MOL M-Bp.-176f.2/236/4ö.e., 130; MOL M-Bp.-143f./6ö.e., 49.

49. For concern at this pattern see *Pamut Újság*, 27 June 1952; OSA RFE Magyar Gy.6/ Item No. 08794, 2; MOL M-Bp.-95f.4/60ö.e., 133–4; PtSzL A Volt Politikatörténeti Intézet Levéltára anyaga (Materials of the former Institute for the History of Politics, herafter PIL) 867f.1/d-50, 76.

50. MOL M-Bp.-95f.4/143ö.e., 2; MOL M-Bp.-95/4/62ö.e., 55–6; MOL M-Bp.-95f.4/60ö.e., 119–20.

51. Tatabánya Városi Levéltár (Tatabánya City Archive, hereafter TVL) Tatabánya VB ülések jegyzökönyvei (Minutes of Tatabánya City Council meetings); 29 September 1950, Item No.4, 6 October 1950, Item No.2/b.

52. PtSzL SZKL Komárom SZMT/42d./1950; *Titkári jelentés 1950 év november hóról (Secretarial report about November 1950)*, 1.

53. PtSzL SZKL Komárom SZMT/43d./1950; *Szakszervezetek Országos Tanácsa Esztergom-Komárom Megye Bizottság 393./1950 sz. Hangulat jelentés (National Council of Trade Unions. Komárom-Esztergom County Committee. Report on the climate of opinion 1950/303)*, 1–2; PtSzL SZKL Komárom SZMT/43d./1950; *Szakszervezetek Országos Tanácsa Esztergom-Komárom Megye Bizottság 419./1950 sz. Hangulat jelentés (National Council of Trade Unions. Komárom-Esztergom County Committee. Report on the climate of opinion 1950/419)*, 2.

54. The exception to this has been anthropological work on Romania during the 1980s. Katherine Verdery has argued that the regulation of consumption through shortage was part of the attempt of the state socialist regime in the country to 'confiscate' the time of its citizens, forming part of the general process that she identified as the 'bureaucratisation of time'. See her *What Was Socialism and What Comes Next?*, Princeton, New Jersey, 1996, Ch. 2.

55. For a useful synthesis of these arguments in so far as they have been made for early industrial England see R.E. Pahl, *Divisions of Labour*, Part One, Oxford, 1984; for scientific management see some of the contributions in Haruhito Shiomi and Kazuo Wada, eds, *Fordism Transformed. The Development of Production Methods in the Automobile Industry*, Oxford and New York, 1995.

56. *Mit adott a népi demokrácia a dolgozóknak?* (What has the Peoples' Democracy Given the Workers?), 12–3, Kiadja a Magyar Dolgozók Pártja Központi Vezetösége Agitációs és Propaganda Osztály, Budapest, 1953.

57. MOL M-KS-288f.21/1958/20ö.e., 272.

58. *Sztálin Vasmű Épitöje* (Builder of the Sztálin Steel Works), 19 March 1954.

59. PtSzL SZKL Komárom SZMT/61d./1950; *Jelentés a bányász falvakról (Report on the mining villages)*, 1–2.

60. Zala Megyei Letéltár (Zala County Archive, hereafter ZML), Magyar Szoxialista Munkáspárt Zala Megyei Bizottság iratai (Papers of the Zala County Committee of the Hungarian Socialist Workers Party, hereafter MSZMP ZMBA ir.) 57f.2/Ipar/66ö.e.; *Kedves Nagy elvtárs (Dear Comrade Nagy)*; ZML MSZMP ZMBA ir. 57f.2/Ipar/66ö.e.; *Kedves Elvtársak ! (Dear Comrades !)*, 1.

61. Fejér Megyei Letéltár (Fejer County Archive) Magyar Szocialista Munkáspárt Fejér Megyei Bizottság iratai (Papers of the Fejér County Committee of the Hungarian Socialist Workers Party, hereafter FML MSZMP FMBA ir.) 17f.1/24ö.e.; *Jegyzökönyv felvétetett 1952.junius 3.-*

án megtartott pártbizottsági ülésen, a P.B. tanácstermében 9 Minutes of a meeting of the party committee held on 3 June 1952 in the party committee meeting room), 2.

62. PtSzL SZKL SZOT Szociálpolitika/9d./1951; *Kereskedelmi és Pénzügyi Dolgozók Szakszervezete Feljegyzés a kenyér és húsjegyek bevezetésével kapcsolatos hangulatról (Report of the Commerce and Finance Workers' Union on the climate of opinion in relation to the rationing of bread and meat)*, 2.

63. OSA RFE Magyar Gy.300/40/4/43, Item No. 8349/56.

64. FML MSZMP FMBA ir. 17f.1/24ö.e.; *Jegyzőkönyv felvétetett 1952.junius 3.-án megtartott pártbizottsági ülésen, a P.B. tanácstermében (Minutes of the party committee meeting held on 3 June 1952 in the party committee meeting room)*, 2.

65. PtSzL SZKL SZOT Szociálpolitika/22d./1952; *A 1952 II.negyedév kiskereskedelmi forgalomról (About shopping in the second quarter of 1952)*, 5.

66. PtSzL SZKL SZOT Szociálpolitika/13d./1953; *Adatok és példák a Szakszervezetek Országos Tanácsa III. Teljes Ülésének beszámolóhoz (Data and examples for the third full sitting of the National Council of Trade Unions)*, 1–5.

67. OSA RFE Magyar Gy. 6./ Item No.11555/55, 4.

68. László Földes ,'A város peremén. Leírás Nagy-Budapest szeméttelepéről, 1954–ben (On the fringes of city. A description of the rubbish dumps of Greater Budapest in 1954)', *Mozgó Vílág (Moving World)*, no.5 (May 1994): 22–9.

69. OSA RFE Magyar Gy.6/ Item No. 08371/52, 1.

70. OSA RFE Magyar Gy.6/Item No. 10820/54, 1–5.

71. OSA RFE Magyar Gy. 6/ Item No. 10820/54, 4–5.

72. FML MSZMP FMBA ir. 9f.2/PTO/48ö.e.; *A Sztálinvárosi Tanács végrehajtó Bizottságba .... (To the implementation committee of Sztálinváros City Council)*, 1.

73. For evidence of this kind of gender division of labour in areas characterised by commuting see the example of Tárnok, close to Budapest (OSA 400/40/4/43; Item No. 7095/54); for allusions to this as a reason for the 'weakness' of agricultural co-operatives in the rural mining areas in Komárom-Esztergom see PtSzL SZKL Komárom SZMT/168d./1956; *Jelentés a Falusi Osztályharc Helyzetéről (Report on the state of the class struggle in the villages)*.

74. FML MSZMP FMBA ir. 17f.1/29ö.e.; *Jelentés a város közellátásának helyzetéről és az üzlethálózat fejlesztéséről (Report on the state of supply in the town and the development of the network of shops)*, 1.

75. PtSzL SZKL SZOT Szociálpolitika/21d./1952; *Szénszállító és Szólgáltató Vállalat Szakszervezeti Bizottsága, Tatabánya – Jegyzőkönyv Társadalmi ellenőrök részére megtartot értekezelről*, 2.

76. PtSzL SZKL SZOT Szociálpolitika/21d./1952; *Szénszállító és Szólgáltató Vállalat Szakszervezeti Bizottsága, Tatabánya – Jegyzőkönyv Társadalmi ellenőrök részére megtartot értekezelről*, 1.

77. OSA 300/40/4/43; Item No. 6700/54, 1–5.

78. PtSzL SZKL SZOT Szociálpolitika/22d./1952; *Feljegyzés a dolgozók hangulatáról (Report on the opinions among the workers)*, 3.

79. PtSzL SZKL SZOT Munkásellátás/15d./1953; *Tatabánya. Ótelepi gépüzem, 1953. január 31 (Tatabánya. The machine factory on the old site. 31 January 1953)*, 4.

80. ZML MSZMP ZMBA ir.57f.2/Agit/10ö.e.; *Nagykanizsa Városi Pártbizottság, 1951. január 2. du. 4.30 (Nagykanizsa City Party Committee. 2 January 1951. 4.30 p.m.)*.

81. PtSzL SZKL SZOT Munkásellátás/15d./1953; *Tatabánya VIII.akna. 1953. február 9. (Tatabánya. Pit No. VIII. 9 February 1953)*, 2.

82. FML MSZMP FMBA ir.9f.2/PTO/48ö.e.; *A Sztálinvárosi Tanács végrehajtó Bizottságba ....,* 1; PtSzL SZKL SZOT Szociálpolitika/21d./1952; *Szénszállító és Szolgáltató Vállalat Szakszervezeti Bizottsága, Tatabánya – Jegyzőkönyv Társadalmi ellenőrök részére megtartot értekezelről*, 2.

83. OSA RFE Magyar Gy.6; Item No. 11699/52, 1.

84. PtSzL SZKL SZOT Szociálpolitika/9d./1951; *Jelentés a Miskolc, diósgyőr munkásellátási kérdésekről (Report on workers' provision in Miskolc and Diósgyőr)*, 1.

85. MOL M-KS-276f.53/145ö.e.; *Tájékoztató az üzemi dolgozók és az üzemi vezetők által felvetett szociális és kultúrális problémákról*, 40.

86. *Kétlakiság* (Worker Peasant-ness), 8, Szakszervezeti Ismeretterjesztő Előadások, Népszava, Budapest, 1952; for the programme see Mátyás Rákosi, *Visszaemlékezések. 2 kötet. 1940–1956*, Budapest, 1997, 845.

87. ZML MSZMP ZMBA ir. 61f.2/Agit/7ö.e.; *Hangulat jelentés (Report on the climate of opinion)*, 1; ZML MSZMP ZMBA ir.61f.2/Agit/7ö.e.; *MDP MAORT Lovászi üzemi pártszervezet titkársága jelentés (Hungarian Workers' Party – MAORT Lovászi factory party organisation secretariat report)*.

88. Pittaway, 'Stalinism, Working Class Housing and Individual Autonomy'.

89. For the situation in one poor county in 1954 see ZML MSZMP ZMBA ir. 57f.2/63ö.e.; *Kimutatás a Zalamegyében engedélyzett.... (Family house construction approved in Zala county)*.

90. For this see Mark Pittaway, 'The Victory of Production over Consumption: Reform, Workers and the Possibilities of a New Course' (unpublished manuscript, Southport, 1999).

91. Quoted in Bill Lomax, 'The Working Class in the Hungarian Revolution of 1956', *Critique* 13, no.32 (1981).

92. For a useful description of the ideological role private home ownership has played in the United Kingdom see Pauline Hunt, 'Gender and the Construction of Home Life' in *The Politics of Domestic Consumption. Critical Readings*, eds Stevi Jackson and Shaun Moores, London and New York, 1995, especially 310–12.

93. MOL M-KS-276f.66/36ö.e., 31.

94. MOL M-KS-288f.23/1957/2lö.e., 54.

95. MOL M-KS-288f.23/1957/2lö.e., 49.

96. OSA RFE Magyar Gy.6/ Item No.1646/55, 1–8.

97. PtSzL SZKL SZOT Bér és Munkaügyi Osztálya (Wage and Labour Department)/21d./1953; *Közlekedés- és Postaügyi Minisztérium Vasúti Főosztálya levél Varga Jánosnak, Szakszervezetek Országos Tanács titkára, 21 November (1954) 1953 (Ministry of Transport and Post. Railway Department letter to János Varga, Secretary of the National Council of Trade Unions, 21 November 1953)*.

98. FML MSZMP FMBA ir.18f.2/lö.e.; *Jelentés a Dunai Vasmű Pártbizottság augusztus havi munkájáról (Report on August work of the Danube Steel Works party committee)*, 1.

99. Personal interview with T.J-né, Dunaújváros, 6 May 1996.

100. MOL M-KS-276f.94/886ö.e., 141; MOL M-KS-276f.94/886ö.e., 230.

101. MOL M-KS-288f.23/1957/2lö.e., 59.

102. OSA RFE Magyar Gy.6; Item No. 08371/52, 2.

103. OSA 300/40/4/24; Item No. 8183/55, 5.

104. See OSA 300/40/4/25; Item No.9394/54, and OSA 300/40/4/25; Item No. 09153/53.

105. 'A Magyar Munkásosztály Fejlődése' (unpublished manuscript, 1954, library of Hungarian Statistical Office); Pittaway *Industrial Workers, Socialist Industrialisation and the State*, 150–229.

106. MOL M-KS-288f.23/1958/27ö.e., 19.

107. OSA 300/40/4/22, Item No. 8027/55, 2.

108. OSA 300/40/4/22, Item No. 04759/53, 3; OSA 300/40/4/22, Item No. 8501/55, 1.

109. OSA 300/40/4/22, Item No. 3242/54, 1.

110. OSA 300/40/4/23; Item No. 267/54, 3; OSA 300/40/4/41; Item No. 12232/53, 3.

111. OSA 300/40/4/22, Item No. 14271/52, 8–9; OSA 300/40/4/22, Item No. 4154/55, 7.

112. Kh stand for *kasztrális hold*. It is a measurement equivalent to 0.58 hectares.

113. Nándor Pálfalvi, *Mint fához az ág (Like the Branch to the Tree)*, Budapest, 1958, 149–55; OSA RFE Magyar Gy. 6/ Item No. 06802/53, 5; OSA 300/40/4/42, Item No. 7929/54, 1; OSA 300/40/4/41, Item No. 12232/53, 3.

114. MOL M-KS-288f/23/1958/27ö.e., 54; ZML MSZMP ZMBA ir.1f.1958/12ö.e.; *A tapasztalatok összefoglalása (A summary of our experiences)*, 9.

115. Rákosi, *Visszaemlékezések 1940–1956*, 845; PtSzL SZKL Komárom SZMT/59d./1950; *Építők Szakszervezet Komárommegyei Bizottsága Havijelentés (Monthly report of the Komárom County. Committee of the Construction Workers' Union)*, 2; MOL M-KS-276f.116/7ö.e., 28; MOL M-KS-276f.116/7ö.e., 99; on tiredness see ZML MSZMP ZMBA ir.58f.3/4ö.e.; *MDP Olajüzemi Szervezet Nagylengyel Jegyzőkönyv felvétetett a Nagylengyeli Olajüzem M.D.P. Szervezetének kibővített vezetőségi ülésén, 1955. augusztus 22.-én (Hungarian Workers' Party*

Nagylengyel Oil Factory Organisation – Minutes of an expanded leadership meeting, 22 August 1955), 3; ZML MSZMP ZMBA ir. 61f.4/2/26ö.e.; *Feljegyzés a Párt Bizottsága megbízásából a kapott feladatot – A pártszervezet munkája a fegyelem megszilárdítása érdekben (Report on the fulfilment of tasks allocated by the party – the work of the party organisation in improving work discipline)*, 1.
116. KEML MSZMP KMBA ir.32f.4/53ö.e., 10–11.
117. MOL M-KS-288f.21/1958/20ö.e., 260.

Bibliography

Bokovoy, M.K. *Peasants and Communists. Politics and Ideology in the Yugoslav Countryside, 1941–1953.* Pittsburgh, 1998.

Crampton, R.J. *A Short History of Modern Bulgaria.* Cambridge, 1987.

Erdei, F. *Futóhomok (Running Sands).* Budapest, 1977.

Földes, L. 'A város peremén. Leírás Nagy-Budapest szeméttelepéről, 1954–ben (On the fringes of city. A description of the rubbish dumps of Greater Budapest in 1954)', *Mozgó Világ (Moving World)*, no.5 (May 1994): 22–9.

Fulbrook, M. *Anatomy of a Dictatorship: Inside the GDR, 1949–1989.* Oxford and New York, 1995.

Garai, T. *A Kultúrtényező Jelentősége a Versenyszellem Kialakításában (The Importance of the Factor of Culture in Creating the Mentality of Competition).* Budapest, 1948.

Gerő, E. *A vas, az acél és a gépek országért (For a country of iron, steel and machines).* Budapest, 1952.

Gille, Z. 'Wastelands in Transition: The Three Waste Regimes in Hungary, 1948–1998', PhD dissertation, University of California at Santa Cruz, 1999.

Hunt, P. 'Gender and the Construction of Home Life', in *The Politics of Domestic Consumption. Critical Readings*, eds Stevi Jackson and Shaun Moores. London and New York, 1995.

Kenney, P. 'The Gender of Resistance in Communist Poland', *American Historical Review* 104, no.2 (April 1999): 399–425.

Kozák, G. and Molnár, A., eds. *'Szuronyok Hegyén Nem Lehet Dolgozni' Válogatás 1956-os munkástanács-vezetők visszaemlékezéseiből ('It isn't possible to work with a bayonet at your head'. A collection of interviews with 1956 workers' council leaders).* Budapest, 1994.

Lomax, B. 'The Working Class in the Hungarian Revolution of 1956', *Critique* 13, no.32 (1981).

Markus, I. 'A Demokrácia Két Éve Martonvásáron (Szociográfiai vázlat) (Two Years of Democracy in Martonvásár (A Social Report))', *Forum* (1946): 251–61.

Montias, J.M. 'Observations on Strikes, Riots and Other Disturbances' in *Blue Collar Workers in Eastern Europe*, eds Jan F. Triska and Charles Gati. London and New York, 1981.

Őrszigethy, E. *Asszonyok Férfisorban (Women Adopting the Roles of Men).* Budapest, 1986.

Pahl, R.E. *Divisions of Labour*, part 1. Oxford, 1984.

Pálfalvi, N. *Mint Fához az Ág (Like the Branch to the Tree).* Budapest, 1958.

Pittaway, M. 'Industrial Workers, Socialist Industrialisation and the State in Hungary, 1948–1958', PhD thesis, Department of Economic and Social History, University of Liverpool, 1998.

———. 'Rejecting Class Solidarity', unpublished paper given at the American Association for the Advancement of Slavic Studies Thirtieth National Convention, Boca Raton, Florida, United States, 24–27 september 1998.

————. 'The Social Limits of State Control: Time, the Industrial Wage Relation and Social Identity in Stalinist Hungary, 1948–1953', *Journal of Historical Sociology* 12, no.3, (September 1999): 271–301.

————. 'The Victory of Production over Consumption: Reform, Workers and the Possibilities of a New Course'(unpublished manuscript, Southport, 1999).

————. 'Stalinism, Working Class Housing and Individual Autonomy: the Encouragement of Private House Building in Hungary's Mining Areas, 1950–1954' in *Style and Socialism. Modernity and Material Culture in Post-War Eastern Europe*, eds S. E. Reid and D. Crowley. Oxford, 2000, 49–64.

————. 'The Reproduction of Hierarchy: Skill, Working Class Culture and the State in Early Socialist Hungary', *Journal of Modern History* (forthcoming).

Port, A. 'When workers rumbled: the Wismut upheaval of August 1951 in East Germany', *Social History* vol.22, no. 2 (1998): 145–73.

Rákosi, M. *Visszaemlékezések. 2 kötet. 1940–1956.* Budapest, 1997.

Rév, I. 'The Advantages of Being Atomized: How Hungarian Peasants Coped with Collectivisation', *Dissent* (Summer 1987): 335–50.

Scott, J.C. *Domination and the Arts of Resistance: Hidden Transcripts.* New Haven and London, 1990.

Shiomi, H. and Wada, K., eds, *Fordism Transformed. The Development of Production Methods in the Automobile Industry.* Oxford and New York, 1995.

Szabó, Z. *Cifra Nyomorúság. A Cserhát, Mátra, Bükk Földje és Népe (Poverty Covered with a Superficial Show of Wealth. The Peoples and Lands of the Cserhát, Mátra and Bükk).* Budapest, 1938.

Ulc, O. 'Pilsen: the unknown revolt', *Problems of Communism* 14, no. 3 (1965).

Verdery, K. *What Was Socialism and What Comes Next?* Princeton, NJ, 1996.

CHAPTER 11

CONCLUSION

Marcel van der Linden

The preceding essays confirm that in order to spread risks more widely, work-ing-class families usually prefer not to make themselves dependent on a single household strategy. They tend to prefer a combination of different strategies, a *strategic repertoire*. Essentially then, the question is how families revise this repertoire, in response to changes in the environment in which they live and work, in such a way that at least one strategy of collective protest is included. The answer cannot be found simply by studying the families themselves, since, as Justin Byrne rightly remarks, 'family and household are only part of the story'. In the introduction I argued that an understanding of the strategic options of families/households is a necessary condition for understanding col-lective protest – or its absence. However, it is equally clear that such an under-standing is not in itself a sufficient condition. Obviously, labour relations and the social networks of the various members of the family also play an impor-tant role, as does the extent to which the institutional environment facilitates or impedes the various components of a strategic repertoire.[1]

Naturally, when a repertoire is being compiled the relative advantages and disadvantages of individual strategies will be assessed and compared. The essays in this volume show that two sorts of considerations play a role in this process:

- Instrumental considerations: Which combination involves the fewest risks, offers the greatest gains, or involves the least effort?
- Normative considerations: Which combination is the most dignified, pleas-ant, and justified?

Both sorts of consideration are closely related, and their mutual boundaries are sometimes vague. For example, a strategy might be considered dignified either because it is hazardous or, depending on the circumstances, because it is not. The arguments for or against adopting a certain combination of strategies might be mutually inconsistent. There are so many potential considerations, and it is impossible to predict what the outcome will be. Naturally, not everyone takes the same things into account. This is true both of individual family members and of a family as a whole. Every judgement about the reasons for adopting a certain repertoire must thus take account of the fact that it involves contingent processes.

We can therefore formulate the question posed above, about how the transition to collective action is made, in another way: *Why is it that working-class households decide to include or exclude certain forms of collective action from their strategic repertoire?* Two remarks should be made here. First, the threshold for some forms of collective action is significantly higher than for others. The level of that threshold is determined partly by (i) the investment in terms of time and money (in that sense, organising a trade union with a strike fund is more costly than a short-lived riot); (ii) the likely negative and positive consequences of the action (wage increase, dismissal, imprisonment, etc.); and (iii) the degree to which the action is compatible with the group's moral and cultural norms. Secondly, and related to this, the thresholds for forms of action are gendered. The different position of men and women in the household, as well as cultural norms concerning what constitutes appropriate 'female' and 'male' behaviour, mean that men and women differ in their access to different forms of action and the value they attach to them.[2] In their own way, the contributions by Christina von Hodenberg, Mark Pittaway, Bruce Scates, Bonnie Stepenoff and Henk Wals all provide strong evidence for this. Many earlier studies have already noted that the barriers to women becoming active trade-union members are higher than those faced by men.[3] Strikes by female workers and led by women are organised differently from 'male' strikes.[4] Mutual benefit societies have often refused to accept women as members, while for a long time consumer co-operatives had women as customers but men as administrators.[5] By contrast, the role of women in food riots was often considerable.[6] In male-breadwinner families the housewife, as manager of the household budget and of the household more generally, is often more aware than her husband of the 'sacrifices' implied by contributions to trade unions and other organisations.

With these remarks in mind, the essays presented here suggest a number of factors that play a role in constructing household repertoires.

1. First, *cost-benefit analyses* play a role in the selection of household strategies. Henk Wals shows how families made 'calculations' before deciding whether or not to join a trade union. This is an important observation, supported by much of the relevant literature.[7] That in itself is not the full story though – nor does Wals suggest it is. To begin with, such cost-benefit analyses are often much more complex than they initially seem. Using a rational-choice approach, Debra Friedman, for example, has devised a quasi-mathematical formula to ascertain the influences contributing to a worker's decision to join a strike. Her list included no less than ten factors.[8] In her analysis she shows clearly that – in terms of the rational-choice approach – a host of different cost-benefit analyses have to be made all at the same time. One wonders

whether, in practice, individuals do actually weigh up the advantages and disadvantages of their potential strategies in this way. The 'cost-benefit analysis'
carried out by each individual can become so complex that people are likely to
take it less seriously than many theorists presume; in such cases people rely on
more practical formulas, *algorithms of everyday life*. The decision whether or not
to participate in a strike might also often be based on such an algorithm.[9]

2. The rational-choice approach assumes decisions are always 'rational' –
even though it remains unclear what that means precisely.[10] However, the
essays in this collection draw our attention again to the fact that choices are
also shaped by 'habit, impulse, dispositions, emotions, and desires, many of
which are not notably rational'.[11] Not only might household members seriously differ from one another in their opinions regarding the composition of
a strategic repertoire, they might also have doubts and defer decisions longer
than would be 'necessary' in rational terms. In relation to a strike among textile workers in Manchester (New Hampshire), Tamara Hareven observed the
following: 'Whether or not to strike divided some families and caused conflicts that took years to overcome. Some relatives, in fact, have not spoken to
each other since their split over the strike in 1922'.[12] Fear was an important
factor in these sorts of conflict, particularly the fear that collective action
would be repressed. Historically, workers have used all sorts of remedies to
reduce fear – varying from alcohol to prayer.[13] The process of organisation
itself can help reduce fear.[14] In many cases a collective action is also – but not
only – a 'collective attempt to avert fear'.[15]

3. Some of the household methods that appear to be rational are not actually included in a strategic repertoire, because they are *'inconceivable' strategies*
for the household in question and thus excluded by definition from the cost-
benefit analysis. There are a number of different reasons for this. First, it is
apparent from Christina von Hodenberg's case study that 'the people who
rioted were those who still had something to lose'. She points out that the
general material situation of families should be taken into account. Do families succeed only in surviving from day to day, or do they have sufficient scope
to plan their lives to some extent? Maurice Merleau-Ponty has wondered 'why
a return of prosperity frequently brings with it a more radical mood among
the masses. It is because the easing of living conditions makes a fresh structure
of social space possible: the horizon is not restricted to the most immediate
concerns, there is economic play and room for a new project in relation to living'.[16] A working-class family on the edge of subsistence is, in the words of
Ditmar Brock, 'a sort of emergency organisation for mutual assistance (*Not-
gemeinschaft*)', whose survival depends more on their skill in improvising than
their ability to plan long-term. Such a situation 'permits only *the short-term,
situative realisation of needs*'.[17] Only with the development of more material
'opportunities' does participation in longer-term activities (trade-union membership, etc.) become possible. Pierre Bourdieu has gone further and suggested that even people with extremely limited material opportunities make
'plans', but these 'plans' tend to resemble daydreams rather than projects
rooted in the present: 'It is not surprising to find that aspirations tend to
become more realistic, more strictly tailored to real possibilities, in proportion

as the real possibilities become greater'.[18] It is therefore conceivable that forms of collective action that require sacrifices today in order to effect possible improvements in the more distant future will find support among working-class families only where there are 'material opportunities' in the sense outlined above. Secondly, like theatrical repertoires, strategic repertoires are also path dependent. The 'players' have a limited number of pieces in their repertoire, and if these are insufficient a learning process is necessary before a new repertoire becomes available.[19] In this way, the composition of the old repertoire influences the composition of the new repertoire. Thirdly, some household strategies are not included in a repertoire because they are culturally unacceptable and contravene norms of decency and justice. A simple example will suffice to illustrate this. When beef and pork became far too expensive for many Berlin working-class families, in 1848 the city authorities tried to persuade them to eat horsemeat instead. This led to food riots. Although a 'rational' analysis would show that horsemeat is every bit as healthy and nourishing as beef or pork, Berlin's working-class families regarded eating horsemeat as degrading.[20]

4. In weighing up the pros and cons of certain household strategies, the *information* to which family members had access is also important. The 'newer' and less familiar the household strategy, the greater the reluctance to employ it. This reluctance can be overcome if people become aware that others have used the method successfully. In their study into the diffusion of strike techniques, Carol Conell and Samuel Cohn note that 'Other workers' protests provide demonstrations of the tactical opportunities that are available in parallel settings …. Innovative strikes provide information about the viability of new strategies. These can include the introduction of novel demands, innovations in bargaining itself, attempts to form coalitions with unusual outsiders, or the use of atypical defenses of the integrity of the picket line'.[21] Something similar might well have influenced Theresa Moriarty's Dublin strikers, who evacuated their children from the scene of the conflict; the same strategy had been employed not long before in other strikes.[22] News of a strike can also 'open up debate and offer the interpretive frameworks required to transform amorphous dissatisfaction into concrete, articulate demands. Hypothetically, news that strikers elsewhere have won limitations on work hours may encourage workers who have limited their demands to wage gains to start a campaign newly focused on shop floor disputes'.[23] This sort of process of information diffusion by means of exemplary forms of collective action is most probably the reason why workers' protests often occurred in cycles (waves of strikes, an upsurge in the founding of separate organisational forms, etc.) and that, geographically speaking, forms of collective action often spread 'like measles'.[24]

5. The risks associated with strategies are social constructs, not 'objective facts'; and the perception of those risks is extremely susceptible to social pressures and rhetorical strategies.[25] People rate a risk as being less when an influential person from their immediate environment does the same, since *trust* is crucial for everyone who has to operate in situations about which she or he has insufficient information.[26] The daughters from the silk factories who imitated the strike behaviour of their coal-mining fathers (see Bonnie Stepenoff's

chapter) were prepared to take that leap into the unknown because their fathers supported them and provided an example. More generally, the importance of *social networks* for the emergence of collective protest – to which a number of the present contributors have referred – might sometimes be related in part to trust mechanisms. The fact that 'extra-movement interpersonal networks' often form the basis of collective action is nothing new.[27] However, the essays presented here suggest that one reason these networks are so important is that they can give families the confidence to try out certain household strategies of which they have little experience. For similar reasons, many collective actions result from day-to-day social contacts. H.A. Turner, for example, has argued plausibly that the short-lived early English cotton unions were merely the formalised expressions of continuous informal meetings.[28] On the other hand, Rosanne Rutten's chapter shows that the influence of social networks can run counter to the immediate interests of households, while also having a mobilising effect.

The essays in this collection demonstrate two advantages in focusing on the strategic repertoires of households as opposed to the 'classical' approach, in which the choice of form of collective action adopted by individuals was central. First, it provides a greater insight into the hitherto somewhat concealed motives of working-class people in deciding whether or not to contribute to the development of labour movements. Secondly, it permits the 'keeping in focus at all times of the lives of both men and women, young and old, and the variety of paid and unpaid work necessary to maintain the unit'.[29] I do not wish to suggest though that the perspective presented here might be a panacea for all the analytical problems of labour history. There is no such perspective. Analytical progress is more likely to be achieved by a *combination* of different perspectives, those of households, of other social networks, of labour relations, but also of the public authorities and employers. The 'history from below' must be completed with a 'history from above', since, as Perry Anderson once remarked, without the latter the first becomes 'one-sided (if the better side)'.[30] Moreover, each of the multiple perspectives requires an understanding of a wide variety of cultural, social, economic and political aspects.

Our essays also make something else clear: even though the perspective of household strategic repertoires can contribute to a better understanding of popular rebellion, countless questions still remain unanswered. These questions are at two levels. First, many aspects of the household strategic repertoires remain unclear. I shall mention just two here. One question is that of the family life cycle. In her study of the artisan radicals in Lyon 1848, Mary Lynn Stewart-McDougall concluded that, particularly in their early adult years, male artisans radicalised 'when they were married and supporting young children' because of 'the pressures on the family economy' during that stage of the family cycle.[31] This sort of observation could stimulate further research into the shifts in strategic repertoires during the various developmental stages of the household.

Another question concerns the 'specific gravity' of wage labour within a strategic repertoire. The research data suggest apparently contradictory conclusions. Some historians argue, for example, that families will be more inclined to take collective action the more dependent they are on one employer. Harold Benenson has argued plausibly that forms of trade unionism in which workers with differing skill levels worked together (as in the industrial unionism in the US coal-mining and garment industries at the beginning of the twentieth century) sometimes benefited from the fact that more than one member of the same family worked in the same industry: 'Workplace issues affecting one occupational group had direct bearing on the welfare of family members employed in other job categories. Industrial conflicts, refracted through the family, mobilized working class communities *en bloc* and drew support from nonemployed persons as well as those on strike, and from family-centered community institutions (small merchants and boardinghouse keepers, some churches and ethnic associations, and settlement houses)'.[32] Mats Greiff came to a similar conclusion in a comparative study of trade-union activism among female textile workers in two Irish cities (Belfast and Lurgan) around 1900. In Belfast, working-class families often had a range of income sources: while one family member worked in the textile factory, others had a job in shipbuilding, engineering or other sectors. In Lurgan, on the other hand, families were entirely dependent on the textile industry. 'In Lurgan it was necessary to invest money in union strike funds to withstand a dispute. Belfast women required no such funds ....'[33]

Other historians though have concluded that dependence on a single employer paralyses families. In her study of the Amoskeag Manufacturing Company in Manchester, New Hampshire, in the first few decades of the twentieth century, Tamara Hareven noted the following: 'When most family members worked for a single employer, the family unit was vulnerable to the vicissitudes of the company. Because of the dependence of a major portion of a family group on one employer, relatives were unable to assist each other when layoffs occurred .... Unable to save on their subsistence budgets, they had few or no reserves left to share during the strike and shutdown'.[34] The question, naturally, is how such apparently contradictory insights can be reconciled. Perhaps the relationship is curvilinear: if they have little trust in collective action, families dependent on *one* employer will be inclined to deference, but once that trust exceeds certain limits they will immediately turn to collective action in a highly organised way, precisely because they are dependent on one employer. In the case of families with more than one source of income, one might expect the relationship to be more diffuse. All this, of course, is mere speculation at this stage.[35]

These examples show that there is still considerable scope for research into household strategic repertoires. However, there is a second level at which further research and reflection is also desirable – namely *the wider embedding of the household strategies*. Rosanne Rutten raises the problem of the relationship between the demands made of individuals by households and the demands made of those same individuals by other social networks. Sometimes these demands will be more or less congruent, at other times they will conflict. Not all forms of collective action therefore can be explained in terms of the strategic actions of households. There are forms of rebellion that have little to do with budget pooling. The longer-term rebellions – often with a powerful political or religious component – are probably furthest removed from day-to-day household strategies. However, one often sees the metaphors and language of the family also being used in the mobilisation of individuals for such 'higher' aims. Ferdinand Tönnies pointed out long ago how in communities the members think of their relationship in terms of consanguineal ties ('brother', 'sister', 'father', 'mother', etc.); and this also holds true for many imagined or abstract communities.[36]

In conclusion then, in a number of respects the analysis of the strategic repertoires of households cannot fully explain why people do or do not rebel. That analysis is just one significant component of such an explanation. No more, but no less either.

Translation: Chris Gordon and Lee Mitzman

Notes

1. Adversaries (employers, the state and legal customs, but sometimes religious bodies too, etc.) partly determine the *opportunity structure* (Sidney Tarrow) for collective action. The effect can be to impede or facilitate. See Doug McAdam, John D. McCarthy and Mayer N. Zald, eds, *Comparative Perspectives on Social Movements: Political Opportunities, Mobilizing Structures, and Cultural Framings*, Cambridge, UK, 1996.

2. The so-called 'Taylor Thesis' claims that women exposed to the same industrial culture as men will also develop the same attitudes as men. In other words, women who have the same jobs as men will react in the same way as men in terms of collective action. Stan Taylor, 'Parkin's Theory of Working Class Conservatism: Two Hypotheses Investigated', *Sociological Review* 26 (1978): 827–42, esp. 835–8. See too Ian Watts, 'Linkages between Industrial Radicalism and the Domestic Role among Working Women', *Sociological Review* 28 (1980): 55–74; and Ida Harper Simpson and Elizabeth Mutran, 'Women's Social Consciousness: Sex or Worker Identity', *Research in the Sociology of Work* 1 (1981): 335–50. Alison Woodward and Håkon Leiulfsrud have qualified this thesis to some extent, arguing that 'the similar situation includes not only location in the class structure and similar work situations but also location in the family'. Production and reproduction should not be seen as a dichotomy but as a whole. Alison E. Woodward and Håkon Leiulfsrud, 'Masculine/Feminine Organization: Class versus Gender in Swedish Unions', in *Organization Theory and Class Analysis: New Approaches and New Issues*, ed. Stewart R. Clegg, Berlin and New York, 1990, 407–25, here 412.

3. As early as 1914 Adolf Braun summarised the main reasons: (i) the double burden of women (wage labour plus household labour); (ii) place and time of meetings; and (iii) psychological barriers. Adolf Braun, *Die Gewerkschaften, ihre Entwicklung und Kämpfe. Eine Sammlung von Abhandlungen*, Nuremberg, 1914, 192. Typical of much of the newer literature on this issue is Alice H. Cook, Val R. Lorwin and Arlene Kaplan Daniels, *The Most Difficult Revolution: Women and Trade Unions*, Ithaca and London, 1992.

4. See the study by Margaret Maruani and Anne Borzeix, *Le temps des chemises: la grève qu'elles gardent au coeur*, Paris, 1982. The authors analysed a series of strikes by women in a French shirt-manufacturing firm, July 1975–July 1978. They describe, for example, how the times of the meetings were arranged to coincide with school hours and the hours their husbands worked, how jobs were rotated, how responsibilities were allocated democratically. These egalitarian arrangements meant that none of the women's leaders achieved prominence.

5. Marcel van der Linden, 'Mutual Workers' Insurance: A Historical Outline', *International Social Security Review* 46, no. 3 (1993): 5–18, and 'Working-Class Consumer Power', *International Labor and Working-Class History* 46 (1994): 109–21.

6. For a time it was assumed that food riots were dominated by women. See for example Olwen Hufton, 'Women in Revolution, 1789–1796', *Past and Present* no. 53 (1971): 90–108. More

recent research has qualified this strong thesis, but it remains undeniable that women were overrepresented among those who participated in food riots. John Bohstedt, 'Gender, Household and Community Politics: Women in English Riots 1790–1810', *Past and Present* no.120 (1988): 88–122; Cynthia A. Bouton, 'Gendered Behavior in Subsistence Riots: The Flour War of 1775', *Journal of Social History* 23 (1990): 735–54; Carola Lipp, 'Frauenspezifische Partizipation an Hungerunruhen des 19. Jahrhunderts', in *Der Kampf um das tägliche Brot: Nahrungsmangel, Versorgungspolitik und Protest 1770–1990*, eds Manfred Gailus and Heinrich Volkmann, Opladen, 1994, 200–13. See also Karen Hagemann, 'Frauenprotest und Männerdemonstrationen: Zum geschlechtsspezifischen Aktionsverhalten im großstädtischen Arbeitermilieu der Weimarer Republik', in *Massenmedium Straße: Zur Kulturgeschichte der Demonstration*, ed. Bernd Jürgen Warneken, Frankfurt am Main and New York, 1991, 202–30.

7. There is now a considerable literature reconstructing the development of collective workers' action in terms of Rational Choice. See for example Norbert Eickhof, *Eine Theorie der Gewerkschaftsentwicklung*, Tübingen, 1973; Claus Offe and Helmut Wiesenthal, 'Two Logics of Collective Action', *Political Power and Social Theory* 1 (1980): 67–115; reprinted in Claus Offe, *Disorganized Capitalism. Contemporary Transformations of Work and Politics*, Cambridge, 1985, 170–220, 334–40; Colin Crouch, *Trade Unions: The Logic of Collective Action*, Isle of Man, 1982; Christiane Eisenberg, *Frühe Arbeiterbewegung und Genossenschaften. Theorie und Praxis der Produktivgenossenschaften in der deutschen Sozialdemokratie und den Gewerkschaften der 1860er/1870er Jahre.* Mit einem Vorwort von Walter Hesselbach, Bonn, 1985; Adam Przeworski and John Sprague, *Paper Stones. A History of Electoral Socialism*, Chicago, 1986; Debra Friedman, 'Toward a Theory of Union Emergence and Demise', in *Social Institutions. Their Emergence, Maintenance and Effects*, eds Michael Hechter, Karl-Dieter Opp and Reinhard Wippler, Berlin and New York, 1990, 291–306.

8. Debra Friedman, 'Why Workers Strike: Individual Decisions and Structural Constraints', in *The Microfoundations of Macrosociology*, ed. Michael Hechter, Philadelphia, 1983, 250–83.

9. I discuss this in more detail in my essay 'Old Labour Movements and "New Political Economy": Uses and Drawbacks of Rational Choice Theory', *Traverse: Zeitschrift für Geschichte / Revue d'histoire* 4, no. 1 (1997): 128–43.

10. George C. Homans' remark about Rational Choice theory is apposite: 'Since it is exceedingly difficult to define the word *rational*, I should prefer to call it simply choice-theory and have it refer to the ways in which people actually choose between alternatives, relegating the word *rational* to the normative theory of decision …'. George C. Homans, 'Rational-choice Theory and Behavioral Psychology', in *Structures of Power and Constraint: Papers in Honor of Peter M. Blau*, eds Craig Calhoun, Marshall W. Meyer and W. Richard Scott, Cambridge, UK, 1990, 77–89, here 78.

11. Clayton Roberts, *The Logic of Historical Explanation*, University Park, PA, 1996, 162. See also James M. Jasper, 'The Emotions of Protest: Affective and Reactive Emotions In and Around Social Movements', *Sociological Forum* 13 (1998): 397–424.

12. Tamara Hareven, *Family Time and Industrial Time. The Relationship between the Family and Work in a New England Industrial Community*, Cambridge, UK, 1982, 114.

13. A remarkable example from Russia at the end of the nineteenth century can be found in Daniel R. Brower, 'Labor Violence in Russia in the Late Nineteenth Century', *Slavic Review* 41 (1982): 417–31, here 421.

14. Robert De Board, *The Psychoanalysis of Organizations*, London, 1978, 117.

15. Detlev Puls, '"Ein im ganzen gutartiger Streik". Bemerkungen zu Alltagserfahrungen und Protestverhalten der oberschlesischen Bergarbeiter am Ende des 19. Jahrhunderts', in *Wahrnehmungsformen und Protestverhalten: Studien zur Lage der Unterschichten im 18. und 19. Jahrhundert*, ed. Detlev Puls, Frankfurt am Main, 1979, 175–227, here 195. Puls adds further: 'Explanations of protest behaviour must include the analysis of structures of fear'. (Ibid.)

16. Maurice Merleau-Ponty, *Phenomenology of Perception*, trans. Colin Smith, London and New Jersey, 1992, 446.

17. Ditmar Brock, *Der schwierige Weg in die Moderne: Umwälzungen in der Lebensführung der deutschen Arbeiter zwischen 1850 und 1980*, Frankfurt am Main and New York, 1991, 66, 77.

18. Pierre Bourdieu, *Algeria 1960*, trans. Richard Nice, Cambridge, UK and Paris, 1979, 51.
19. There is a clear parallel here with Charles Tilly's concept of 'repertoire of contention', which as such relates to the multitude of collective action methods. See for example Charles Tilly, 'Getting It Together in Burgundy, 1675–1975', *Theory and Society* 4 (1977): 479–504; Louise Tilly and Charles Tilly, eds, *Class Conflict and Collective Action*, Beverly Hills, CA, 1981, Introduction. An assessment and historical criticism of Tilly's concept of repertoire can be found in Mark Traugott, 'Barricades as Repertoire: Continuities and Discontinuities in the History of French Contention', *Social Science History* 17 (1993): 309–323.
20. Manfred Gailus, *Straße und Brot: Sozialer Protest in den deutschen Staaten unter besonderer Berücksichtigung Preußens, 1847–1849*, Göttingen, 1990, 13–20.
21. Carol Conell and Samuel Cohn, 'Learning from Other People's Actions: Environmental Variation and Diffusion in French Coal Mining Strikes, 1890–1935', *American Journal of Sociology* 101 (1995–96): 366–403, here 369–70.
22. See for example Ardis Cameron, 'Bread and Roses Revisited: Women's Culture and Working-Class Activism in the Lawrence Strike of 1912', in *Women, Work and Protest: A Century of US Women's Labor History*, ed. Ruth Milkman, Boston, 1985, 42–61. Analogous to Moriarty, Cameron points out that the so-called 'children's exodus' during the Lawrence strike was an extension of older practices: 'Typically (before the strike) working mothers had turned to neighbours who took in children at modest fees, or, in some cases, had sent their young into the countryside during the working week and collected them again on Sundays'. (50)
23. Conell and Cohn, 'Learning from Other People's Actions', 369.
24. Peter Hedström, 'Contagious Collectivities: On the Spatial Diffusion of Swedish Trade Unions, 1890–1940', *American Journal of Sociology* 99 (1993–94): 1157–79. See also Carville Earle, *Geographical Inquiry and American Historical Problems*, Stanford, CA, 1992, chs 9 and 10.
25. Kathleen J. Tierney, 'Toward a Critical Sociology of Risk', *Sociological Forum* 14 (1999): 215–242, especially 219–22 and 226. Extensive support for this argument can be found in Mary Douglas and Aaron Wildawsky, *Risk and Culture: An Essay on the Selection of Technological and Environmental Dangers*, Berkeley, 1982.
26. Peter Preisendörfer, 'Vertrauen als soziologische Kategorie', *Zeitschrift für Soziologie* 24 (1995): 263–272. See also Diego Gambetta, ed., *Trust: Making and Breaking Cooperative Relations*, New York, 1988.
27. See for example James Petras and Maurice Zeitlin, 'Miners and Agrarian Radicalism', *American Sociological Review* 32 (1967): 578–86; Jo Freeman, 'The Origins of the Women's Liberation Movement', *American Journal of Sociology* 78 (1972–73): 792–811; David A. Snow, Louis A. Zurcher, Jr and Sheldon Ekland-Olson, 'Social Networks and Social Movements: A Microstructural Approach to Differential Recruitment', *American Sociological Review* 45 (1980): 787–801. Charles Tilly has even developed a formula (Catness x Netness = Organisation) to illustrate the fact that two aspects are important for an understanding of collective action: (i) common identity and (ii) internal networks. The common identity corresponds to the number of categories people share (Catness). According to Tilly, the stronger the common identity and the denser the mutual networks (Netness), the greater the capacity of a group of households (or members of households) to take collective action. Charles Tilly, *From Mobilization to Revolution*, Reading, MA, 1978, 63–64. Whether Tilly is correct though is an empirical question; it is also conceivable that strategic innovations actually occur more quickly in less dense networks. See Mark Granovetter, 'The Strength of Weak Ties', *American Journal of Sociology* 78 (1972–73): 1360–80; and Frances Fox Piven and Richard A. Cloward, 'Collective Protest: A Critique of Resource-Mobilization Theory', in *Social Movements: Critiques, Concepts, Case-Studies*, ed. Stanford M. Lyman, Basingstoke and London, 1995, 137–67, in particular 145–50.
28. H.A. Turner, *Trade Union Growth, Structure and Policy*, London, 1962, 50–4.
29. Jean H. Quataert, 'Combining Agrarian and Industrial Livelihood: Rural Households in the Saxon Oberlausitz in the Nineteenth Century', *Journal of Family History* 10 (1985): 145–62, 158.
30. Perry Anderson, *Lineages of the Absolutist State*, London, 1974, 11.
31. Mary Lynn Stewart-McDougall, *The Artisan Republic: Revolution, Reaction, and Resistance in Lyon, 1848–1851*, Kingston and Montreal, 1984, xvi.

32. Harold Benenson, 'The Community and Family Bases of U.S. Working Class Protest, 1880–1920: A Critique of the "Skill Degradation" and "Ecological" Perspectives', *Research in Social Movements, Conflicts and Change* 8 (1985): 109–32, here 118.

33. Mats Greiff, '"Marching Through the Streets Singing and Shouting": Industrial Struggle and Trade Unions among Female Linen Workers in Belfast and Lurgan, 1872–1910', *Saothar* 22 (1997): 29–44.

34. Hareven, *Family Time and Industrial Time*, 113–14.

35. Perhaps the presumed difference between families with one wage income and those with more than one wage income can also be accounted for partly in terms of the gendered power relations within the family unit. Take the following example: Many early nineteenth-century English mines employed family teams, in which more than one member of the same family worked together under the supervision of the male household head. The introduction in 1842 of the Mines (Regulation) Act, which excluded all females under the age of eighteen from working in the mines, immediately precipitated a 'rapid spread of unionization among the miners' workforce, as struggles over the size of the wage became the only element of control left to the previously independent master, the collier'. Jane Mark-Lawson and Anne Witz, 'From "Family Labour" to "Family Wage"? The Case of Women's Labour in Nineteenth-Century Coalmining', *Social History* 13 (1988): 151–74, here 168.

36. Ferdinand Tönnies, *Gemeinschaft und Gesellschaft. Abhandlung des Communismus und des Socialismus als empirischer Culturformen*, Leipzig, 1887, 9–12; Paul James, 'Forms of Abstract "Community": From Tribe and Kingdom to Nation and State', *Philosophy of the Social Sciences* 22 (1992): 313–36.

Bibliography

Anderson, P. *Lineages of the Absolutist State*. London, 1974.

Benenson, H. 'The Community and Family Bases of U.S. Working Class Protest, 1880–1920: A Critique of the "Skill Degradation" and "Ecologica" Perspectives', *Research in Social Movements, Conflicts and Change* 8 (1985): 109–32.

Bohstedt, J. 'Gender, Household and Community Politics: Women in English Riots 1790–1810', *Past and Present* no. 120 (1988): 88–122.

Bourdieu, P. *Algeria 1960*, trans. Richard Nice. Cambridge, UK and Paris, 1979.

Bouton, C.A. 'Gendered Behavior in Subsistence Riots: The Flour War of 1775', *Journal of Social History* 23 (1990): 735–54.

Braun, A. *Die Gewerkschaften, ihre Entwicklung und Kämpfe. Eine Sammlung von Abhandlungen*. Nuremberg, 1914.

Brock, D. *Der schwierige Weg in die Moderne: Umwälzungen in der Lebensführung der deutschen Arbeiter zwischen 1850 und 1980*. Frankfurt am Main and New York, 1991.

Brower, D.R. 'Labor Violence in Russia in the Late Nineteenth Century', *Slavic Review* vol. 41 (1982): 417–31.

Cameron, A. 'Bread and Roses Revisited: Women's Culture and Working-Class Activism in the Lawrence Strike of 1912', in *Women, Work and Protest: A Century of US Women's Labor History*, ed. R. Milkman. Boston, 1985, 42–61.

Conell, C., and Cohn, S. 'Learning from Other People's Actions: Environmental Variation and Diffusion in French Coal Mining Strikes, 1890–1935', *American Journal of Sociology* 101 (1995–96): 366–403.

Cook, A.H., Lorwin, V.R., and Daniels, A.K. *The Most Difficult Revolution: Women and Trade Unions*. Ithaca and London, 1992.

Crouch, C. *Trade Unions: The Logic of Collective Action*. Isle of Man, 1982.

De Board, R. *The Psychoanalysis of Organizations*. London, 1978.

Douglas, M., and Wildawsky, A. *Risk and Culture: An Essay on the Selection of Technological and Environmental Dangers*. Berkeley, 1982.

Earle, C. *Geographical Inquiry and American Historical Problems*. Stanford, CA, 1992.

Eickhof, N. *Eine Theorie der Gewerkschaftsentwicklung*. Tübingen, 1973.

Eisenberg, C. *Frühe Arbeiterbewegung und Genossenschaften. Theorie und Praxis der Produktivgenossenschaften in der deutschen Sozialdemokratie und den Gewerkschaften der 1860er/1870er Jahre*. Bonn, 1985.

Fox Piven, F., and Cloward, R.A. 'Collective Protest: A Critique of Resource-Mobilization Theory', in *Social Movements: Critiques, Concepts, Case-Studies*, ed. S.M. Lyman, Basingstoke and London, 1995, 137–67.

Freeman, J. 'The Origins of the Women's Liberation Movement', *American Journal of Sociology* 78 (1972–73): 792–811.

Friedman, D. 'Why Workers Strike: Individual Decisions and Structural Constraints', in *The Microfoundations of Macrosociology*, ed. M. Hechter. Philadelphia, 1983, 250–83.

———. 'Toward a Theory of Union Emergence and Demise', in *Social Institutions. Their Emergence, Maintenance and Effects*, eds M. Hechter, K.-D. Opp and R. Wippler. Berlin and New York, 1990, 291–306.

Gailus, M. *Straße und Brot: Sozialer Protest in den deutschen Staaten unter besonderer Berücksichtigung Preußens, 1847–1849*. Göttingen, 1990.

Gambetta, D. ed. *Trust: Making and Breaking Cooperative Relations*. New York, 1988.

Granovetter, M. 'The Strength of Weak Ties', *American Journal of Sociology* 78 (1972–73): 1360–80.

Greiff, M. '"Marching Through the Streets Singing and Shouting": Industrial Struggle and Trade Unions among Female Linen Workers in Belfast and Lurgan, 1872–1910', *Saothar* 22 (1997): 29–44.

Hagemann, K. 'Frauenprotest und Männerdemonstrationen: Zum geschlechtsspezifischen Aktionsverhalten im großstädtischen Arbeitermilieu der Weimarer Republik', in *Massenmedium Straße: Zur Kulturgeschichte der Demonstration*, ed. B.J. Warneken. Frankfurt am Main and New York, 1991, 202–30.

Hareven, T.K. *Family Time and Industrial Time. The Relationship between the Family and Work in a New England Industrial Community*. Cambridge, UK, 1982.

Hedström, P. 'Contagious Collectivities: On the Spatial Diffusion of Swedish Trade Unions, 1890–1940', *American Journal of Sociology* 99 (1993–94): 1157–79.

Homans, G.C. 'Rational-choice Theory and Behavioral Psychology', in *Structures of Power and Constraint: Papers in Honor of Peter M. Blau*, eds C. Calhoun, M.W. Meyer and W.R. Scott. Cambridge, UK, 1990, 77–89.

Hufton, O. 'Women in Revolution, 1789–1796', *Past and Present*, no. 53 (1971): 90–108.

James, P. 'Forms of Abstract "Community": From Tribe and Kingdom to Nation and State', *Philosophy of the Social Sciences* 22 (1992): 313–36.

Jasper, J.M. 'The Emotions of Protest: Affective and Reactive Emotions In and Around Social Movements', *Sociological Forum* 13 (1998): 397–424.

Linden, M. van der, 'Mutual Workers' Insurance: A Historical Outline', *International Social Security Review* 46, no. 3 (1993): 5–18.

———. 'Working-Class Consumer Power', *International Labor and Working-Class History* vol. 46 (1994): 109–21.

———. 'Old Labour Movements and "New Political Economy": Uses and Drawbacks of Rational Choice Theory', *Traverse: Zeitschrift für Geschichte/Revue d'histoire* 4, no. 1 (1997): 128–43.

Lipp, C. 'Frauenspezifische Partizipation an Hungerunruhen des 19. Jahrhunderts', in *Der Kampf um das tägliche Brot: Nahrungsmangel, Versorgungspolitik und Protest 1770–1990*, eds M. Gailus and H. Volkmann. Opladen, 1994, 200–13.

Mark-Lawson, J., and Witz, A. 'From "Family Labour" to "Family Wage"? The Case of Women's Labour in Nineteenth-Century Coalmining', *Social History* 13 (1988): 151–74.

Maruani, M., and Borzeix, A. *Le temps des chemises: la grève qu'elles gardent au coeur*. Paris, 1982.

McAdam, D., McCarthy, J.D., and Zald, M.N., eds. *Comparative Perspectives on Social Movements: Political Opportunities, Mobilizing Structures, and Cultural Framings*. Cambridge, UK, 1996.

Merleau-Ponty, M. *Phenomenology of Perception*, trans. Colin Smith. London and New Jersey, 1992.

Offe, C., and Wiesenthal, H. 'Two Logics of Collective Action', *Political Power and Social Theory* 1 (1980): 67–115.

Offe, C. *Disorganized Capitalism. Contemporary Transformations of Work and Politics*. Cambridge, 1985.

Petras, J., and Zeitlin, M. 'Miners and Agrarian Radicalism', *American Sociological Review* 32 (1967): 578–86.

Preisendörfer, P. 'Vertrauen als soziologische Kategorie', *Zeitschrift für Soziologie* 24, (1995): 263–72.

Przeworski, A., and Sprague, J. *Paper Stones. A History of Electoral Socialism*. Chicago, 1986.

Puls, D. '"Ein im ganzen gutartiger Streik". Bemerkungen zu Alltagserfahrungen und Protestverhalten der oberschlesischen Bergarbeiter am Ende des 19. Jahrhunderts', in *Wahrnehmungsformen und Protestverhalten: Studien zur Lage der Unterschichten im 18. und 19. Jahrhundert*, ed. D. Puls. Frankfurt am Main, 1979, 175–227.

Quataert, J.H. 'Combining Agrarian and Industrial Livelihood: Rural Households in the Saxon Oberlausitz in the Nineteenth Century', *Journal of Family History* 10 (1985): 145–62.

Roberts, C. *The Logic of Historical Explanation*. University Park, PA, 1996.

Simpson, I.H., and Mutran, E. 'Women's Social Consciousness: Sex or Worker Identity', *Research in the Sociology of Work* vol. 1 (1981): 335–50.

Smith, J., Wallerstein, I. and Evers, H.-D., *Households and the World-Economy*. Beverly Hills, 1984.

Snow, D.A., Zurcher Jr, L.A., and Ekland-Olson, S. 'Social Networks and Social Movements: A Microstructural Approach to Differential Recruitment', *American Sociological Review* 45 (1980): 787–801.

Stewart-McDougall, M.L. *The Artisan Republic: Revolution, Reaction, and Resistance in Lyon, 1948–1851*. Kingston and Montreal, 1984.

Taylor, S. 'Parkin's Theory of Working Class Conservatism: Two Hypotheses Investigated', *Sociological Review* 26 (1978): 827–42.

Tierney, K.J. 'Toward a Critical Sociology of Risk', *Sociological Forum* vol. 14 (1999): 215–42.

Tilly, C. 'Getting It Together in Burgundy, 1675–1975', *Theory and Society* 4 (1977): 479–504.

———. *From Mobilization to Revolution*. Reading, MA, 1978.

Tilly, L., and Tilly, C., eds. *Class Conflict and Collective Action*. Beverly Hills, CA, 1981.

Tönnies, F. *Gemeinschaft und Gesellschaft. Abhandlung des Communismus und des Socialismus als empirischer Culturformen*. Leipzig, 1887.

Traugott, M. 'Barricades as Repertoire: Continuities and Discontinuities in the History of French Contention', *Social Science History* 17 (1993): 309–23.

Turner, H.A. *Trade Union Growth, Structure and Policy*. London, 1962.

Watts, I. 'Linkages Between Industrial Radicalism and the Domestic Role Among Working Women', *Sociological Review* 28 (1980): 55–74.

Wellman, B., and Berkowitz, S.D, eds. *Social Structures. A Network Approach*. Cambridge, 1988.

Woodward, A.E., and Leiulfsrud, H. 'Masculine/Feminine Organization: Class versus Gender in Swedish Unions', in *Organization Theory and Class Analysis: New Approaches and New Issues*, ed. S.R. Clegg. Berlin and New York, 1990, 407–25.

NOTES ON CONTRIBUTORS

Justin Byrne is a researcher at the Instituto Juan March's Centre for Advanced Study in the Social Sciences in Madrid, and a lecturer at New York University in Madrid and on the Madrid programme of Vassar-Wesleyan-Colgate universities. Author of a number of articles on Spanish labour and social history, his main current areas of interest are labour markets and relations in the building industry. He is also writing a cultural and social history of one of nineteenth-century Madrid's most famous music hall and theatres, the *Teatro Eslava*.

Christina von Hodenberg is Assistant Professor of History at the University of Freiburg in Germany and currently a John F. Kennedy Memorial Fellow at the Minda de Gunzburg Center for European Studies, Harvard University. Her research interests concern the legal and social history of nineteenth century Germany and the liberalization of West German political culture after 1945. She is author of the book *Aufstand der Weber*, Bonn, 1997 on the uprising of the Silesian weavers in 1844 and its place in German memory. Also among her publications is the book *Die Partei der Unparteiischen*, Goettingen, 1996, a collective biography of Prussian judges in the first half of the nineteenth century with special regard to their role in early liberalism and the revolution of 1848–49.

Jan Kok is a senior researcher at the International Institute of Social History in Amsterdam and writes on various subjects in historical demography and family history. Also he is one of the Research Directors of the programme 'Family and Labour – A Comparative Approach to Changing Labour Relations' of the N.W. Posthumus Institute, the Netherlands Research Institute and Graduate School on Economic and Social History.

Marcel van der Linden is Research Director at the International Institute of Social History in Amsterdam, Professor of Social Movement History at the University of Amsterdam, and Executive Editor of the *International Review of Social History* (Cambridge, UK). He has published widely on labour history and the history of ideas.

Theresa Moriarty is a staff member of the Irish Labour History Museum (Dublin). She has published on the history of women's health in Northern Ireland and on women's trade unionism in Ireland, 1880–1920.

Mark Pittaway is Lecturer in European Studies in the Faculty of Arts at the Open University in the United Kingdom. He works on the social history and popular culture of post-war Hungary and is currently completing a book on the social history of industrial labour in the country between 1945 and 1958.

Rosanne Rutten is Lecturer in Anthropology at the University of Amsterdam. She wrote *Women Workers of Hacienda Milagros: Wage Labor and Household Subsistence on a Philippine Sugarcane Plantation*, 1982, and *Artisans and Entrepreneurs in the Rural Philippines: Making a Living and Gaining Wealth in Two Commercialized Crafts*, 1990. She is currently working on a book on the rise and decline of popular participation in the Philippine revolutionary movement CPP-NPA, based on field research in two rural communities over the last two decades.

Bruce Scates lectures in Australian history at the University of New South Wales Sydney. He is active in the Labour History Society and an executive member of the History Council of NSW. His major monograph *A New Australia: Citizenship, Radicalism and the First Republic* was published by Cambridge University Press in 1997. He is also co-author of a number of studies with Rae Frances, including the prize-winning *Women and the Great War*, Cambridge, 1997. He is currently completing a study of unemployment in the 1890s' depression and a book examining war, memory and pilgrimages to cemeteries of the Great War.

Bonnie Stepenoff is Associate Professor of History at Southeast Missouri State University, Cape Girardeau, Missouri, USA. Her book, *Their Fathers' Daughters: Silk Mill Workers in Northeastern Pennsylvania, 1880–1960*, was published in 1999 by Susquehanna University Press. She has published articles in *Labor History*, *Labor's Heritage*, *Pennsylvania History*, *The Missouri Historical Review*, and other journals. She is completing a book-length biography of Thad Snow, a cotton planter who supported a farm workers' protest in Missouri in 1939.

Henk Wals is Deputy Director of the International Institute of Social History in Amsterdam. His research interests are labour, labour relations and the living strategies of working-class families. His doctoral thesis on the living strategies of Amsterdam construction workers appeared in 2001.

Eileen Janes Yeo is Professor of Social and Cultural History at the University of Strathclyde in Glasgow and has published widely on the culture of radical movements. She has also recently written *The Contest for Social Science: Relations and Representations of Gender and Class* (1996), and edited *Mary Wollstonecraft and 200 Years of Feminisms* (1997) and *Radical Femininity: Women's Self-Representation in the Public Sphere* (1998).

INDEX